LOOKOUT AMERICA!

INTERFACES

Studies in Visual Culture

Editors Mark J. Williams, Dartmouth College,
and Adrian W. B. Randolph, Northwestern University

This series, sponsored by Dartmouth College Press, develops and promotes the study of visual culture from a variety of critical and methodological perspectives. Its impetus derives from the increasing importance of visual signs in everyday life, and from the rapid expansion of what are termed "new media." The broad cultural and social dynamics attendant to these developments present new challenges and opportunities across and within the disciplines. These have resulted in a transdisciplinary fascination with all things visual, from "high" to "low," and from esoteric to popular. This series brings together approaches to visual culture—broadly conceived—that assess these dynamics critically and that break new ground in understanding their effects and implications.

For a complete list of books that are available in the series, visit www.upne.com

Kevin Hamilton & Ned O'Gorman, *Lookout America!: The Secret Hollywood Studio at the Heart of the Cold War*
Nathaniel Stern, *Ecological Aesthetics: artful tactics for humans, nature, and politics*
Christina Braun, *Thomas Hirschhorn: A New Political Understanding of Art?*
Daniel Harkett & Katie Hornstein, eds., *Horace Vernet and the Thresholds of Nineteenth-Century Visual Culture*
Meredith Hoy, *From Point to Pixel: A Genealogy of Digital Aesthetics*
James Housefield, *Playing with Earth and Sky: Astronomy, Geography, and the Art of Marcel Duchamp*
William Kaizen, *Against Immediacy: Video Art and Media Populism*
Steve F. Anderson, *Technologies of History: Visual Media and the Eccentricity of the Past*
Robin Veder, *The Living Line: Modern Art and the Economy of Energy*
Tanya Sheehan, ed., *Photography, History, Difference*
Ory Bartal, *Postmodern Advertising in Japan: Seduction, Visual Culture, and the Tokyo Art Directors Club*
Erina Duganne, *The Self in Black and White: Race and Subjectivity in Postwar American Photography*
Ruth E. Iskin, *The Poster: Art, Advertising, Design, and Collecting, 1860s–1900s*
Heather Warren-Crow, *Girlhood and the Plastic Image*
Heidi Rae Cooley, *Finding Augusta: Habits of Mobility and Governance in the Digital Era*
renée c. hoogland, *A Violent Embrace: Art and Aesthetics after Representation*
Alessandra Raengo, *On the Sleeve of the Visual: Race as Face Value*

LOOKOUT AMERICA!

THE SECRET HOLLYWOOD STUDIO AT THE HEART OF THE COLD WAR

KEVIN HAMILTON & NED O'GORMAN

Dartmouth College Press
Hanover, New Hampshire

Dartmouth College Press
An imprint of University Press of New England
www.upne.com

Manufactured in the United States of America
Designed by Kevin Hamilton and Ned O'Gorman
Typeset in Albiona by Rian Hughes and Trade Gothic Next by Akira Kobayashi

Library of Congress Cataloging-in-Publication Data available upon request

Paperback ISBN: 978-1-5126-0327-9

5-4-3-2-1

For our children

This is the excellent foppery of the world that when we are sick in fortune—often the surfeit of our own behavior—we make guilty of our disasters the sun, the moon, and the stars, as if we were villains by necessity, fools by heavenly compulsion.

—Edmund in *King Lear*

The movie, by sheer speeding up the mechanical, carried us from the world of sequence and connections into the world of creative configuration and structure. The message of the movie medium is that of transition from lineal connections to configurations.

—Marshall McLuhan in *The Medium Is the Message*

CONTENTS

1948

PREFACE

The Bomb really did change everything. As critical lights such as Garry Wills, Elaine Scarry, and Joseph Masco have argued, America's creation of the Bomb and subsequent stockpiling of nuclear weapons during the Cold War not only militarized the whole of American society and taught citizens in America and abroad to live facing the prospect of a horrifyingly dangerous future, but also transformed the federal government itself into a national security state and reconfigured the presidency as a "thermonuclear monarchy."[1] In tracing the origins and genealogy of what Wills calls "Bomb power," some have explored government histories; others science, technology, and sociotechnical systems; and yet others symbols, images, and spectacle. But with a small number of important exceptions, few have explored where government, technology, and nuclear spectacle intersected in the context of the Cold War.[2] Such is the way of the book before you.

Images of nuclear detonations have operational, technical, and rhetorical origins. They played a key role in the big science of the Bomb. But they also were integral to the rhetoric of Bomb power. America's Cold War national security state used images—sometimes the very same images—to manage both the technological operations of nuclear weapons and the cultural anxieties and appetites of the Cold War world. The producers of these images faced extraordinary demands. As Masco writes, "After World War II, the cinematic atomic bomb became the crucial way in which the government communicated the weapon's power to soldiers, civilians, and policy makers alike. It achieved two main purposes: First, it documented the effects of the exploding bomb; second, it shaped and controlled the meaning of the technology for each of these domestic audiences."[3] Official nuclear filmmakers and photographers therefore faced the challenge of producing images that could both further weapons research and tell stories of the Bomb as a controlled physical and political instrument before a variety of audiences: enthusiastic technophiles, skeptical decision

1959

makers, aggressive generals, mystified military personnel, wary publics, and so on.

As we will see, from the start the US government took nuclear images very seriously, especially cinematic images. As Jerome Shapiro notes, cinema and the atomic bomb were "two of the most significant technological innovations of the past century"; and when fused together in atomic-bomb films, they became a "paradigmatic site of struggle over cultural power"—and not just cultural power, but political, economic, and operational power.[4] The burgeoning nuclear state, however, was initially ill equipped to manage and produce atomic imagery, leaving the struggle for the direction and meaning of the Bomb to the speculations of the press and the worries of the public.

This book relates the story of how the government, through the Air Force, tried to take hold of both the science and significance of the Bomb by creating a secretive film unit in Hollywood, branded "Lookout Mountain Laboratory." Also known over time as the 4201st Motion Picture Squadron [1947-1949], the 4881st Motion Picture Squadron [1949–1951], the 1352nd Photographic Squadron [1952–1961], and the 1352nd Photographic Group [1962–1969], Lookout Mountain Laboratory opened in the Hollywood Hills during the run-up to a series of nuclear tests in 1948 known as Operation Sandstone. It would become the government's largest film studio during the Cold War and among Hollywood's most comprehensive ones, producing over eighty-seven thousand hours of film footage [a decade's worth] and millions of still photos during its twenty-year history. And more than any other Cold War government film unit, and there were others, it drew upon the styles and systems of Hollywood as a means not simply of reporting on nuclear and other defense activities, but also of making sense of the Bomb and the Cold War more broadly.

Lookout Mountain Laboratory—later known as "Lookout Mountain Air Force Station"—was located in Laurel Canyon in the Hollywood Hills. Over the course of its two-decade history, it grew in size to be over forty thousand square feet and included a sound stage, screening rooms, a processing facility, an editorial department, giant film vaults, an industrial machine shop, and an animation studio. Well over one hundred people worked in the complex, mostly civilians: they shot, developed, cataloged, stored, and distributed hundreds of thousands of feet of film footage and photographs, and produced, scripted, and edited thousands of scientific, technical, and training films, together with official film reports and "informational" motion pictures for the public. The studio employed a wealth of Hollywood experts and brought in on an ad hoc basis such Hollywood notables as Jimmy Stewart, Walt Disney, Marilyn Monroe, Susan Hayward, and John Ford. Over its two-decade history, its clients included not only the Air Force and other branches of the Department of Defense, but also the Atomic Energy Commission, the Civil Defense Agency, NASA, and private government contractors such as Douglas Aircraft Company and Western Electric.

Moreover, as its name suggested, Lookout Mountain was a *laboratory*, a site for ambitious experiments in film and other technologies of visual representation. Its technical pursuits included high-speed camera kits, stereoscopic photography, underwater cameras, and new film storage and archiving techniques. Whereas other military film units made 16 mm film stock the mainstay of their routine training and educational films, Lookout Mountain made heavy use of 35 mm and even 70 mm stock. They helped test CinemaScope, Superscope, and Cinerama technologies, and did early work with stereophonic sound. The unit had an active and highly skilled animation department, staffed by animators who had worked on *Fantasia*, *Dumbo*, and other Disney features; it experimented with various sorts of special effects, including optical printing work; and it built innovative camera mounts for filming nuclear detonations, missile launches, and aerial bombardments from ground-based or airborne platforms. Custom-mounted Lookout Mountain cameras peered out of bombers into atomic clouds, tracked missiles and later manned rockets into

1968

space, and recorded sorties from the bellies of planes over Korea and Vietnam. Moreover, Lookout Mountain would serve as a secretive site for numerous meetings among nuclear-related military, political, scientific, and technical personnel attempting to steer a course for nuclear weapons development. As such, it was in its own way a nuclear weapons laboratory, like the better-known nuclear weapons laboratories at Los Alamos or Lawrence Livermore.

Government agencies and contractors preferred Lookout Mountain for film work because it possessed cutting-edge technical capabilities and staff with the high-level security clearances required for producing and storing nuclear weapons images. Always in demand, the studio constantly struggled to balance requests for labor-intensive, highly produced documentaries or training films with the demand for ready-response crews at multiple points around the globe to capture on film the innumerable activities of the secretive Cold War state. The group also provided extensive still photographic services and made thousands of charts, graphs, and other visual illustrations. It became, in short, a massive Cold War "information" system.

While the vast majority of Lookout Mountain's work was secretive, not all of it was. Many Lookout Mountain–produced films had public lives, and footage shot by the studio was spliced into newsreels, Hollywood films, and television broadcasts seen across the country, and sometimes around the globe. The unit's work was put up for an Oscar, won a "Cindy" award from the Industry Film Producers Association, and garnered awards at numerous smaller film festivals. Their work also earned recognition in technical journals for innovations in sound recording and scientific photography. Lookout Mountain's employees regularly presented at film industry conferences and won a number of patents for their innovations. NASA counted on Lookout Mountain–invented technology for records of its launches for years; Secretary of Defense Robert McNamara relied on Lookout Mountain camera crews for film used in the quantification of military action in Vietnam; and Hollywood producers depended on Lookout Mountain for stock footage for virtually any film that featured nuclear mushroom clouds, Stratojets, or Thunderbirds. Of the various Department of Defense photographic units, Lookout Mountain was closest in proximity to continental and Pacific atomic testing grounds, and to significant strategic facilities such as California's Vandenberg Air Force Base and the Strategic Air Command Headquarters and Command Center at Offutt Air Force Base. Its geographical location, together with its organizational location within the Air Force's Military Air Transport Service, combined to keep the facility operating at maximum capacity for twenty years.

There has never been a film studio like it, and until now no book has thoroughly told its history. This book, however, does more than tell the story of Lookout Mountain Laboratory; it also offers an account of the vision and sensibilities of the American Cold War state of which Lookout Mountain was a part. We tell the story of Lookout Mountain Laboratory as a story of America's Cold War, and vice versa. Given that Lookout Mountain was at the heart of the Cold War state, what did it see? And what do we learn about America's Cold War by looking at and through the cameras of Lookout Mountain? Our story begins with an account of America's atomic image problems and their redress in Lookout Mountain Laboratory. We then follow the work of the studio in support of the Cold War state as the latter created fearsome new technologies and engaged in the technical and rhetorical management of those technologies. In the course of our story, we travel from Hollywood to the Marshall Islands to Nevada, Florida, coastal California, the Arctic, and Vietnam. We of course also move through time, from the postwar atomic operations of the Navy to the air war in Vietnam. In each place and at each moment we see Lookout Mountain Laboratory working to produce compelling images and coherent narratives amid conflicted and contradictory Cold War conditions, above all the condition of the Bomb.

LOOKOUT AMERICA!

INTRODUCTION

Believe it. At the close of 1947 the United States Air Force, newly forged as an independent branch of the US Department of Defense, opened a cutting-edge film studio in Hollywood. Named "Lookout Mountain Laboratory," the 1352nd Photographic Group of the United States Air Force, as it was officially known throughout much of its career, was set up not just to take pictures and shoot film—by then established practices in the US military—but to make "movies," with all that entailed in postwar Hollywood.

The studio operated for some twenty years at the intersection between what President Eisenhower called the "military-industrial complex" and what German émigré intellectuals Max Horkheimer and Theodor Adorno called the "culture industry."[1] It stands, as such, at the origins of what James Der Derian describes as today's "military-media-entertainment network," the billion-dollar industry that fuses gaming, moviemaking, and war fighting into a seamless whole.[2] Lookout Mountain Laboratory provided photographs and film footage and edited feature films for a variety of clients across the Department of Defense and the Atomic Energy Commission, as well as for Hollywood studios. The facility also functioned as a film processing laboratory, storage facility, and regular meeting spot for atomic scientists and military brass. It employed hundreds of Hollywood veterans and summoned the services, as needed, of film luminaries such as John Ford, Jimmy Stewart, and Marilyn Monroe. Moreover, Lookout Mountain Laboratory worked closely with the most important innovators in scientific photography in midcentury America, above all the government contractor EG&G, or Edgerton, Germeshausen, and Grier, founded in 1947 by MIT's Harold Edgerton and his colleagues to support America's atomic weapons program.

In fact, most of the images of nuclear fireballs and mushroom clouds that we have today, including those later circulated in films such as *Hiroshima Mon Amour* and *Dr. Strangelove*, were shot by the cameras of Lookout Mountain Laboratory or EG&G, often functioning as the cinematic crescendos of Lookout Mountain movies. So, too, members of Lookout Mountain or its affiliates shot most of the footage of the early US space program, including launch and recovery photography for the Mercury, Gemini, and Apollo programs. Still later, footage from cameras originating in Lookout Mountain captured images of bombings and dogfights over Vietnam, broadcasted across the nation on the nightly news and rebroadcasted recently in Ken Burns and Lynn Novick's *The Vietnam War*. That is to say, though its history has been neglected and all but forgotten, Lookout Mountain is responsible for some of the most enduring iconography of America's Cold War. It is the most important and least known film operation of its era.

Why the neglect? Why forgotten? Two reasons suggest themselves. First, though the group produced a great number of films for the public, and even at times measured its success by such public exposure, secrecy was its day-to-day modus operandi. The vast majority of Lookout Mountain's films were classified, and many remain so today. Even its public films were more likely to carry the brand of the Air Force or other sponsoring agencies than "Lookout Mountain Laboratory" or the "1352nd Photographic Group." Moreover, upon its closing in the late 1960s, its archives were dispersed, lost, or otherwise neglected by the federal government. Hence, even though Lookout Mountain Laboratory was consumed with the creation of images and information and produced for the world a vast Cold War archive, it was a behind-the-scenes operation and was forgotten as such. Second, Lookout Mountain's history may be neglected because so many of its films now ap-

pear bygone. When viewers look at these films today on websites such as YouTube, the Internet Archive, or our own site, lookoutamerica.org, they may come across as not just dated but hokey, camp, affected, stylized, and overplayed. They seem to trumpet rather than document America's Cold War activities, even when those activities were manifest disasters. It's hard to take them seriously. Few have.

Indeed, if the government of the United States was under a king-like sovereign in the 1950s, today that king might be a bit embarrassed about his adventures, even ashamed. For not only did he play with the worst sort of fire—atomic, even thermonuclear—he also made secret movies about his atomic affairs, screening them in private viewing rooms, convinced [at the time] of his technological superiority not just by the big bangs he set off on Pacific isles and in Southwestern deserts, but by the fact that he could watch them replayed on-screen in sophisticated [at the time] motion pictures. If he were to look back at these movies today, if he had any sense at all, their stylized seriousness would probably make him feel a bit squeamish. Or he might react as one commenter on the Internet Archive did in 2006, with "quite a hoot."[3] To which we say again, as a kind of evangelistic counterpoint, hoot or not, believe it. Lookout Mountain Laboratory was a serious operation, deadly serious, and we offer here a serious book about its activities, artifacts, and filmic subject matter. This is not to say that we have not hooted [and gasped, laughed, cried, and more]. We have. But rather than trust our reactions, we have learned to question them.

One of the goals of this book is to resist the most obvious categories—camp, kitsch, cool, and so on—and instead show the seriousness of Lookout Mountain's work. To be sure kings and presidents have been fools, but the foolish king or president is a serious subject. So here in the opening pages of this history of what was arguably the most important film studio of America's Cold War, we lay out the most basic problems we have faced in writing this book, together with some of our initial arguments.

Why did Lookout Mountain make movies? "Documentation" of America's Cold War activities was the official answer. But their movies did far more than "document"; they dramatized America's Cold War, employing cutting-edge film technologies such as CinemaScope, VistaVision, new forms of high-speed photography, stereophonic sound, and a plenitude of props, sets, professionally written scripts, and animation. Who watched these movies? The American public had irregular access, and global publics even less so. Rather, the most typical audiences for Lookout Mountain movies were American officials working at various levels of state and military authority. Lookout Mountain frequently made training films for Air Force personnel. Meanwhile, military brass, defense brains, atomic scientists, high-level bureaucrats, members of Congress, and sometimes the president himself regularly watched their "documentary" productions.

As a rule, almost all Lookout Mountain films were designated initially as "restricted," and often "secret," even "top secret," with the special disposition "for public release" infrequently given. In this sense, Lookout Mountain Laboratory was a "secret" film studio: it is not that its existence was altogether unknown by Hollywood, but rather that the vast majority of its movies were unseen by the public because of their secretive nature. Instead, the main job of Lookout Mountain was to produce movies for the officials and operators of the American Cold War state. Indeed, Lookout Mountain films constituted a kind of "cinematic self-talk" for the state. Amid all the dire Cold War circumstances and rapid and dramatic technological and geopolitical changes in the 1950s and 1960s, America's leaders needed some positive narrative reinforcement. Lookout Mountain offered it on film.

We can therefore learn a lot about the American Cold War state by watching Lookout Mountain films. America's Cold War was a highly fluid and artificial affair that nevertheless produced a remarkably fixed sense of a bipolar global conflict together with a new and powerful generation of resilient institutions, technologies, and practices. Lookout Mountain not only worked amid the paradoxical instability and stability of the American Cold War state, but also mediated it in important respects by producing pictures, both still and moving, of the emerging Cold War. Above all, at Lookout Mountain, as at no other official US Cold War site, narratives and visual rhetorics could be produced that joined together what America's nuclearized Cold War was tearing asunder: namely, American moral agency and American technological agency. The studio was told to "document." But they realized that they needed to do considerably more: they needed to style America's Cold War, to engage in aesthetic and rhetorical negotiations of meaning, power, and politics. More broadly, extending Jacques Rancière's thesis that politics always entails "distributions of the sensible," we might say that Lookout Mountain realized it had to render America's Cold War activities, above all its nuclear activities, sensible, and we mean here something more than just "reasonable."[4]

"Sensibility" is a term with a broad set of meanings: it can denote an ability to sense, an ability to be sensed, a means by which to denote the "common sense" or "sensible" character of some action or idea, as well as a synonym for something like "taste" or what Raymond Williams referred to in more contemporary language as a "structure of feeling."[5] To claim that political orders are aesthetic orders among other things, as Rancière, Williams, Clifford Geertz, and other critics have done, is to claim that political orders sense, are sensed, and establish a common sense, both in the sense of the "reasonable" and in the sense of a structure of feeling.[6]

The camera is a sensibility medium, and Lookout Mountain was a sensibility operation. Its job was not only to use cameras to record American Cold War activities, but to transform film records into aesthetic objects to be sensed by others. And during all of this, the studio worked rhetorically and narratively to represent America's Cold War operations as both "reasonable" and as in conformity with dominant tastes, appetites, and desires.

For governments are not just born from the Earth, though they sometimes claim to be. They have to be made, formed, and constituted. So too with states (as in nation-states). They are artifacts, albeit very complex ones; they have to be built, rebuilt, and maintained. As such, states have actively sought to construct sensibilities: to sense, to be sensed, and to construct a common sense. As the political scientist and anthropologist James C. Scott has influentially argued, modern nation-states such as the United States have attempted to render the world "legible" (or understandable and workable) by, among other things, mapping, classifying, and abstractly organizing the everyday world, the lifeworld, into schemas and systems.[7] The boundaries of a state and corresponding maps are the most

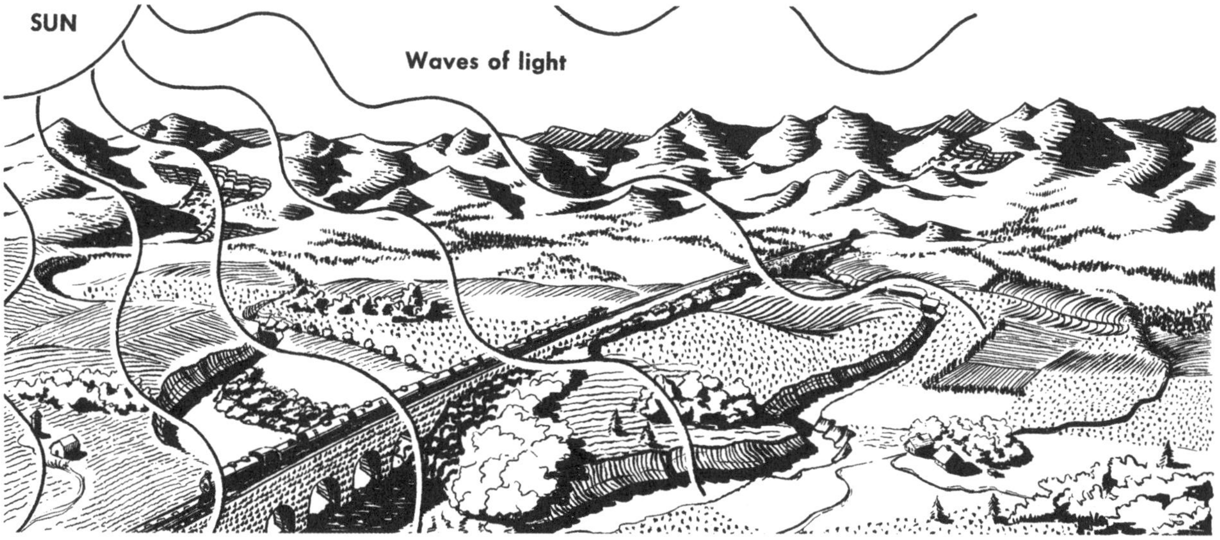

Fig. 1. Waves of Light

blatant example by which modern states have sought to make the world legible [as boundaries are never natural], but census figures, economic measures, polling, and social-scientific metrics each can seek similar ends.[8] Census figures, for example, help determine everything from voting districts to the allocation of funding for hospitals, public housing, and other social services.

However, states not only seek to make the world legible, they also attempt to render *themselves* legible to publics and other states, particularly in the form of legitimacy appeals: acts, arguments [broadly construed], or symbols calling for the recognition of the state's authority and rule as valid. Here the state must render itself, in part at least, like a text or image open to interpretation—for there is no other way to make legitimacy appeals other than to invite interpretive responses.[9] Indeed, legibility and legitimacy constitute two complementary poles of modern state authority, and both rest on what we have been calling sensibility: legibility entails a capacity to sense and legitimacy to be sensed. Moreover, both work together to establish a "common sense," both in the sense of the "reasonable" and in the sense of conforming to a common style and "structure of feeling."[10]

But in considering this twofold quality of what we are calling the "sensibility of the state," we need to add another consideration, technology. Technologies, especially technologies of communication, relate to our senses and to our "common sense" in all sorts of ways. The well-known media scholar James Carey, remarking on the work of Marshall McLuhan, once wrote, "The media of communication affect society principally by changing the dominant structures of taste and feeling, by altering the desired forms of experience."[11] Both legibility and claims of legitimacy have, for example, appealed to the paradigm of writing: legibility in obvious ways [it would make the world "readable"], and legitimacy in subtler interpretive or "hermeneutic" ways. Literacy and interpretation have hence been pivotal in the construction of modern statehood, which makes the written law central. The imposition of order by legislation, mapping, classifying, and abstractly organizing the everyday world into a governed system of rules and laws is a basic state function, as is the attempt of the state to render itself symbolically meaningful in the context of the "nation."[12]

As media scholars such as Paul Virilio, Friedrich Kittler, and Roger Stahl have shown,

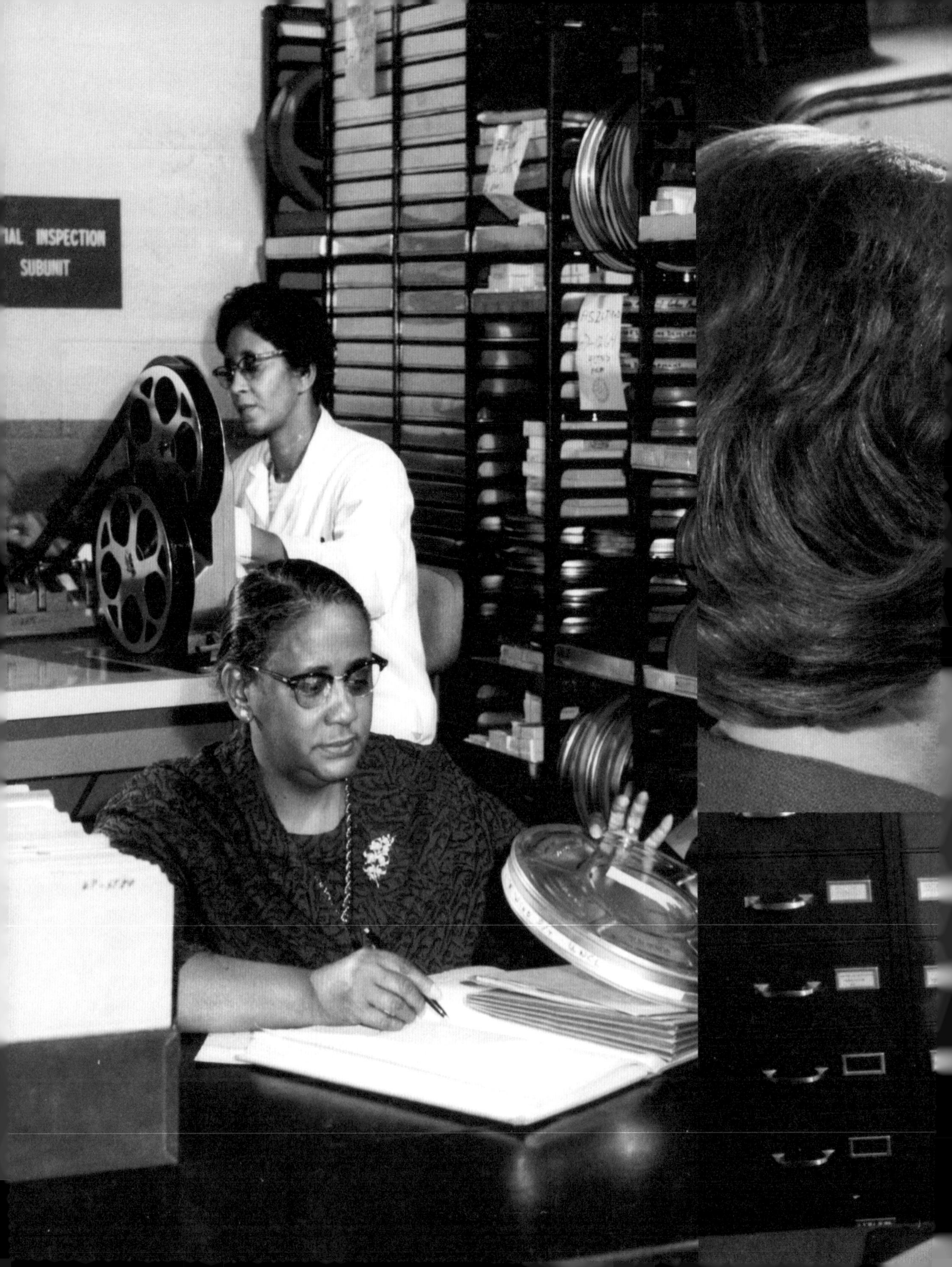
IAL INSPECTION
SUBUNIT

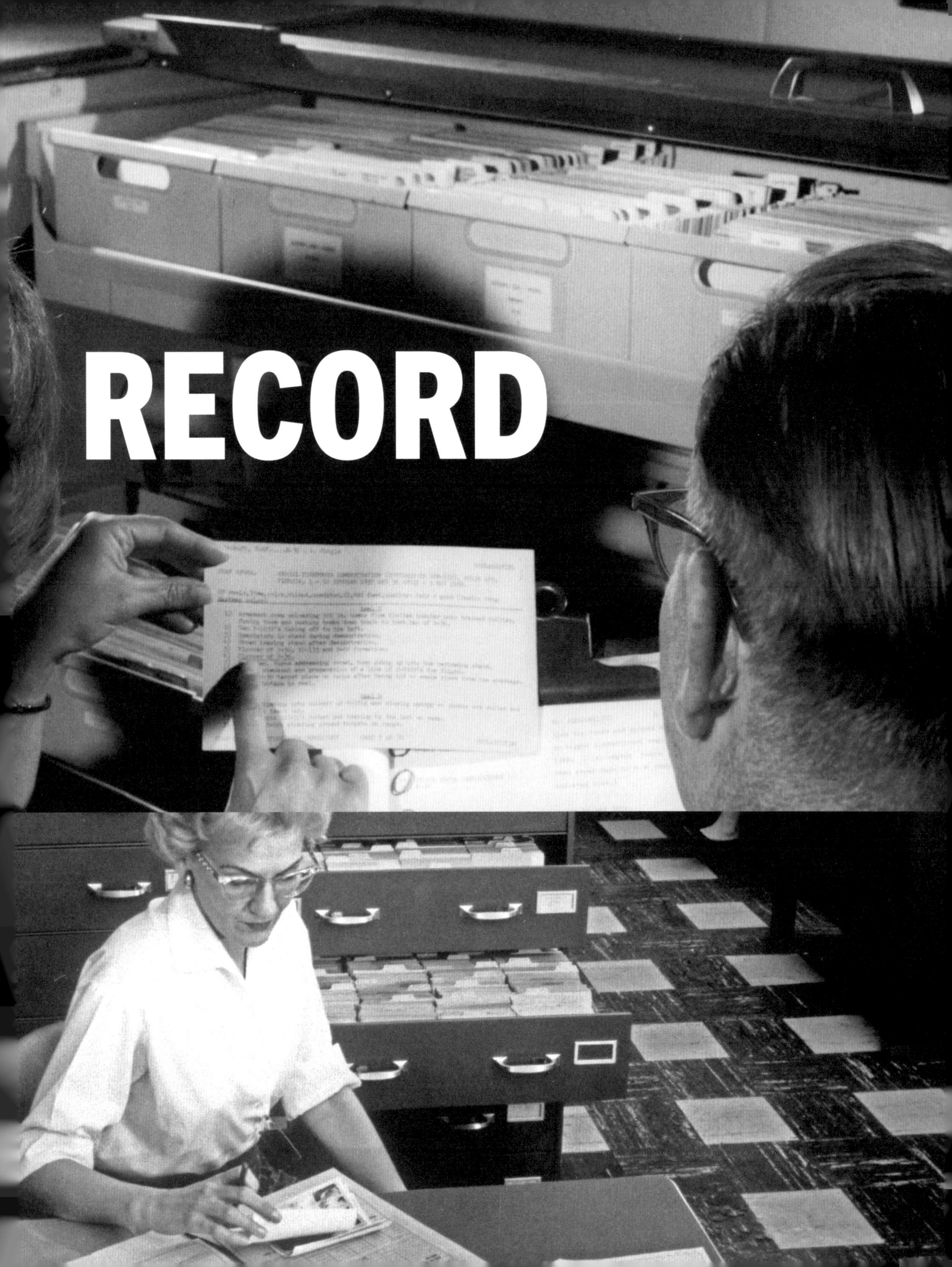
RECORD

in addition to writing the modern state has also made heavy use of other visual media like scopes, sights, and screens, particularly in war-making activities.[13] Such visual media have had more than instrumental importance for the state; they have contributed, with writing, to the solidification of state power through violence.[14] But even here we have perhaps underestimated the role of one of the most crucial developments in modern visual media, *film*. Film may be no more than an elaborate writing technology (though Kittler and others would differ), but exposed film, unlike most forms of writing, has itself been acted upon by the world, via light, and indexes that act. Ariella Azoulay writes, "Writing in light is what transpires when the camera shutter opens and light rays, reflected off that which stands in front of the camera, penetrate the lens and are inscribed upon a certain surface." Who or what does this writing? "[N]ature," Azoulay concludes, "now inscribes itself by itself," and this makes photography an altogether peculiar sort of writing.[15]

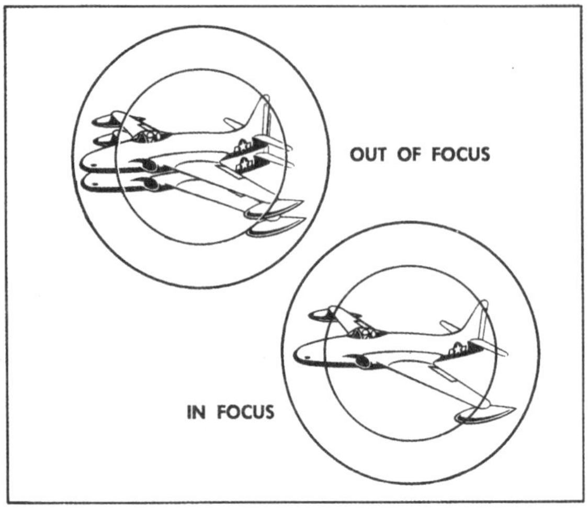

Range Finder Focus

As such, film—especially when coupled with recorded or manufactured sound—may approach a direct relationship to the world more aggressively than writing, charting, accountancy, and so on. Think about all the controversy on whether statistics "really" reflect the world as it is, or whether they are "manipulated" to serve ulterior motives, contrasting that debate with the relatively mild intensity of the discussion about whether photojournalists "really" capture the events of war in their images. In the middle of the twentieth century, film's apparent capability to directly absorb and factually record the world granted it a seemingly immediate connection to flesh, action, surroundings, and life, an immediacy that eluded traditional writing or numerical calculations. It even offered an apparent window into the inner workings of otherwise invisible phenomena.[16] And in the reanimation of motion-picture projection, film offered something more than the schema of legibility; it offered story and spectacle. It was no coincidence that film offered the state the tantalizing possibility of something beyond laws and statistics: a "realism" that could also serve spectacle and powerful, meaningful story.

In the last decade, critical scholars of photography have significantly complicated the purported "direct" relationship of film to the world. Azoulay has argued that photography is an ongoing negotiation among human subjects, camera technologies, photographic subjects, photographic objects, media systems, political systems, and collective civic and moral commitments.[17] Robert Hariman and John Lucaites have argued that interpretation is basic to photography, despite the widespread cultural assumption, particularly in mid-twentieth-century America, of photographic realism (the camera merely reproduces that which is front of the lens). Hariman and Lucaites argue that while realism is "the first principle of photographic meaning, it cannot be achieved completely without imaginative presentation and response. The camera records the surface of the world like no other instrument, but the truth of what is shown can be realized only through an act of imagination."[18] In writing in light, film, like all writing, opens itself up to *reading*, with all that entails. Indeed, visual studies scholar Nicholas Mirzoeff has eloquently argued that just as we need to learn how to read, so we need to learn how to look.[19]

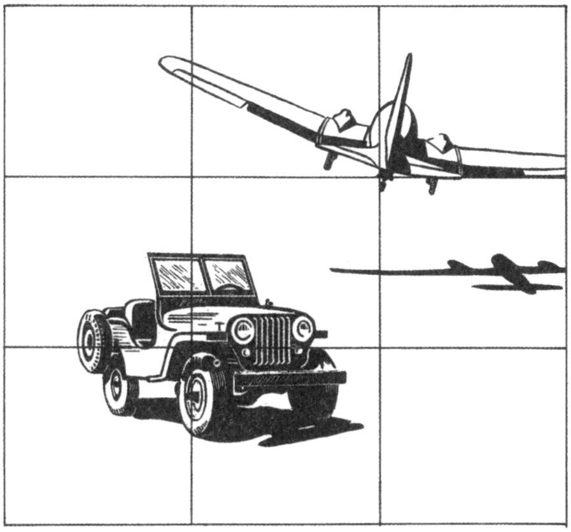

Fig. 84. Division of Area for Balance

In addition, recent film scholarship has produced a strong body of work on nontheatrical, scientific, and industrial films such as those produced by Lookout Mountain Laboratory in the middle of the twentieth century.[20] Vinzenz Hediger and Patrick Vonderau describe the "three Rs" of such films: film as *record*, *rhetoric*, and *rationalization*. "Record" refers to the ways in which film serves institutional memory; "rhetoric" to strategies of inducing audience cooperation and consent; and "rationalization" to the ways in which films are used to "improve organizational performance."[21] To be sure, the films of Lookout Mountain fulfilled each of these "three Rs." They were crucial to the Atomic Energy Commission, Department of Defense, and larger governmental institutional memories, both in the strong material sense of storing scientific data central to weapons development and in the more ephemeral sense of institutional and national legacies and ideologies. At the same time, Lookout Mountain films represented far more than reels of memory. They were actively produced to get things done, especially to support Air Force weapons development, and they got this done through the production of cinematic rhetorics. Finally, these films were a means of maintaining and sometimes enhancing the vast machinery that made up the military-industrial complex in the first decades of the Cold War.

That twentieth-century states made broad use of film, ranging from police photo books to surveillance footage to propaganda films, suggests that the camera offered modern states the range of possibilities to which Hediger and Vonderau point. Film, that is, should not be understood as only a potential organ of state power for surveillance or propagandistic control, though it is that. It also has been a means by which states in crisis have approached and sought to secure memory and meaning. Most broadly, film and cameras have addressed the state's manifold attempts at sensibility: its efforts at perception, an ability to see and sense; its attempt at materialization, an ability *to be* sensed; and its work to form and conform to a shared "common sense" about the way the world works.

Indeed, in World War II the camera moved into the heart of the sensibility of the US warfare state. The entrance of the camera was a factor of both analytics and appetite. Photographers and cameras were conscripted by the War Department in large numbers to document combat operations and their effects. Film provided defense analysts with target images, damage data, and other measures of American operational efficiencies. But far more than documentation and data, the US government also saw in the camera, as Thomas Doherty has argued, a vital inroad into "cultural meaning," specifically in the form of Hollywood motion pictures. Amid the emergency conditions of World War II, Washington and Hollywood formed an "unprecedented alliance" that "generated not only new kinds of movies but a new attitude toward them."[22] All sorts of films—educational, documentary, comedies, musicals, melodramas, newsreels, and film reports—were spun out of Hollywood and its affiliates on behalf of the war effort with breathtaking rapidity, with both Hollywood and the government richly benefiting from these war efforts.[23]

It is therefore not surprising that the camera remained a primary state organ after the war. In the early days of the Cold War, the Department

RHETORIC

PARCHMENT
BRAND

of State, the Atomic Energy Commission, and the various branches of the US military integrated film production units into their day-to-day organizational and operational structures. Images of the effects of atomic weapons and devices were more than emblematic here; they were "representative," in a political sense, standing in for the state and its ambitions, performing them, realizing them. In America's experiments with atomic power, film absorbed light so that the state could construct its own sensibility. In film and through the camera the United States came to see, to see itself, and to be seen. And Lookout Mountain Laboratory became the preeminent official film unit of America's Cold War.

Two forms of sensibility framed Lookout Mountain's operations, what we refer to as the "cinematic" sensibility and the "cybernetic" sensibility. Starting with the former, in his 1951 book, *White Collar*, sociologist C. Wright Mills commented on the "numbness" of Americans before the disasters of World War II:

> People sat in the movies between production shifts, watching with aloofness and even visible indifference, as children were "saturation bombed" in the narrow cellars of European cities. Man had become an object; and in so far as those for whom he was an object felt about the spectacle at all, they felt powerless, in the grip of larger forces, having no part in these affairs that lay beyond their immediate areas of daily demand and gratification. . . . It was as if the expert angle of the camera and the carefully nurtured, pompous voice of the commentator had expropriated the chance to "take it big." It was as if the ear had become a sensitive soundtrack, the eye a precision camera, experience an exactly timed collaboration between microphone and lens, the machines thus taking unto themselves the capacity for experience.[24]

For Americans both during and after the war, cinema was far more than Hollywood stars and starlets; it was part of the broader fabric of American culture. What scholar Anne Friedberg describes as the "classical spectatorship" associated with Hollywood cinema—immobile viewers in the dark, dwarfed by larger-than-life images that conflate the temporalities of diegesis and of viewing—had by then found expression in all manner of media and culture as a style, as well as a mode of production and reception.[25] Newsreels constituted a major source of news and information, and noncinematic media such as *Look* and *Life* magazines, especially the latter, took on a distinctly cinematic style, with compelling stories focused on identifiable characters that drew on vivid pictures more than vivid text for their rhetorical force. Meanwhile, other art forms took up cinema as a subject: Tennessee Williams's *The Glass Menagerie* featured Tom Wingfield filling up his off-hours from his warehouse work at the movies; Walker Percy's *The Moviegoer*, which won the National Book Award in 1962, followed Binx Bolling in and out of movies as he embarked on his existential "search"; and designers such as Charles and Ray Eames began taking up the screen as an architectural and design motif.[26]

The cinematic sensibility, therefore, represents a midcentury American cultural formation that emerged from decades of production and reception in "classical cinema" around the globe. Its typical features can be approached in aesthetic, epistemological, and ethical terms. Aesthetically, the cinematic sensibility moves between the neoclassical aesthetic poles of the beautiful and the sublime, and the romantic

poles of heroism and sentimentalism. It seeks to focus, intensify, and heighten experience, rather than just leaving experience to be. But this heightened subjectivity always risks taking experience unto itself, as Mills notes, thus leaving the spectator numb. Similarly, the cinematic sensibility tends to heighten reality, but this can quickly turn into a sense of unreality, even hyperreality [a point where the cinematic and cybernetic sensibilities will later converge, well before the rise of mobile media in the 1990s].[27] Epistemologically, the cinematic sensibility is characterized by a hermeneutic or interpretive impulse. This impulse is related to not only spectatorship, but voyeurism—the capability of the camera to manipulate perspective, to switch angles, to zoom in and out—that is, to move. Movement means the viewer has to actively interpret what she sees not only as an observer but as a participant, to recognize a change of angle as a change in perspective, to fill in the gaps between edits, and so on. The cinematic sensibility therefore approaches meaning in terms of interpretation. Ethically, the cinematic sensibility approaches something like a "virtue ethic."[28] As the cinematic screen is a site of story, so the cinematic sensibility is narratively oriented, characterized by motifs of adventure, adversity, antagonism, and the "quest."[29] The cinematic sensibility presents the ethical life—be it individual or collective—in terms of a movement from tensions to their resolutions in terms of characters, plot, and action.

But Mills's *White Collar* suggested the rise of another sort of sensibility, what we refer to as the cybernetic sensibility: "You are the cog and the beltline of the bureaucratic machinery itself; you are a link in the chains of commands, persuasions, notices, bills, which bind together the men who make decisions and the men who make things; without you the managerial demiurge could not be. But your authority is confined strictly within a prescribed orbit of occupational actions, and such power as you wield is a borrowed thing. . . . You are the servant of decision, the assistant of authority, the minion of management."[30]

Cybernetics was a term famously created by the midcentury mathematician Norbert Wiener and is the title of his 1948 book *Cybernetics: Or Control and Communication in the Animal and the Machine*. In that book, Wiener argued for a marriage between solutions to the problems of control and those of communications: by approaching problems of control as problems of communications [and vice versa], one could move beyond any one technique or technology to think in a "much more fundamental" manner about control problems.[31] As such, cybernetics, as Wiener suggested in coining the term, pursued the perfection of "steersmanship" by means of refining complex systems via the processes of feedback systems and control loops.

But cybernetics encompassed far more than a project by a single, if singular, mathematician. It was part of a far-reaching sensibility that too can be approached in aesthetic, epistemological, and ethical terms. Aesthetically, the cybernetic sensibility turns on *seeing systems*: it sees everywhere schemes, feedback loops, circuits, and so on, and understands all things—human, nonhuman, and human-machine—in terms of information flows, and ultimately modes of "control" through "commands." Inputs and outputs form the schematic boundaries of the cybernetic sensibility, creating the assumption of what Paul Edwards has described as the "closed world" of cybernetics.[32] In terms of epistemology, the cybernetic sensibility privileges heuristics over hermeneutics. Assuming

REFLEX ACTION BOMBER
WEATHER

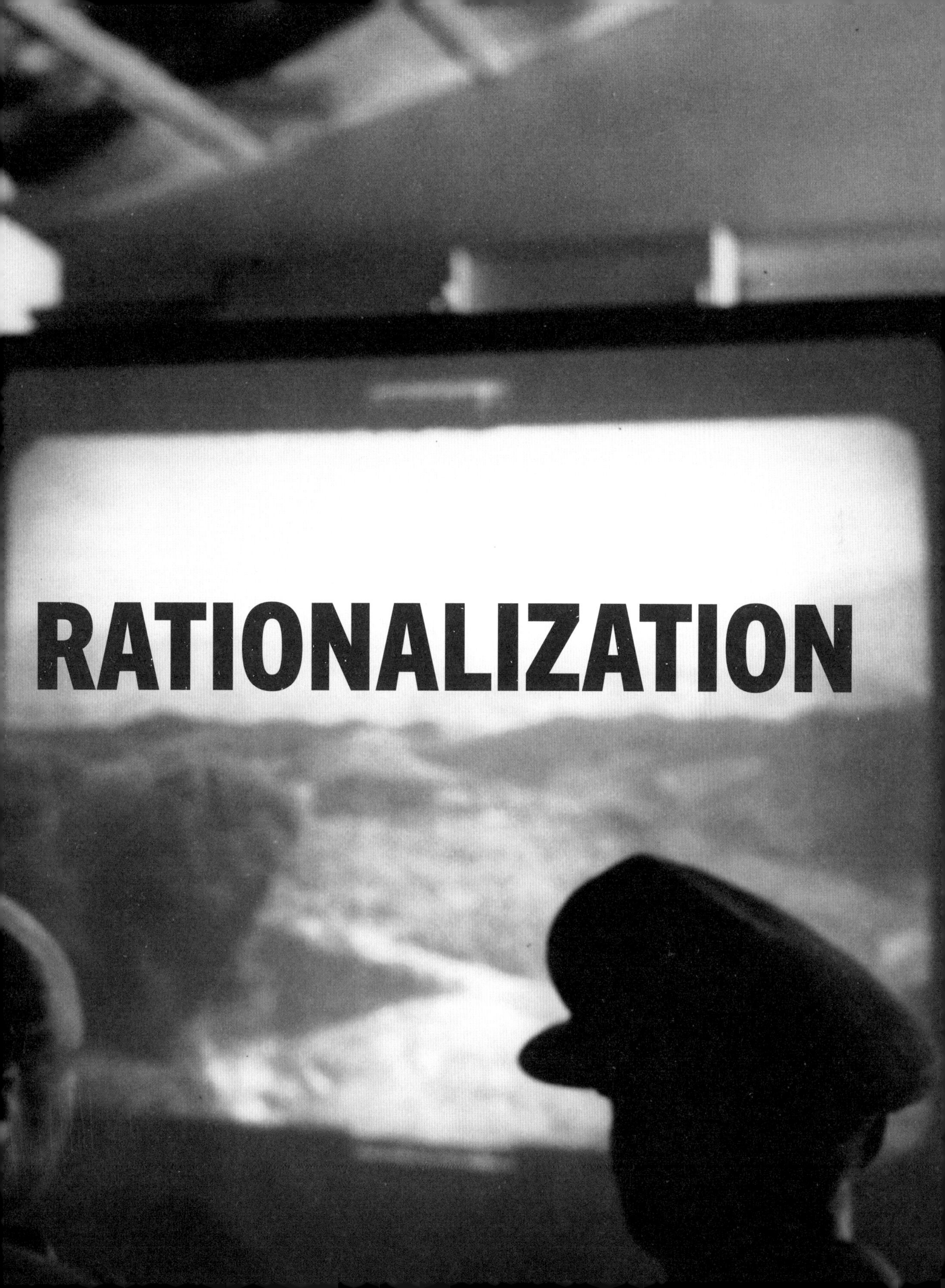

RATIONALIZATION

an "informational surfeit," a proliferation of data, methodology, organization, and rule systems took precedence over interpretive judgments.[33] In this postwar moment, as Orit Halpern argues, "Vision and cognition were rendered equivalent, a 'process.'"[34] The cybernetic sensibility moved between the aesthetic-epistemological poles of modernist abstraction and utilitarian documentation, and between the ethical poles of a kind of scientific, even stoic, objectivity and utilitarian cost/benefit calculus. Ethics was a problem of control. And of course, the iconic technological analog of cybernetics was electronic computing, rather than cinema. As operating machines, computers, in the words of Edwards, "served not only as military devices and tools of policy analysis but as icons and metaphors in the cultural construction of the Cold War."[35] And computer interfaces condensed communications and control, knowledge, and action into a single visible screen. Computers as such exemplified in their operations and their visual presentation the power of systemic communications and control. Within the cybernetic sensibility, computers came to symbolically span "mind," "machine," and indeed the state itself.

As suggested here, the cinematic and cybernetic sensibilities offer a window into not only the work of Lookout Mountain, but also the world of America's Cold War more broadly. Indeed, in significant respects America's Cold War from the age of George Kennan to that of Robert McNamara can be understood as a movement from the cinematic sensibility to the cybernetic one, as hermeneutic modes of inquiry, so typical of Kennan, were displaced by the heuristic ones so typical of McNamara. In the 1960s, the ignoble "killing machines" of Vietnam overcame the heroic ethos of World War II, and cost-benefit analyses replaced romantic ideals of heroism and freedom.

Take the word "information."[36] In the summer of 1950, the Department of Defense's Ad Hoc Committee on Chemical, Biological, and Radiological Warfare—established in 1949 by Secretary of Defense Louis Johnson—urged the defense department to take the lead in coordinating public information on "weapons of mass destruction" [a phrase that the report urged publicists not to use]. It sought an "organic" public information campaign, one that did not appear forced, coordinated with the Department of State and aimed at offering "information" free of both "emotion" and "moral implications." The goal was "making the public aware in a nonhysterical sense" through a "factual and objective viewpoint" so as to avoid "panic," "speculation," and "exaggerated fear." Such an "educational" program, the Ad Hoc Committee reported, could prepare Americans to withstand with relative calm chemical, biological, or atomic attacks on their cities and encourage them to support America's ongoing chemical, biological, and atomic weapons programs. The committee therefore recommended that the government carefully measure the "impression," "tone," "indications," and "terms" used to directly or indirectly [through leaks] manage publicity about "wonder weapons."[37] This was all part of its "information" campaign.

Now compare this sense of "information"—that which one agent communicates to another via a medium and framed in terms of "tone," "emotion," and "moral implications"—with the official definition of "command and control" offered by the US Joint Chiefs of Staff in 1961, the first definition of its kind: "An arrangement of personnel, facilities, and the means for information acquisition, processing, and dissemination employed by a commander in planning, directing, and controlling operations."[38] "Information" is here not simply something that is communicated by one agent to another, but something that is acquired, processed, and disseminated within a larger "operational" process. It is part of a "system," such that "information" and "communication" become virtual synonyms [electronic computers could be called "information systems" or "communication systems"]. The United States Air Force was at the heart of the rise of "command and control" in the 1950s, and with it, this different, cybernetic sense of "information."[39]

"Command and control" took hold in the US military after World War II and before the prospects of atomic warfare: these weapons were so powerful that their command had to be centralized, or *controlled*.[40] A hierarchical structure was put in place, with the president at the top, and elaborate systems built so that rapid decisions could be made. These systems were called "communication" or "information" systems, a (con)fusion that suggested a more basic melding between processes and substances, rendered virtually identical within larger operational systems. Thus government, industry, and media began to speak as much of "information processes" as of "information programs"; and in computing, programs would indeed be processes.

Lookout Mountain felt the effects of the transformation from the cinematic to the cybernetic sensibilities of the American Cold War state. For its first ten years, its main work revolved around recognizable cinematic subjects: characters, stories, action. It engaged, we might say, in informational programming in the sense of media production and so-called edutainment. But as it moved into the 1960s, Lookout Mountain found itself pulled more strongly in the direction of "data" production, so that by the beginning of the Vietnam War in 1965, the studio was busy building, fitting, and operating camera mounts on fighter planes to record bombardment footage. Such work was as old as aerial war photography itself, but the difference was not only that the Pentagon was stripping the studio of its cinematic subjects, but it was processing Lookout Mountain's film footage as one set of "data" among others, incorporated into a giant modern war computer. To be sure, even in its early years Lookout Mountain generated plenty of footage for use in postdetonation, postlaunch, or postattack data analysis; but the studio was originally set up for edited film productions more than for data analysis. In the late 1950s and 1960s, with the rise of a cybernetic sensibility, Lookout Mountain restructured its technical, organizational, and communicative practices to facilitate the efficient flow of images-as-information, including setting up internal review and critique processes to improve the functional quality of such "informational" images. The unit's leaders grew ever more focused on getting the right images before the right eyes at every level of decision making, from the pilot over Vietnam to the adviser in the White House. Lookout Mountain had become a cybernetician's dream: a kind of living information processing machine.

But the story of Lookout Mountain is not really the displacement of a cinematic sensibility with a cybernetic sensibility. It is more complicated than that, for the cybernetic was the subject of so many of Lookout Mountain films during its "cinematic" phase. Over and over again, Lookout Mountain films featured men and machines, and men at machines, working in "systems" and executing operations. Early on Lookout Mountain framed the Cold War state as what we call a "state of operations." The cinematic sensibility helped construct the cybernetic sensibility, and both helped build the American Cold War state into a state of operations comprising discrete, distributed, and ideally coordinated geopolitical actions. As Lookout Mountain dramatized the rise of men, machines, and the Cold War, they drew on the peculiar capacity of the camera to bring together technique and art, engineering and imagination, objectivity and subjectivity—the very poles that the rest of America's Cold War activities seemed to be driving apart. Their cameras offered the state imaginative and narrative forms for conceiving of and waging an American-style "scientific" Cold War.

Their cameras, however, were rarely directly seen. While their images were everywhere—from mushroom clouds, to missile launches, to space monkeys—Lookout Mountain was hardly noticed even by government officials, let alone members of the public. And this brings us back to the most significant challenge we faced in writing this book, and to a central argument. Lookout Mountain, like the camera, but unlike many other Cold War sites and institutions, was

TRANSFERRED TO THE FEDERAL RECORDS CENTER 18 May 68

MASTER CARD

UNCLASSIFIED

SFP 1028. PHOTOGRAPHY IN THE USAF - OPTICAL INSTRUMENTATION AT VANDENBERG AFB, CALIFORNIA (1960).

2 reels, 35mm, color, sound, edited, 1508 feet, quality: Good (Basic: Orig color "A&B" Rolls)

Covers mission of 1352nd Motion Picture Squadron in providing optical instrumentation and record photography for 1st Missile Division and for AFBMD in support of research and development launches and SAC training exercises. (Photo'd by 1352nd)

1 reel, 16mm, analyzed)

1) Scenes of Atlas launch -- show missile veering off course and being destroyed.
2) Shows telemetry control panels.
3) Technicians screening film on light table.
4) Scenes of Thor/Discoverer launch -- shows missile veering off course and being destroyed.
5) Scenes of remote and manned camera installations surrounding launch area -- shows crews setting up equipment, checking electrical circuits and manning tracking camera mounts.

603' Total footage in reel.

THE END

USAF MOTION PICTURE FILM DEPOSITORY CARD 1 OF 1 UNCLASSIFIED

MASTER CARD

UNCLASSIFIED

FOR OFFICIAL USE ONLY

FR-743. AIR STRIKES, SOUTHEAST ASIA (REPORT ENDING 25 AUGUST 1966).

2 reels, 16mm, color, sound, edited, 744 feet, quality: Good (Basic: Mas ektachrome "A,B & C" rolls

Documentary footage of July and August air strikes on concentrated structures, bridges, watercraft, observation post and POL utilizing F-4C, F-100 and F-105 aircraft. Many scenes have North and South Vietnam outline map superimposed at beginning of mission run with pop-ons of location. (Photo'd by 1352nd)

(1 reel, 16mm, analyzed) Reel 1

11' Forward PMC footage of F-4C dropping napalm on Viet Cong structure west of Chu Lai -- shows napalm burst and damaged buildings. (24 July 1966)
23' Forward PMC footage of rockets striking Viet Cong area along river and striking objects in water and densely wooded area.
41' Aft PMC footage of incendiary bomb burst in area west of Saigon. (27 July)
63' ALS of F-4C dropping napalms at low level on Viet Cong structures -- map of North and South Vietnam superimposed over scene.
89' Aft PMC footage of CBU passes along river and structures -- shows bomblets bursting.
113' ALS of F-4C dropping napalm south of Pleiku in wooded area.
117' Forward PMC footage of rocket attack on Viet Cong village -- shows launch and impact near Da Nang.
140' ALS of F-4C dropping bombs on structures.
152' ALS's of F-4C going in over wooded target and dropping napalms.

USAF MOTION PICTURE FILM DEPOSITORY CARD 1 OF 3 UNCLASSIFIED a "behind the scenes" operation. More properly, they were "before the scenes," both chronologically and spatially. Their scripts, cameras, and editorial units did the framing, but Lookout Mountain itself was rarely framed as a subject. They operated, in a certain sense, invisibly. Lacking the financial incentives of an MGM or a Universal Studios to "go public," Lookout Mountain invested relatively little in its own brand or imprimatur. To be sure, its commanding officers tried to promote the value of the unit to the Air Force and the Atomic Energy Commission. But once that value diminished, there was little will to remember and preserve the memory of the unit and its work.

Archives are not automatic. Like states, they have to be made and preserved. Typically, when researching histories having to do with the activities of the US government, scholars rely on relatively well-organized discrete official archives. No such archive exists for Lookout Mountain Laboratory, for the makers of archives have to have some reason to make an archive, as well as resources. It is apparent that when Lookout Mountain was closed in 1969—though the studio was itself a kind of archive, holding thousands of films and hundreds of thousands of still photos, cataloged through meticulously constructed caption sheets to aid in retrieval—no one cared to archive its records and holdings, at least not as an archive of Lookout Mountain Laboratory. Instead, these artifacts were treated like the contents of a grandparent's attic upon his or her death. Some of Lookout Mountain's holdings were sent to Los Alamos or other Atomic Energy Commission sites, where they were added to research libraries. Some films followed other personnel and equipment to a new operation at nearby Norton Air Force Base, where the Air Force and eventually other defense units would consolidate their audiovisual labor. Other items slowly and haphazardly made their way to the National Archives. The Air Force's Historical Research Agency managed to get some documents, largely as they were sent up the chain of command. But a large portion of Lookout Mountain's holdings, including thousands of film canisters, negatives, photographer's logbooks, various reports, and many still photographs, were trucked off to an Air Force warehouse in California, where they were piled (rather than compiled) and either discarded or forgotten.

It took the curiosity of a nuclear test scientist some years later to help recover what survived. Dr. Byron Risvet, a geologist working for the Department of Defense, wanted to learn more about the effects of nuclear blasts on sand and soil. At Los Alamos he came across some Lookout Mountain footage of nuclear blasts in the Pacific, and he set out to locate more. This brought him eventually to the pile of stuff in an Air Force warehouse. Dr. Risvet summoned some government trucks to go get the pile and ship it back to Kirtland Air Force Base in Albuquerque, where it was put under the custody of Dr. Risvet's organization, the Defense Threat Reduction Information Analysis Center (or DTRIAC, since we are now in the acronymed world of the Department of Defense—we are, in fact, going to try to avoid acronyms in this book). DTRIAC, of course, is not open to the public, definitely not—not even to the scholarly public, unless you are a government or government contractor "scholar" with security clearances. Scholars like us have a hard time getting access to DTRIAC. If they do, they have to be constantly watched or "escorted." All electronic devices, let alone all electronic recording devices, have to be left at the gate. Only pencils and paper are allowed. And once you get in, unless you have security clearances, you can see only a small number of items: the logbooks, some reports, a few films.[41]

The point of all of this is not to chronicle our research adventures—of which there are numerous others (see our "Epilogue and Acknowledgments")—but rather to present a research problem. The scattered, deteriorating, disorganized, neglected, and often inaccessible archives of Lookout Mountain Laboratory are not just a challenge for research, but a basic research problem calling for critical answers. Part of the history of Lookout Mountain Laboratory is the virtual disappearance of its archives. That its holdings were relegated to the emptying of the "attic" of the Air Force says much about the climate of the Cold War in America in the late-1960s. It also says much about the structure of the Cold War state. Finally, it says quite a bit about the invisibility of the camera to historiographical optics.

And this history presents us, as critics and historiographers, with a basic question: Do we write the history of Lookout Mountain as if there were no history of neglect, as if there were a relatively organized and coherent archive from which to work? Do we ignore, in fact hide, the problems of the archives, as historians often do? Or do we instead make the problem of the archive a subject of the book? We have chosen a middle path. This book is a critical history. We want to tell the story of Lookout Mountain Laboratory, but in a way that does not glide over its fraught, complex, and often covert history. To be sure, we have written a history of Lookout Mountain Laboratory that, for the most part, smooths over the major challenges we, as researchers, faced in reconstructing its history. But we do not smooth over the tensions and contradictions that typify this history, for the basic aim of the book is to tell not only a history of Lookout Mountain Laboratory, but also a history of the United States' Cold War as it appeared in and through Lookout Mountain's cameras and operations. Lookout Mountain stood in a dialectical relationship to the US Cold War state: it was both its chronicler and its producer. As such, the studio was every bit as complex and contradictory as the state that sponsored it, and which it projected. In the pages that follow, telling that complex and contradictory story is our central aim.

The first two chapters concern the advent of Lookout Mountain Laboratory and its place at the postwar cultural nexus of the military-industrial complex and the culture industry. In chapter 1, "Hollywood's Nuclear Weapons Laboratory," we trace its beginnings in Hollywood amid America's postwar nuclear weapons regime; in chapter 2, "Colonels, Cameras, and Security Clearances," we climb up the chain of command, so to speak, and look at the military and government organizations with which Lookout Mountain worked and to which they directly reported. Subsequent chapters focus on Lookout Mountain's films and operations, and are organized around the main geographic sites of their operations: the Pacific, the Nevada Test Site, Vandenberg Air Force Base, the Arctic, and to a lesser but still crucial extent, airspace and outer space. America's Cold War was very much a "staging" operation, premised on the power of technological spectacle. In chapter 3, "Strategies of Containment," we consider the way in which the Pacific was staged in the cameras of Lookout Mountain as a "pristine laboratory" much more than what it was: an imperial site for adventurous, dangerous, and indeed highly destructive nuclear experiments. Chapter 4, "Sense and Sensibilities," looks at the production history of Lookout Mountain's most famous and controversial film about the Pacific nuclear tests, Operation Ivy. Here we find the American nuclear state using narrative film to try to make nuclear weapons make sense to members of Congress, mayors, and the public. Chapter 5, "Routine Reports," focuses on Lookout Mountain films about nuclear tests in the Nevada desert, a space that also appeared as a laboratory, but a barren rather than pristine one, and thus a far more reconfigurable stage for the "routine" engineering operations of nuclear testing. Both the Pacific atolls and the Nevada desert were sites of political conquest as well as technological dominion. In chapters 6 and 7, "The Vectors of America" and "Engineering Geographies" respectively, we look at the ways in which in the Arctic and in outer space the logics of political conquest and technological dominion were fused in accounts of Air Force missile, radar-defense, and space activities. Chapter 8, "The Vietnamization of the Cold War Camera," turns to Lookout Mountain's activities in Vietnam, activities that ended up spelling the studio's end through absorption into a larger system largely of its own invention, and the culmination of the transformation of the American Cold War state from cinematic sensibility to a cybernetic one. Chapter 9, "Mushroom Cloud Cameras," steps back from the particulars of Lookout Mountain's history to critically reflect on the power of cameras in the American nuclear state; and chapter 10, "Closure," relates the story of Lookout Mountain's closing, arguing for its significance for understanding the changing nature of the national security state at the end of the 1960s.

The back matter of this book matters a lot. We encourage not only reading the "Epilogue and Acknowledgments," but also skimming through the Sources. There you will learn more of our own research adventures and find other routes into the history of Lookout Mountain and our research materials. We hope that when you are finished reading this book, you will believe that one of the most important sites for America's Cold War was this little-known Air Force film studio up in the Hollywood Hills, and you will continue to critically reflect with us and others on the ongoing configurations of the American military-media-entertainment network.

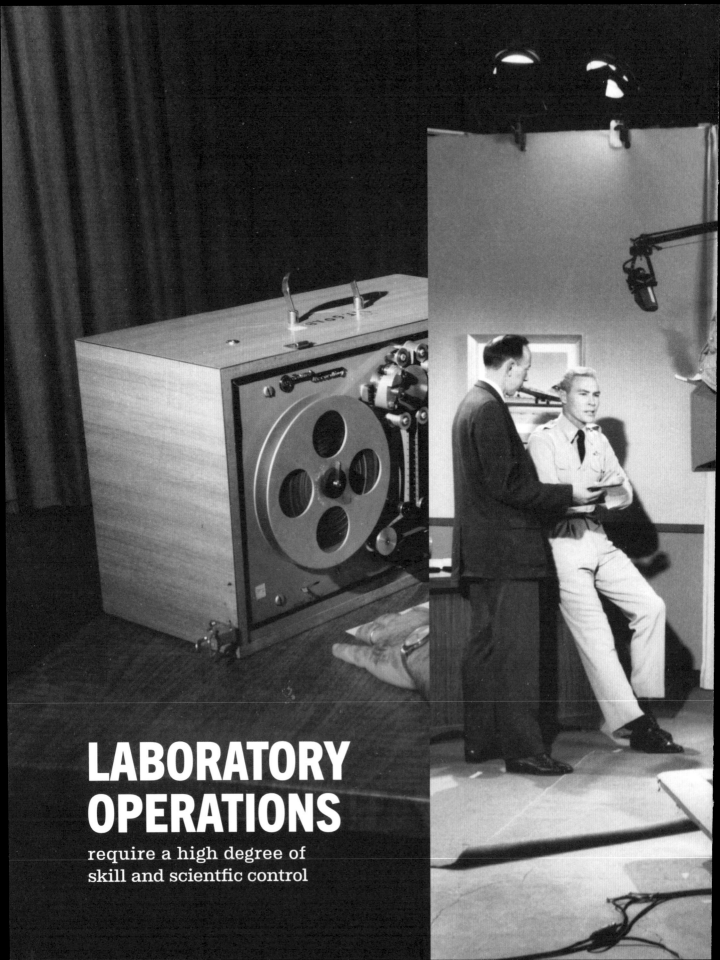

LABORATORY OPERATIONS

require a high degree of skill and scientfic control

Chapter One

HOLLYWOOD'S NUCLEAR WEAPONS LABORATORY

It was a scene from the 1960s, set in 1954. Angry protesters lined up outside a government defense facility, carrying placards decrying its activities. A petition, directed to the "Government of the United States," was circulated. Congressmen were called. And court options were considered. The *Los Angeles Times* picked up the story. Its front-page report on June 19, 1954, began, "Bitter protests that the city building code is being violated, that traffic conditions are endangering children's lives and that nearby property is being damaged by operations at a 'top secret' Air Force film-processing laboratory now being expanded at 8900 Wonderland Ave., in a canyon of the Hollywood Hills, were voiced yesterday by a score of residents of the area."[1]

According to the newspaper account, a neighbor to the facility complained that when her car backfired one night she found herself the subject of Air Force floodlights. Others reported that the facility's armed guards threatened children. And another said his mailbox was knocked down four times by construction crews working on additions to the government building.[2]

But the most befuddling aspect of the story, the *Los Angeles Times* reported, "is what they [the protestors] call the 'lack of logic' in building a film-processing plant, believed to be a multi-million-dollar project, in a remote canyon where there is little chance for it to remain secret because of the publicity it has received from irate citizens."[3] The commanding officer in charge of the facility, Lt. Col. James Gaylord of the US Air Force, could not untangle this publicity knot. He went on the record with the *Los Angeles Times* saying that while he wanted to placate the concerns of Wonderland Avenue's residents, for "security reasons" he would have to remain mum about the nature and necessity of the facility that so infuriated them.[4] When it came to the Air Force's activities in the Hollywood Hills, Gaylord was loud and clear about just one thing: secrecy.

So the *Los Angeles Times* sheepishly speculated about Lookout Mountain's activities,

reporting, "It was generally believed that most of the photographic work concerned processing of pictures of the H-bomb test and other highly secret operations."[5] Certainly they could have been bolder, for earlier that spring the Atomic Energy Commission and the Federal Civil Defense Administration had released for public viewing a twenty-eight-minute film about the 1952 test of an American hydrogen device detonated in the Pacific, the first "thermonuclear" device of its kind. The film, *Operation Ivy*, was shown in movie theaters across the country, including Los Angeles, and even on television [see chapter 4]. And it had emblazoned on its title screen, "Produced by United States Air Force Lookout Mountain Laboratory" in "Hollywood, California." To be sure, though Lt. Col. Gaylord would not say, and though the *Los Angeles Times* was reticent to report too much, the residents did not have to think too hard to figure out that their neighbors made films about "the H-bomb test and other highly secret operations."

As this episode suggests, the logic of Lookout Mountain's publicity and secrecy was very knotty indeed. So were its activities. The logic was knotty because the mission and activities of the Air Force film unit were entangled in the tensions, indeed contradictions, of the nuclear deterrence system the United States constructed out of the rubble of Hiroshima and Nagasaki. In this chapter we begin to untangle these knots by reconstructing the beginnings of Lookout Mountain Laboratory. As we will discuss, the logic of Lookout Mountain's publicity was in one respect quite blunt: the Department of Defense and the Atomic Energy Commission wanted to have Hollywood's imprimatur to persuade publics, and even more so state personnel, of the power, procedures, and strategic and tactical philosophies of the nuclear deterrent state. Yet the logic of Lookout Mountain's secrecy was just as blunt: almost everything that went on in the facility pictured, quite literally, America's secret defense activities, especially its nuclear-weapons activities. These two countervailing logics, when tied together, made for quite a knot indeed. What Lookout Mountain's Wonderland Avenue neighbors could not have imagined was in fact the case: Lookout Mountain was both a Hollywood-style film studio, featuring some of Hollywood's biggest stars to promote the Air Force cause, and a highly secretive nuclear weapons laboratory, albeit of a most unusual kind.

As early as the 1920s, Hollywood films filled the big screens of America, and the world, with tales of flying adventures. Films such as the 1927 *Wings* [which won Academy Awards for both Best Picture and Best Engineering Effects], Howard Hughes's 1930 *Hell's Angels*, and the 1933 *Night Flight*, starring Clark Gable, presented the pilot as an aerial adventurer, maneuvering through the clouds with the brave solitude of a man on horseback but with far more mechanical daring. Pilots appeared on-screen as the future-oriented counterparts to the cowboys that filled the Hollywood films of the 1930s, a sign of a new, rapidly approaching America rather than a nostalgic token of America's fading past. So Hollywood became an early promoter of "air power." As historian Steve Call writes, when it came to propagating the power of flight, "Nothing could beat the power of cinema, and much about aerial warfare made it natural for this new medium: action, speed, danger, heroics, even gripping pathos."[6] After World War II, the Air Power League, a self-described "non-profit, non-partisan corporation" that was in fact made up of a who's who of American airplane manufacturing titans, recruited to the air-power cause Hollywood notables such as Samuel Goldwyn, David O. Selznick, Darryl F. Zanuck, and Clark Gable to exploit the cinematic affordances of flight to the advantage of air manufacturers.[7]

Indeed, in addition to movies Southern California was the capital of the world's other great globalizing technology: the airplane. In the 1930s, as part of his expansive vision for Los Angeles, the *Los Angeles Times*'s Harry Chandler became a major "booster of airpower," working to make the area the center of American air manufacturing.[8] Supported by Chandler's efforts, Douglas Aircraft Company, Lockheed Aircraft Company, Vultee Aircraft, North American Aviation, Vega Aircraft Corporation, and Northrop Corporation all set up shop in the area, eventually coming to employ several times as many people in Los Angeles County as Hollywood did. In 1952, for example, 160,000 people worked for the aircraft industry in the county, compared with just 31,000 for the movie industry.[9] Southern California was home as well to the California Institute of Technology's Jet Propulsion Laboratory, which had been founded in 1944 by German air-power guru Theodore von Kármán and helped solidify air power within the military-industrial-university complex.

During World War II, the United States Army Air Forces, established in 1941 under the leadership of General Henry "Hap" Arnold, was a main beneficiary of Hollywood's projected air heroism and the robust Southern California aircraft industry. Thanks in part to Hollywood publicity, when World War II hit, the Army Air Force had no problem drawing young men from across the country into their ranks—most, no doubt, with movie-inspired fantasies of being aerial acrobats. But pilots were not the only recruits to the Army Air Force in the war. It also recruited photographers, and lots of them. Reconnaissance photography played a crucial role in planning and assessing bombardments of enemy lines and cities; documentary film and photographic work helped people back home learn of the Air Force's contributions to the war effort; and training films played a central role in teaching World War II airmen how to go about their work. So too the Army, along with other branches of the military services, recruited large numbers of personnel from Hollywood to perform a range of photographic functions. The most famous recruit, of course, was Frank Capra, whose *Why We Fight* series powerfully presented America's war aims.[10] But beyond Capra's work, the Army sent Hollywood men and machines across the world on behalf of the war cause, even as it incorporated film production into the chain of command, establishing in 1942 the Army Pictorial Service, which oversaw major film units in Washington, DC; Orlando, Florida; Wright Field

The First Motion Picture Unit

Lookout Mountain Laboratory's predecessor was the World War II–era First Motion Picture Unit of the Army Air Forces. Active from 1942 to 1945 and situated at the famous Hal Roach Studios in Culver City, California, the First Motion Picture Unit produced over three hundred films with titles such as *Winning Your Wings* (1942), *The Rear Gunner* (1943), *Recognition of the Japanese Zero Fighter* (1943), *Memphis Belle: A Story of a Flying Fortress* (1944), and *Wings for this Man* (1945). Like Lookout Mountain Laboratory, the First Motion Picture Unit was a full-service studio capable of producing films that met the highest standards of Hollywood at each stage, from scripting to set construction, cinematography to editing, and postproduction to promotion and distribution.

The First Motion Picture Unit recruited heavily from industry, counting among its members a number of recognized actors such as Ronald Reagan, Clark Gable, and DeForest Kelley. William Wyler and John Huston both directed films for the unit. Their productions, ranging from recruitment shorts to training films to celebratory documentaries, reached broad audiences across the United States and were seen by most Army Air Forces personnel.

A number of Lookout Mountain Laboratory staff, civilian and military, got their start at the First Motion Picture Unit. *The Last Bomb*, produced in 1945, featured many cinematic ingredients that Lookout Mountain would adopt later in films such as *Operation Ivy*, including the voice of Reed Hadley and a culminating image of a mushroom cloud. The First Motion Picture Unit helped demonstrate for the Army Air Forces (soon to be the United States Air Force) the contributions that Hollywood could make to Air Force identity.

See also

Betancourt, "World War II: The Movie"; Cunningham, "Imaging/Imagining Air Force Identity."

in Ohio; and Astoria, New York, the last the former site of Paramount Studios.[11]

In 1942, as the Army Air Force was ramping up and the Army Pictorial Service getting established, Hap Arnold—who had himself considered a movie career earlier in his life—worked with the Hollywood mover and shaker Jack Warner to establish the Army Air Force's "First Motion Picture Unit" in Culver City. The First Motion Picture Unit would be in many respects the forerunner to Lookout Mountain Laboratory. The explicit mission of the First Motion Picture Unit was to produce "training, operational, and inspirational films" concerning Army Air Force activities in World War II. But as film scholar Douglas Cunningham has argued, the implicit mission of the unit was to forge a distinct Air Force identity for Army Air Force personnel, government officials, and the publics who would watch the Army Air Force on the big screen.[12] The First Motion Picture Unit became part of a sustained "cinematic battle for that group identity and operational autonomy" of the Air Force.[13] The studio, which incorporated into its operations everything from writing and shooting to animation and special effects, produced over three hundred films during the war. Indeed, in 1944, at the height of the war, it made more films than any other Hollywood studio, distributing them to war plants, town theaters, and civic organizations, and of course to airmen.[14] The sheer proliferation of First Motion Picture Unit films helped craft "a cinematic sense of Air Force identity."[15] This identity would revolve around a combination of heroic actors, above all pilots, and technological spectacle, in the form of both bombs and planes. The aura of the Army Air Force was therefore projected to fit the big screen.

The Army Air Force's cinematic identity would also entail forms of narrative and visual control over the meaning of its central strategic practice in World War II, so-called strategic bombing.[16] A controversial new war tactic made possible by technological advancements in airplanes and bombs, strategic bombing used heavy aerial bombardment to destroy not only enemy forces, but war production facilities, lines of transportation and communication, and above all, enemy morale. General Curtis Lemay, who would earn infamy in the 1950s as the firebrand leader of Strategic Air Command's nuclear deterrent force, gained special notoriety in the war for his ruthless and belligerent leadership of strategic bombing operations in Europe and the Pacific. Lemay, Arnold, and other Army Air Force leaders in 1940s trumpeted the advent of the air age and "total war" and argued for the centrality of air operations in the future of warfare. The advent of atomic weapons only strengthened their case. In terms of Air Force identity, one of the First Motion Picture Unit's most iconic films was also one of its last: *The Last Bomb*, which featured Lemay and chronicled, in cinematic form, the Army Air Force's strategic bombing operations over Japan, culminating in an image of the atomic cloud, the first such "mushroom cloud" to appear on the big screen.[17]

Lookout Mountain Laboratory, like the First Motion Picture Unit, was formed from the union of Hollywood power and air power. Indeed, Lookout Mountain's most immediate origin lay in the First Motion Picture Unit. Though the latter was closed in 1945, a new First Motion Picture Unit opened in 1947 in Astoria, New York, with a Los Angeles detachment located at the site on Wonderland Avenue.[18] The Astoria unit was redesignated as the 4201st Motion Picture Squadron in 1948, but then abruptly closed in 1949. The Los Angeles detachment lived on however, first as the 4881st Motion Picture Unit under the Air Proving Ground, and then later as the 1352nd Motion Picture Squadron of the Military Air Transport Service. This newly autonomous unit relied on not only the old First Motion Picture Unit equipment, but its style, dramatizing as it did Air Force technological spectacles against backdrops of blue skies, engineered acrobatics, and orchestrated sounds. Its main subject matter, however, was different, as it was charged with providing "specialized photographic documentation of atomic weapons tests," beginning

Lookout Mountain Air Force Station

MARCH AIR FORCE BASE
PHOTO LAB.
UNITED STATES AIR FORCE
APCS
PHOTOGRAPHIC GROUP
THE END

0-377
(1963)

with Operation Sandstone, a series of nuclear tests carried out in 1948 at the Pacific Proving Grounds in the Marshall Islands.[19] The difference, that is, was the mushroom cloud.

To make room for big-screen atomic film productions, Lookout Mountain began to expand its facility on Wonderland Avenue, despite the protests of neighbors. The site had been but a small flight control station in World War II; by the middle of the 1950s, the facility would cover over forty thousand square feet, complete with soundstage, carpenter's shop, maintenance shop, lunchroom, processing labs, storage vaults, editing rooms, animation studio, and an auditorium equipped with CinemaScope projection capabilities. It became, arguably, the most comprehensive film production site in all of Hollywood, capable of taking a film from scripting to shooting to long-term storage all in one secure location.

In addition to directly adopting Hollywood methods and styles, Lookout Mountain experimented widely with new film methods, from 3-D cinema to color processing to new audio techniques. In fact, Lookout Mountain's first 3-D film was finished in February of 1952, some nine months before the Hollywood studios achieved their first 3-D film, and CinemaScope was tested at Lookout Mountain some eight months before Twentieth Century Fox released the first Hollywood studio picture using it, *The Robe*.[20] In light of their experimental work, Lookout Mountain's cadre of technicians and engineers, most of them civilians drawn from the ranks of the Hollywood film industry, found themselves presenting at industry conferences and winning accolades: in 1962 the Lookout Mountain film *Breaking the Language Barrier*, featuring the Thunderbirds, would earn a nomination for an Academy Award in the documentary, short-subject category.[21]

During the 1950s, Lookout Mountain would work with a range of Hollywood luminaries or semiluminaries: Jack Warner, George Owen, George Sidney, Carey Wilson, Bob Hope, Susan Hayward, James Garner, Kim Novak, Gregory Peck, Reed Hadley, Tyrone Power, George Murphy, Harold Lloyd, Walter Cronkite, Glenn Ford, Walt Disney, Robert Stack, Cathy Crosby, Vic Morrow, Jerry Colonna, Robert Cummings, James Arness, and Marilyn Monroe among them. The unit's art and animation division included Jules Engel, an influential artist who worked on *Dumbo*, *Bambi*, and *Fantasia*. Indeed, Lookout Mountain's ties to Disney were strong: after a fire at the Wonderland Avenue facility, Lookout Mountain's sound department was invited to temporarily relocate to Disney's studio, earning Walt himself a formal award of recognition from the Air Force. Jimmy Stewart, who in addition to his acting career remained in the Air Force Reserve until 1959, was frequently featured in Lookout Mountain films and took an active interest in their operations. And John Ford directed at least two films for the unit, and offered his ranch in the San Fernando Valley for employee picnics.

Meanwhile, the Hollywood commercial film industry reciprocated by regularly requesting stock footage from Lookout Mountain of nuclear mushroom clouds, fighter jets, missile launches, and other Cold War iconography. The unit advertised and sold "unedited stock film footage in black and white and color on nuclear or thermonuclear detonations" in trade magazines such as *Business Screen Magazine*.[22] Notably, a montage of footage shot by uncredited Lookout Mountain photographers ended up in Stanley Kubrick's *Dr. Strangelove*. Lookout Mountain's work found its way into television as well: not only did a significant portion of aerial footage of the Vietnam War screened on the nightly news emanate from Lookout Mountain's cameras, but specialized footage shot by unit personnel found its way into the *Perry Mason* series; and the studio maintained a reciprocal relationship with the producers of *Steve Canyon*, a popular television adaptation of the comic strip series.[23]

Of course, while Lookout Mountain worked in and with Hollywood in Cold War productions in the late 1940s and 1950s, Hollywood was fighting its own cold war, with the Hollywood "blacklist" being its most infamous product.[24] In World

John Ford

Director John Ford may have been a Navy man during World War II, but that didn't stop him from offering regular support to the Air Force at Lookout Mountain Laboratory. During the war, Ford served with the Office of Strategic Services, and then became founding commander of a naval motion-picture unit, where he supervised the production of at least eighty-seven documentary and training films. After the war, he took a less official role with Lookout Mountain Laboratory.

Throughout the 1950s and 1960s, Ford hosted an annual staff picnic for Lookout Mountain at his Field Photo Farm, the San Fernando Valley property he purchased for gatherings of his former navy colleagues. But Ford's role at Lookout Mountain was more than social. The influence of his distinct film style is seen in a variety of Lookout Mountain films, especially its treatment of desert landscapes. Ford's most direct role within the unit was as supervisor and director of two films Lookout Mountain produced for the Pacific Command, *Korea: Battleground for Liberty* (1961) and *Taiwan: Island of Freedom* (1963). These films were produced for American military personnel and their families. In tone, voice, and story they resemble travel guides, presenting Oceanic landscapes as grandly and pastorally as the deserts of Ford's westerns and depicting servicemen interacting respectfully with locals. As such, they also implicitly challenged communist claims of American imperialism in Asia by showing American "respect" for the Pacific.

See also

McBride, *Searching for John Ford*.

Facility Expansion at Lookout Mountain Laboratory

8935 Wonderland Avenue, Hollywood, California

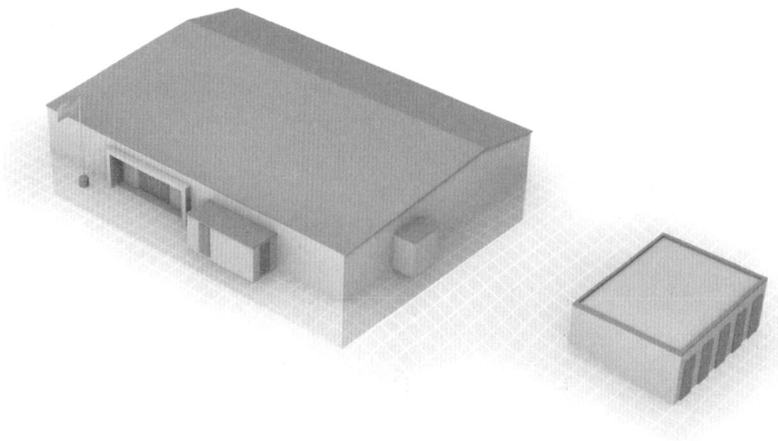

1947 ~11,000 sq ft

The original structure served as a radar station for Los Angeles air traffic control.

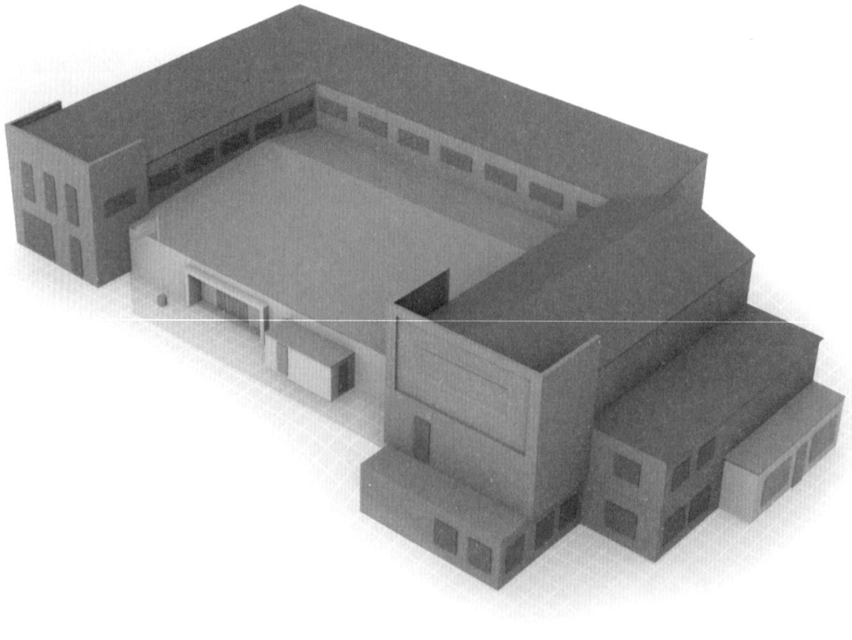

1950 ~26,000 sq ft

Conversion of the radar station to a film studio required the addition of a soundstage, screening rooms, processing labs, and other spaces for editing and production.

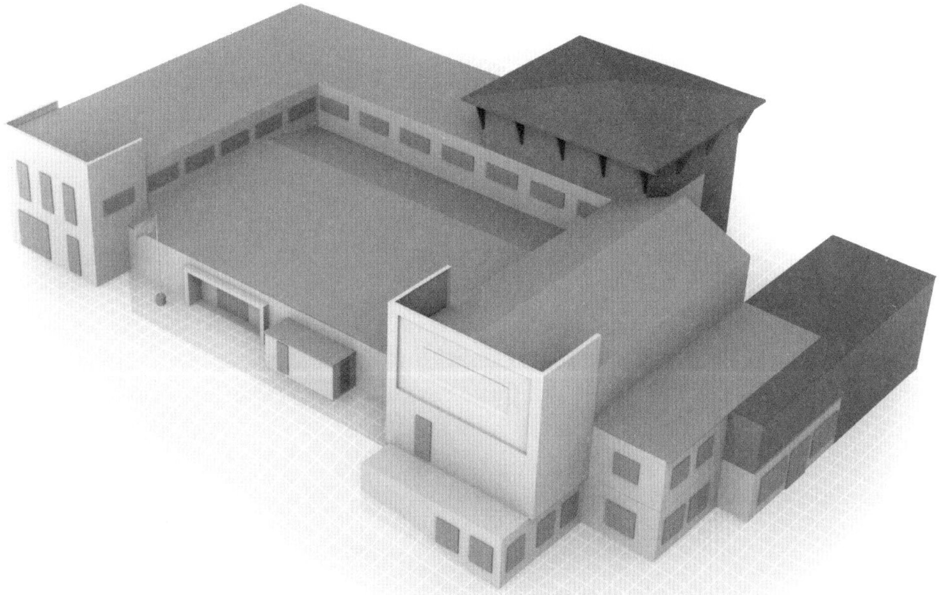

1953 ~31,000 sq ft

The animation studio added above provided light for the artists, while a new machine shop and loading dock below served the engineers.

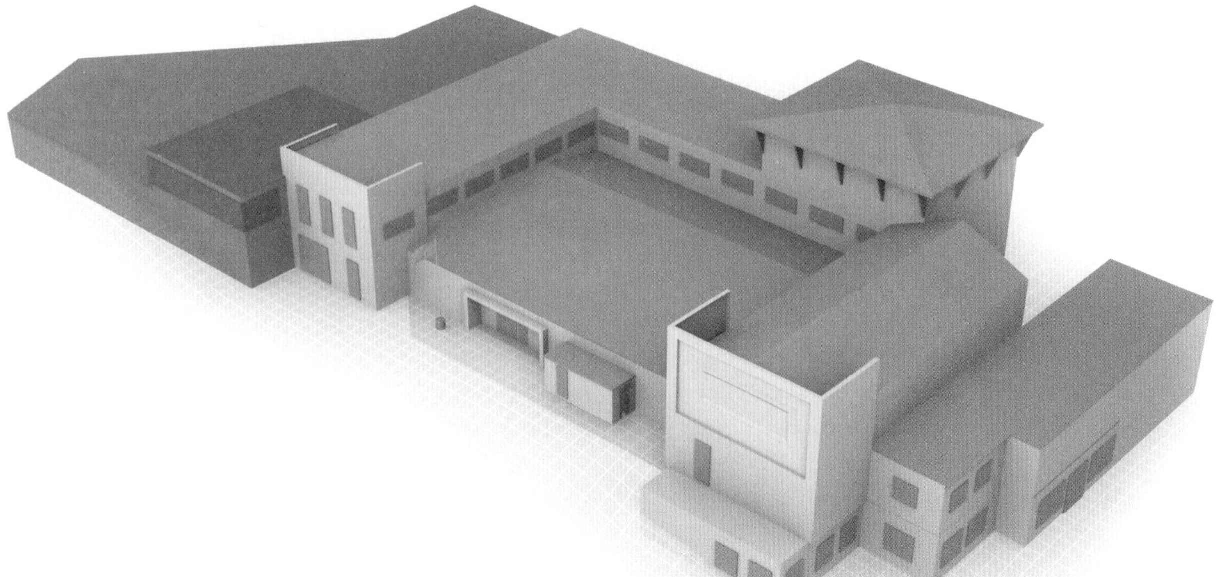

1955 ~40,000 sq ft

A final ambitious addition provided a new security checkpoint and offices above ground, and capacious film processing and storage facilities below.

War II, Hollywood had taken on a strongly patriotic cast, turning from what film historian Larry May refers to as a 1930s "non-Marxist republican radicalism" to what Thomas Doherty, another film historian, calls "message mongering" on behalf of the war effort.[25] Doherty argues that World War II also represented the period when "the educational import and ideological impact of the movies" hit home for American war makers. "The motion picture industry became the preeminent transmitter of wartime policy and a lightning rod for public discourse. The unique, unprecedented alliance between Washington and Hollywood generated not only new kinds of movies but a new attitude toward them. Hereafter, popular art and cultural meaning, mass communications and national politics, would be intimately aligned and commonly acknowledged in American culture."[26]

Nevertheless, the Hollywood stars Lookout Mountain pulled into its Cold War operations were not "message mongers." Nor were they hunting for communists. They were products of, and participants within, a new American postwar vision premised on the virtues of liberal capitalism and consumer culture.[27] To be sure, there would be plenty of cold warriors willing to exploit Hollywood, as evidenced in films such as MGM's *The Beginning or the End*, which dramatized the Manhattan Project with the cooperation of the Truman administration, or the Paramount picture *Strategic Air Command*, produced at the behest of General Curtis Lemay. Indeed, Cecil B. DeMille himself would join the Eisenhower administration as chief motion-picture consultant for the US Information Agency.[28] But most of the Hollywood fixtures to which Lookout Mountain turned merely seemed to be "doing their part" rather than "leading the charge." Lookout Mountain took little interest in ardent anticommunists such as John Wayne and Ronald Reagan (though the latter did participate in at least one Lookout Mountain project), preferring instead the dutiful types such as Jimmy Stewart and (the lesser-known, to be sure) Reed Hadley.[29] Even as John Ford was hosting Lookout Mountain employees at his ranch, his films—for example, the 1949 *She Wore a Yellow Ribbon*, featuring no less than anticommunist crusader John Wayne—were at best ambivalent about the costs of war. Lookout Mountain, in short, managed to capitalize less on Hollywood's overt patriotism or nationalism, as the Air Force had in World War II, than on a more general, relatively nonpartisan sense in Hollywood and elsewhere that in a dangerous world peace and prosperity could be achieved through only the vigilant, if at times ambivalent, projection of American power. In the 1950s, you didn't have to be an ardent anticommunist crusader to believe that.[30]

Though devastating for the careers of many in Hollywood, the impact of the House Un-American Activities Committee investigations on Lookout Mountain's work were relatively slight. In 1954 the FBI investigated the facility, apparently in response to a phone call from Representative Joe Holt, who had been contacted by Lookout Mountain's neighbors amid their fury over its construction noise, floodlights, and armed guards. (The Pentagon had been contacted too, and considered for a bit closing the site.) The FBI responded to Holt's call in the way it seems they responded to all calls at the time, treating it as a case of potential communist infiltration. They sent a special agent to the site to investigate. He reported to his superiors that of the 130 civilian employees at Lookout Mountain, most belonged to guilds and unions. A Lookout Mountain employee told him there were "at least six people" who were "favorable to all causes," and even "openly sympathetic to such organizations as the Independent Progressive Party and to Henry Wallace." Another employee, the special agent reported, complained of a lack of security and of the "mental attitude" of Lt. Col. John Harvey, the installation officer. Harvey, in turn, told the investigator that his accuser was just bitter over being reprimanded at work. Needless to say, the FBI investigation was fruitless: the special agent could find "no Communist Party or subversive activity in the plant," and the case was closed.[31]

Of course, *had* communists "infiltrated" Lookout Mountain Laboratory, the fallout would have been very great—and not just because of the nuclear secrets the unit photographed, processed, and stored. Everyone at the time, it seems, presumed the great power of movies. Next to military power, movies were America's greatest export, and they were unquestionably its biggest "soft power" export.[32] Indeed, as one film scholar has noted, during the 1930s it was quite possible that Greta Garbo was better known in Prague than Franklin D. Roosevelt.[33] What seems outlandish to the contemporary reader—the infamous Hays Code and the HUAC investigations—makes sense only because movies were presumed to be so powerful. Hollywood was an axis in the pursuit and regulation of cultural and political power. It is no wonder that cold warriors wanted to exploit the movies and, likewise, may have worried about communist "infiltrators" learning their secret arts.

The Soviets served as an imaginary reinforcement for cold warriors wanting to grab hold of the movies. "Cinema," Tony Shaw and Denise Youngblood write, "occupied a place of honor in Soviet culture," and many in the West believed that the Reds were riding cinema to power across the globe.[34] Charles R. Norberg, a member of Truman's Psychological Strategy Board, made the worry official, claiming that the Soviets, far more than the Americans, understood the power of film. He wrote in a White House memo in October 1952, "I have seen some very excellent examples of Soviet motion pictures which have been made specifically for propaganda purposes." America, he argued, should take the cue. "The use of motion pictures for propaganda work is a major weapon in any government's arsenal and I do not believe that our Government has, as yet, gotten into this field extensively."[35] That would soon change. In the 1950s the US government would rely heavily on film to propagate its "peaceful message," especially in Eisenhower's massive "Atoms for Peace" campaign, which featured several Lookout Mountain films and used, in the films of other agencies, a great deal of footage shot by the unit.[36]

In sum, in the 1950s Lookout Mountain Laboratory would be caught up in the "soft propaganda" of the US-Soviet Cold War. Assuming with many world leaders that film was the most powerful mass medium ever created, government agencies of a variety of types—from defense, to civil defense, to the scientific laboratories—would turn to Lookout Mountain to produce persuasive films aimed at convincing government decision makers and publics alike of the worthiness of their activities and operations, even as film became a primary means of instructing soldiers and citizens on how to think and behave in the age of the Bomb. As such, Hollywood power became Cold War power, with Lookout Mountain serving as a primary nexus point in the articulation of this power.

But Lookout Mountain was much more than a government Hollywood film studio; it was a *laboratory*, indeed, a nuclear weapons laboratory. We are used to the idea of nuclear weapons laboratories. The experimental work of the Manhattan Project took place in a network of laboratories, not only at Los Alamos, Oak Ridge, and the Metallurgic Laboratory at the University of Chicago, but also in labs at Princeton, Columbia, Harvard, Berkeley, and the Alamogordo Bombing and Gunnery Range in New Mexico, where the "Trinity" test took place. After the war, these laboratories were publicly celebrated as having helped win the war, and more important, with having definitively *ended* it. Indeed, while the laboratories of the state, universities, and industry could claim a thick dossier of wartime accomplishments, it was the belief that the Bomb had ended the war that would help turn these provisional wartime laboratories into permanent fixtures of a Cold War "peace." For all the heroism of those who fought in the battlefields of Europe, Africa, and the Pacific, it was the men and, to be sure, the women of the defense laboratories who would end up driving the star system of the Cold War national security state.

In postwar America, laboratories were sites of great technological and ideological power. They

Nuclear Testing and Photography

in the contiguous United States, 1945-1968

- Nuclear tests
- Manhattan Project locations
- Lookout Mountain Laboratory detachments

were the source of what came to be known as "big science," the big-budget, large-scale, government-sponsored and industry-driven experimental and engineering ventures that would bring about intercontinental ballistic missiles, televised moonwalks, satellite communications, and many other Cold War marvels.[37] The ideological power of laboratories was predicated in part on such products; but it was also tied to a capacity to see the unseen, to disclose "nature's secrets." If the postwar world in America was a world of engineering marvels, it was also a world in which, as Hannah Arendt wrote of laboratories, "that which does not appear [or had not appeared] of its own accord is forced to appear and to disclose itself."[38] Laboratories offered insights as counterintuitive as the regnant Keynesian economics [which posited deficit spending as a means of economic stimulus], but apparently from a basis that was far more "real" and empirically verifiable—scientific instrumentation.

Historians have devoted a great deal of attention to the nuclear weapons laboratories of America. However, they have tended to focus heavily on the scientific, military, and political personalities who worked in and around these laboratories, as if laboratories were merely the elaborate instruments of great men.[39] Yet if we follow the instruments themselves, as scholars in the field of science, technology, and society studies [or simply STS] have encouraged us to do, we will inevitably find ourselves looking at cameras and related optical instruments.[40] Motion-picture cameras were, along with mechanical and later digital computers, the most important "new" information technology in America's rise to nuclear power in the 1940s, 1950s, and 1960s.[41] Motion-picture cameras were scientifically crucial, as they could be rigged to record the otherwise indiscernible visual facets of nuclear detonations, especially those phenomena that human or electronic computers failed to model and which scientists therefore could not anticipate. In addition, as seen in the films of Lookout Mountain, motion pictures were vital because they brought ready-at-hand rhetorics as yet unheard of in computing, including editing, mise-en-scène, and narrative. Consequently, government cameras traveled in droves to every corner of the planet where nuclear weapons were tested or deployed, and the resulting films were carefully dispersed through the scientific, military, governmental, and sometimes public channels of the nation and the world.

And if we follow these nuclear cameras very far at all, we will come back to Lookout Mountain Laboratory, a unit charged with "specialized photographic documentation of atomic weapons tests."[42] Indeed, Lookout Mountain produced not only images that were essential to the nuclear weapons development program, but also image instruments. Its engineers and technicians worked closely with government contractors, especially EG&G, to figure out ways to capture still and motion pictures of nuclear detonations, missile flights, and other defense-related engineering feats, all for "scientific" purposes. By freezing nuclear blasts on film, scientists could measure yields, observe otherwise invisible effects, and document experiments. By capturing a missile disaster on film, engineers could figure out what went wrong and fix it. And by recording a monkey or man being subjected to g-forces, scientists could better understand the physiological effects of acceleration. But to do all this well, various sorts of cameras and film instruments had to be modified, and sometimes built from scratch. Beginning in the late 1940s, but especially in the mid-1950s, Lookout Mountain took on a "scientific" mission, producing, as they wrote, "motion picture photography in 35 mm and 16 mm both black and white and color, silent or sound, on the ground or in the air, for instrumentation analysis, time and motion studies, engineering reports, and special photography required for support of the Atomic Energy Commission, the Armed Forces Special Weapons Project, Joint Task Force Seven, and the United States Air Force."[43] Lookout Mountain was in this sense every bit the weapons laboratory that Los Alamos or Lawrence Livermore was.

Lookout Mountain personnel sometimes worked around the clock to get test films shot, edited, and distributed to scientific or military authorities as rapidly as possible for analysis. In addition to equipment, their photographers put a premium on preparation, not wanting to waste any time on reshooting scenes. And in many cases, of course, Lookout Mountain photographers did not have the luxury of reshooting, because of the documentary nature of their projects. Meanwhile, at their capacious but still overcrowded film storage vaults lodged underground at the Wonderland Avenue facility, Lookout Mountain staff struggled to keep up with demand for storing and retrieving security-sensitive audiovisual material for government engineers and scientists to use on request. During the 1950s and 1960s, Lookout Mountain held the preponderance of visual records of America's atomic experiments, and by extension the photographic annals of America's most secretive Cold War science-and-engineering adventures. Their holdings included motion pictures, still photos, negatives, slides, and transparencies. By 1960, the unit's official mission would include not only storage of such material, but the inspection and identification of developed film for content and quality, so that defense and Atomic Energy Commission personnel and contractors could get what they needed when they needed it with minimum fuss. Indeed, Lookout Mountain Laboratory came to be a major weapons library, a central node in a Cold War network of secretive defense information.

Still, for all its importance, the creation of Lookout Mountain was in many respects the result of postwar happenstance. In fact, the extension of the atomic bomb program into the postwar period was not at all a given, as there was considerable official and public resistance to further atomic testing and even production.[44] Most notably, the Federation of Atomic Scientists, founded in 1945 by scientists who worked for the Manhattan Project, publicly denounced further tests, declaring them scientifically unnecessary, a military caprice, but part of a competition between the Army, Navy, and Army Air Force for power and prestige in the postwar military hierarchy. In spite of such august opposition, back-to-back atomic tests using "Fat Man"-style bombs were held at Bikini Atoll in the Pacific Ocean in 1946 under the name Operation Crossroads. The tests, "Able" and "Baker," proved to be a crossroads in the history of nuclear weapons development. Among other things, they vaulted the Army Air Force to the helm of atomic test photography.

Crossroads took place, just as the Federation of Atomic Scientists had claimed, in the spirit of intramilitary rivalry: the Navy hoped to prove that its ships could withstand atomic attacks at sea, whereas the Army Air Force—approaching a hard-won independence from the Army—was eager to capitalize on Crossroads as proof that neither the ground nor the sea could provide a suitable basis for the future of warfare: only the air could.[45] A massive operation involving forty-two thousand servicemen, Operation Crossroads was a public relations spectacle, even as the joint task force in charge of the operation struggled to maintain control of the narrative in the run-up to the tests. The scale of the operation, together with the military rivalries and tensions that filled it, made Crossroads "a public relations nightmare," as historian Jonathan Weisgall writes.[46]

And as things turned out, Crossroads not only would be a public relations nightmare; it also would be an experimental one. At first, the Navy seemed to come out looking quite good. Their newer, stronger ships survived the bomb drops with relatively little structural damage. However, before long it became apparent, much to the chagrin of the Navy, that even if a ship could sustain an atomic blast, the health of the crew could not.[47] The radiation effects on the sailors, not to mention the hundreds of animals used in the test, kicked in days after the blasts but were deadly.

The Army Air Force did not look so good at Crossroads either. During the "Able" test, the B-29 long-range bomber *Dave's Dream* [the same plane, under the name the *Big Stink*, had been used as a camera plane in the atomic bomb drop on Nagasaki] missed its target by a good half mile, destroying a large cadre of equipment set to record essential data from the test.[48] But more than this, the Army Air Force seemed even less prepared for taking radiation seriously than the Navy. Of the 130 military officers enrolled in a Navy course on radiological defense shortly after the test, only five were from the Army Air Force.[49] Hence, when it came to atomic war, the Army Air Force seemed both a bit incompetent and a bit oblivious.

Except in two crucial respects. First, it was the Army Air Force, not the Navy, that seemed to intuit that no amount of training in radiological defense would make an atomic war a winnable war. But weeks after Hiroshima and Nagasaki, Army Air Force General Hap Arnold—the same Hap Arnold who had helped found the First Motion Picture Unit—articulated in nascent form what would become the doctrine of nuclear deterrence: "Real security against atomic weapons in the visible future will rest on our ability to take immediate offensive action with overwhelming force," he wrote at the conclusion of World War II. "It must be apparent to a potential aggressor that an attack on the United States would be immediately followed by an immensely devastating air-atomic attack on him."[50] And so some five years before John Foster Dulles's infamous doctrine of "massive retaliation" was popularized, Arnold's Army Air Force seemed to understand that advancing an atomic arms race could lead to the perverse paradox that would become nuclear deterrence, wherein "peace" and "security" would rest on the very real prospect of total, irrevocable, and unrecoverable atomic destruction.

Second, it was the Army Air Force, not the Navy, which ended up securing some of the best film footage of the Crossroads test. Because of misfires and misunderstandings, much of the Navy's photographic equipment was destroyed at Crossroads. The Army Air Force's photographers, however, had the distinct advantage of shooting from the air. Under the leadership of Col. Paul T. Cullen [later promoted to brigadier general of the Air Force's Strategic Air Command], they fitted an array of drones and piloted airplanes with a myriad of still and motion-picture cameras and camera lenses to create what were dubbed "flying cameras."[51] Working high above ground zero, safe from the atomic fires and misfires, the photographic output of Colonel Cullen's "flying cameras" was spectacular and would help establish the reputation of the Air Force as having the best photographic cadre in the world for atomic tests.

The two strategies, deterrence and atomic spectacle, as we now know, would be as one in the decades to come. For the only way to threaten massive atomic retaliation, or so it was held, was to demonstrate the power of atomic destruction. But demonstrating the power of atomic destruction meant [in history as it happened, if not in logic] continued experimentation with atomic bombs. For many atomic scientists and strategists, the demonstration of nuclear destruction would become the most compelling reason for nuclear testing. But the test was not enough. It had to be seen, or at least potentially seen; therefore, it had to be filmed and photographed, processed and produced, and depending on circumstances, printed and projected on screens and in magazine pages so that the world could see the power of atomic destruction.

Hence, the Air Force came back to Hollywood: when Lookout Mountain Laboratory was opened in the late 1940s, America was becoming a nuclear deterrent state. Indeed, the coincidence was coordinated, for nuclear deterrence was a "big picture" strategy that found a counterpart in the big-picture cameras and screens of Hollywood. Formally speaking, the major documentary motion picture, produced in the idiom of the Hollywood spectacle, enclosed into a singular aesthetic system each of the main components of nuclear deterrence: surveillance, spectacle, story, and epochal temporalities. American-style nuclear deterrence was, historically speaking, inseparable from the cinematic sensibility that dominated midcentury American culture. But cameras, as we have seen, were also a means of scientific diagnostics and data [as cameras were in various scientific and

engineering laboratories worldwide]. Lookout Mountain therefore had strong connections to Los Alamos and other Atomic Energy Commission and Department of Defense weapons laboratories.

Lookout Mountain Laboratory in this way did double duty: they offered the Cold War state a means of persuasion, proof, and propaganda, *and* a means of scientific analytics and mechanisms of control. It was often the same cameras that provided scientists and engineers with data and outside audiences with proof of America's nuclear might. Lookout Mountain, therefore, would become doubly central to the nuclear deterrence system that would unfold in the 1950s and to the overall operations of the American deterrent state.

In 1948 the United States would carry out its second postwar nuclear test, "Operation Sandstone." Held at Eniwetok Atoll in the Pacific, a couple hundred miles west of the Crossroads site, the purpose of Sandstone was to build bigger, better bombs, not just assess military effects on extant ones.[52] And at Sandstone all photographic efforts would be centrally organized and run by the Air Force, which had just won independence from the Army. At Crossroads, the Air Force and other military brass recognized that photographic operations were integral to atomic tests. However, to provide adequate photographic coverage for Crossroads, the military had to sequester camera and film supplies from civilian locations back in the United States; and camera operators, many from Hollywood, had to be summoned to special assignments. "As a result of these operations," one internal Air Force history states, "it was decided at the conclusion of Operation Crossroads that a permanent photographic unit should be established, specially trained, equipped and organized to obtain scientific, technical, and documentary photography or recurring atomic tests."[53] That permanent unit would become Lookout Mountain Laboratory.

All photographic work at Sandstone was put under the command of Colonel Cullen of the Air Force's Strategic Air Command.[54] Cullen split photographic responsibilities at the test into two principal wings: Los Alamos Laboratory, operating under the auspices of the newly formed Atomic Energy Commission, and the Air Force. Los Alamos would oversee "scientific" photography, and the Air Force would do "technical" and "documentary" photography. The distinctions had less to do with technologies and techniques and more to do with the intended purposes of the photographic work: scientific photography was aimed at gauging yield and effects, whereas technical and documentary photography was intended to document the tests for both operational and historical purposes.

Colonel Cullen also worked to set up a production facility and clearinghouse for all Sandstone photography. He looked for a location in Hollywood for the practical reason that Hollywood had the personnel and facilities capable of handling the large volume of film footage Sandstone would produce. After an extensive search in the area, Cullen acquired an abandoned flight control center on Wonderland Avenue in Laurel Canyon. It was big enough to set up shop, close enough to the heart of Hollywood to be accessible, and tucked away enough not to draw attention to itself, or so Cullen thought.[55]

Unlike any other Air Force film unit, the new facility was given a brand name, "Lookout Mountain Laboratory," a move that intimated the knotty logic of secrecy and publicity which would characterize Lookout Mountain's history. The brand signaled its Hollywood status, but it also suggested that it would be a laboratory working alongside Los Alamos and other Atomic Energy Commission laboratories in the service of nuclear weapons development. "Laboratory operations," as a Lookout Mountain officer explained, "require a high degree of skill and scientific control."[56] But Lookout Mountain was also a nuclear deterrence laboratory. Its Hollywood location meant it had, ready at hand, the symbolic means for doing the work of reassuring publics and allies while threatening adversaries. For while nuclear weapons development needed film for diagnostic and operational purposes, nuclear deterrence needed film for rhetorical purposes. Indeed, Lookout Mountain would be both a scientific laboratory and a Hollywood studio; and deterrence, as a rhetorical strategy, would draw on these dual capacities. While these various functions would make explaining Lookout Mountain Laboratory's purpose to neighbors and the press very difficult, throughout the 1950s it made it crucial to the workings of the Atomic Energy Commission, the Armed Forces Special Weapons Project [the part of the Department of Defense charged with nuclear weapons development], and the Air Force as they did the work of constructing a nuclear deterrent state.

Lookout Mountain's story, therefore, is in part the story of the ambition of the US Cold War state, especially as it was centered on the Air Force, the Armed Forces Special Weapons Project, and the Atomic Energy Commission, to secure a seat within the control room, so to speak, of midcentury cultural production. For a young pilot to see Brig. Gen. Jimmy Stewart gracing the screen of a training film on the strategy of nuclear deterrence [as in a 1958 episode of *The Airman's World*, an Air Force–produced series regularly hosted by the actor] was to overlay a premier cultural imprimatur on the Air Force's own imprimatur. Or for a moviegoer in rural Kansas to have a cowboy actor such as Reed Hadley guide him on the big screen into the dawn of thermonuclear weaponry, as in Lookout Mountain's 1953 *Operation Ivy*, was for the Air Force and the Atomic Energy Commission to wrest from Hollywood a ringing cultural endorsement.

But Lookout Mountain's relationship with Hollywood suggested, as well, an anxiety that the aims and methods of the Air Force, the Armed Forces Special Weapons Project, the Atomic Energy Commission, and the Federal Civil Defense Administration might not be seen as "American" enough. Hollywood was needed to supplement, and in some way bring legitimacy to, the messages of "command and control," "massive retaliation," and "civil defense" that dominated official Cold War rhetoric during the 1950s and into the 1960s. The burgeoning Cold War military-industrial complex, in short, badly needed the culture industry. Of course, it must not be forgotten that the military-industrial complex had its own powers that Hollywood could hardly resist—air power and atomic power. Indeed, in the 1950s and into the 1960s airplanes, missiles, and mushroom clouds were the foci of the optics of Hollywood nearly as much as they were the optics of the national security state. At Lookout Mountain, these optics were entangled on a daily operational basis.

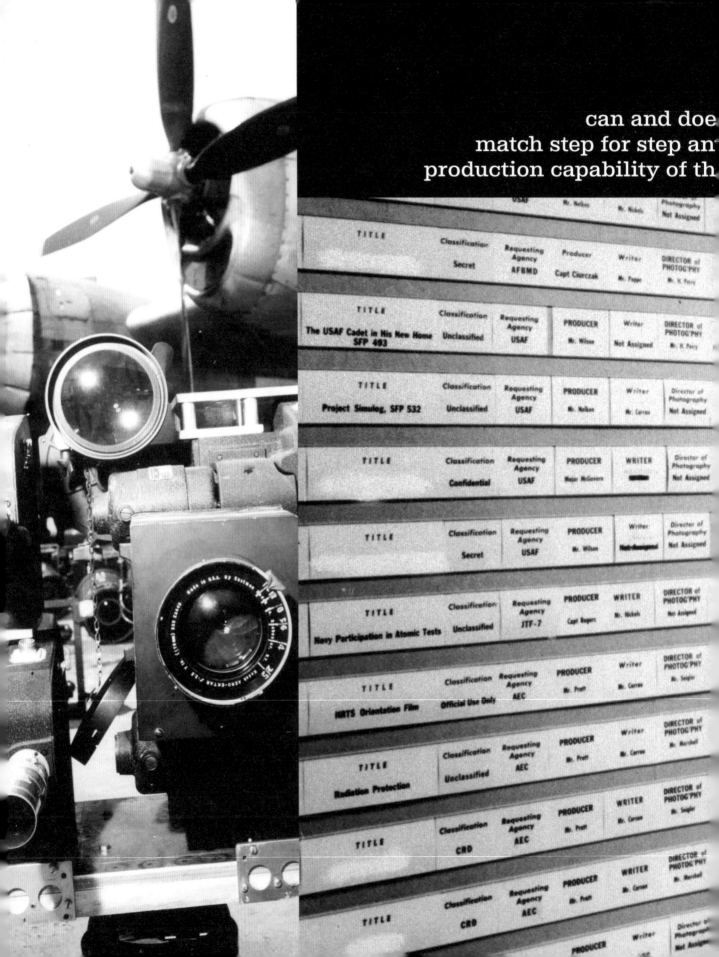

can and doe
match step for step an
production capability of th

AVERAGE INDUSTRY STUDIO

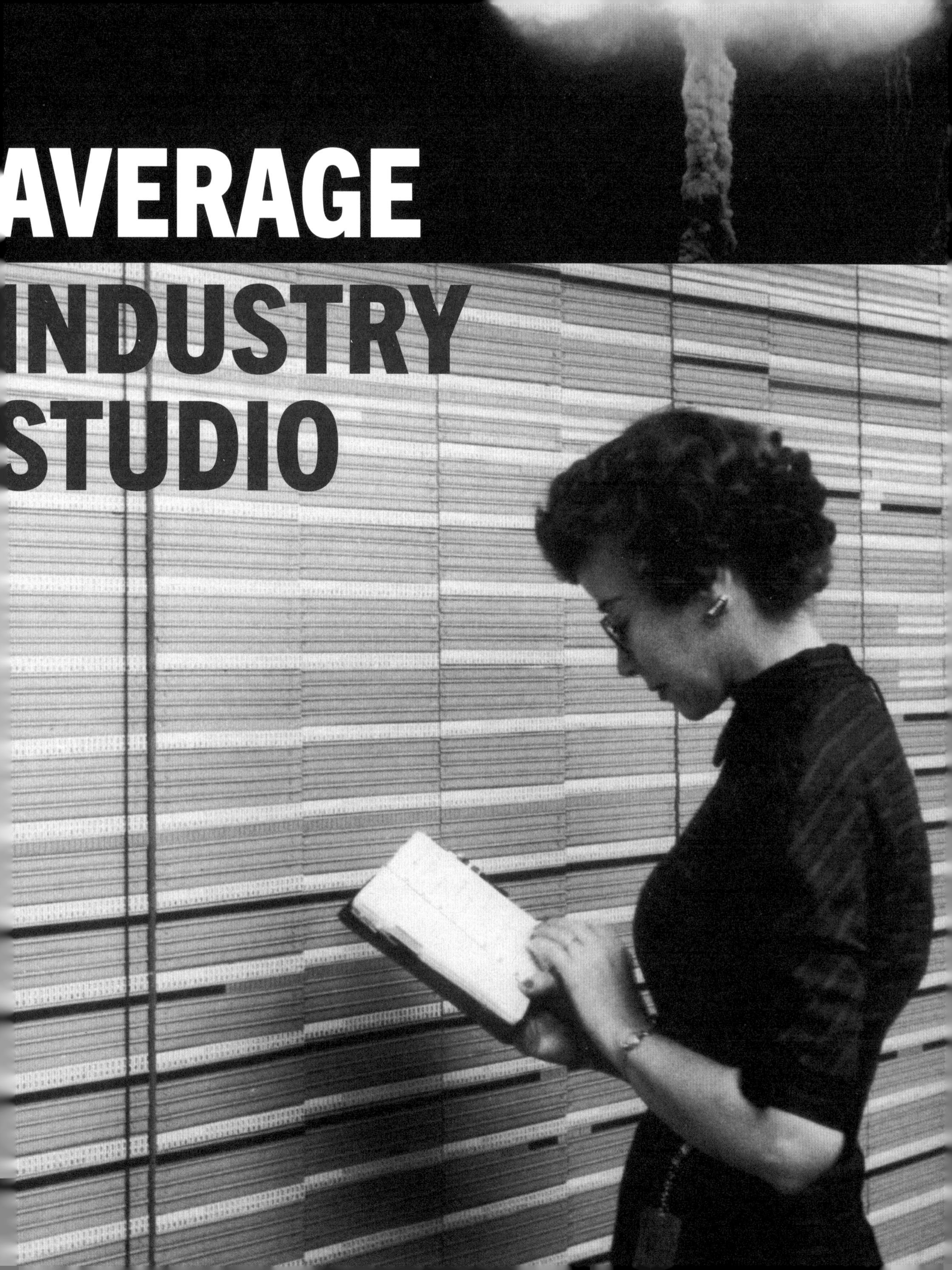

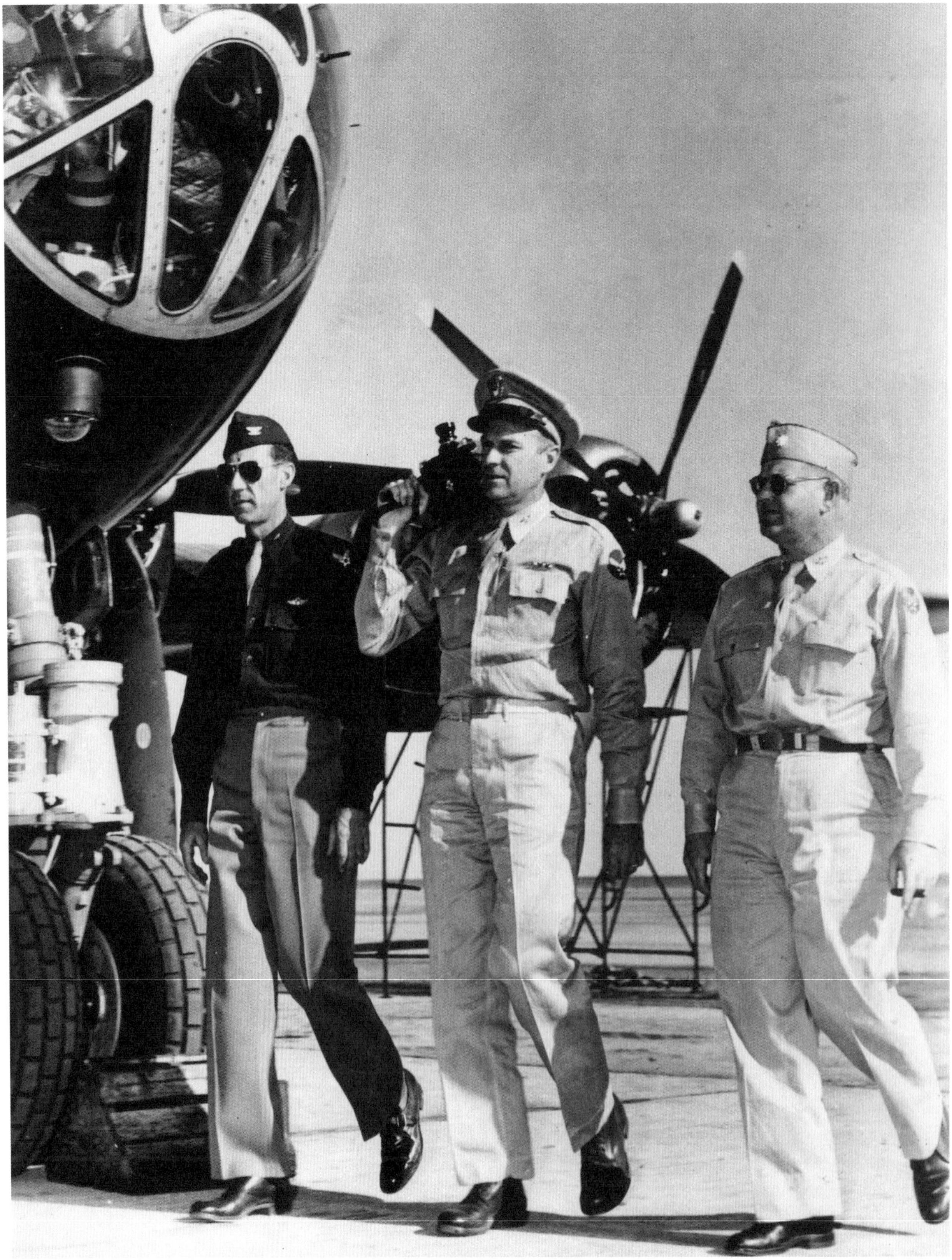

Chapter Two

COLONELS, CAMERAS, AND SECURITY CLEARANCES

The 1983 film *The Right Stuff*, the now classic Hollywood tale of the Mercury astronauts, is punctuated by a repeated interlude in which the president and other top government officials sit in a conference room, lights out, watching newly produced movies bearing the latest stories and images of America's space highlights and mishaps. More than a narrative device, these scenes in *The Right Stuff* reflect the actual practice of presidents, government elites, and military leaders in the 1950s and 1960s. Before official written reports on state-sponsored science-and-technology efforts were even completed, state officials were often sent specially made, typically secret "film reports" and "accident briefings" from government film studios documenting in narrative, visual, aural, and graphic form the latest news from the brave new world of big science.

Narrative film played a vital role in the official political culture of Cold War science and technology, beginning with the most terrifying big science venture, the nuclear weapons program. Indeed, in the 1950s the technological developments, strategic promise, explosive power, and Cold War perils of nuclear weaponry were almost always first presented to top officials, whether civilian or military, through classified photographs and motion pictures, many of them produced by the film units of the Air Force. As such, the government participated in a curious and complex form of cinematic self-talk, wherein the successes and failures of the nuclear weapons development program were met with positive rhetorical reinforcement in these filmic first reports from the agencies—the Department of Defense and the Atomic Energy Commission—responsible for the fate of nuclear America.

But film did far more than report. By the 1950s, aerial tactical reconnaissance photography was already, in the words of early adopter Brig. Gen. George W. Goddard, "as old as the airplane," with aerial strategic photography in growing demand as a way of keeping tabs on the Soviet Union.[1] As early as the 1930s, the

Army Air Corps maintained a photography training school at Chanute Field in Rantoul, Illinois. The new branch of the Army Air Corps Technical School that opened in Denver at Lowry Field in 1938 boasted a three-story building dedicated to a department of photography.[2] Ground photography had also long served a variety of crucial roles in American armed forces and combat operations, if inevitably "supplementary" compared to the central role of aerial photography. Though less "informational" in nature than the aerial images that would find their way into maps, ground photography's mobility as a technical and representational form lent it unusual flexibility, even ubiquity. As one 1959 Air Force manual on "basic photography" explained to the budding photographer:

> An Air Force ground photographer's assignments include [a] wide variety of phases. Pictures of recreation and sports, of routine operations and special events, of scientific advancements and "spot" news are required to illustrate public information articles. Other pictures are not intended for public release but are for the archives of the armed forces—to be used for reference and record. These include photographs of all types of activities with emphasis on construction, development, and progress. Air Force photographers cooperate with research engineers and scientists to record pictures of their experiments and technical developments for research and study. During hostilities they photograph war equipment and scientific materiel of foreign nations for study and analysis. Pictures of crashes and accidents are necessary to aid in determining the causes and contributing factors. Identification photographs are required for admittance passes to restricted areas of Air Force installations. The ground photographer must make official portraits of personnel for public release.[3]

And this was just ground photography. Aerial photography included strike photography, reconnaissance, surveillance, and mapping, as well as photographing the aerial maneuvers of other airplanes, rockets, and parachutes. As recent thinkers such as Paul Virilio and Friedrich Kittler have emphasized, cameras and film technologies enjoyed a preeminent place in the twentieth-century warfare state.[4]

Lookout Mountain Laboratory, as we will see in the following chapters, was caught up in what Joseph Masco describes as the US Cold War "theater of operations," an ever-expanding imaginary and geopolitical realm of "American self-fashioning through technoscience and threat projection" that targeted, far more than "enemies," the affect and emotions of American citizens.[5] "Theater," of course, can refer to a place where dramatic performances are given, as well as a site of warfare; and the theater of war, as Masco, Virilio, and others have observed, is no less a place of staging, performance, spectacle, and story than the dramatic theater.[6] Both forms of theater took hold of the cameras of Lookout Mountain Laboratory. As they staged and screened dramas, and they also helped define the limits of officially sanctioned violence. It was their cameras that captured the theatrical performances of the deterrent state, and it was their cameras that helped constitute regions of the Earth as a "test site," a "staging ground," or an "outdoor laboratory" to "prove" American military powers.

In chapter 1 we considered the beginnings of Lookout Mountain Laboratory within the broad cultural contexts of Hollywood, the rise of the Air Force, and the advent of postwar atomic testing. In this chapter, we consider how Lookout Mountain fit—or didn't fit, as was sometimes the case—within the operations of the Air Force, the Atomic Energy Commission, and the official structures of the nuclear deterrent state. Our goal is to explain how and why Lookout Mountain was a military unit, situated within a chain of command, and at the same time, often hardly recognizable as a military unit in both its culture and operations.

The Air Force opened Lookout Mountain in 1947 to serve the needs of Operation Sandstone, a series of three nuclear tests carried out at Eniwetok Atoll in the Pacific Proving Grounds. Sandstone, unlike Crossroads, was

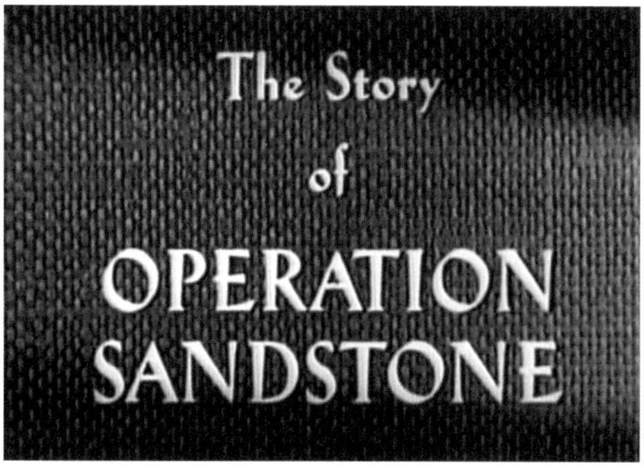

a highly secretive operation. It was the first nuclear test carried out after the passage of the Atomic Energy Act [1946] and was subject to a new regime of security clearances [for example, eleven of the test's thirteen thousand workers were screened out of service for "communistic tendencies"].[7] The tests were closed to journalists and VIPs, and the joint task force in charge of the tests studiously avoided any form of publicity at all in the run-up to the blasts. The whole operation was to be kept under wraps. In this way, Sandstone represented a return to the secrecy of the Manhattan Project, and for evident reason: with the Cold War heating up, the aim of the tests was to evaluate new techniques and technologies so as to build atomic weapons which could surpass in destructive power that of "Fat Man" and "Little Boy."

Still, for all the secrecy, filmic records of the events were crucial for scientific and political purposes. Cameras would record operational procedures and the details of the blasts themselves, and provide the basis for the official "film reports" that would be shown to Atomic Energy Commission officials, military brass, members of Congress, and even the president himself. In the run up to the tests, the Air Force, which had distinguished itself at Crossroads for its camerawork, was put in charge of all test photography. As we saw in the last chapter, Brigadier General Cullen split major photographic responsibilities between Los Alamos and the Strategic Air Command's 311th Air Reconnaissance Division, the former responsible for scientific photography and the latter for documentary footage.[8] But their duties overlapped. As the official report on photography at Sandstone stated, the 311th's work was not strictly for official film reports; it was meant to "gather scientific data and operational facts upon which an Atomic striking force must be built."[9] A cadre of Navy, Army, and Marine Corps cameramen joined the 311th, as did a small crew of Air Force–employed photographers, who had been helping to get Lookout Mountain Laboratory off the ground back in Hollywood.[10] Meanwhile, Lookout Mountain's operations were put under the charge of Strategic Air Command. They were commissioned to produce a series of film reports about Sandstone, each covering a different aspect of the tests.[11] [See the following chapter for more on Lookout Mountain's work at Sandstone.] In look and feel, these secret films adopted the style of the First Motion Picture Unit, complete with musical scores, offscreen narrators, dramatic scripts, and—following the First Motion Picture Unit's *The Last Bomb*—a crescendo in a nuclear blast.

After Sandstone, in the fall of 1949, then Maj. Gen. Curtis Lemay, who had recently taken over Strategic Air Command, asked that Lookout Mountain Laboratory be reassigned to another Air Force branch. He didn't seem to care which branch, as long as it was not Strategic Air Command. It seemed to him that the work of the film studio had little directly to do the mission of the command, as Lookout Mountain did nothing in the way of reconnaissance

Operation Sandstone

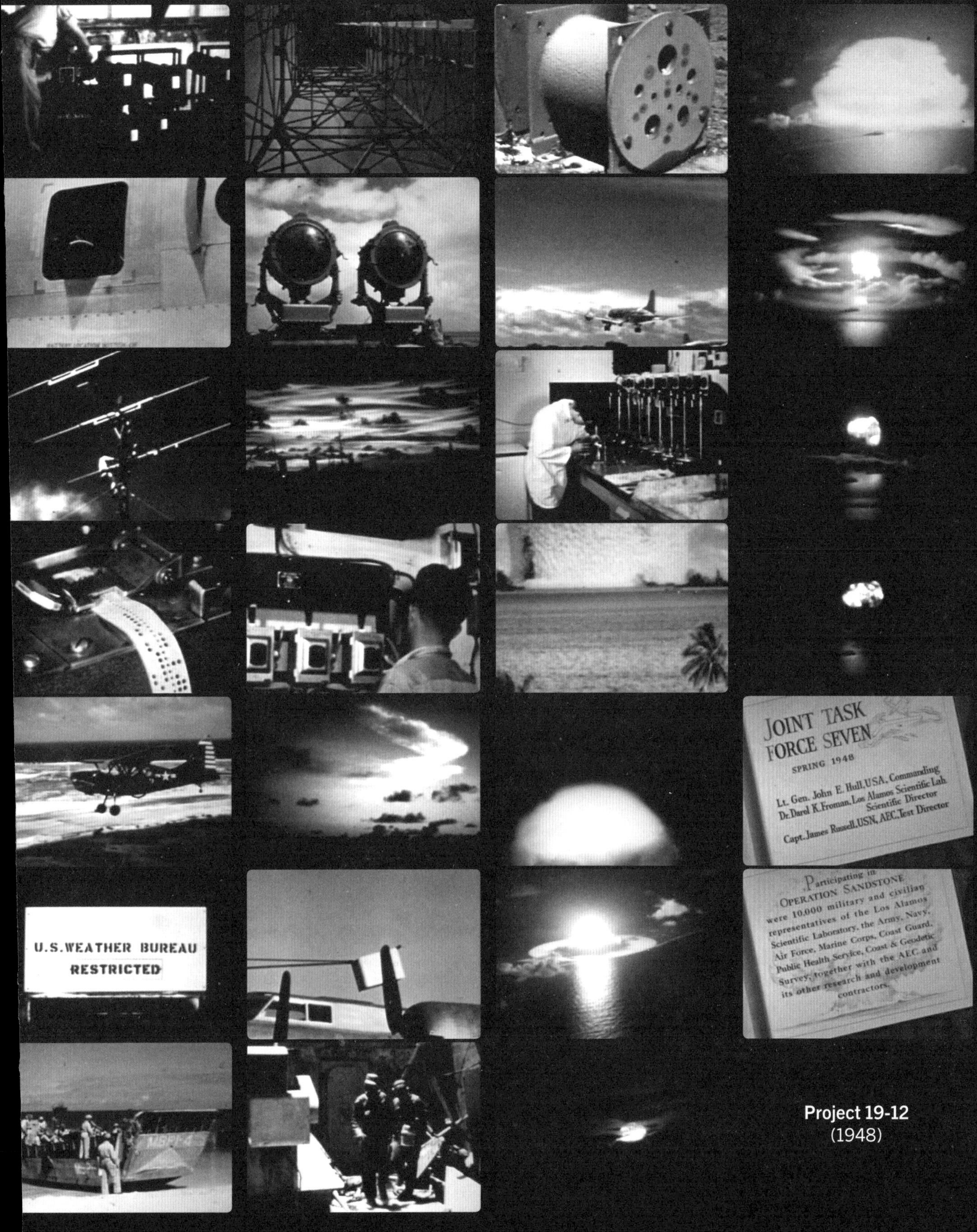

JOINT TASK
FORCE SEVEN
SPRING 1948
Lt. Gen. John E. Hull, USA, Commanding
Dr. Darol K. Froman, Los Alamos Scientific Lab.
Scientific Director
Capt. James Russell, USN, AEC, Test Director
U.S.WEATHER BUREAU
RESTRICTED
Participating in
OPERATION SANDSTONE
were 10,000 military and civilian
representatives of the Los Alamos
Scientific Laboratory, the Army, Navy,
Air Force, Marine Corps, Coast Guard,
Public Health Service, Coast & Geodetic
Survey, together with the AEC and
its other research and development
contractors.

Project 19-12
(1948)

and targeting. Lt. Gen. William Kepner of the Air Force's Air Proving Ground, who had overseen overall Air Force operations at Sandstone, saw in Lemay's request an opportunity and requested that Lookout Mountain be put under his command.[12] As one Air Force report states, "General Kepner knew from experience as Commander of Air Forces on Operation Sandstone, and from his experience on Operation Crossroads, of the vitally important function of photography in support of these tests, and recognized the necessity for retaining on a permanent basis a unit capable of obtaining such photography and completing its production into the finished form."[13]

In fact, the reassignment of Lookout Mountain from Strategic Air Command to Air Proving Ground was not merely a matter of chain-of-command minutiae. It portended conflicts that would lie at the heart of the Air Force's approach to nuclear weapons over the next decade and beyond. General Lemay, of course, was happy to buy into the strategy of nuclear deterrence, as it kept his atomic flying force in business. But he was always ready to target and use nuclear weapons. For Lemay, nuclear deterrence was but a kind of preface to nuclear destruction. However, others in the Air Force, not to mention the White House, were slower to think of nuclear weapons as usable weapons of war. Especially as the weapons grew in power, they were increasingly seen as strictly a means of a catastrophic threat, or of deterrence, and therefore of a kind of international spectacle. To threaten adversaries and to assure allies, you had to have the capacity to show them your stuff. Here Lookout Mountain's location in Hollywood would come to mean far more than proximity to photographic equipment and resources; it would mean access to Hollywood directors, actors, editors, animators, musicians, and above all, access to Hollywood cinematic styles.

The reassignment of Lookout Mountain from Strategic Air Command to Air Proving Ground also suggested tensions around the relative prestige of photography in Air Force operations. Outside of aerial reconnaissance, photography was yeoman's work in the Air Force of the 1940s. It had been used in World War II in a vital but still supplementary fashion: public relations, historical documentation, damage assessment, and so on. With respect to prestige, photography would never lose this supplementary, even secondary, status in the Air Force. From the earliest years, airmen received training in motion-picture and still photography as part of the Air Technical School, next to others learning how to maintain guns, engines, or bombsights. Cadets at the newly established Air Force Academy would learn how to read and understand aerial photographs, but not how to produce images.[14] Within the Air Force ranks, photographers were viewed as technicians, strict subordinates in cachet to pilots, navigators, gunners, and other "real" airmen. And yet during the 1950s, as Eisenhower sought to get more for America's defense bucks, it became increasingly apparent to many Air Force brass that photography was even more vital to the projection of Air Force identity than it had been in World War II, capable of persuading presidents, politicians, publics, allies, and adversaries alike of the economies and capacities of American air power. Hence, while in the late 1940s General Lemay wanted to rid himself of Lookout Mountain, Strategic Air Command's later attempts to produce compelling cinematic stories about its mission suggest that he may have come to regret the move.[15]

In the early 1950s, as more destructive atomic weapons were being designed, Lookout Mountain Laboratory's responsibilities began to grow exponentially. Whereas the studio had been created as a motion-picture production unit for Operation Sandstone, at Operation Greenhouse—a series of nuclear tests held in 1951 in the Pacific—Lookout Mountain became a full-scale nuclear testing shooting and production unit, displacing the 311th Air Reconnaissance Division. The Air Force and the Atomic Energy Commission made Lookout Mountain responsible for all "documentary" motion-picture and

Air Photographic and Charting Service (APCS)

Command Structure, June 1953

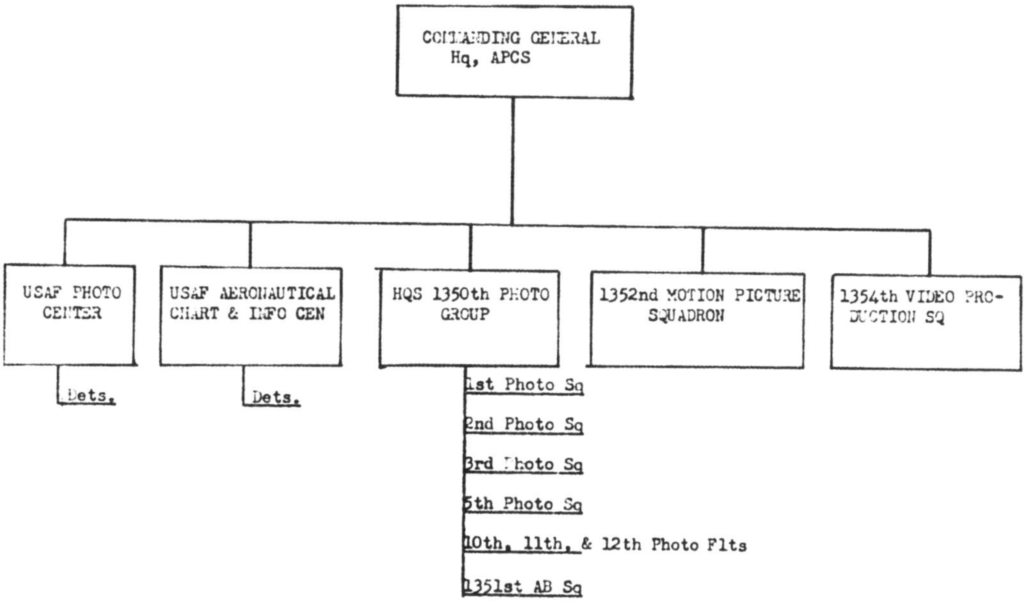

still work at the Greenhouse blasts. Photographers from the Atomic Energy Commission and its contractors still did scientific photography, but Lookout Mountain was the most prominent photographic unit at the Greenhouse tests. A year later, at Operation Ivy—the first test of a thermonuclear device—Lookout Mountain was reassigned to the scientific division of the test task force, even encroaching on the domain of Atomic Energy Commission photographers. Lookout Mountain, however, was not received as a threat to the photographic work of the commission, but rather as serving it, for the cinematic story of "scientific progress" was becoming more and more important to elites in the Atomic Energy Commission, the Pentagon, and the White House; and Lookout Mountain could tell that story better than any of the Atomic Energy Commission photographers [see chapter 4].

In 1951 the Air Force created the Air Pictorial Service, and Lookout Mountain was put under its command. Formed during the Korean War, the idea behind the Air Pictorial Service was to put all Air Force photographic services, excepting some reconnaissance photography, directly under the command of the Air Force chief of staff, who could centrally manage it. A year later, in 1952, the Air Pictorial Service was redesignated the Air Photographic and Charting Service, taking on, in addition to photography, cartographic and geodetic responsibilities. The newly formed Air Photographic and Charting Service was put under the Military Air Transport Service, a vast Air Force command that took care of the strategic air transport needs of all US military services.[16] The Air Photographic and Charting Service would oversee a wide range of mapping, charting, and filming activities for the Air Force.[17] Its geodetic work, comprising the mathematical measuring of the earth's precise shape, would be critical to the calculations needed for targeting nuclear weapons. However, as important as mapping and charting were to the Air Photographic and Charting Service, film and photography was the largest mission of the command.[18] Aerial photography was, of course, the primary means by which the new maps were drawn. But Air

Geodetic Survey

As critical as the work of Lookout Mountain was in the nation's nuclear adventures, other units of the Air Photographic and Charting Service (APCS) were engaged in an equally ambitious effort: the construction of an accurate map of the planet.

With the new possibility of global air war, pilots—and more to the point, bombardiers—needed to know where in the world they were at any given time, day or night, cloudy or clear. The problem was that huge parts of the world were as yet unmapped, especially in environments that were not amenable to line-of-sight survey techniques. Indeed, after World War II the Air Force had no reliable way to navigate from North America to Europe, Russia, or Asia with the precision that transatlantic, transpacific, or transarctic reconnaissance and bombing runs demanded.

Though satellite technology would eventually come to the rescue, in the years following World War II the Air Force had to rely on other techniques and technologies. Principal among them was the radar-based Short Range Navigation, or SHORAN, technique. The technique was used to construct maps by plotting triangle meshes from the United States and Canada northward into the Arctic, westward from Europe across the Atlantic, and across the waters of Oceania. SHORAN also played a critical role in bombing, allowing bombers to measure with relative precision their distance from ground-based transponders, which in turn kept them on course and ultimately on target. The technique was used effectively for bombing for the first time in the Korean War.

The work of the APCS was central to SHORAN and related aerial mapping techniques. Guided by transponders on the ground, APCS mapping planes flew prescribed paths while cameras rolled in the bomb bays, resulting in both a mathematical model of the planet's precise three-dimensional shape in space—its *geoid*—and a corresponding visual model, composed of innumerable aerial images of the Earth's surface.

See also

Martin-Nielsen, *Eismitte in the Scientific Imagination; Measuring and Mapping the World*, a 1961 APCS profile of the 1370th Photo Mapping Wing of the Military Airlift Transport Service, available at https://archive.org/details/342FR165MeasuringMapping.

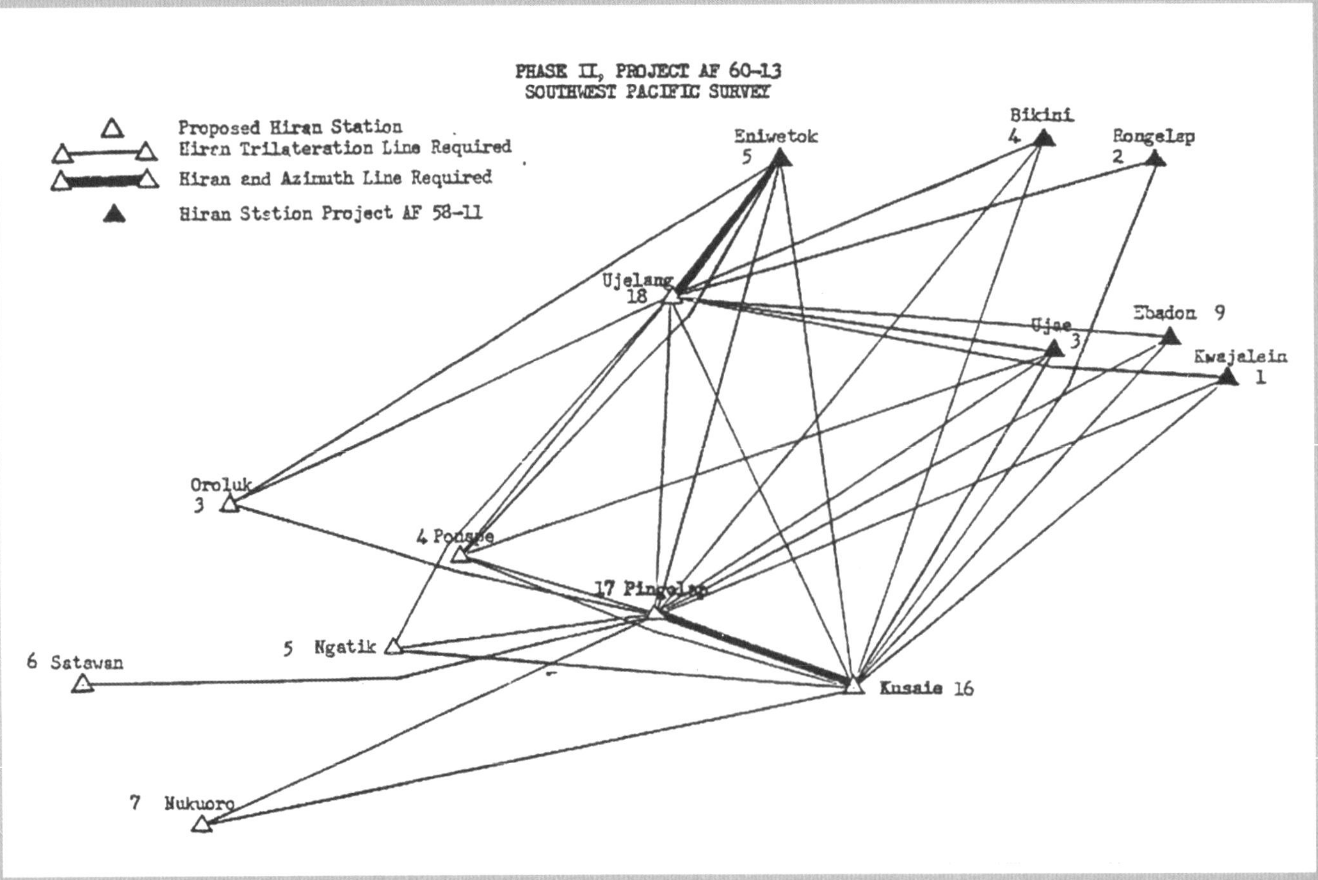

Photographic and Charting Service units also produced thousands of training films, orientation films, documentary, and "information" films, essentially becoming the primary system by which the Air Force produced and distributed visual information for its personnel.

The stated mission of the Air Photographic and Charting Service was "to produce a wide variety of materials, including various types of photographic items—moving pictures, still pictures, film strips, charts—pertaining to all phases of aeronautics, terrain mapping, flight information, pilot's handbooks, and television or kine recordings"—and all of this "world-wide."[19] To meet their mission, the service relied on a cadre of Air Force film units in addition to Lookout Mountain (as well as outside contractors, when needed). In 1953, as Lookout Mountain was in its fifth year, there were fourteen photographic units under Air Photographic and Charting Service command. Along with Lookout Mountain, the 1365th Photographic Group at Orlando Air Force Base and the 1350th Motion Picture Squadron at Wright-Patterson Air Force Base in Ohio played especially active roles in the Air Force's photographic and motion-picture work.[20] Lookout Mountain regularly worked alongside these other Air Force film units on various projects.

The films of the Air Photographic and Charting Service units fell into several generic types. The most ambitious films were designated as "Special Film Projects." They narrated noteworthy events or special concepts, providing scripted and often scored documentary overviews of new techniques and technologies, or of particular military operations. "Film Training Aids," which could range from edited montages of existing footage to location shoots with paid actors, functioned as curricular instruments on topics ranging from nuclear flash protection for pilots to survival skills for downed crews. Finally, "Film Reports" provided an edited, often narrated, montage of documentary footage without much additional context or background. These were typically aimed at providing particular audiences—especially those in leadership—with an official visual "report" on how particular military efforts were advancing. Lookout Mountain made all of these types of films.

With the redesignation of the Air Pictorial Service as the Air Photographic and Charting Service under the Military Air Transport Service, Lookout Mountain Laboratory itself was redesignated the 1352nd Motion Picture Squadron of the Air Photographic and Charting Service (from the 4881st Motion Picture Squadron of the Air Pictorial Service). In one respect, this redesignation put Lookout Mountain on the same level as other motion-picture and photographic units within the Air Force chain of command. Yet Lookout Mountain never operated according to the top-down logic of Air Force Command and had a very different social culture from other Air Force film units. While subject to Air Force orders and regulations, the day-to-day operations of the unit were quite flexible. When should a film open with a musical score and animated titles? When are paid civilian actors needed to accurately portray military personnel? How can a single script result in three or more integrated final edits for differing security clearances among various audiences? What character arcs and motivations should drive the narrative of a particular film "report," given the different ways in which a story of technological progress, success, or failure might be told? And after the film report has been made, what artifacts need to be retained for the future, and who will have access? Such questions were day-to-day problems at Lookout Mountain, and despite the chain of command, top-down decision making rarely resolved them. Rather, Lookout Mountain personnel addressed each new project on a case-by-case basis, sometimes by referring to precedent, sometimes improvising, and sometimes working provisionally and experimentally.

Moreover, as civilians far outnumbered military personnel at Lookout Mountain [representing nearly 70 percent of the unit's workforce at its height], a distinct social culture developed at the unit, relative to other film units in the Air Photographic and Charting Service. Uniforms were optional for military personnel, who also had to find residence and provisions in or around Hollywood rather than on a big base.[21] Office picnics and parties had the feel of Hollywood carnival more than drinks at the officers' club, and informal gatherings of staff took place in comfortable suburban Los Angeles homes around music, drink, and food. Though some staff spent long periods away from home in uncomfortable remote locations, for those who worked daily at the base the job was considered one of the best in Hollywood.

That is, Lookout Mountain was not just another Air Force film unit. From its very inception, it stood apart from other Air Photographic and Charting Service photography units, even with respect to its operations. Much more than its counterparts, the 1352nd participated in "joint" defense activities, especially joint Atomic Energy Commission and Department of Defense nuclear operations. No other film unit in the entire Department of Defense—including those in the Navy and the Army—was, like Lookout Mountain, systematically and structurally attached to these joint activities. It meant that Lookout Mountain faced significantly more stringent demands for secrecy; but it also meant that the unit could, and sometimes did, operate with relative independence from the Air Photographic and Charting Service.

In 1952 the commander of Lookout Mountain at the time, Lt. Colonel Gaylord, made an explicit case for the unit's independence from other Air Force film units in a memo to his superiors. Lookout Mountain Laboratory, he argued, was founded to handle motion-picture and photographic responsibilities for the joint Department of Defense and Atomic Energy Commission nuclear testing operations. This was a "highly specialized mission," demanding, among other things, "strict security requirements" as well as direct work with Los Alamos Laboratory and the Atomic Energy Commission. Gaylord suggested that Lookout Mountain was nearly as much an Atomic Energy Commission film unit as it was an Air Force one. In fact, when the Wonderland Avenue facility was first acquired, it was the Atomic Energy Commission, not the Air Force, who footed the $25,000 needed to get the facility up and running [this would be about $250,000 today].[22] Therefore, Gaylord argued, Lookout Mountain warranted relative independence from the day-to-day operations of the Air Photographic and Charting Service.[23]

Gaylord prevailed: in 1952, even as Lookout Mountain was redesignated the 1352nd of the Air Photographic and Charting Service, the unit won nominal independence from other Air Force photographic units with instructions from the Air Force that it was "not to be included in any other subordinate photographic echelon."[24] Lookout Mountain's official mission became explicitly tied to the Atomic Energy Commission: "To provide in-service production of classified motion pictures and still photographs for the Department of the Air Force in support of the Atomic Energy Program." By 1955 its mission had expanded to include "scientific" photography related to Air Force activities in support of nuclear weapons development.[25] Throughout the 1950s, the primary clients of Lookout Mountain—in terms of importance, if not always in terms of workload—were the Atomic Energy Commission and the Armed Forces Special Weapons Project. Indeed, by 1957 Lookout Mountain held in its vaults seventeen million feet of film footage, the majority of the archive being nuclear weapons–related footage shot for the Atomic Energy Commission and the Armed Forces Special Weapons Project.[26] At the same time, nearly one-third of its expenses were covered by agencies other than the Air Force, especially by the Atomic Energy Commission.[27]

Lookout Mountain became central to the broader nuclear-weapons program because it could promise its clients the highest security standards. To keep the lid on its activities, it did virtually all of its work in-house. It was certainly one of the most, if not the most, comprehensive film studio in all of Hollywood. Moreover, many of its workers had "Q" clearances, among the Atomic Energy Commission's highest security clearances, as well as Department of Defense top secret clearances. Such secrecy meant that Lookout Mountain personnel could work closely, indeed often side by side, with the men and women at the laboratories of the Atomic Energy Commission and government contractors working on top secret projects. The reputation of Lookout Mountain Laboratory for security kept it a favorite in the Q-cleared world.

Along with this, Lookout Mountain promoted its services to the Department of Defense, the Atomic Energy Commission, and military contractors as "top quality" work.[28] They wrote of their operations:

> Lookout Mountain Laboratory can and does match step for step any production capability of the average industry studio. In the 36 steps in motion picture production, LML lacks no facility or capability, although an occasional specialist—actor, narrator or director—may be called upon for a particular task. In fact, because of specialized photographic assignments, LML has developed skills, equipment and knowledge beyond that of the normal service men. . . . [O]n one mission alone LML was charged with scientific, underwater, high-speed, aerial and conventional photography, and as a considerable portion of this photography was used in a diagnostic study of atomic blast phenomena, it had to be of critical first-rate quality.[29]

Lookout Mountain employees would sometimes boast that they worked for the best film studio not just in the US government, but in Hollywood. Even if this was only a boast, the reputation of the studio was not: while the Air Force, Army, and Navy had their own film units, and while many government contractors and Atomic Energy Commission laboratories had their own specialized film operations, these agencies would come to Lookout Mountain if they were particularly keen on high-quality production.[30]

And they came often. By the early 1950s, Lookout Mountain's reputation and institutional practices were firmly established. Their regular clients—the Atomic Energy Commission and branches and divisions of the Department of Defense—provided steady demand for new projects, while other clients such as civil defense and aircraft industry contractors provided additional jobs. Requests for work centered on three modes, each of which required distinct pathways of intake, processing, and output: didactic films, film reports, and documentary features, produced largely in support of nuclear tests and military exercises; scientific and diagnostic photography, resulting in imagery sent to engineers or scientists in support of their work on new technologies; and documentary field photography, in still or motion-picture form, provided to clients in unedited form as an official record of an event, or to producers of feature films who needed images in support of particular scripts or stories. Much of Lookout Mountain's work through the 1950s would consist in developing ever more efficient workflows for processing these demands.

In the case of scripted and edited motion-picture projects, the process began with a questionnaire of sorts, asking the requesting agencies things such as: [1] Why is the motion picture being made? [2] Who will use it? [3] What are the audience's security-clearance and educational levels? [4] What do you want to stress in the film? [5] Do you want the picture to be shot in 16 mm or 35 mm? Black and white or color? What sort of music or sound expectations do you have? [6] Is animation needed to explain technical points? And last but not least, [7] Could there possibly be a picture in existence that would already fill your needs?[31] Writers typically led the way on Lookout Mountain's bigger productions, often visiting the laboratory, manufacturer, or test site for script research, and consulting with the requesting agency—be it the Armed Forces Special Weapons Project, the Atomic Energy Commission, or Strategic Air Command—before setting out to write the script. Then a producer would be assigned to oversee, coordinate, and expedite production of the film. A director or assistant director would break the script into scenes, and the producer would select scenes for on-location shoots, studio shoots, and so on [depending on the film, Lookout Mountain might or might not rely heavily on stock footage]. Location shoots would be planned and sets designed, and any assignments to the animation department would be made. The shooting for the film would take place: actors would be called in to the studio or, if shooting on location, sent to sites. Sometimes a Hollywood director would be called in to direct a scene. Meanwhile, animators would be at work in the animation studio. The film would then be edited, and a first rough-cut viewing would be shown to key personnel at Lookout Mountain. An Air Force commander would request criticism and give some of his own. And then representatives from the requesting agency or agencies would view the film, offering their own feedback. Finally, based on all the feedback, the final changes would be made and prints of the film would be couriered off to the requesting agency or to designated distribution centers.[32]

In the 1950s, demand for projects increased to such a point that a new production management office was created in 1957 just to track progress and coordinate labor, space, and resources.[33] In September 1963, Lookout Mountain operationalized this process even further through reorganizing a significant portion of its efforts under a Motion Picture Services division that followed what they self-described as "the Producer-Director system."[34] The edi-

1352nd Motion Picture Squadron

Command Structure, June 1953

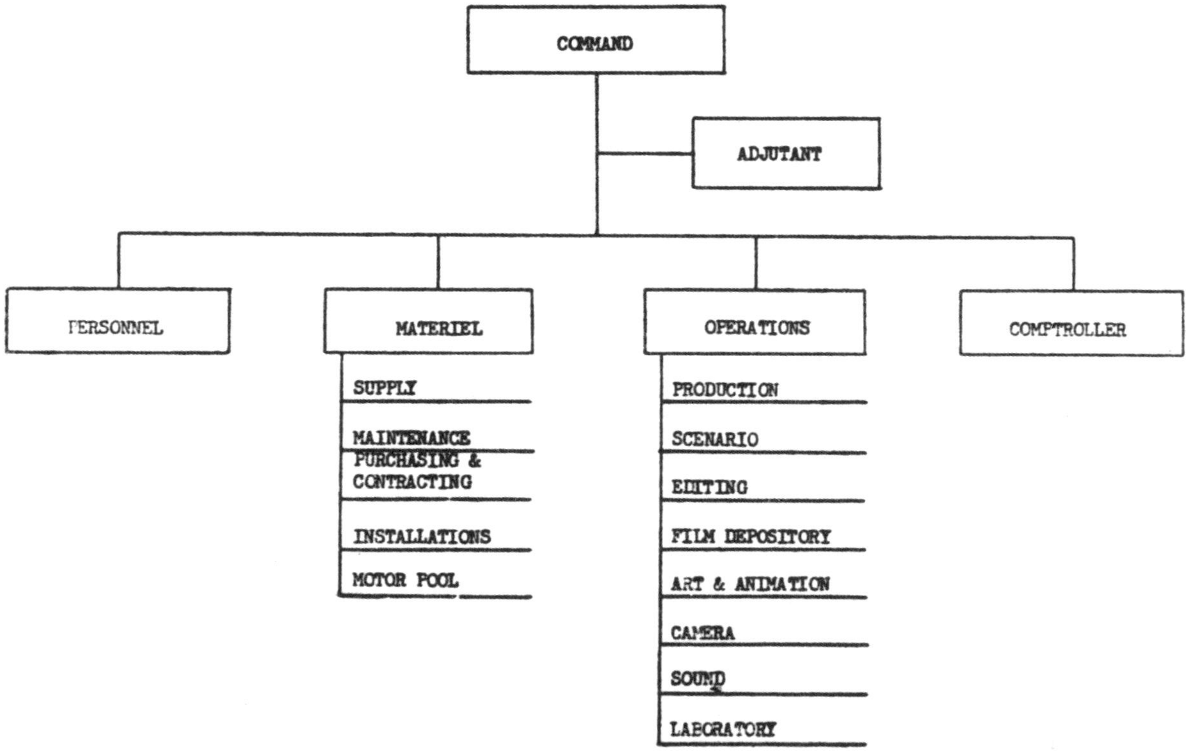

torial, camera, art and animation, writing, and sound divisions all reported to this new division, which was run by a chief, assisted by producer-directors and project officers.[35] Each new project would be assigned to a producer-director and project officer, who together would see it through to completion, deploying whatever Lookout Mountain resources they needed. Both producer-directors and project officers would oversee numerous projects at once, most of them taking less than a year and sometimes less than a month, resulting in a workflow and organizational structure that sometimes looked more like a major network television news outfit than a Hollywood studio.

To meet its workload, Lookout Mountain repeatedly sought to build and maintain centralized, efficient, and repeatable processes. In fact, however, the studio was constantly improvising and engineering, especially with respect to their on-location shoots, where camera rigs would have to be built, wires run, cameras repaired, film stock searched out, and so on. Back on Wonderland Avenue, if a client was not happy with a production, scripts would have to be rewritten, films reedited, sequences reanimated, and new scenes added.

Despite their capacity for high-quality film production, many—indeed, most—of Lookout Mountain's films were average, institutional productions: training films that looked like training films, film reports that sounded report-like, and informational, promotional, and propaganda films that were overwrought because they were too hastily done. Some Lookout Mountain films barely rival some of the lesser low-budget flicks of the period. Sometimes, to be sure, they produced what might well be celebrated as *art*,

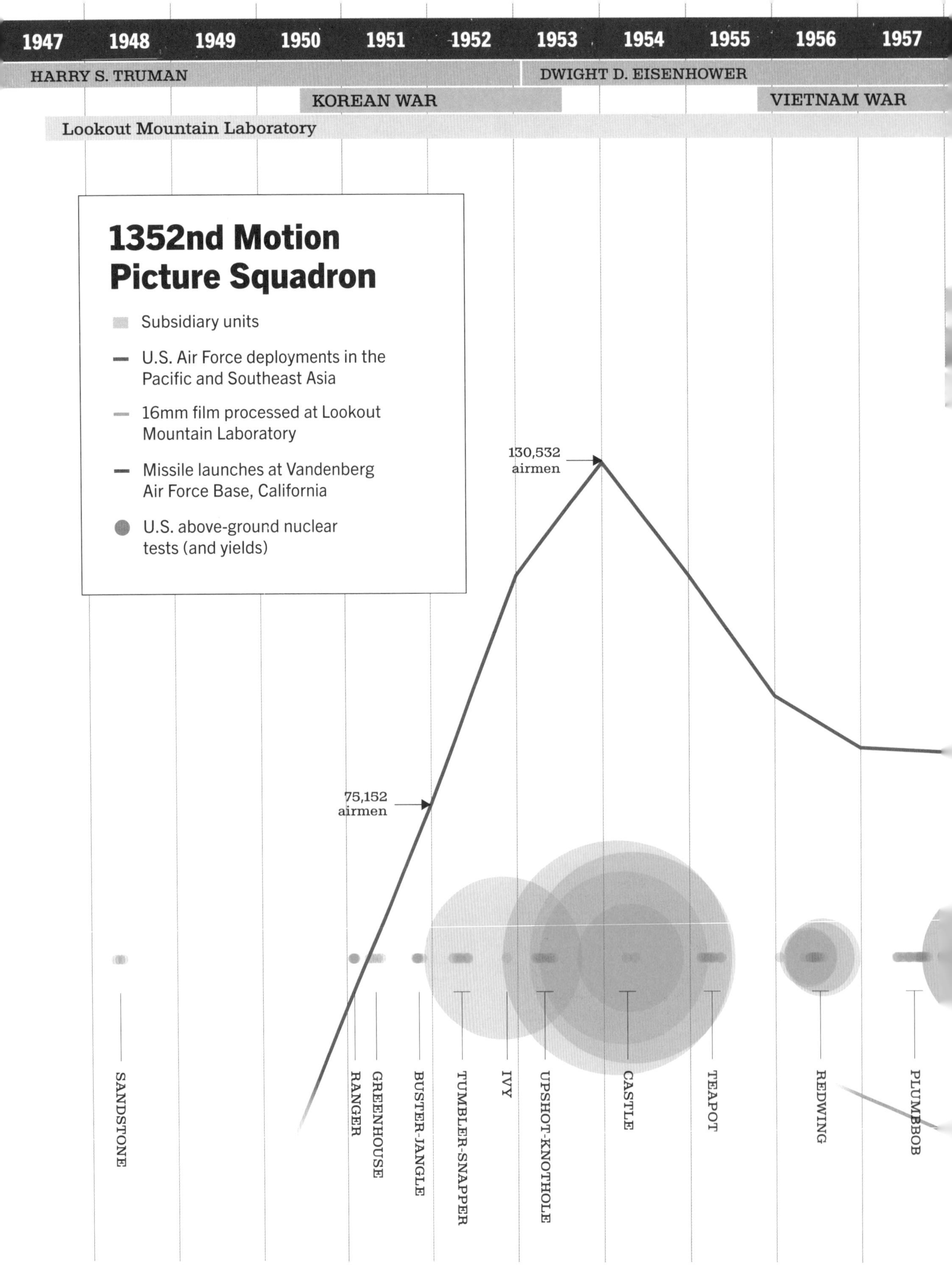
1947
1948
1949
1950
1951
1952
1953
1954
1955
1956
1957
HARRY S. TRUMAN
DWIGHT D. EISENHOWER
KOREAN WAR
VIETNAM WAR
Lookout Mountain Laboratory
1352nd Motion Picture Squadron
Subsidiary units
U.S. Air Force deployments in the Pacific and Southeast Asia
16mm film processed at Lookout Mountain Laboratory
Missile launches at Vandenberg Air Force Base, California
U.S. above-ground nuclear tests (and yields)
130,532 airmen
75,152 airmen
SANDSTONE
RANGER
GREENHOUSE
BUSTER-JANGLE
TUMBLER-SNAPPER
IVY
UPSHOT-KNOTHOLE
CASTLE
TEAPOT
REDWING
PLUMBBOB

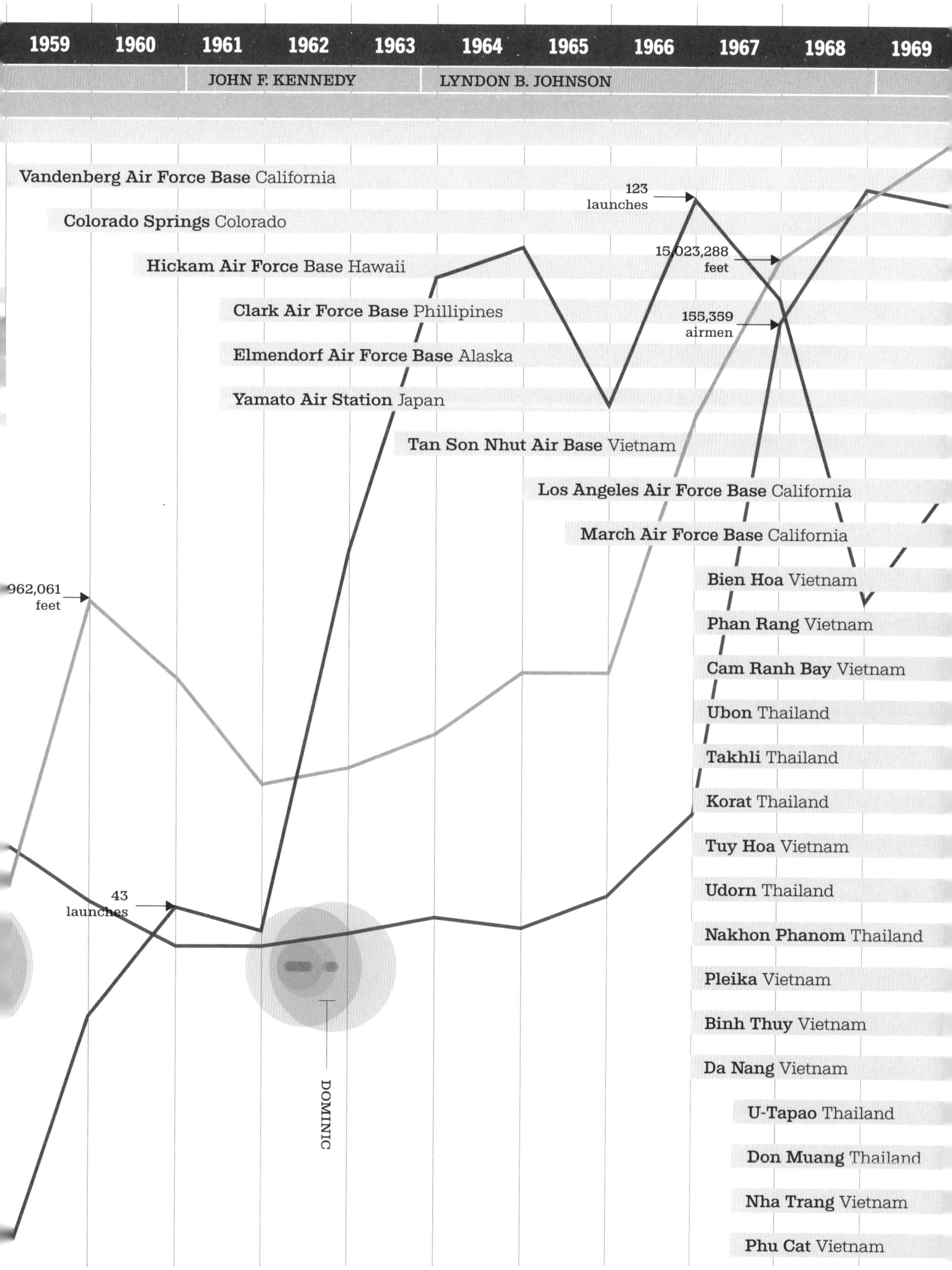

1959
1960
1961
1962
1963
1964
1965
1966
1967
1968
1969
JOHN F. KENNEDY
LYNDON B. JOHNSON
Vandenberg Air Force Base California
Colorado Springs Colorado
Hickam Air Force Base Hawaii
Clark Air Force Base Phillipines
Elmendorf Air Force Base Alaska
Yamato Air Station Japan
Tan Son Nhut Air Base Vietnam
Los Angeles Air Force Base California
March Air Force Base California
Bien Hoa Vietnam
Phan Rang Vietnam
Cam Ranh Bay Vietnam
Ubon Thailand
Takhli Thailand
Korat Thailand
Tuy Hoa Vietnam
Udorn Thailand
Nakhon Phanom Thailand
Pleika Vietnam
Binh Thuy Vietnam
Da Nang Vietnam
U-Tapao Thailand
Don Muang Thailand
Nha Trang Vietnam
Phu Cat Vietnam
123 launches
15,023,288 feet
155,359 airmen
962,061 feet
43 launches
DOMINIC

especially in their animation and atomic blast work, and especially in films focused on the nuclear deterrent system. But this was more the exception than the rule; more times than not, getting a film done took precedence over getting it done well. Moreover, as we will see, Lookout Mountain's requesting agencies frequently had rhetorical reasons for wanting "no-frills" documentary films, and the unit's producers wielded its capacity for high production values carefully to match style to substance.

At no point in Lookout Mountain's twenty-year history did things go smoothly, yet at every point the studio was extraordinarily productive. The thing that may have most marked Lookout Mountain as an Air Force film studio was not the guards outside, nor even the colonels within, but its incapacity to say "no." The best that could be done was to ask requesters, "Could there already be a picture that fills your needs?" The fact that Lookout Mountain had "Q" and top secret clearances, the fact that it specialized in nuclear-test photography, and the fact that it was all but a functional wing of the Atomic Energy Commission—none of this kept the studio from being called into a wide array of Air Force activities that were not directly about nuclear testing. To the contrary, as nuclear weaponry became less "special" and more and more central to the Air Force's overall mission activities, so too did Lookout Mountain's work blend into that of other Air Photographic and Charting Service units such as the 1350th and 1365th. And as budgetary pressures weighed down the Air Force during the 1950s and again in the 1960s, Lookout Mountain was asked to fill in where other Air Force film units could not meet demand. Hence, its work tacked back and forth between nuclear testing work and more "mundane" responsibilities such as photographing Air Force ceremonies, construction projects, and military exercises.

Subsequent chapters in this book focus on different theaters of Lookout Mountain Laboratory's operations: the Pacific, Nevada, the California coast, the Arctic, and Vietnam. While allowing us to concentrate on different arenas of Lookout Mountain's work, they can be misleading; at no point after Sandstone did Lookout Mountain focus singularly on any one project, or even on one kind of photographic service, to the exclusion of others. The staff were always multitasking. Their history is characterized by scope, complexity, and even chaos. So as to offer a sense of the multifaceted character and frenetic pace of their work, we conclude this chapter by comparing Lookout Mountain Laboratory's work in 1954 with its operations in 1964.

In 1954 Lookout Mountain was making prints of a film concerning America's 1952 thermonuclear detonation, *Operation Ivy*, for distribution to movie theaters and television stations across the country. At the same time, it was dealing with the protests of its Wonderland Avenue neighbors and facing the scrutiny of the FBI. As all this was going on, Lookout Mountain was wrestling with the fallout, literally and metaphorically, of a major thermonuclear debacle in the Pacific, the "Bravo" shot at the 1954 Operation Castle. Scientists predicted a yield at "Bravo" ranging from four to eight megatons [the equivalent of four to eight million tons of TNT]. "Bravo" instead yielded fifteen megatons—the largest detonation of its kind by the United States—and spewed dangerous radioactive fallout well beyond any semblance of a legitimate theater for such state violence, leaving islanders in the Pacific atolls, and more infamously a group of Japanese fishermen, sick and dying. In 1954 Lookout Mountain was charged with producing a range of films for Operation Castle: a full-length "report" to the Joint Chiefs of Staff; seven different scientific reports for the Atomic Energy Commission and the Defense Nuclear Agency for each of the seven components of the Castle test series; a film report on Department of Defense participation at Castle; a series of film trailers stressing to servicemen the importance of security and secrecy at Castle; a full-length film on Castle for public release; a range of scientific and diagnostic photography for the Castle shots, including fireball photography [to help measure yield] and crater surveys; motion-picture coverage of the emergency and evacuation efforts made after the "Bravo" debacle; and still-photo documentation of the entire Castle operation.[36]

As if this were not enough, Lookout Mountain took on in the second half of 1954 forty-two additional film projects, twelve of which were for government agencies outside of the Air Force or Atomic Energy Commission—among them the Federal Civil Defense Administration film *Let's Face It*. Of the forty-two film projects, thirty-four were classified. The extent of the work meant motion pictures were "made under completely dissimilar circumstances."[37] While they were prepping specialized cameras for photography of the underwater test Operation Wigwam, they were shooting the *Bob Hope Show* in Greenland, producing TV shorts aimed at recruiting airmen to the Air Force, and doing regular newsreel-style coverage of Air Force activities. A Lookout Mountain report summed up the work of their cameramen alone:

> LML [Lookout Mountain Laboratory] cameramen worked in a variety of places and under some very unusual conditions. While one group was on location in New York City, another was shooting underwater scenes at Bikini in the Marshall Islands [the site of Operation Castle], and [a] third was photographing from an RB-36 [airplane], 40,000 feet above Eniwetok. Some of these same cameramen photographed Marilyn Monroe in scenes for the Castle security films, and others accomplished interior photography in a general's office in Washington, and then in an Army barracks in Virginia. They photographed from seagoing tugs, helicopters, DUKW's [an amphibious vehicle], aircraft carriers, C-54's, trucks, atomic test towers, T-boats, and in one case from high atop a construction crane. Their assignments took them from Hollywood to Micronesia and from Alaska to the coastal waters off Cuba. They worked in sand, coral dust, snow and water, and often under conditions that could not tolerate personnel or equipment failure. On the Castle project alone, they flew well over 600,000 miles, logging some 3,000 hours in the air.[38]

And this was just six months' worth of work. One might expect not only some exhausted cameramen, but also film technicians, editors, animators, engineers, and other Lookout Mountain personnel. In fact, in 1954 the unit suffered the greatest turnover in their six-year history to date, with airmen getting transferred and civilians, who made up the great majority of the workforce, leaving the unit for better offers at commercial studios. The problems Lookout Mountain faced in 1954, however, went further. They were dealing with a range of technical challenges, from the specialized underwater photography needed for Castle and Wigwam, to tweaking CinemaScope technologies, to a crisis created when Kodak decided to stop processing 16 mm Kodachrome film, forcing the studio to hastily modify their film-processing laboratory.

Ten years later, in 1964, major new bureaucratic, political, and cultural pressures were being felt at Lookout Mountain, and the nature of their assignments had changed dramatically. But the extent of their activities had not. The stated mission of the unit in 1964, which would vary slightly over the years, indicated that the range of their work had barely contracted:

> The mission of the 1352d Photographic Group is to accomplish still and motion picture documentary photography and motion picture productions; operate laboratories for processing motion picture and still photographic film; operate a facility to inspect, identify, catalogue, store and maintain motion picture film and still photographs; provide photographic archive services; accomplish instrumentation and technical photography; provide technical and administrative direction to assigned Squadron and Detachments in the CONUS and overseas; operate and maintain the facility occupied by the 1352d, known as Lookout Mountain Air Force Station, Los Angeles, California.[39]

In 1964 Lookout Mountain worked on ten training films covering matters ranging from nuclear safety to vehicular safety; fifty-five "news review films" or "film bulletins" on topics such as "Airlift to Bankok" [*sic*], "Moon Spots," and "New X-15 Rollout"; twenty-six "film reports" on subjects

The Marilyn Monroe Shoot at Greenacres

Fans and historians of Marilyn Monroe have long wondered about the origin of some elusive clips of the actress lounging by a pool, sipping Coca-Cola, and addressing the camera with such phrases as "I hate a careless man." Some have imagined it was an advertising shoot for the soda company; others have wondered whether the images stem from a publicity session for Monroe's film *How to Marry a Millionaire* (1953), in which she wears the same red swimsuit. In fact, this footage was the work of Lookout Mountain Laboratory, done on behalf of America's thermonuclear weapons program. Photographs of the session were captured by silent screen star Harold Lloyd while hosting the shoot at his Greenacres estate. These images portray camera equipment boldly emblazoned with the name of "Lookout Mountain Laboratory."

The shoot appears to have been part of the run-up to Operation Castle, the fateful 1954 thermonuclear test that, exceeding expectations for yield, rained radiation on Marshallese Islanders, test personnel, and a boat of Japanese fishermen. A 1954 Lookout Mountain report describes a collection of secrecy- and security-stressing "trailers" made for personnel arriving at the Pacific test site for Operation Castle. These trailers, which seem to have been the idea of Lt. Colonel Gaylord, the unit's influential commander, were meant to discourage leaks about the tests.

Lookout Mountain produced ten such trailers, each starring Monroe, cajoling men to keep secret their atomic affairs. Though none of these trailers can be found in publicly available archives, excerpts surfaced in other Air Force work over the years, as later editors found ways to reuse the footage. Though Lookout Mountain reports don't name Lloyd's estate as the site for the shoot, a later report names Lloyd as among the industry leaders who lent a hand to the unit's work, and Lloyd's camera captured ample images that confirm the event.

extending from the Mercury space program to Arctic warfare; seven "special film projects" meant for public release; and some hundred films categorized simply as "miscellaneous," "other," or "documentary."[40] Their motion-picture and still photographers covered not only nuclear tests, but also Pacific Air Command activities in Vietnam, various tactical military exercises, coverage of an earthquake disaster in Alaska, a high-altitude balloon launch, aircraft tests, missile tests, NASA activities, and many other subjects. Meanwhile, if more quietly, another portion of the unit's staff dedicated itself to inspecting and archiving the resulting footage, facilitating an additional 150 requests over six months from other units or studios seeking material for use in their own productions. Finally, 1964 also saw Lookout Mountain supervising the work of eight "detachments" around the world, whose projects merited their own processes and reports.

As if the extent of the work were not enough, in 1964 Lookout Mountain and its detachments faced constant shortages of personnel. This meant backlogged projects, equipment malfunctions, and significant declines in the production quality of Lookout Mountain films. Moreover, the unit suddenly found itself with a shortage of suitable Hollywood actors willing to cut their hair short [they were afraid of losing a chance to be cast in the popular westerns of the time period]. Indeed, amid the feverish activities of the national security state in the 1960s, Hollywood was becoming a less and less compelling place for the Air Force to be: not only did actors not want to cut their hair, but technicians and other industry professionals were consistently finding better pay and less stress elsewhere. Meanwhile, the Department of Defense under Robert McNamara was clamping down on purchasing and pushing for more centralized forms of military organization. Though it would take five years to come to fruition, in 1964 the Air Force notified Lookout Mountain that plans were in pace to close the Wonderland Avenue facility and move the 1352nd Motion Picture Squadron to Norton Air Force Base in San Bernardino.

In fact, the theater of Lookout Mountain's operations was always at risk of fragmenting under the pressures of the Cold War tensions and contradictions, and eventually it would. What began in 1947 as a Hollywood-based unit charged with the production of Hollywood-style films about America's nuclear weapons tests grew in the 1950s into an operation tasked with documenting the full, frenetic scope of the nuclear deterrent state and much more. By the middle of the 1960s, America's deterrent operations were so extensive, so diverse, and so furious that Lookout Mountain and its detachments simply could not keep up. While the footage would be historic and sometimes spectacular—the 1960s was the period in which Lookout Mountain helped cover the space race—the filmscripts became more programmed and predictable. Efficiency, not creativity, was the watchword. Indeed, Hollywood itself was undergoing profound changes in the 1960s, leaving the heyday of classical Hollywood cinema behind in favor of rougher-cut stories. Even more, film as a medium was changing with respect to its cultural and political functions: once closely knit to the sensibilities of big-studio dramas, the medium was arguably becoming more democratized—screened on television and shot on home-movie cameras—even as it was being absorbed by a national security state bent on the cybernetic management of not just nuclear deterrence, but the full orbit of America's defense activities, as one of several means of "data." As we have seen and will see further in later chapters, using film as a means of defense data was built into Lookout Mountain's mission from the start. Nevertheless, the Hollywood studio of 1948 could never have envisioned the cybernetic transformation of their work that was to come.

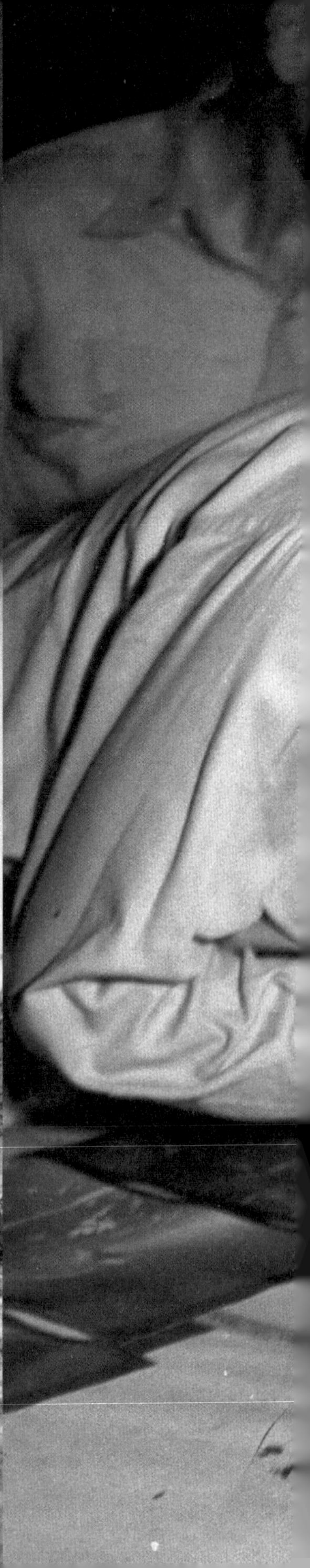

PSL

LIKE A PORCELAIN TABLETOP

in a physics laboratory

Chapter Three

STRATEGIES OF CONTAINMENT

Lookout Mountain's Oceanic Operations

Lookout Mountain Air Force Station, a crisp, twenty-minute self-promotional film made by Lookout Mountain Laboratory in the mid-1960s, culminates in an animated map of the Pacific Ocean, bordered by the American West on the right and Southeast Asia on the left. Like blips on an electrified screen, nine lights pop up in sequence on the map, each representing a Lookout Mountain site: a dot appears over Colorado Springs, another at the Aleutian Islands, one in central Los Angeles, another southeast of Los Angeles, another over Hawaii, one in Japan, and a seventh in South Vietnam. Then a small illuminated square appears at the site of Lookout Mountain's Vandenberg Air Force Base operations in California. Finally, like the crown of a Christmas tree, a star appears over Hollywood, the home, of course, of Lookout Mountain Laboratory itself. Over a rising orchestral score, we see the world as it appeared in the cameras of Lookout Mountain: pivoting on America's Pacific operations. The film's narrator concludes, "It adds up to camera crews covering over 98 million square miles—half of the world."[1]

Though its reach would in fact extend well over half the world, the history of Lookout Mountain Laboratory begins and ends with Pacific operations. Viewed on European- and American-made maps for centuries as "tiny, isolated dots in a vast ocean," the islands of the Pacific would become in the middle of the twentieth century the building blocks of an immense military network for mobilizing machines and troops, and for projecting American power.[2] As Epeli Hau'ofa writes, the islands of the Pacific—which Hau'ofa notes, is better called Oceania—are constantly shifting with tectonic and oceanic flows.[3] The mapping of those islands by European explorers as isolated dots, rather than as a continuous land connected undersea, was itself inseparable from European colonization, a means of turning a dynamic world into a static frontier.[4] Ironically, in a distorted echo of the Polynesian understanding of Oceania as a "sea of islands" rather than a collection of "islands

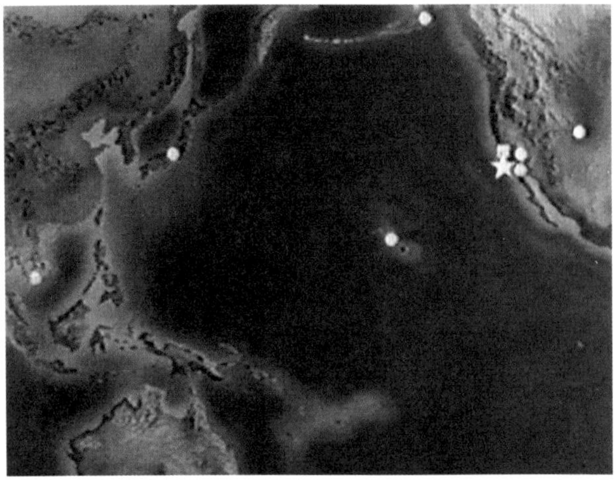

in a far sea," the postwar American empire would also come to see Oceania's islands as nodes in a mobile assembly of vectors, as the paths of ships, signals, jets, missiles, and satellites would leap from the ground of sovereign claimants to the air, and eventually to the very stratosphere. Though American imperial incursions into Micronesia began in and around the Spanish-American War, the Pacific had long appeared to many Americans variously as a defensive barrier; a demarcation of race, ethnicity, and nationality; or as the void on the far side of the "closing" of the American frontier.[5] The war with Japan, however, made the Pacific a bloody and fiery site of "total war." It was in the Pacific that American troops fought Japanese soldiers in some of the most infamously ruthless and relentless combat of the war. It was in the Pacific that naval battles took on new mythologies and magnitudes. And it was in the Pacific that the Army Air Force aggressively pushed forward air power, strategic bombing, and atomic war to revolutionize the meaning of war.

After the war, the United States would claim victory in the Pacific and rule vast portions of it. The United States occupied Japan until 1952, and it exercised sovereignty over the oceanic region of Micronesia for forty-plus more years after that, transforming the latter into not only a nuclear proving ground, but a vast site of radioactive slow violence.[6] Micronesia was a kind of spoil of war. In 1947 the whole area of Micronesia, including the archipelagos of the Marshalls, Carolines, and Marianas, was named an official Trust Territory of the United States by the United Nations, giving America official sovereignty over the territory. It was made an atomic colony, the site of over sixty American nuclear tests from 1946 to 1958.[7] It became a space for endless American military operations and for the exponential expansion of American technological and symbolic power.[8] It also became a site of great controversy, especially after reports began to appear that Micronesians (hundreds of whom had been forced to migrate from the test islands of Bikini and Eniwetok) were growing sick, and even dying, because of radiation exposure, as were others who relied on the Pacific for their livelihood (most infamously a crew of Japanese fisherman that was pummeled with radiation in 1954 from an out-of-control US nuclear test). All told, US nuclear tests in Micronesia would radiologically spoil an area exceeding the size of the continental United States and spread fallout globally.

In the early 1960s America's Pacific nuclear tests, having created so much global controversy, were pushed from Bikini Atoll in Micronesia 1,700 miles eastward to Johnston Atoll, and 4,300 miles westward to Christmas Island. Johnston Atoll had been in US possession since the 1920s, and Christmas Island was a long-standing colonial possession of Great Britain until, in 1958, it was ceded to Australia. While moving nuclear tests outside of the Trust Territory freed the United States from

Etak Navigation in Oceania

Timeworn approaches to navigation, mapping, and even to the very definition of an island among the peoples of Oceania enabled them to traverse much of the southern hemisphere thousands of years before Europeans began leaving their shores for far-off destinations. Scholar Vincente Diaz explains that *etak*, which often translates as "moving islands," entails a remarkable navigational technique for "calculating distance traveled, or position at sea by triangulating the speed of islands of departure and destination with that of a third reference island."

"You get on your canoe and you follow the stars in the direction where lies your destination island," writes Diaz. "As your island of departure recedes from view, you pay attention to a third island, as it is said to move along another prescribed star course." In stark contrast to the navigators of the US military who made their way by air and sea through the Pacific during World War II and the Cold War, for the Oceanic navigator, "the canoe remains stationary and the islands zip by." Along the way, changes in sea life also serve as landmarks, as called out through song and story.

Drawing from the work of Epeli Hau'ofa, Diaz describes Oceania as not only a geographic region, but also an approach that regards islands not as dots in a vast empty seascape, but as moving entities within a larger body. The islands move around the static traveler within the frame of etak, but they also move because they are tectonic, because seagulls and sea creatures carry pieces of them across the waters, and because the volcanic earth spits them out and takes them back again. This makes possible a conception of the world and one's place within it that contrasts sharply with the practices used by the US military during the twentieth century, which approached the Pacific as a network of static islands differentiated chiefly by their distance from fueling stations and other key ports.

See also
Diaz, "Voyaging for Anti-Colonial Recovery."

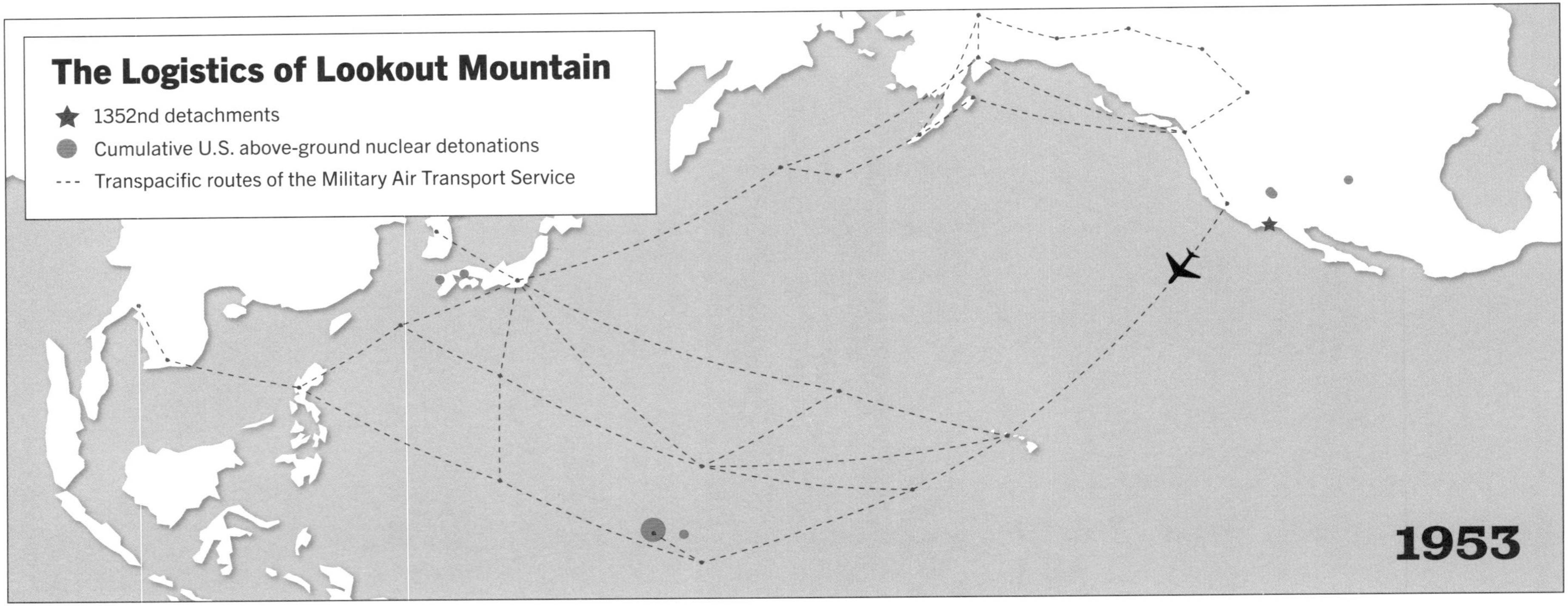
The Logistics of Lookout Mountain
1352nd detachments
Cumulative U.S. above-ground nuclear detonations
Transpacific routes of the Military Air Transport Service
1953

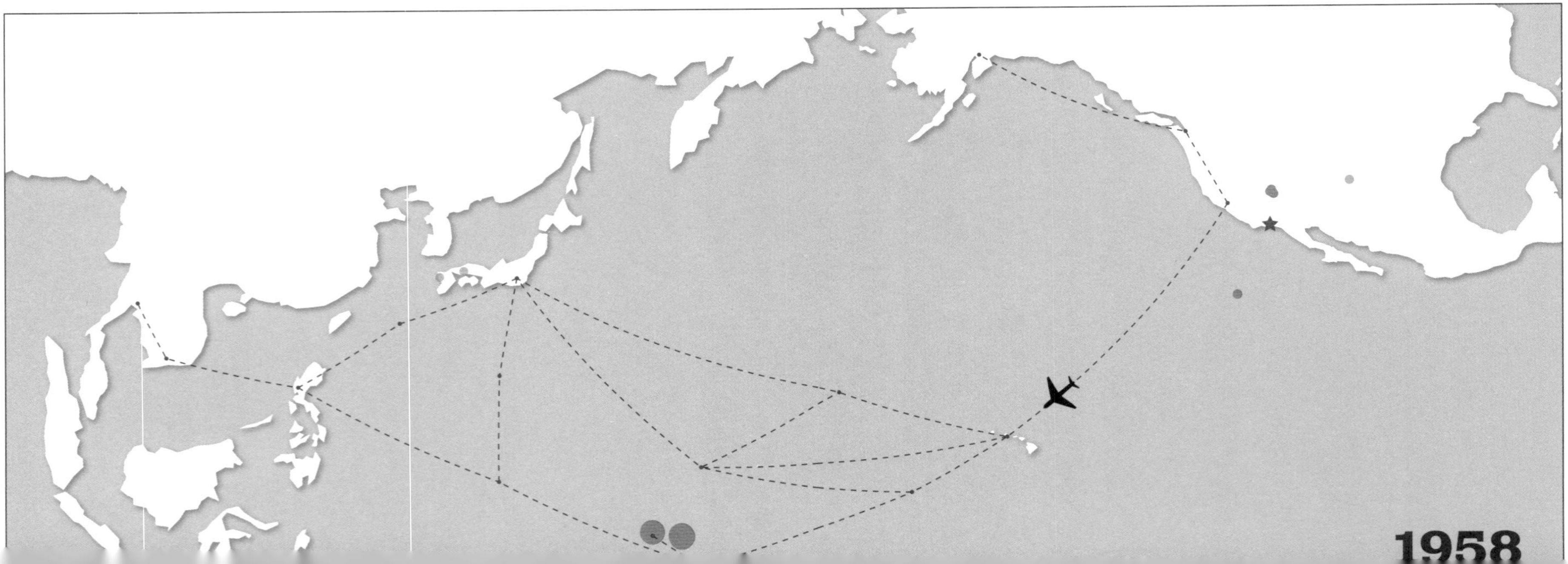
1958

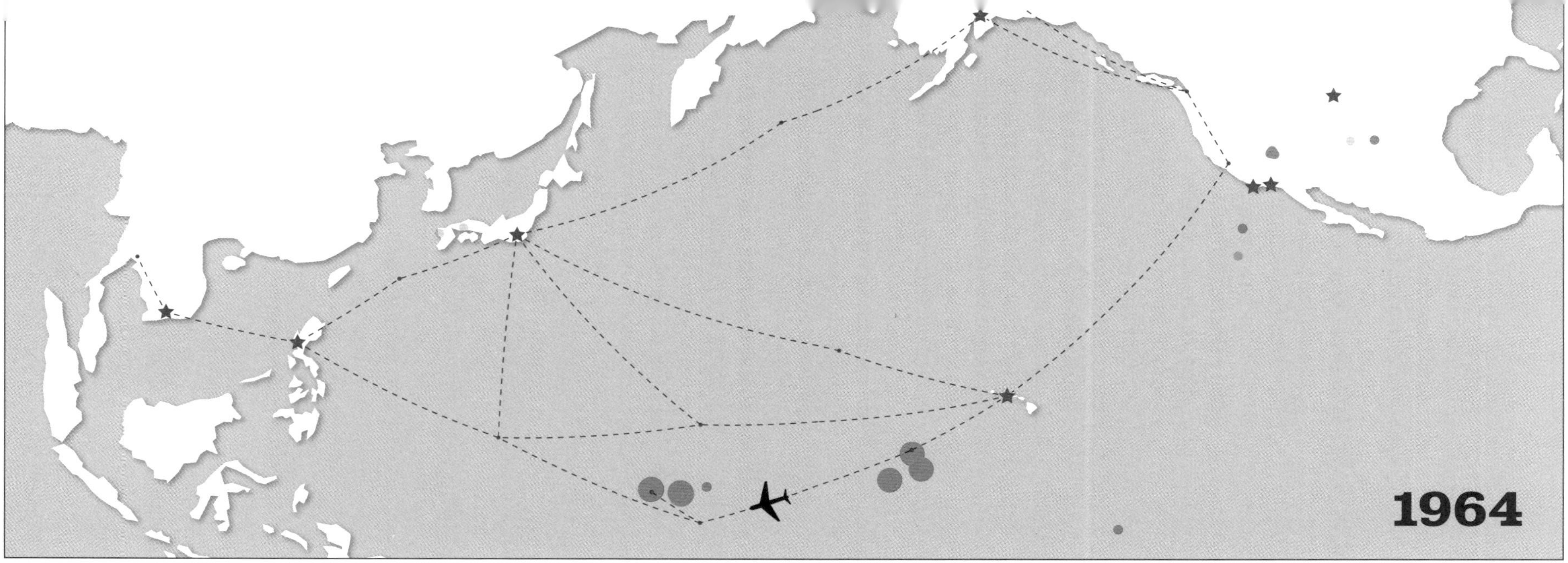
1964

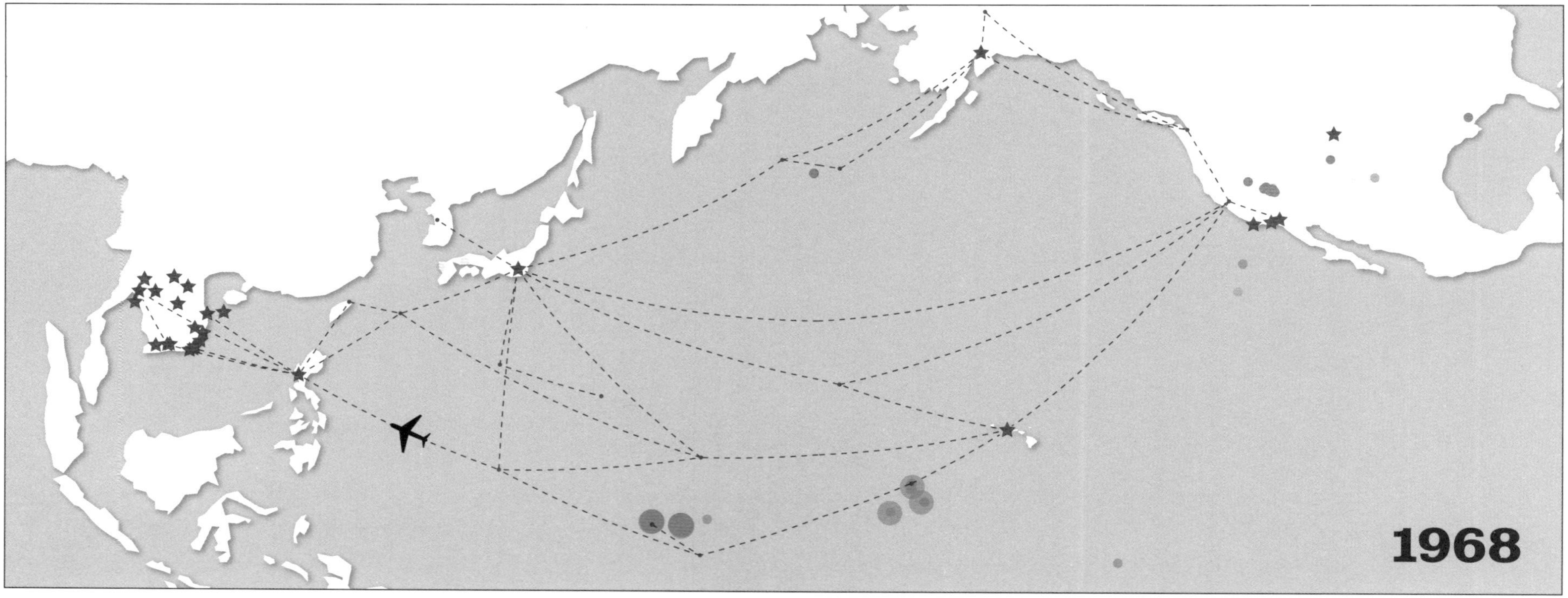
1968

accusations that it was not executing its United Nations "trust" faithfully, the move expanded the extent of America's atomic empire in the Pacific—reaching, as we shall see, not only laterally, but vertically, up into the atmosphere. Altogether, the Pacific would come to represent an American nuclear test site of millions of square miles of the Earth's surface, and vast regions of space extending well up into the heavens above.[9]

If the stage was the Pacific, the script was nuclear deterrence. Why repeatedly test such unprecedented weapons of mass destruction? Government officials gave numerous reasons, but wrapped all their arguments into an overall strategy of deterrence intended to warn adversaries and reassure allies by means of nuclear techno-spectacle. Still, the deterrent script always risked alarming, even horrifying, global allies and domestic citizens, rather than reassuring them. And in fact, despite the "test" designation, the United States was engaged for two decades in the nuclear bombing of the places and peoples of Oceania—there is no other way to accurately put it. Thus, for the Atomic Energy Commission and the Department of Defense, the symbolic and rhetorical fallout of Cold War Pacific nuclear bombing, more than the nuclear fallout itself, had to be contained and recontained. The US government had to manage not only a technological system and its biochemical artifacts, but also the collection of images, stories, and data that inherently threatened to upset America's place within a precarious postwar international order.

So we come back to the blips on Lookout Mountain's animated map in *Lookout Mountain Air Force Station*: operationally, Lookout Mountain's various detachments spanned and contained, like a net, the Pacific space of American power during the 1950s and 1960s. Functionally, Lookout Mountain worked to cinematically contain the Pacific as a site of nuclear experimentation and spectacle, even as it provided a range of photographic services to the Department of Defense for measuring and monitoring airplane and missile technologies that were not easily bound by land or water. Rhetorically, Lookout Mountain's Pacific films, ranging from *Operation Sandstone* (1948) to *Operation Dominic* (1962), present ever-changing arguments and justifications for Pacific testing, while redefining the very space over which America claimed control and re-presenting the nature and means of that control. Indeed, from Sandstone to Dominic the execution and representation of American nuclear tests in the Pacific underwent a set of interrelated transformations: as the tests moved from sea and land to the atmosphere, sovereignty claims shifted from bounded land claims to the rights of free movement across air-and-sea logistical networks, and Lookout Mountain's work shifted in emphasis from the production of strategic spectacles to the collection of data in the service of geopolitical data games. These transformations in approaches to geography, sovereignty, and representation can be seen across the series of Lookout Mountain Laboratory Pacific test films we consider in this chapter: *Sandstone* (1948), *Greenhouse* (1951), *Ivy* (1952), *Castle* (1954), and *Dominic* (1962).

As we saw in chapter 1, America's first postwar nuclear test, Operation Crossroads, set the stage for Lookout Mountain's rise. We therefore need to take a further look at the test in order to make better sense of what was to come. Crossroads was simultaneously a photographic bonanza and a public relations fiasco. Dubbed "Operation Camera" by the *New York Times*, the 1946 test can be characterized only as massive: it comprised over forty-two thousand personnel, ten thousand instruments, nearly six thousand test animals, seven hundred cameras, some five hundred photographers, and three bombs, two yielding the explosive and radiological destruction equivalent to the Nagasaki "Fat Man" bomb and the third never detonated for fear of creating too much controversy. Crossroads, unlike Hiroshima and Nagasaki, resulted in an onslaught of press pictures and newsreels, as well as a vast array of photographic prints and unedited footage shot by photographers from the Navy and Army.[10] The operation resulted in more than fifty thousand stills and 1.5 million feet of exposed film, making Crossroads the most photographed nuclear test in history, and according to one historian, "the most thoroughly photographed moment in history."[11] Not surprisingly, to this day images from Crossroads are among the most widely circulated and reproduced in popular culture, fine art, film, and journalism.[12]

However, Crossroads ended up teaching American officials as much about what not to do as what to do in the future of nuclear testing images. The operation was intended to both test the fortitude of naval vessels before an atomic blast and provide ample images to US and global publics of America's newly invented weapons [something, again, that both Hiroshima and Nagasaki failed to do]. As such, photography was as critical to Crossroads as ballistics, and in certain respects more critical, as the United States had never set up a photographic operation quite like this, whereas the bomb designs had already been "proven" in Japan.

In the run-up to the July 1946 tests, hundreds of Navy and Army photographers were summoned, some of them pulled out of postwar civilian life and sent to Bikini Atoll in order to document Crossroads. To supply the photographers, camera equipment and film had to be sequestered on an emergency basis from laboratories and photographic centers across the United States and shipped to the test site.[13] The preponderance of the photographers—some 412 men—were assigned to Task Unit 1.5.2, the photographic unit responsible for much of the official "technical" photography at Crossroads; and most of these men were Army Air Force personnel [the Air Force had not yet won its independence from the Army].[14] Their mission was to record the effects of the blasts on naval ships, equip-

ment, personnel, and the thousands of animals that had been shipped to Bikini Atoll for the purpose of blast and radiation exposure. Photography was here officially framed a matter of "information gathering." As Maj. Perry Thomas, chief of the Army Air Force's Photographic Engineering section at Crossroads, explained, "In the entire history of the Army Air Forces there had been no function which depended so much upon the success of this [photographic] mission to obtain the vast information from one bomb burst."[15] Central to the Army Air Force's photographic efforts here were the so-called flying cameras, specially modified C-54s designed to photographically contain the atomic fireball image by circling it from the air. The entire right side of these planes was filled with portals and racks for photographic equipment, making the planes fit for nonstop photographic exposure as they flew in a loop.[16]

Ironically, the overwhelming presence of cameras at Crossroads worked as much to undermine the government's aims as it did to further them. As we saw in chapter 1, many of the Navy's cameras were destroyed or badly damaged by the blasts, leaving the Army Air Force in the fortuitous place of being responsible for some of the best images of Crossroads. But even more significantly, the images themselves—no matter what their source—failed to produce the rhetorical impact the government, especially the Navy, had hoped for. To be sure, Crossroads was a massive image event, a great American spectacle, resulting in iconic images of nuclear clouds set within palm-tree-laden vistas. And yet Crossroads was an image event for which America lacked anything like a *compelling story*. Indeed, because the images depicted awful atomic might set against the backdrop of Pacific serenity, with no clear-and-present danger even remotely in sight, the US government ended up looking as if it were blowing to bits "a new Eden."[17] What sense was there in this? The question was explicitly asked by E. B. White in the pages of the *New Yorker* in the run-up to Crossroads: "Bikini lagoon, although we have never seen it, begins to seem like the one place in all the world we cannot spare; it grows increasingly valuable in our eyes—the lagoon, the low-lying atoll, the steady wind from the east, the palms in the wind, the quiet natives who live without violence. It all seems unspeakably precious, like a lovely child stricken with a fatal disease."[18] White later lamented that America had not only turned Bikini into a laboratory, but also engaged in "an experiment in befouling the laboratory itself."[19] A 1946 issue of *National Geographic* featured Bikini's men and women moving from their beautiful Oceanic home so the United States could blow it up.[20] To many, it all seemed so out of whack, so incongruous.[21]

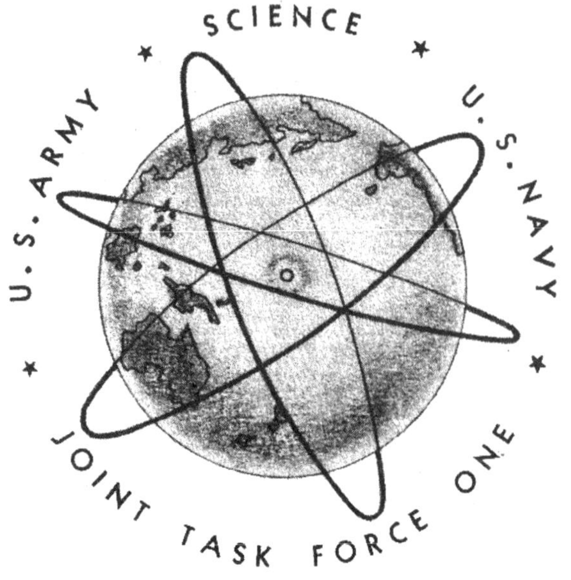

The story of Crossroads threatened to become the story of American military recklessness.[22] The Navy tried to avert this public relations fiasco by making the images, and indeed the cameras themselves, the story. Newsreel-type films on Crossroads prominently featured the photographic mission through depictions of the "flying cameras" and an array of cameras hoisted into towers, bolted tightly for the blast, and secured from radiation effects by lead shields. If this was to be an atomic spectacle, the Navy wanted the story to be how the armed forces pulled off the visual feat itself. But cameras could not contain the story. Crossroads offered the nation and the world a powerful

The Flying Cameras of Operation Crossroads

A single plane dedicated to photography followed each of the bombers that delivered destruction on Hiroshima and Nagasaki. For Operation Crossroads, which saw the world's fourth and fifth atomic explosions, ten bombers retrofitted as "flying cameras" flew in elliptical orbits around Kwajalein, the Pacific Island target. The resulting footage from just one of these tests amounted to over sixty thousand feet of film exposed over the ten minutes surrounding the detonation.

Cameras filled every existing portal of these planes, and many newly cut portals as well, secured in ways to minimize vibration. Turret domes and "blisters," usually filled with guns, now held cameras, with aerial gunners retrained as cameramen operating them. Among the most enduring of the engineering solutions involved in this effort was a mount developed for use in the doorway of the aircraft, enabling the stable positioning of multiple cameras aimed in the same direction. Sophisticated new timing-control systems also ran the course of the planes to ensure the synchronized operation of banks of cameras manned by a single operator.

The transformation of these bombers took place over the first half of 1946 by a group of photo engineers that included Berlyn Brixner, the man responsible for overseeing photography at the "Trinity" test. Engineers worked on the planes at night under the light of jeep headlamps, leaving the planes free to fly training missions during the day. The resulting footage not only produced some of the earliest and most iconic images of the Bomb, but established within the military the identification of nuclear photography with engineering and the Air Force.

image palette, but no compelling narratives, other than the awful might of atomic explosions.

To be sure the image palette would become iconic. It revolved around two photographic objects: the "Pacific" and the "mushroom cloud." To Americans, and many others who would see Bikini through the Crossroads cameras, the Pacific island would represent a place at once alluring and pristinely removed.[23] The allure was not only Edenic, it was erotic—as indicated by the choice of Parisian fashion designer Louis Réard to name his new two-piece bathing suit a "Bikini."[24] The cultural conjunction, in Paris of all places, between atomic bombs and nearly nude women was not merely a matter of the microscopic scale of the basic materials, though that was certainly part of Réard's point. In the mid-1940s, both the female body and the explosive military spectacle appeared as objects of eroticism, as indexed by the pervasiveness of pinup girls and Hollywood starlets posted next to GI bunks and emblazoned on Army Air Force bombers, and as indicated by the innumerable rape stories, as well as war stories, American GIs could have told about their wartime exploits.[25] Indeed, both bombs and "babes" became subjects of the postwar camera. Metro-Goldwyn-Mayer made the point precisely only weeks after Hiroshima and Nagasaki, presenting their newest starlet, Linda Christians, as their "Ms. Anatomic Bomb," which *Life*'s cameras photographed poolside in a two-piece, soaking up radiation.[26]

Operation Crossroads officially embraced the eroticism. A picture of Rita Hayworth was painted on the first of the two Crossroads bombs that were detonated, which was called "Gilda" after Hayworth's movie.[27] The second bomb was named "Helen."[28] Meanwhile, soldiers at Bikini tried to recreate the semblance

of a Pacific paradise, constructing a tiki bar on Bikini Atoll, gesturing toward a Pacific resort and to the eroticized Don the Beachcomber and Trader Vic's bars back in the States.[29] Indeed, when Crossroads soldiers returned home after the tests, they brought with them a new cultural fusion that joined atomic kitsch with tiki culture and scantily clad women, all within a cloak of secrecy. Las Vegas, located but a morning's drive from the Nevada Test Site for nuclear testing, would become the epicenter of this cultural fusion.

If images of the Pacific covered half of the image palette, the now iconic, puffy, white "mushroom cloud" and vertical blast of seawater from Crossroads covered the other. As we discuss the mushroom cloud as a nuclear icon at length in chapter 9, we will not dwell on it here, other than to stress that while the mushroom cloud would become "a condensation symbol of modern destructiveness," as Robert Hariman and John Lucaites have argued, it was not such a stable signifier at Crossroads.[30] Indeed, at Crossroads the mushroom cloud was just beginning its process of transformation from a photographically recorded phenomenon—seen in the grainy images of Nagasaki—to an aesthetic object, beautified and stylized for popular consumption.[31]

At Operation Sandstone in 1948, the second postwar nuclear test carried out by the United States, the scene was the same, but the cloud appeared different. By 1948 the radiation effects of atomic testing were becoming more apparent not just to nuclear scientists, physicians, and military strategists, but to the general public. Meanwhile, or perhaps because of the fallout of Crossroads, the government had lost interest in making atomic tests public relations spectacles. Nevertheless, against major opposition, President Truman and his advisers decided to push

the atomic weapons program further forward, seeking to build more deadly bombs. The newly formed Atomic Energy Commission worked with the newly formed Department of Defense—the latter incorporating the newly independent Air Force—to organize a test program under the auspices of Joint Task Force Seven. In the spring of 1948, as part of Operation Sandstone, Joint Task Force Seven performed a series of three tests at Eniwetok Atoll, a chain of some forty islands located about two hundred miles west of Bikini [where Crossroads took place], but still within the Trust Territory.[32] To make room for the devastation, Eniwetok's 145 "inhabitants," as official memos referred to the people who lived there, were forcibly removed.[33]

In sharp contrast to Crossroads, Sandstone was a highly secretive affair, closed off to journalists, newsreel cameras, or to any kind of firsthand public reports. The ten thousand American personnel involved in the tests were forbidden from talking to family and friends about the nature of their Pacific adventure. Pictures of the test would not be released to the public until over a year after it concluded.[34] And the comprehensive motion picture Lookout Mountain produced about Sandstone, *Operation Sandstone*, was not released until several years after the test.[35]

The intense secrecy was in part because Sandstone was focused on weapons development, specifically on testing newly designed bomb cores. Truman publicly argued that strict secrecy was necessary for hiding America's nuclear science from the Soviets.[36] Yet as important as keeping nuclear secrets was felt to be, it was as much the emotive and symbolic power of nuclear testing that the government implied needed containing—even as, indeed especially because, the toxic material effects of nuclear detonations were still, quite literally, up in the air. The Atomic Energy Act of 1946 had given the Atomic Energy Commission extraordinary powers to operate secretly. Information or artifacts could be classified as "secret" for the mere reason that they could "cause serious injury to the interests or *prestige* of the nation" [emphasis added]. And the information need not even be all that damaging to national prestige to be kept from public view: materials could be labeled "restricted" and thus "denied public circulation" for the simple and ambiguous reason of "administrative privacy."[37]

Behind this wall of secrecy, the Air Force was put in charge of photography for the Sandstone tests, with the understanding that all the film exposed in the operation would be under the control and supervision of the Atomic Energy Commission.[38] The Air Force's Colonel Cullen, who had overseen the "flying cameras" of Crossroads, was given charge of all photographic operations. He turned to Los Alamos to handle technical photography and to Lookout Mountain Laboratory to handle documentary motion pictures.[39] Initially, it seemed that Lookout Mountain's documentary tasks would be quite narrow: the Atomic Energy Commission requested a two-hour documentary film, and the Department of Defense's Armed Forces Special Weapons Project, the military agency responsible for nuclear weapons testing, requested a single training film suitable for servicemen.[40] However, once Lookout Mountain's producers and directors got to work, the requests kept coming: the Air Force, the Army, the Navy, and even the private contractor EG&G each decided they wanted films made featuring their respective work on Sandstone. When it was all said and done, Lookout Mountain made not two, but seventeen Sandstone films, spanning a continuum from top secret to unclassified.[41]

As they would with other nuclear tests in the years to come, Lookout Mountain staff started writing the stories of the Sandstone tests before the tests were even carried out, an odd practice for purportedly "documentary" work. Lookout Mountain instead followed standard Hollywood studio practice, composing "shooting scripts" months ahead of time, allowing Lookout Mountain producers to instruct film crews on which parts of the operation to shoot.[42] After the tests were completed, the footage was sent directly to Lookout Mountain in Hollywood, where it was processed, classified, stored, and used to make the films.[43] With later projects, additional scenes were shot either in the studio or at locations other than the test site, and ample animation work was done.[44] With the Sandstone films, however, all shooting was done at the test site itself. While Lookout Mountain did use some stock footage for the Sandstone films, there were no studio shoots. Moreover, all sound was nondiegetic—no one speaks to the camera, and no sound was recorded with the film on-site. Lookout Mountain instead took the soundless footage from Sandstone, processed and edited it, revised the script, had the Air Force Band compose and record music, and recorded a narrator reading the final script, telling the story of the operation. As such, it was narrative more than spectacle that drove Lookout Mountain's early work.

Among the many films Lookout Mountain produced for Sandstone, the most comprehensive was a color film simply titled *Operation Sandstone*. It was produced as a short, twenty-minute "film report," suitable for public release (though not released to the public until 1952). *Operation Sandstone* was no *Operation Crossroads*. Whereas the latter appeared as an elaborate newsreel, *Operation Sandstone* looked and sounded like a Hollywood production, complete with an elaborate title sequence, original music, props, and MGM's Carey Wilson as its offscreen narrator. In *Operation Sandstone*, for the first time in America's young but fraught nuclear weapons history, the government had an official filmic story about nuclear weapons testing and development.

Operation Sandstone prepared viewers from the outset for a "story." The film opens to the music of trumpets with an image of a book displaying the words, "The Atomic Energy Commission presents."[45] A hand opens the book to the pages of the film's title sequence: [*a page turn*, page 1] "Operation Sandstone: Sixth, Seventh, and Eighth Atomic Bomb Tests, Eniwetok Atoll Marshall Islands"; [*a page turn*, page 2] "Produced by United States Air Force Lookout Mountain Laboratory, Hollywood, California"; "Music by United States Air Force Band"; [*a page turn*, page 3] "Narrated by Carey Wilson, courtesy of Metro-Goldwyn-Mayer Studio"; and then a fade to a long shot from the shores of Eniwetok Atoll. This bookish prop would be reused in some of Lookout Mountain's subsequent nuclear test films, and it said as much about the beginnings of Lookout Mountain as Lookout Mountain would say about nuclear weapons testing. The studio presented America's nuclear testing program as part of the story of America. As America's nuclear tests would accumulate, so the storybooks would accumulate on the studio set's bookshelf (or as secrecy required, performatively locked in a drawer). At the same time, in each film Lookout Mountain presented *itself* as the storyteller of America's nuclear weapons testing program. As props, these were "books" presented as by Lookout Mountain Laboratory, on behalf of the Atomic Energy Commission. For *Operation Sandstone* to open in this way was for Lookout Mountain to say from the very start, as they would more modestly say later in a documentary film they made about their own work, that they "told the story of nuclear weapons testing by the United States."[46] But if Lookout Mountain Laboratory would be the storyteller of America's nuclear testing program, what would be the story? *Operation Sandstone* was unequivocal: it was the story of laboratory science.

After the storybook title sequence, *Operation Sandstone* opens with footage of hazmat-suited workers combing the beaches of Eniwetok Atoll. Carey Wilson, the film's offscreen narrator, introduces the scene as one from science fiction: "On a certain spring day, in a remote corner of the world, a handful of men like strange voyagers from another planet set foot to a small Pacific island," he begins.[47] "Who are these weirdly garbed visitors who so gingerly pick their way forward?" he asks. They are, as if in a reveal, "men . . . from the United States." Such an opening would seem to make aliens of these men, but in fact, as the narrative unfolds, it is Eniwetok that is made alien. The atoll, Wilson explains, was "just a spot on a map" until the Americans showed up. Their arrival meant

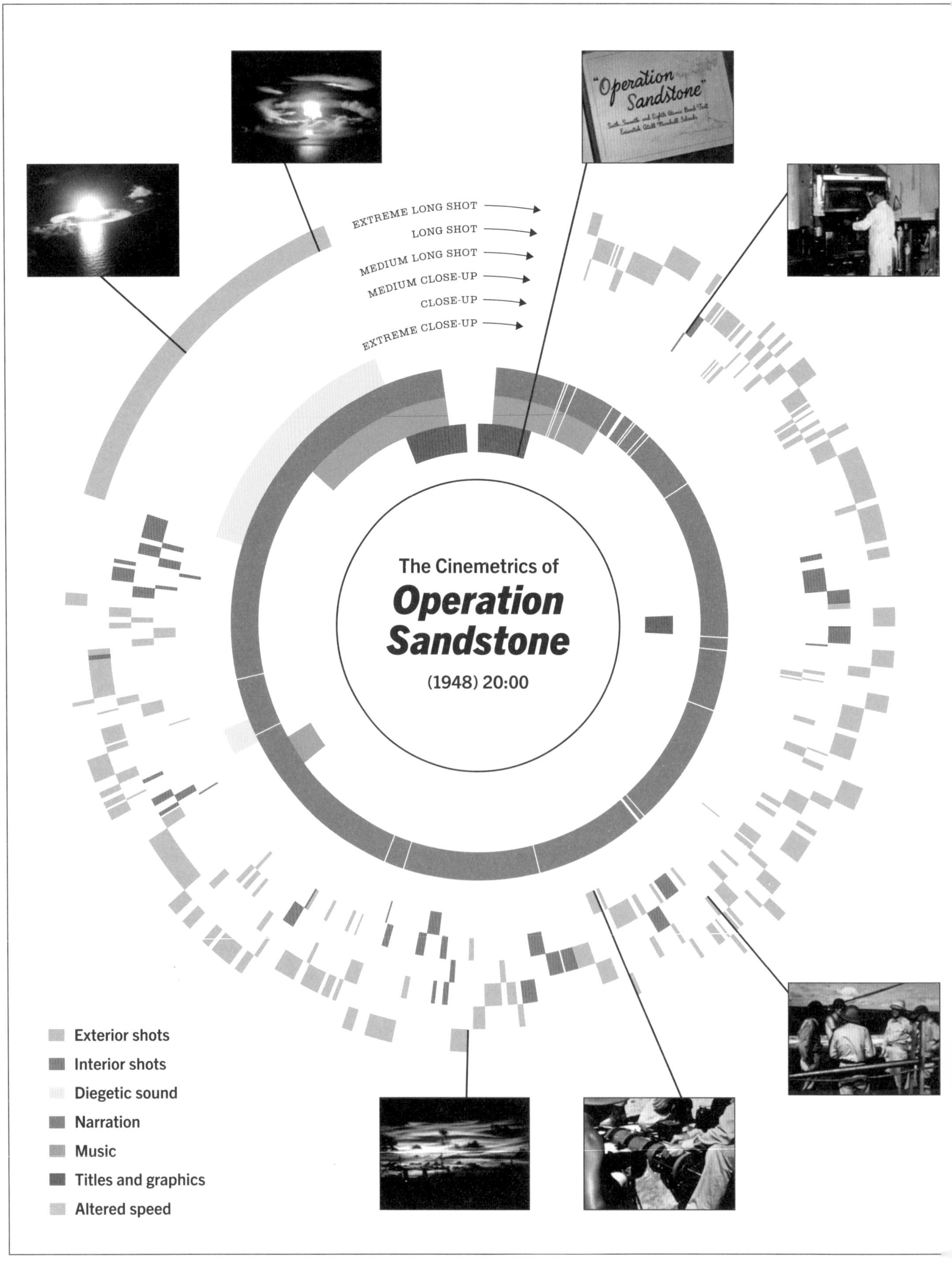
The Cinemetrics of
Operation Sandstone
(1948) 20:00
EXTREME LONG SHOT
LONG SHOT
MEDIUM LONG SHOT
MEDIUM CLOSE-UP
CLOSE-UP
EXTREME CLOSE-UP
"Operation Sandstone"
Exterior shots
Interior shots
Diegetic sound
Narration
Music
Titles and graphics
Altered speed

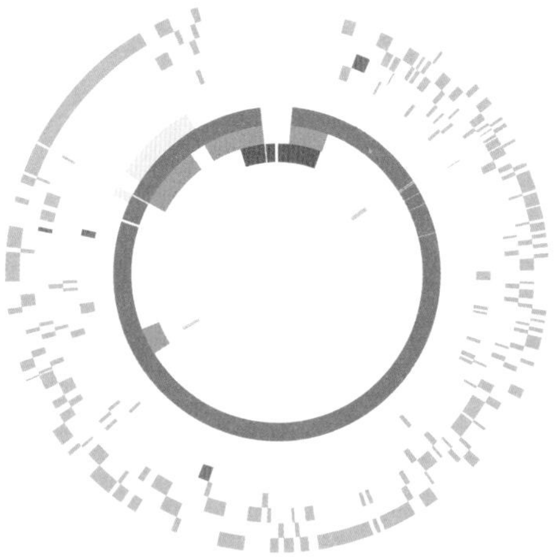

United States Army Engineers in Operation Sandstone (1948) 20:00

Blast Measurement Group in Operation Sandstone (1948) 18:35

EG&G in Operation Sandstone (1948) 15:40

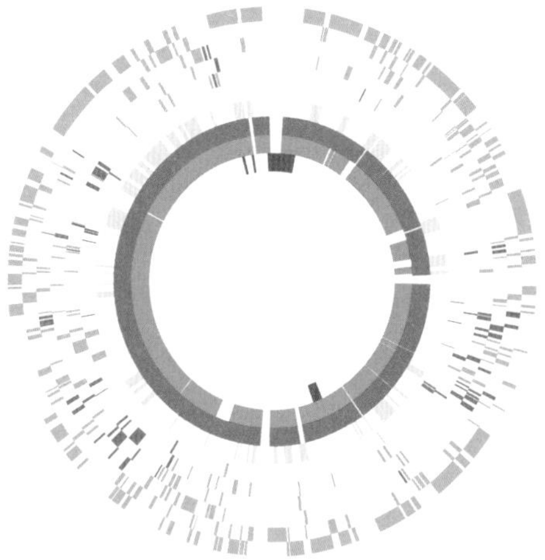

The Navy's Part in Operation Sandstone (1948) 41:30

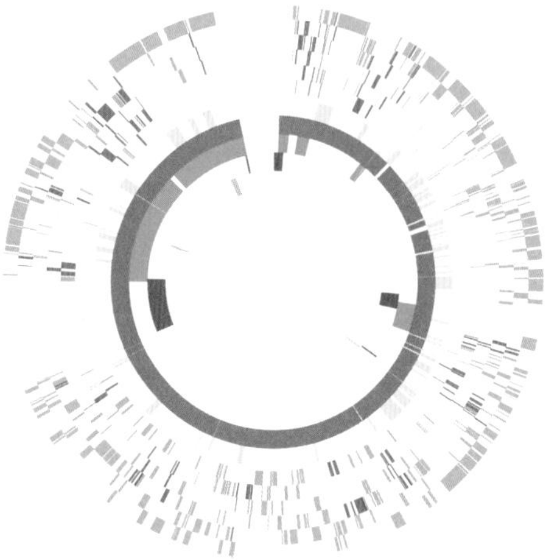

Atomic Proving Ground: The Story of Operation Sandstone (1948) 1:13:50

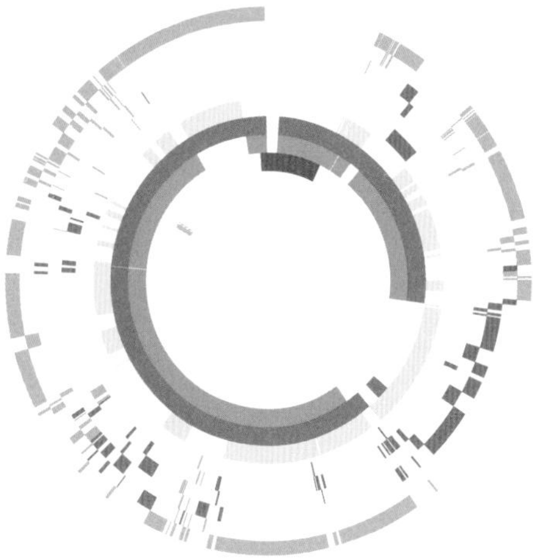

The United States Air Force in Operation Sandstone (1948) 30:00

clearing the vegetation of the "virgin land," leveling the soil, and laying pavement. "And so it is," Wilson concludes as the film presents a series of scenes of men moving earth, laying cables, and building towering structures, "that tropical Eniwetok comes to know the mechanical prowess of men who have changed many a similar island during the late Pacific war." Operation Sandstone is, in this respect, but another iteration of the incursion of American military engineering into the Pacific, another introduction of the American machine into the garden.[48] Or is it?

In fact, Wilson explains, despite the similarities to the engineered islandscapes of the former war, "This is not an ordinary island. This is not just another supply base. Not just another landing strip. This tower [*a tower is shown*] rising in the sky to be the holder of fissionable material, this zero tower gives us the essential clue. This is an atomic island. A test island. A gigantic laboratory island."

And so the central metaphor of *Operation Sandstone* is introduced. Eniwetok, in the hands of the Atomic Energy Commission, is an alien space in the way that a laboratory would be a reified space: specialized, removed, and engineered to achieve experimental ends. Laboratories, Wilson explains, are means of gaining vital knowledge, given "how little we really know about atomic energy." Wilson spends much of the remainder of the film expanding on the laboratory metaphor: the pavement is "like

a porcelain tabletop in a physics laboratory." "This tabletop, barely ten feet above the level of the sea, and on this, the machines' spit of sand, the test instruments are installed. All facing the zero towers. Instruments which will give dimension, depth, and character to what exists in the minds of the scientists. Instruments designed to capture, record, measure in a hurried millionth of a second."

The film devotes over a minute to the cameras of the operation: normal-speed, high-speed, color, black-and-white; cameras in towers, cameras in planes; "cameras capable of shooting ten thousand individual pictures every second. Cameras with lenses powerful enough to record the dust on a flea's whisker at five miles." Indeed, it is cameras, more than any other sort of instrumentation, Wilson suggests, that make the remote atoll a laboratory. Evoking claims that had been made about Operation Crossroads, Wilson claims that Operation Sandstone "is to have the most complete photographic coverage in human history." But here the pictures are not about publicity, but about scientific surveillance: "for this oversized workshop demands eyes which can see in all directions at the same time."

At Sandstone, Oceania—and the whole world with it—was being transformed into a laboratory for nuclear science.[49] However, transforming the Pacific into a laboratory in *Operation Sandstone* was a less a means of justifying the incursion of the United States into its remote "entrusted" territory than it was a means of containing the meaning of atomic bombs. From the outset, as Peter Hales discusses, the atom bomb was described by scientists and journalists alike as a "marvel of nature."[50] The very term "mushroom cloud" suggested as much: the atomic detonation took on both the form and the power of nature. But the "laboratory" metaphor was also drawn from the Manhattan Project, and indeed from the larger twentieth-century industrial laboratory complexes such as Edison's laboratory and Bell Labs. Laboratories, that is, did not represent a reified space of "pure research," but a locus of applied science, of engineering, of experimenta-

tion meant to further knowledge so as to change the world. "Nature" thus belonged in the laboratory if it was going to become useful; and if "virgin land" itself had to be made a laboratory, *Operation Sandstone* suggested, so be it.

Still, *Operation Sandstone* did not ignore a pressing question: Why *this* place? The film answers the question directly: "Why not," Wilson asks, use instead "the laboratories of the Atomic Energy Commission, or the laboratories of our colleges and universities, or even the New Mexico desert?" Because a nuclear detonation cannot be easily contained: "There is no such thing as a small atomic explosion." Eniwetok is "an open-air laboratory," Wilson explains. "No blower fans here, no fume hoods to diffuse and dispense the radioactive cloud." So *Operation Sandstone* implies that only by virtue of Eniwetok's remote location—some 7,500 miles from America's atomic planning centers, the film claims—are the atomic blasts contained. The United States had gone to extraordinary lengths, the film implies, to perform a "controlled experiment" with atomic weaponry, moving men and machines thousands of miles over many months to protect Americans from the hazards of atomic experimentation.

No mention, of course, is made of the forced movement of those people for whom Eniwetok had been home. No mention is even made of why this particular island was chosen, or how it was that the United States assumed sovereign rule over it. Eniwetok is but an "isolated, primitive island," a space seemingly without a sovereign and without a history, and therefore acceptable to destroy. As no particular place, Eniwetok offers Lookout Mountain's scriptwriters an ideal space for illustrating the apparent lessons of atomic power: "Scientific knowledge in itself is not a bad thing. It is tragic that in the case of atomic power, destruction goes hand in hand with construction. The age-old story of good and evil, keeping step with man in his fight for a better life. No, the answer to man's greatest problem is not atomic energy in itself. The answer lies in the hearts and minds of men."

Indeed, in a remarkable instance of idealism for a film so preoccupied with instrumentation, destruction, and empirical experimentation, Wilson summarizes, "The *minds of men* are creating this laboratory in the middle of an ocean" [emphasis added]. What the metaphor of the laboratory in *Operation Sandstone* does more than anything else is remove this particular site of atomic experimentation from the vexed contests, questions, and contexts of politics, morality, and history. Eniwetok is a terra nullius, a no-man's-land, empty and ready for formation like Prospero's isle in Shakespeare's *The Tempest*; its scientific and political exploitation is thus a matter of moral indifference because it seemingly stands outside of moral law, its historical status unknown.[51]

For all of its emphasis on telling the story of Operation Sandstone, the film, as a story of science and as a story of America, left the narrative open, stretching it indefinitely into the future. If Eniwetok was a massive outdoor scientific laboratory—a metaphor that would be widely used to describe the Nevada Test Site too—this meant that what the film calls "the *real* story" of the tests was in the scientific data, not in its filmic representation. Even as *Operation Sandstone* ends with a four-minute montage of fireballs and mushroom clouds, the film, in making Sandstone a story of science, resists wrapping up the story. *Operation Sandstone* qualifies its own narrative as secondary, provisional, and even unreal before the open and incomplete story of not only scientific discovery but American global power. While, as Wilson states in the last words of the film, "In the long perspective of human history, Operation Sandstone may well have been Operation Milestone," it may well not have been—for there is no "history" in the data and seemingly no end to America's nuclear experimentation.

Near the end of the summer of 1949, the Soviet Union detonated their first atomic bomb. The event, called "Joe One" by the Americans [after Stalin], would confirm a sentiment that had already been stirring in the Truman White House and defense establishment more broadly: a nuclear arms race with the Soviets was inevitable. The Joe One test was used to justify not merely the expansion of America's nuclear weapons development program into the thermonuclear age, but the permanent operationalization of the atomic weapons complex. No longer an artifact of interservice rivalry, as it had been at Crossroads, or even a matter of refining World War II–era atomic technologies, as had been the goal at Sandstone, nuclear weapons development was transformed in the wake of Joe One into a massive standing state operation. As Lewis Strauss, chairman of the Atomic Energy Commission, told his fellow commissioners but a month after the Soviet test, it was time for the United States to make a "quantum jump" in its atomic arsenal.[52]

In the 1950s, the Atomic Energy Commission and the Department of Defense carried out five nuclear test operations in the Pacific: Operation Greenhouse, Operation Ivy, Operation Castle, Operation Redwing, and Operation Hardtack. Each of these five tests dwarfed in yield the Crossroads and Sandstone tests, and—combined with a slew of tests at the Nevada Test Site—were part of a permanent nuclear weapons development and testing regime, centered at the Atomic Energy Commission laboratories at Los Alamos and Lawrence Livermore, but extending well beyond the delimited spaces of these laboratories. Lookout Mountain became, in turn, the official film chronicler of this permanent testing regime, working side by side with not only the Air Force—indeed, not even primarily with the Air Force—but also the scientists and engineers of the Atomic Energy Commission and their contractors. As one official Air Force history states, Operation Greenhouse, held in 1951, "was the first time that a photographic unit, specifically staffed and equipped for documentation of atomic weapons tests, existed during the planning stages of such test" [emphasis added].[53]

Of the hundreds of films they produced during the 1950s, Lookout Mountain's Pacific films index the Atomic Energy Commission's shifting strategies for containing the symbolic and rhetorical fallout of their expanding operations. If *Operation Sandstone* offered to its viewers the story of the scientific laboratory as a confined and controlled space, the films chronicling Operation Greenhouse—a 1951 series of preliminary tests used to work toward the construction of thermonuclear bombs—argued for a more aggressive and dangerous testing regime. As the operation's commander, Elwood R. Quesada, stated while smiling into one of Lookout Mountain's cameras, "Greenhouse was routine in one sense, but should not be confused with previous tests. Greenhouse has a place distinct and apart."[54] It was, as the Greenhouse films explained, of an entirely new scope and significance, aimed at weapons many times more powerful than those dropped on Hiroshima and Nagasaki.

Lookout Mountain's official film report, *Operation Greenhouse*, was produced for Atomic Energy Commission, Department of Defense, White House, and congressional elites. At the same time and under the same title, Lookout Mountain produced a "public release" film that, set to a different script, retold the story of Greenhouse for an American audience presumed to be worried about the acceleration of the new nuclear arms race between the United States and the Soviet Union, and about the [im]possibilities of civil defense.[55] The official film report—which we will refer to as *Operation Greenhouse*—attempted to provide an overview in a single production of the entire Greenhouse operation, which included four detonations ranging from 46- to 225-kiloton yields [the Hiroshima bomb had a 15-kiloton yield, and Nagasaki a 21-kiloton one], with eight different testing aims planned, ranging from testing devices that could be later used in thermonuclear weapons, to further measuring the physical and biological effects of nuclear weapons.[56] The much shorter film for public release—which we will refer to simply as *Greenhouse*, eventually cleared for public airing in 1954—instead focused on the work of the scientists at Los Alamos on behalf of national security, asking Americans to entrust their fate to these "men of science."[57]

Both films emphasized the new scale of Greenhouse's nuclear explosions, and the new and permanent scale of the secret national security state necessary for the accelerated pursuit of bigger, more powerful, and yet more efficient bombs. As Carey Wilson, who narrates both films offscreen, states in *Operation Greenhouse*, "Even while still unpacking our suitcases for the Sandstone operation, thinking was in order for the next operation, for a new test program, Greenhouse." No longer an exceptional work reserved for exceptional spaces, Wilson explains, "testing at a proving ground is to be a permanent element of our work." Indeed, *Operation Greenhouse* emphasizes the imperative of testing even amid the fragile and potentially volatile contingencies of the Korean War. Showing on-screen a table surrounded by policymakers busily deliberating, *Operation Greenhouse* asserts, "National policy dictates that [despite Korea] the vital atomic test program must be maintained and," nodding to Truman's ballooning defense budget, "weapons development work must continue at any cost."[58]

Operation Greenhouse's tone of inevitability was reinforced by the fact that the film was unconcerned with justifying this particular series of tests—a notable absence given that the Greenhouse tests inaugurated the thermonuclear weapons program. Indeed, neither the secret film report nor the public-release movie offers explicit justification for the tests. Rather, both films simply offer the dangerous world of the atomic arms race itself as the motive force behind Greenhouse. In *Operation Greenhouse* viewers see a fifteen-second series of headlines—"Russia Has A-bomb," "Find Fuchs Atomic Spy," and "Truman Orders H-bomb." The reasons for America's nuclear acceleration are apparent enough in the headlines, or so it seems. The only things that need explaining are the scientific and operational means of that acceleration.

As they would throughout the 1950s, Lookout Mountain turned in the Greenhouse films to Los Alamos scientists, featured on-screen, to explain the designs and dangers of the new nuclear age. In *Operation Greenhouse*, no less than famed physicist Edward Teller, the so-called father of the hydrogen bomb, is featured. Taking over from Cary Wilson, Teller explains the possibilities hydrogen offers, through fusion, for engineering exponentially more powerful bombs—this as we see scenes of him at work in his Los Alamos office. There is an "urgent need to know if a man-made thermonuclear reaction is possible," he explains, "and we are going to burn the midnight oil until we have an answer." Like Sandstone, Eniwetok Atoll was the site of the Greenhouse tests; and like *Operation Sandstone*, the Greenhouse films feature the massive engineering efforts on and around the islands. But more than *Operation Sandstone*, *Operation Greenhouse* and *Greenhouse* focus on the way in which the Pacific "outdoor laboratory" is but one node in a network of testing operations extending from Washington, DC, to Los Alamos to San Francisco, a network so large that secrecy could not be achieved through the mere containment of activities on a remote Pacific island.

Before Hiroshima, secrecy had of course been paramount to atomic weapons development, achieved through the Manhattan Project's compartmentalization of labor and its selection of geographically remote locations.[59] At Crossroads publicity rather than secrecy was the goal. But the ascent of national and global anxieties about nuclear weaponry, together with the advent of the Soviet bomb, had returned secrecy to the fore of the US nuclear testing complex, even as the tests themselves grew harder to contain because of the size of the weapons and the infrastructure required to detonate them. The deputy task force commander of Sandstone described the test as conducted in "relative privacy" compared to Crossroads.[60] The planners of Operation Greenhouse went further, thinking explicitly about the control of information, and not only controlling access to the test site. They commissioned two films from Lookout Mountain: one at the highest possible security clearance [top secret] and a second much shorter one intended for public release.[61] In this we see early signs of the need to control secrecy not so much through the choice of a remote test location, but through careful mediation and communication.

So too Lookout Mountain's *Operation Greenhouse* and *Greenhouse* are far less concerned with geographically containing the nuclear subject than the Sandstone films. To the contrary, both films stress the geographical and operational expanse of the new, permanent nuclear testing regime, and the need for test workers to keep state secrets. The publicly released *Greenhouse* film goes to great pains to make this point. "During the tense days of World War II," the film begins as viewers are shown domestic

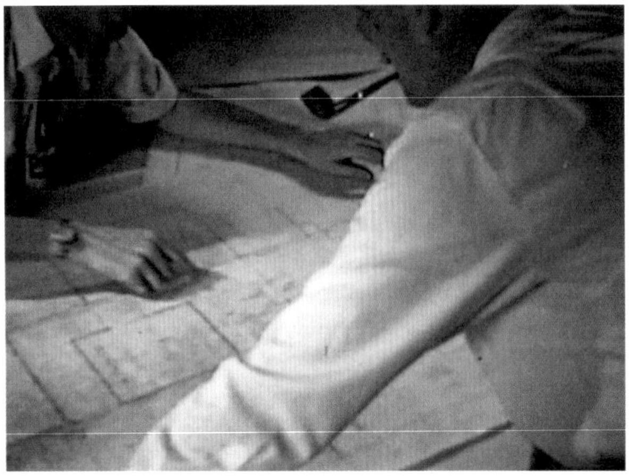

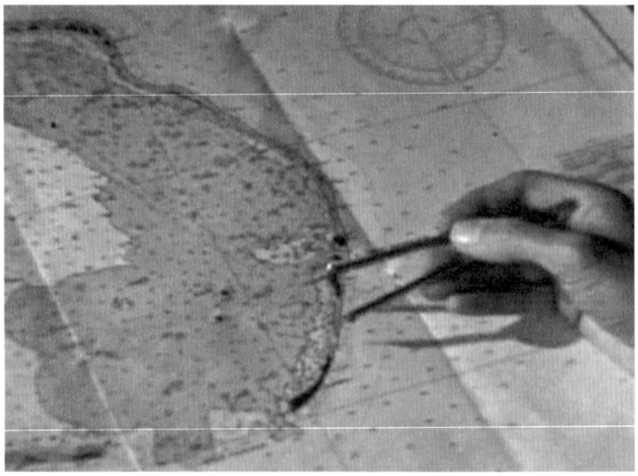

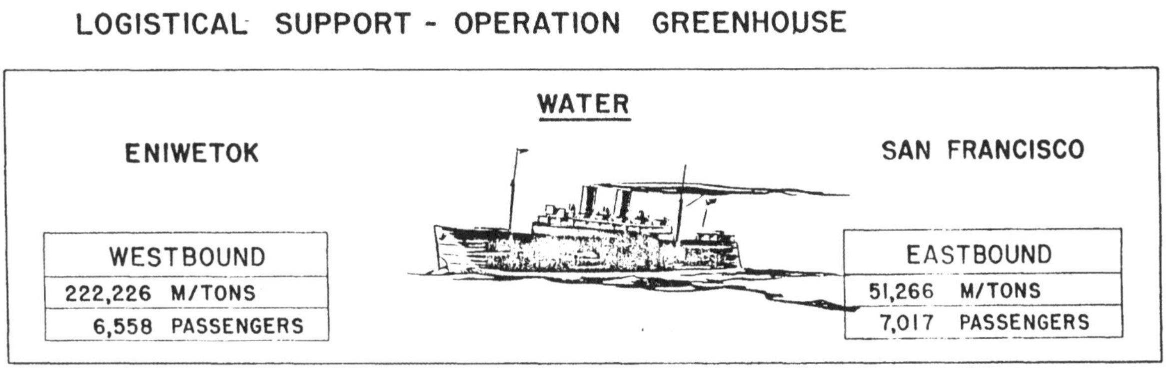

scenes of postwar life in Los Alamos, "an entire American city of men, women, and children was hidden behind a seemingly unimportant postal number." "Today," narrator Wilson continues, "such secrecy is no longer possible." Nevertheless, *Greenhouse* insists that Los Alamos is not "an ordinary city." To prove the point, Lookout Mountain's sound department brought to the film the sounds of atomic blasts. The residents of Los Alamos, shown at play or at work in what the film describes as their "modern pueblo," suddenly freeze at the blast sounds. In a remarkable instance of overt film fantasy for a "documentary" operation, the scene is offered as real, as if atomic tests took place in the backyard of Los Alamos. The sounds function as a metaphor for the proximity of not only the "ordinary" citizens of Los Alamos, but also the citizens of America more generally, to atomic testing.

Greenhouse would introduce those Americans who saw it to the scope of the military-industrial complex years before President Eisenhower christened it as such. As the film explains, "Even though Los Alamos is the parent laboratory, so to speak, scientists and technicians from other government agencies, from American industry, colleges, universities, and other organizations across the country, men working in related fields, are asked to participate, to help in instrumenting the operation." Whereas *Operation Sandstone* was content to paint a picture of a tightly run and well-organized scientific operation, *Operation Greenhouse* cowers before any comprehensive picture of its subject. "The largeness of the total project," Wilson states amid a sequence of shots featuring disparate groups of sun-drenched men working on different aspects of the Pacific test, "means that individual experiments have been farmed out to dozens of different bureaus, laboratories, institutes, and offices." Attempting a summary of the operation near the end of the film, Wilson states, "In the large frame of the atomic program, Operation Greenhouse was a soundly successful experiment. New and priceless information and statistics were secured. Previously unknown factors were established. We have learned importantly about transit times, alpha measurement, booster fission reactions, yield computations, radiochemical results, temperatures, thermal burns, clinical and pathological findings, all of the thousand and one ramifications of the atomic idea." Here the appeal to the "idea," which we also saw in *Operation Sandstone*, is less oriented toward the reification and removal of America's atomic testing adventures from politics, morality, and history, and more about rendering nuclear science as knowledge, *secret* knowledge.

In this way, the Pacific atolls are themselves represented in the film as security sites as much as remote scientific ones. Their advantage, *Operation Greenhouse* suggests, is not their isolation, but in the fact that they can be so readily secured, surrounded by an expansive zoned-off "danger area" patrolled by the military. What Elizabeth DeLoughrey has noted of the Pacific nuclear testing films more generally is certainly true for *Operation Greenhouse*: "The US military films of Micronesia excessively employ an aerial view that renders the atolls into a panopticon."[62] The repeated aerial shots of the Pacific atolls reinforce the argument of the film that the advantage of these sites lay in their capacity to be secured. Greatest among those lessons in *Greenhouse* was the necessity for a vast and nuclearized military-industrial complex, stretching the span of the globe and working within in the strictures of secrecy. The Greenhouse films were a means of publicizing and promoting this new Cold War reality.

In the 1950s, publicity was a giant conundrum for the nuclear-military-industrial complex. Even as the official Greenhouse film report was being watched in secret screening rooms, Robert Oppenheimer was pushing the White House to adopt a policy of "candor" with the American people, and by default the world. In 1952 and 1953 Oppenheimer led a State Department–sanctioned panel of experts that urged the government to take "new initiative in deciding to inform the public of the facts as to the armaments race and its official analysis of those facts."[63] When Eisenhower took office, he seemed amenable to the idea, asking his staff to explore a policy of candor. But before long he retreated, fretting about public panic and more generally about a breakdown in trust among Cold War allies.[64] Thus, a great paradox of the Eisenhower administration emerged: it aggressively pursued a policy built on nuclear power, even as it worried that the selfsame policy would destroy the Cold War balance of power.[65] This dilemma, however, was subsumed within the even greater one of deterrence, which entailed building an arsenal of global nuclear catastrophe only to prevent such a disaster. As such, deterrence necessitated what Cold War scholar Ira Chernus has called strategies of "apocalypse management."[66]

As the unit that, more than any other, was officially charged with telling the story of America's burgeoning nuclear weapons program, Lookout Mountain Laboratory was also caught between these logics of publicity and secrecy. The studio constantly faced the basic problem of containing the rhetorical and symbolic effects of America's nuclear adventures, especially *fear*, while seeking to promote those selfsame adventures as necessary, and even positively good. Lookout Mountain's strategies of containment changed with each new step in weapons development. In the Sandstone films, as we saw, Lookout Mountain crafted a strong narrative of laboratory science. In the Greenhouse films, however, the narrative was transformed to accentuate the way in which the scientific laboratory—be it at Los Alamos or at Eniwetok—was but one node in a vast, nuclearized military-industrial complex, and secrecy in this network the only means of containing nuclear ballistic and symbolic power.

But in the 1950s, the exploding weapons program became impossible to contain, symbolically or otherwise. In 1952 the United States detonated at Eniwetok its first thermonuclear device, the "Mike" device of Operation Ivy, sending America into the era of megaton yields. In 1954 the United States outdid even its own best expectations, firing a thermonuclear bomb at Bikini Atoll that reached fifteen megatons, nearly twice as big as expected and some seven hundred times bigger in yield than that delivered at "Trinity." The latter test, code-named "Castle Bravo," sent fallout across the globe and left Marshallese in the northern atolls and the crew of a Japanese fishing trawler irradiated. After these tests, polls suggested that roughly a third of the world's population lived with a conscious fear of nuclear war.[67] If it was impossible to contain the nuclear fallout with the "Bravo" shot, symbolic containment, too, became well-nigh impossible.

Lookout Mountain Laboratory nevertheless tried very hard. In 1953 they produced a set of films about Operation Ivy featuring, on-site and on-screen, a pipe-smoking Hollywood actor, Reed Hadley. Hadley's appearance in the secret official film report as well as the public-release film was Lookout Mountain's most aggressive appropriation of the Hollywood cinematic style to date, and would never be outdone. The Operation Ivy films argued for the world-historical significance of the "Mike" thermonuclear shot, featuring on their big screens not only Hadley but also Disney-inspired animated maps showing the destruction of Washington, DC, and New York City. The only salvation from the age of thermonuclear weapons, the films suggest, is a firm policy of deterrence made possible by the expert work of engineers and operators.

Operation Ivy was a turning point, at least for Lookout Mountain. As such, we devote the entire next chapter to its production history and rhetoric. The film exemplifies not only the convoluted logics of nuclear publicity and secrecy, but also Lookout Mountain's most aggressive attempt to contain the symbolic fallout of nuclear testing through a Hollywood cinematic sensibility. In certain respects, as we will show, the film was a great success, making a major splash at the White House. But for the public, it was an exercise in futility; for once it made its way onto public screens, it was seen as oddly incongruent with the realities of nuclear devastation. The turning point for the public was the 1954 "Bravo" shot of Operation Castle, the largest nuclear blast ever made by the United States and a massive, self-wrought nuclear accident. Over this disastrous shot, Lookout Mountain would not even attempt to assert the sensibilities of Hollywood.

"Multimegaton weapons are here!" So declared the unidentified, offscreen narrator of Lookout Mountain's *Military Effects Studies on Operation Castle*. Operation Castle, held in March and April of 1954 in the Pacific Trust Territory, sought to prove that the warehouse-size "Ivy Mike" hydrogen device of 1952 could be engineered to make an equally powerful, but much smaller, deliverable weapon. This was the aim of the first shot of Operation Castle, theatrically named the "Bravo" shot. The remainder of the operation included more tests, four of which were of a thermonuclear nature, and none of which went as predicted.

But "Bravo" made the entire operation a literal disaster. Scientists miscalculated the yield of the shot by at least two times. It generated a detonation one thousand times bigger than the Hiroshima bomb, casting a cloud of dense radioactive fallout that stretched over three populated islands to the east, two of which were inhabited by Marshallese and the other by US military personnel. Moreover, the explosion destroyed most of the recording equipment and sensors of the technical photography group [Task Group Eight], so that even the scientific mission of the test had to rely heavily on imagery from Lookout Mountain Laboratory's more distant, documentary cameras.[68] "Bravo" is to date the largest atmospheric nuclear blast ever executed by the United States.

Following the precedent established at Operation Ivy [see the next chapter], Joint Task Force Seven, which ran Crossroads and comprised Atomic Energy Commission and Department of Defense officials, assigned Lookout Mountain to the scientific group of the test and charged the studio with the production of a fifty-minute secret *Commander's Report* at the conclusion of the test; a shorter unclassified version of the same film for potential wider, public release; another secret film on military participation and effects measurement on Castle; and a series of "brief visual technical reports" completed after each of the six tests and rushed back to Washington and Los Alamos for review.[69] Of these films, only two have been declassified as of the time of the writing this book [some sixty-five years later!]: *Military Effects Studies on Operation Castle* and *Commander's Report*. But they indicate clearly enough the effects of the Ivy and Castle tests on Lookout Mountain's own sensibilities, and on those of America's nuclear testing regime more generally.

While Lt. Colonel Gaylord, at the helm of Lookout Mountain, initially felt "vindicated" by the inclusion of an unclassified, potentially public, edit in Lookout Mountain's mandate for Castle [there had been prior to this, as we will see, a fight over a public film during Operation Ivy], as early as July of 1953 the Atomic Energy Commission had already expressed doubts about going "big" with the Castle films.[70] By the end of 1954, Gaylord would report that

Military Effects Studies on Operation Castle

WASHINGTON D.C.
AREA
WASHINGTON D.C.
AREA
BIKINI ATOLL
THE END
PROJECT 22-12-54
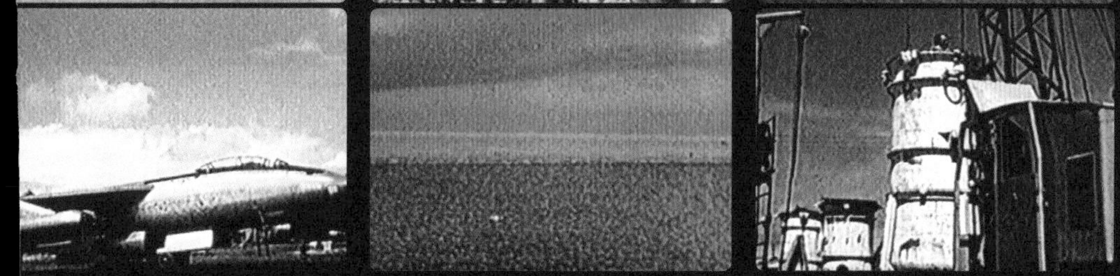

22-12-54
(1954)

the Atomic Energy Commission "has blown hot and cold on this subject."[71] Indeed, initially Atomic Energy Commission Chairman Lewis Strauss instructed Los Alamos's Alvin Graves and Brig. Gen. Kenneth Fields that any public documentary film should be kept "simple with technical information, and Hollywood trimmings to a minimum."[72] A month later, however, Fields bailed on the whole idea of a public film, instructing Major General Percy Clarkson, the commander of Joint Task Force Seven, that "while the AEC recognizes the public information value of an unclassified documentary film, we do not consider the expenditure of funds for this purpose would be justified at this time."[73] Lookout Mountain would oblige: the "public" film on Castle died. Moreover, after Lookout Mountain completed their work on the secret *Commander's Report* and screened it for the Joint Chiefs of Staff and leaders of the Atomic Energy Commission, the atomic energy commissioner, Lewis Strauss, advised the secretary of defense that the film should be disseminated "only to those persons who have the 'need to know' such information."[74] Beyond state secrecy, the Atomic Energy Commission wanted to strictly limit the circulation of the Castle films within the halls of state secrecy themselves.

Though Castle was a disaster unrivaled in the nation's nuclear program, *routine* was the order of the operation's rhetoric. "Enough experience and a wide enough variation of operational contingencies had been encountered to suggest certain major problems *common to all atomic task forces*," the commander of Joint Task Force Seven wrote after the test. "With this in mind, the Castle history is for the most part an attempt to point up broadly those general problems which *any* task force may anticipate" [emphases added].[75] It was as if megaton nuclear accidents were to be the new normal. But that was not the main lesson of Operation Castle for the nuclear elite, at least not according to their film reports. Rather, the lesson was that America's military needed to be ready to deal with megaton nuclear disasters as though they were regular occurrences. Shortly after the "Bravo" disaster, Morse Salisbury, Atomic Energy Commission director of information, wrote to Richard Hirsch of the National Security Council that in reporting on weapons tests, "the subject matter should be routinized, and test series should be portrayed not as isolated dramatic events but as part of a process."[76] Operational routine was the new imperative, a matter of national saving face.

Nevertheless, in Lookout Mountain's *Commander's Report*, General Clarkson—seen standing at a podium on the set of a briefing room built at the Wonderland Avenue studios—opens by suggesting that the only process Castle was a part of was one of adaptation, improvisation, and making it up as you go along. "We feel," he begins, "that the report of this important test should give the failures as well as the successes, should reflect the changes in thinking that occurred during the test." "We hope," he continues, "this will help you understand the problems that were experienced during the course of the operation." At the film' s conclusion, over imagery of officers on phones and writing at desks, Clarkson again describes the tests as "beset by operational problems of a magnitude not encountered previously," but praises the "flexibility" of all those involved.

That flexibility, which *Commander's Report* and *Military Effects* make clear, is the flexibility of experimentation, even when experiments had not been planned. Both films present one of the world's largest fallout disasters not as a cleanup operation or recovery effort, but as an opportunity to study the effects of thermonuclear bombing on humans, machines, treetops, ocean bottoms, and distant shores. Indeed, the films almost suggest the disaster was planned [and indeed, some have maintained that it was]. Here the bodies of those exposed—human, animal, and mineral—are registered as fallout sensors, subjects to measure over space and time. The islands of the Pacific Trust Territory became gauges, as soil samples from affected islands became the basis for drawing out—quite literally in *Military Effects*—the shape and power of the fallout cloud.

The same animated cloud was then superimposed over Washington, DC, as a fantastical originating ground zero, with attendant fallout stretching all the way to New York City. An offscreen narrator explains, "A one-hundred-kiloton weapon at optimum height will cause severe damage over an area of five square miles and moderate damage over twelve square miles. Contrast this five and twelve with eighty square miles of severe damage and two-hundred-and-forty square miles of moderate damage from a fifteen-megaton surface burst like Shot One [the 'Bravo' shot]. Two-hundred-and-forty square miles, more than twenty Hiroshimas in a group, more than ten Manhattans ['Trinity'], in which blast compounded with fire may bring almost total destruction."

And so, in a cinematic moment, a new threat to the United States had emerged, one that originated within the United States, yet was presented as a potential threat from without, and was even literally visited on American soldiers and those America was entrusted to protect, the Marshallese. Yet the source of this threat—America's relentless nuclear gambles—was contained by an emphasis, in not only Lookout Mountain's films but also the official papers more generally, on routine operation and responsive organization—the state of operations.

Indeed, Lookout Mountain's cameras were increasingly incorporated into the state of operations as the 1950s came to a close. Beginning with Operation Ivy, the unit had been assigned to document primarily the scientific and technical aspects of nuclear weapons testing, more than so-called military effects. But by the time of Castle, Lookout Mountain was also doing much of the technical photography at nuclear tests: at Operation Wigwam, a single-shot test

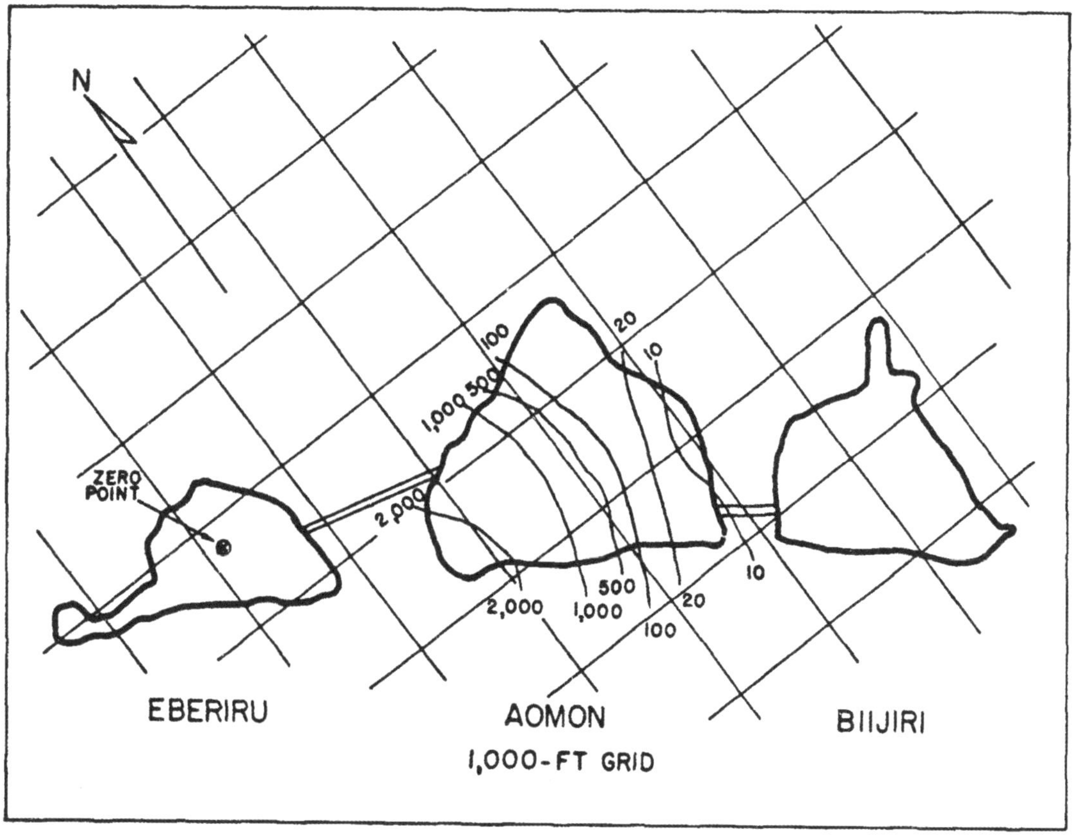

Fig. C.2 Aomon Survey, 1000 11 May 1951, G+2. Intensities are mr/hr.

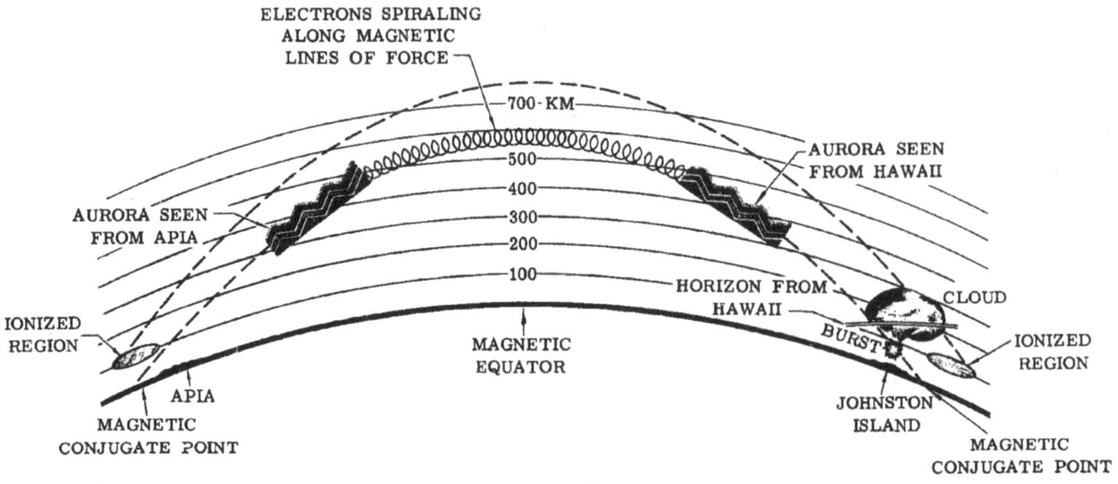

Figure 2.127. Phenomena associated with high-altitude explosions.

held in the Pacific off the coast of California, Lookout Mountain was wiring, installing, and running specialized underwater cameras that had previously been the province of Harold Edgerton's company, EG&G. [For more on EG&G, see chapters 6 and 9.] Lookout Mountain also did such technical work at the Nevada Testing Site.[77] Meanwhile, their documentary work continued, but became more and more focused on the hundreds of small, even mundane, operations of the state of operations. In the second half of 1956, for example, among many other things, Lookout Mountain found itself shooting footage at a parachute test facility, documenting crosswind landing-gear experiments, making a training film for B-52 crews, shooting raft-survival tests on the Colorado River, covering a Rocketdyne motor test, and filming supersonic sled tests.[78] At the same time Lookout Mountain was finishing work on the Redwing tests in the Pacific, but even this work was now reduced to the status of making "film bulletins," which displayed in their look, sound, and script an assumption that the official audience wanted only "information"—forget the "Hollywood trimmings."

Lookout Mountain found itself often frantically trying to keep up with the rapidly changing Cold War state. If military brass and the White House ever had a taste for "money shots" of nuclear tests as a means of publicity and propaganda, the "Bravo" test killed it. Nevertheless, the weapons development work continued, especially in the missile program. In 1959 a Lookout Mountain auxiliary unit, which would become the 1369th Photographic Squadron of Vandenberg Air Force Base in California, was established to document another Pacific operation, America's missile tests off the West Coast. And the missile work ended up launching Lookout Mountain into the space race.

Indeed, during a three-year nuclear testing moratorium between 1958 and 1962, Lookout Mountain and its detachments refined a whole repertoire of technologies and techniques for shooting missiles and other high-speed aircraft in flight, such that by the time nuclear testing resumed in 1962 with Operation Dominic, a thirty-one-test operation in the Pacific that almost exclusively relied on aerial delivery systems [rather than barge, tower, or island-based devices], Lookout Mountain was more than prepared for the technical feats of filming bombs and missiles in flight. For Dominic, Lookout Mountain photographers sailed on ships to document the recovery of test instruments at sea, tracked missiles from specialized mounts, placed pod cameras under missiles to

help diagnose accidents, and ascended Maui's Mt. Haleakala to document aurora effects on a missile-borne stratospheric shot.

Dominic demanded precision, or so Lookout Mountain documentaries insisted. Yet for all the technical expertise they had developed in the 1950s [becoming expert in "scientific" and "technical" photography], the irony of Dominic was that Lookout Mountain would serve at the tests primarily as a "documentary" operation. For here photography and film served less as a witness to the nuclear event than to the logistics of the state of operations. During Dominic, Joint Task Force Eight would attempt thirty-six detonations in six months, starting in early 1962. The tests involved sites that spanned the hemisphere, falling into three general categories: air-dropped bombs that exploded at high altitude; new naval weapons systems launched from submarine or ship; and missile-borne atmospheric tests designed to understand the effects of nuclear detonations on missile guidance systems or global communication networks, particularly in the context of antimissile warfare. Nearly all of the diagnostic information would come from newly developed sensors rather than cameras. In addition, Lookout Mountain's attention to the cinematic quality of nuclear test shots was displaced by scene after scene of antenna arrays, satellite dishes, and other communications equipment.[79]

Like almost all of their post-Castle nuclear test films, Lookout Mountain's Dominic films had a distinct "bulletin" quality to them: a nameless narrator speaking over on-site footage and ample graphics and animations of scientific and engineering processes.[80] The generic quality was more than an aesthetic choice: *time*, more than editorial quality, was of the essence in the work at Dominic. President Kennedy, who authorized the formation of Joint Task Force

Eight in response to Soviet testing with more than a few reservations about the resumption of atmospheric testing, permitted only a very short window for the tests.[81] The film work kept pace: among their various accomplishments at Dominic, Lookout Mountain could boast that they had completed an interim film report on the Starfish Prime component of Dominic for the president in less than twenty-seven hours from receiving the exposed film.[82]

Nevertheless, the narratives were still there. The tests took place far away from the Pacific Trust Territory, tests in the latter having become so fraught with controversy that the United States decided to conduct its new nuclear exploits in territories that they or their allies could less equivocally claim as their own sovereign space.[83] *Operation Dominic: Christmas Island*, one of six films Lookout Mountain produced as part of Joint Task Force Eight's 1962 operation in the Pacific, opens, after an introduction from Cdr. Alfred Starbird, with a shot of the White House. "The decision to plan for the resumption of atmospheric testing," a narrator begins, "was complicated by a basic problem: real estate." The solution, as another Dominic film stated, was a series of tests "spread across some fifteen million square miles of the Pacific," including not only Christmas and Johnston Islands, but other remote locations "carved out of tropical jungle growth."[84]

The expanse of the geography was significant, but its particulars were not, or so both Lookout Mountain's reports on the filming operation and the Dominic films themselves suggested. Yes, the tests meant the by now almost token-like disruption of the lives of Pacific peoples [but in this case, not relocation]. Nevertheless, the Dominic films barely attend to the travails of "natives." The inhabitants of Christmas Island appear in *Operation Dominic*, a short briefing film, as "there [on Christmas Island] under contract to manufacture Copra." Similarly, footage of an island crab and of the tiki-like headquarters of Joint Task Force Eight receive screen attention, but only in passing. If in the Sandstone films Eniwetok could have been another planet, in the Dominic films the Pacific could have been anywhere, or nowhere. Indeed, initial plans for Dominic called for the filming to be carried out strictly over the open sea, but instrumentation challenges pushed the United States to adopt the British-ruled Christmas Island as a terra firma. But this was no longer a stage. Rather, the Pacific and its atolls were simply a space of operations, a zone of controlled, self-referential, placeless logistics. Dubbed sounds of blowing wind are used in the Dominic films to emphasize expanse and emptiness, and not one of the mushroom-cloud sequences in the Dominic films contains objects in the frame to indicate scale. The view is from nowhere.[85]

The operation had the form of a network. Whereas the Greenhouse and Ivy films featured actors—be they Edward Teller or Reed Hadley—the Dominic films feature instrumentation, communications equipment, transportation vehicles, maps, diagrams, and charts. To be sure, men are everywhere on-screen in the Dominic films, but they are men operating machinery, not sitting at office desks or, with the exception of film introductions and conclusions, the podiums of briefing rooms. Dominic appears as an impersonal operation, one precisely executed at the sovereign's command and gauged according to the metrics of systems management. As the anonymous offscreen narrator states of the Christmas Island series of tests in *Operation Dominic Nuclear Tests 1962*, "On 23 April, the president directed the waiting task force to proceed with the first shot, a weapon development drop. The initial airdrop was on the 25th of April, the last on 11 July. During this period, a total of twenty-four weapon development shots were detonated in the Christmas area. All drops were on target and within the precise time and space limitations established by the requirements of diagnostic instrumentation, a record by the B-52 crews, which reflected a high degree of bombardment skill. Detonation technological efficiency also scored high in the fusing and firing systems and the device telemetry."

This was no Crossroads, where the B-29 *Dave's Dream* badly missed its target. Nor was it Castle, where scientists woefully miscalculated the yield their bomb would produce. But the emphasis on precision timing and firing, metrics, and networks in Dominic was not simply a reaction to the nuclear testing regime's history of fumbles. Given the absurdity of the Soviet-US tit for tat in atmospheric atomic displays, an absurdity that Kennedy himself saw, some other rationale had to be invented; and in McNamara's defense department, that rationale was "scoring high."

Unlike Crossroads, Dominic had no press ships and no diplomatic observation party. Unlike Operation Ivy or Castle, there was little scrambling on the part of the Atomic Energy Commission or the White House to manage the diplomatic effects of test images. Consistent with McNamara's goals, public knowledge of the detonations was a test aim, but operational efficiency and effectiveness, rather than images of spectacular shots, was the message McNamara wanted heard. With respect to operations, McNamara succeeded, or so one of Lookout Mountain's Dominic films proclaim: "Despite Dominic's unprecedented . . . complexity, with all the tests prepared under the conditions of the greatest urgency in both time and circumstance, the year 1962 is regarded as the most productive since U.S. nuclear testing began."[86] The state of operations was not only in high gear, but operating at maximal efficiency. Whether or not this meant strategic and diplomatic success is an altogether different question. The Cuban missile crisis, which came but three months after Dominic, suggested not.

Hence, in the span of fifteen years, Oceania went from being framed as home to remote "natural" laboratory sites to the space for large-scale information networks, and Lookout Mountain Laboratory's work went from being story-driven to data-driven. To be sure, as we have suggested, Lookout Mountain was in the business of "information gathering" from the start. Nevertheless, the studio was created not because America's new nuclear complex needed images or information, but because it needed stories to justify its activities, and Hollywood cinema seemed to offer the most efficient and effective means of producing such stories. However, as Lookout Mountain's stories became incorporated into the rhythms and rationalizations of the state of operations, its productions became increasingly iterative and open ended, like reports piling up on a library shelf. And as the stories became more incredible—culminating in weak narrative attempts to justify risking massive-scale nuclear accidents—the whole idea of attempting to tell the story of atomic experimentation, let alone America's Cold War adventures, was largely abandoned. Instead, the studio turned increasingly to developing mobile techniques and technologies for rendering visual information and information visual for the scientific and managerial satisfaction of the overlords of the nuclearized military-industrial complex.

Yet this transformation in Lookout Mountain's work from cinematic to cybernetic practices was riddled with tensions. As we will see in the following chapter, many of these tensions were worked out through the long and laborious attempt by Lookout Mountain Laboratory to make films to tell the story of America's first major thermonuclear test, *Operation Ivy*, held in 1952 at Eniwetok Atoll in the Pacific. In the story of the film Operation Ivy we see close-up not only how Lookout Mountain worked, we also see how the Hollywood-style cinematic sensibilities that were initially so compelling to state officials became implausible. Moreover, as we will argue, we see just how much the advent and development of nuclear weapons challenged the sense and sensibilities of America's Cold War.

a threat looms s
overwhelmingly that it seems to hav

NO ANSWER

the human mind
tends to take refuge

IN ESCAPISM

IVY

Chapter Four

SENSE AND SENSIBILITIES

Lookout Mountain's *Operation Ivy*

In 1950 President Truman, facing considerable opposition, made the momentous decision to pursue the creation of a thermonuclear bomb. Two years later, on November 1, 1952, as part of the Operation Ivy series of nuclear tests, America's first thermonuclear detonation obliterated Eniwetok Atoll in the Marshall Islands, the site of the 1948 Sandstone tests. The blast carried eight hundred times the explosive power of the Hiroshima bomb. It was said to have been powerful enough to destroy most of Manhattan with a single blow; it left thousands of square miles of Oceania toxic with radiation; and it implanted, by means of fallout, radioisotopes in living bodies, human and nonhuman, across the globe.

However, its devastation was not the product of a workable bomb. Rather, Operation Ivy's "Mike" device, as it was called, was so big—weighing between fifty and sixty-five tons—that it had to be detonated from within a large warehouse-like structure built upon the tiny Eniwetok island of Elugelab. As one engineer recalled, the structure was "a massive cryogenic factory," kept cold to keep the device from getting prematurely active.[1] A factory, of course, could never be dropped from a bomber, let alone made to ride on a missile. Consequently, while "Mike" is frequently said to have inaugurated the age of thermonuclear weapons, it was not really the device itself that did the inaugurating, but rather its fantastic images. If the thermonuclear bomb was born at Operation Ivy, it was born in images.

From 1952 to 1954, Operation Ivy dominated Lookout Mountain's agenda. The studio worked tirelessly to shoot, process, edit, and produce a series of films on the "Mike" explosion, complementing them with an array of still photographs. These films and photographs, more than any other record or artifact of the event, would introduce military and government officials, and eventually American and global publics, to the terrifying new realities of the thermonuclear bomb. To produce these images, the studio summoned not only cameras and cameramen but a range of other Hollywood arts—from orchestration to animation to the services of a Hollywood actor, Reed Hadley—to try to satisfy the contradictory demands of officials in the Pentagon, the Atomic Energy Commission, Civil Defense, and even in the White House. The result was a historic film and, even more, a historic attempt to make sense through film of the dawn of the thermonuclear age.

This chapter relates the production history of the 1953 Lookout Mountain documentary *Operation Ivy*, arguably the most important single film of Lookout Mountain's two-decade career. *Operation Ivy*—which in fact was a series of documentaries cut and edited for different audiences—offers us an occasion to consider Lookout Mountain's role as a sense-making institution within the American Cold War state. For what we see in the history of *Operation Ivy* is the US national security state, through Lookout Mountain, trying to justify the creation of thermonuclear weapons and struggling to craft a new shared sensibility for the thermonuclear age. We also see just how difficult it was for the state to do this, let alone to control the meaning of thermonuclear bombs. Rather, *Operation Ivy* ended up doing more to expose the fissures of the Cold War state and the tensions of American Cold War culture than it did to justify the pursuit of the thermonuclear bomb.

Because this chapter is as much about the Cold War state as it is about Lookout Mountain's *Operation Ivy*, it begins by stepping back from the history of Lookout Mountain Laboratory to look at the broader history of the national security state of which it was a part. We start by reflecting on the role of cameras in the dawn of the atomic age, and then proceed to discuss debates and deliberations within the national security state about the pursuit of thermonuclear weaponry. We then turn to Lookout Mountain's role in Operation Ivy, and its subsequent two-year history of cutting and editing films on the test. Here we find Lookout Mountain at the heart of the Cold War state as not only a "witness" but an active participant, producing the artifacts by and before which elected officials, government bureaucrats, military leaders, the press, and publics would contest the meaning of thermonuclear weapons and the future of the world.

Nuclear history implicates not only histories of science, technology, and diplomacy, but also histories of vision and reason.[2] It can be said that atomic science began in a struggle to see the invisible workings of the atom and reached a climax in the struggle to see reason, order, and humanity in the awful power of nuclear weapons.[3] Not surprisingly, a history of vision accompanies the history of nuclear reason: diagrams, schematic charts, blueprints, illustrations, maps, animations, indicator lights, gauges, computer screens, and an array of cameras. Indeed, as we have seen, cameras were everywhere: still and motion, standard and high-speed, ground and aerial, color and black-and-white. Cameras were not only machines by which to see, but also machines that produced artifacts which could be seen; and these artifacts, through rhetorical negotiations, held out the promise of being the means of establishing a common collective vision. Consequently, from the beginning of atomic tests at "Trinity," cameras and their operators accompanied scientists and soldiers to every corner of the planet where America's new weapons were tested or deployed, and the resulting film artifacts were carefully dispersed through the scientific, military, governmental, and sometimes public channels of the nation and the world.

The role of cameras at the dawn of the thermonuclear age was of particular consequence for four interrelated reasons. First, the "Super," the "fantastic weapon," the "ultimate weapon," or the "wonder weapon"—as the thermonuclear device was variously called when it was functionally only a giant gadget but rhetorically a powerful image—would function as a final rather than efficient cause in the American Cold War state. A dark idealism came to displace the realisms of the 1940s: the "Super" was the image *toward* which the state would move with all of the inexorable force of "history," rather than the reality from which it would move.[4] Second, the horrifying images of destruction wrought by America's first thermonuclear device meant that the "Super"—as an image and an idea—would be used *against* the very citizens it was meant to protect, both in the United States and abroad. Citizens would be subjected to a fear they could not dismiss and to a future they did not want. Citizens would therefore become the objects of state management, not the least through images.[5] Third, as we will see, the "fantastic weapon" would also be used as a Cold War weapon *within* the political battles of the American state—for to be sure, the American Cold War state was at war with itself, contesting not only different conceptions of "America" in the world of nations, but the very meaning and significance of its liberal democratic traditions in light of this new and immensely destructive power.[6] Finally, the appearance of the "Super" would present a crisis to the state, a legitimation crisis. America's nuclear activities left American citizens in a state of uncertainty with respect to the government's designs; and in addition, the United States was accused by the Soviets—who, despite their own nuclear program, were publicly calling in 1952 for the abolition of nuclear weapons—of "warmongering" and of unnecessarily accelerating the nuclear arms race to catastrophic dimensions. Indeed, America's European allies were quite anxious about the nuclear arms race and wondered aloud in front of American diplomats whether US nuclear actions were making Europe less rather than more secure.[7]

In sum, the appearance of the "Super" in both image and imagination initiated upheavals in what we described in the introduction to this book as "the sensibility of the state": the ability of the state *to sense*, *to be sensed*, and to establish a *common sense*. Indeed, as the "Super" was an image before it was a workable bomb, the first field of battle it entered was that of collective sensibilities—a capacity culturally achieved more than politically organized. Faced with crises of history, governance, and legitimacy, the American Cold War state sought to render itself, its world, and its activities "sensible," in each of the three senses above, before the immediate prospects of a thermonuclear age. And it used media of the senses—sound, word, and image—to do so, with motion pictures seeming to magically deploy all these media at once. If the "Super" reconfigured the intentional logics of the American Cold War state—moving America inexorably *toward* an awful destiny, setting the state *against* the citizenry, and initiating legitimation crises both *within* and *before* the state—film, it seemed, could bring about a new "distribution of the sensible," to use Jacques Rancière's phrase, a reconfiguration of the "self-evident facts of sense perception" and even a redistribution "of spaces, times, and forms of activity."[8] Film could contain the contradictions of the "Super." Or could it?

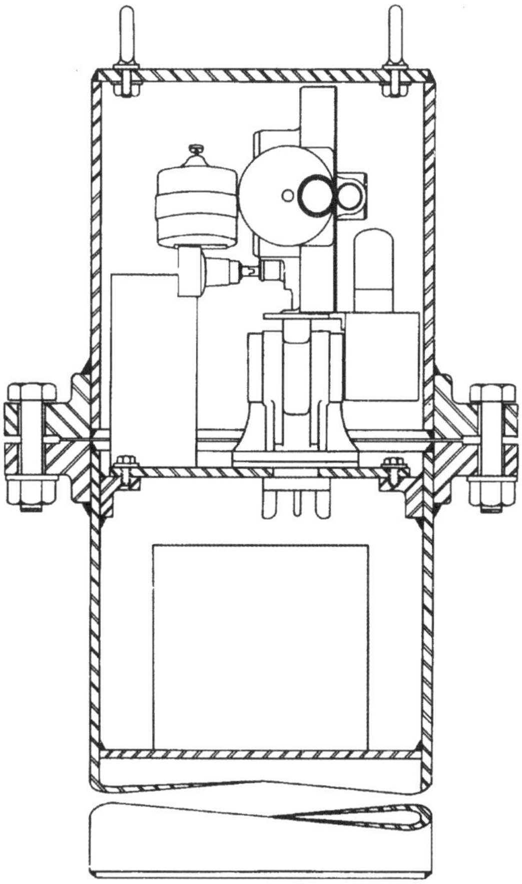

Fig. 1.7—Auto-remote camera installations.

The first atomic bombs seemed destined to kill—so much so that in 1945, when the US Army could well have dropped these kiloton bombs somewhere off the shores of Japan to display their newly discovered military might, they instead dropped them on Japanese cities full of civilians, killing over two hundred thousand and maiming, contaminating, burning, and forever traumatizing many thousands more. Reactions were strong, and it did not take long for some—even some in the highest ranks of the US military—to question whether atomic bombs should ever be used to kill again.[9] Virtually everyone agreed that the atomic bomb was an epochal weapon. It meant a new age. "Yesterday," as Hanson W. Baldwin wrote in the *New York Times* the day after Hiroshima, "man unleashed the atom to destroy man, and another chapter in human history opened, a chapter in which the weird, the strange, the horrible becomes the trite and the obvious. Yesterday we clinched victory in the Pacific, but we sowed the whirlwind."[10] So too, some of the very creators of the Bomb, the scientists of the Manhattan Project, began after the war to publicly question, and indeed oppose, nuclear weaponry, beginning the famous "doomsday clock" to warn the world against pursuing nuclear weapons further.

In light of such worries and warnings, what sense was there in further experimentation to create even more horrible atomic bombs, the thermonuclear bombs? The Truman administration was repeatedly confronted with the question in its passage to the first thermonuclear test, the November 1952 "Mike" detonation. In addition to vigorous moral opposition from the scientific sector, represented by likes of Eugene Rabinowitch of the *Bulletin of Atomic Scientists* and Robert Oppenheimer of the Institute for Advanced Study (and Truman's own ad hoc adviser), there were a host of technical and practical questions as yet unanswered—not the least of which was how to make a thermonuclear device deliverable.[11] Consequently, the "Super" was met with a mixture of superlatives and skepticism. The influential columnist Joseph Alsop echoed the latter sentiments in a September 1951 *Washington Post* column, "The soothing 'wonder weapon' story is getting under way again. President Truman has given it a boost. Senator Brien McMahon has given it a good hard shove. The Air Force has published a series of publicity photographs, lacking nothing but glorious technicolor, of its new 'Matador' guided missile. And now we have the President's request for a supplemental appropriation of more than 400 million dollars for the South Carolina hydrogen bomb plant."

"Maybe there really are wonder weapons," Alsop continued sardonically. "But it is well to remember that the reports about these weapons are generally phony. . . . [I]t is very far from sure, as yet, that this [hydrogen] weapon from which so much is hoped and feared is going to turn out to be a practical question."[12] However, the Truman administration saw in stories and images about "wonder weapons" what Edward Barrett, assistant secretary of state for public affairs in 1951, described in a memo to the White House as "enormous psychological possibilities"—at home, with allies, and against the Soviet Union.[13] Indeed, the atomic bomb was seen even in 1945 as a "psychological" weapon as much as a physically destructive one, and the decision to drop the bombs on Hiroshima and Nagasaki was strongly informed by "psychological" factors.[14]

But these psychological possibilities were far from stable. They could vacillate wildly between creating confidence in the American people (by creating fear in America's enemies) and causing panic and anxiety. In the summer of 1950, the Department of Defense's Ad Hoc Committee on Chemical, Biological, and Radiological Warfare—established in 1949 by Secretary of Defense Louis Johnson—urged Defense to take the lead in coordinating public information on "weapons of mass destruction" (a term that the report urged publicists not to use). It sought an "organic" public information campaign, one that did not appear forced, coordinated with the Department of State and aimed at offering "information" free of both "emotion" and "moral implications." The goal was "making the

The Mike Device

The world's first operational hydrogen device, detonated as part of Operation Ivy, could hardly be called a bomb. The "Mike" device, as it was called, weighed some sixty-five tons and required a massive plant of equipment and instrumentation to, among other things, keep the "heavy" nuclear elements cool enough to keep them stable in the hot tropical sun. According to EG&G engineer Bernard O'Keefe, the device and the cooling plant together took up nearly every inch of the island of Elugelab. In addition, the test included the construction of a two-mile-long wooden structure, large enough for a person to stand in, which was filled with helium at the time of the detonation so as to enable data collection. Many described the overall sight as one of a train of boxcars leaving a station.

For the Operation Ivy "Mike" test, there would be no "Bomb's away!" moment, no images of planes or pilots. The massive device was operated from afar on board a navy ship, the USS *Estes*, via remote control. In an ambitious broadcast engineering feat, the task force in charge of running the test even constructed a microwave television unit atop the "Mike" device to convey live images of its dials and meters to operators aboard the USS *Estes*.

In *Operation Ivy*, the filmmakers at Lookout Mountain seized on the "Mike" experiment as an occasion to feature the work engineers and console operators would do for America's growing nuclear state, anticipating the control rooms of NASA, NORAD, and other interface-filled sites of state operations that would dominate the Cold War imagination for decades to come.

See also

O'Keefe, *Nuclear Hostages*.

public aware in a nonhysterical sense" through a "factual and objective viewpoint," and thus avoiding "panic," "speculation," and "exaggerated fear." Such an "educational" program, the Ad Hoc Committee reported, could prepare Americans to withstand with relative calm chemical, biological, or atomic attacks on their cities and encourage them to support the Department of Defense's ongoing chemical, biological, and atomic weapons programs. The Ad Hoc Committee therefore recommended that the government carefully measure the "impression," "tone," "indications," and "terms" used in directly or indirectly [through leaks] managing publicity about "wonder weapons."[15]

On December 5, 1950, Truman issued a directive instructing government agencies to "take immediate steps to reduce the number of public speeches pertaining to foreign or military policy" and to set up channels of official clearance. "The purpose of this memorandum is not to curtail the flow of information to the American people," Truman wrote to government employees, "but rather to ensure that the information made public is accurate and fully in accord with the policies of the United States." However, as Truman's Psychological Strategy Board confirmed in National Security Council policy document 126, "Public Statements with Respect to Certain American Weapons," released in late winter 1952, emphasis on the accuracy or consistency of information was about creating rhetorical effects conducive to what Truman and his advisers deemed national security interests. All public information, NSC 126 instructed, had to be carefully crafted to consider impacts according to three criteria:

- Will this information strengthen the morale of the free world?
- Will this statement at this time help the American public to understand and accurately appraise the capabilities of these weapons?
- Will this statement create the fear that the U.S. may act recklessly in the use of these weapons?

On the one hand, the Truman administration worried that poorly conceived statements could generate alarm; on the other hand, they imagined "ill-considered statements about these weapons may create a false sense of security, lead to expectations of miracles in war and possibly jeopardize the maintenance of a balanced defense program, both military and civil."[16] The objective was to offer just enough information to spur citizens into alertness and support for defense programs without sending them into hysteria. Under NSC 126, members of the Truman administration were to structure their statements according to the exigencies of such rhetorical aims.

On taking office, Eisenhower began to streamline the process.[17] Initially, the Eisenhower administration tiptoed toward a policy of "candor." Candor was a central policy proposal of the so-called *Oppenheimer Report*, a product of a Truman-era study commission on disarmament led by Robert Oppenheimer. The *Oppenheimer Report* painted a stark picture of the present and future of the nuclear arms race, declaring that it was proceeding at "an ever more rapid pace" and that efforts to limit its speed seemed "hardly thinkable."[18] The report advised instead a policy of "candor" that would frankly acknowledge the scope and speed of the arms race. Americans and the world, it argued, needed to come to terms with the "meaning of armaments."[19] "The destructive power of the atomic stockpiles is of a wholly new order," it insisted.[20] Candor with the world about this fact was badly needed. More than building more weapons and strengthening defenses, the US government needed "a focusing of responsibility . . . for both thought and action."[21] America's allies needed "a new level of understanding . . . on the meaning of atomic weapons."[22] Thus the *Oppenheimer Report*, initially commissioned to appraise disarmament possibilities, turned into a policy paper on the importance of coming to terms with the meaning of nuclear weapons.

"Candor" initially appealed to Eisenhower.[23] He too saw nuclear weapons as of a wholly new order and suspected that American and global publics needed to come to terms with the nuclear age. But candor, the president and his advisers began to worry, could lead to panic. And so, rather than a policy of "candor," they began to pursue an overt campaign against panic. In August of 1953, Val Peterson, head of US Civil Defense, published a widely circulated article in *Collier's Weekly*, "Panic: The Ultimate Weapon." "Ninety per cent of all emergency measures after an atomic blast," he wrote, "will depend on the prevention of panic among survivors in the first 90 seconds."[24] Holding up the snowy owl as "the most panic-proof animal in creation," Peterson continued, "Curiously, tests have shown that the closest human counterpart to the unpanicky owl is the cowboy of the Western high plateaus, where the vast lonely spaces seem to weave into men an attitude of stoic calmness."[25] However, "Less intelligent people are much more panic-prone."[26] Thus Peterson correlated public information with stoic calmness. "Emotion management" would mean controlling both the meaning and the feeling of nuclear weapons.[27]

Indeed, "candor" eventually led not to a policy of frank disclosure, but rather to a carefully crafted propaganda campaign built from Eisenhower's "Atoms for Peace" speech, delivered before the United Nations on December 8, 1953.[28] Eisenhower and his Operations Coordinating Board landed on the position that Americans and the world at large needed to be convinced that the atom, the symbol of such horrible destruction, could become an agent of peace and prosperity by means of nuclear energy and other "peaceful" nuclear technologies. It could be, in a word, economized, made an agent of economic prosperity rather than national destruction.

The turn toward "Atoms for Peace" came as Eisenhower centralized and militarized propaganda and "public information" operations, creating, in Shawn Parry-Giles's words, "a propaganda pyramid of operations [that] allowed Eisenhower to serve as commander-in-chief of the propaganda program, with the White House functioning as the central command post."[29] Central to this effort was the formation of the Operations Coordinating Board, first led by Time-Life executive and World War II psychological warfare expert C. D. Jackson. The Operations Coordinating Board replaced Truman's Psychological Strategy Board but continued its work. The key difference was a greater degree of coordination, centralization, and control.[30] The Operations Coordinating Board worked closely with the CIA to monitor "world opinion," even as it drew upon the professional practices learned in Jackson's Time-Life and World War II experiences to coordinate campaigns that would support American interests without appearing to be "propaganda."

With respect to publicity about nuclear weapons, Eisenhower leaned heavily on the Operations Coordinating Board and the Atomic Energy Commission to make judgments about the nature, timing, and suitability of public statements. Unlike Truman, who had put the Department of Defense and Department of State in the lead, Eisenhower's National Security Council decided in the first year of the administration that all public statements regarding nuclear weapons had to be cleared through the Atomic Energy Commission, in consultation with the Operations Coordinating Board and the CIA—stripping the Departments of Defense and State of authority to speak about nuclear weapons without Atomic Energy Commission clearance.[31] The aim was to locate authority for public information on weapons of mass destruction in the White House, and the effect was chilling. The director of Eisenhower's Foreign Operations Administration, for example, told his staff to limit any statements about nuclear weapons to "quotation of a previous statement made by the President of the United States or by the Chairman of the Atomic Energy Commission."[32]

The key word in Eisenhower's efforts was *control*: even as the arms race seemed to be escalating to a point out of control, the Eisenhower administration was determined to keep the story of America's nuclear ambitions under control. But administration officials could not help but acknowledge that control was hard to maintain. Indeed, the massive propaganda efforts made under the "Atoms for Peace" program were unprecedented in scope and style, constituting, in the words of Kenneth Osgood, "quite possibly the largest single propaganda campaign ever conducted by the American government."[33] Yet it was not just the scale and scope of the "Atoms for Peace" campaign that distinguished it, it was its sophistication. "Atoms for Peace" was aimed at *attitudes* more than opinions and sought to orient more than persuade the world of the virtues of the "peaceful atom," and more importantly America. In its many exhibitions, publications, educational initiatives, speeches, and films, "Atoms for Peace" operated according to the principles of identification more than persuasion.[34]

We cannot attribute this approach, as scholars have tended to do, to the genius of Eisenhower's team alone. Indeed, just as the campaign against panic had begun in the Truman administration, so the turn to the "peaceful" uses of the atom had been anticipated there. Truman had left for Eisenhower the *Possony Report*, named after its author Stefan Possony, which had argued that America should counter Soviet exploitation of the American weapons program—which characterized it as evidence of "the 'barbarous' character of American 'imperialism'"—by positioning the "atom as a peace and prosperity maker" rather than "a war maker." America's aim, the *Possony Report* advised, should be to reorient the world toward the atom as an instrument of peace by foregrounding nuclear energy over nuclear weaponry.[35] At the same time, Truman left Eisenhower with two unsettling precedents: first, his decision to pursue the thermonuclear bomb against the objections of some of his most prominent advisers, and second, his decision to prohibit any public admission of the particulars of America's thermonuclear developments. Under Truman, the Atomic Energy Commission began to take more and more control over public information about America's nuclear pursuits. Indeed, in September 1952 the Atomic Energy Commission concluded, with Truman's concurrence, that all decisions about public information regarding America's thermonuclear pursuits would have to be made through the commission.[36] As we will see, the commission maintained a lock on such information: official acknowledgment of the US thermonuclear program would have to wait till the spring of 1954, over a year after Truman left office and some eighteen months after the "Mike" test.

In sum, the Truman-Eisenhower approach to nuclear weapons pointed to a larger political regime, one that transcended presidential personalities and policies and encompassed what Garry Wills calls "bomb power": the remaking of the American presidency and state around nuclear weaponry.[37] As such, it entailed a new way of seeing the state as a bulwark against extermination.[38] This, in turn, meant new ways of what James Scott refers to as "seeing like a state": new ways of counting, accounting, plotting, mapping, managing, and controlling.[39] Most broadly, therefore, bomb power entailed a revolution in political aesthetics: for as Robert Oppenheimer had recognized, the central crisis before the nuclearized state was one of *meaning* and with it, *feeling*. The national security state sought to make sense of the insensible by constructing a *sensibility*.

The United States carried out Operation Ivy in November 1952. It consisted of tests of two different nuclear devices. The first was a test of a 10.4-megaton fusion, or thermonuclear shot, known as "Mike," and the second a test of a 550-kiloton fission bomb, known as "King." "Mike" was the first detonation of a thermonuclear device by any state. As such, Operation Ivy was a closely guarded state secret, or at least it was supposed to be. News of the test quickly leaked, apparently because of errant radio communications from ships involved in the test, and also owing to some letters written from the test site by personnel to friends and family.[40] Still, the United States refused to officially acknowledge its thermonuclear device, admitting simply that the test was relevant to thermonu-

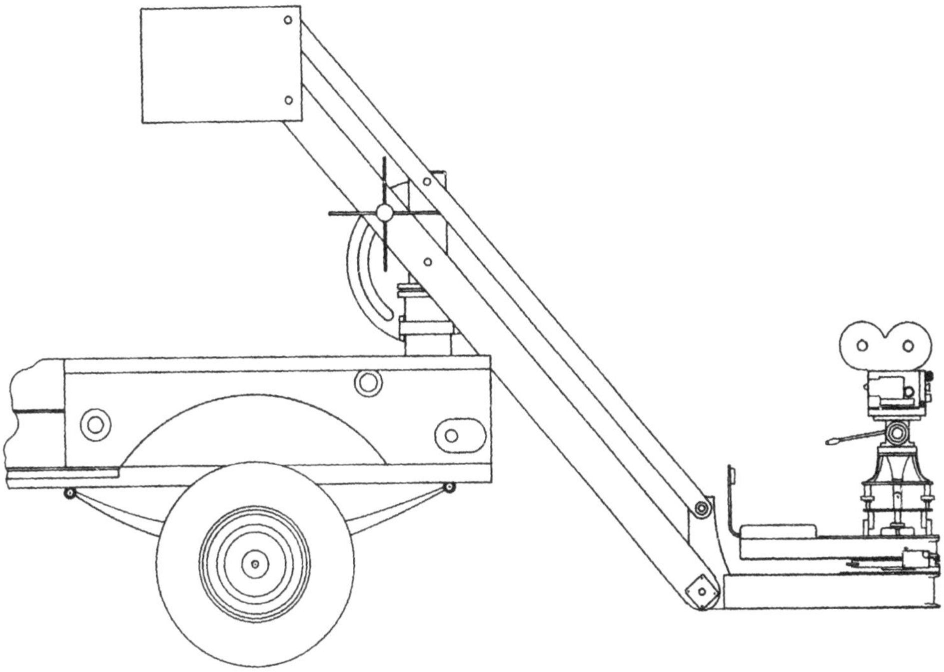

clear questions. In the fall of 1952, the Atomic Energy Commission ordered that information about the test should be strictly secured, as "the outcome of the thermonuclear experiment will exert greater impact upon U.S. Foreign Relations and Domestic Opinion." All information about the "Mike" test was to be cleared at the highest levels of government by Atomic Energy Commission commissioners, who were to be in direct consultation with the president and the National Security Council. Moreover, as the Atomic Energy Commission stated, "The release of photographs or motion pictures of Operation Ivy has not been approved and will not be anticipated in IVY information plans."[41]

Operation Ivy required some fourteen thousand personnel. They were prohibited from taking personal communication or recording devices with them to the test site, which included "personal cameras, film, or other photographic equipment . . . binoculars or telescopes, signaling devices [signaling guns or lights, flares, etc.], radio transmitters, [and] fireworks."[42] They were, moreover, prohibited from writing about the test, or otherwise memorializing it. Bags would be checked. Background checks would be run. Discipline would be kept. Orders to be silent would be given. And yet sixty-three tons of cameras and camera equipment, together with forty-five studio personnel, would be sent by Lookout Mountain to the test area for the filming, from earth and sky alike, of every aspect of the test, from assembly to detonation to departure.

Lookout Mountain's charge was to document the test. Stanley Burriss, commander of the Scientific Group for Joint Task Force 132, reported to his superiors, "A scientific historical documentary motion picture which summarizes the record of the operation will be produced. . . . The film is to document Operation Ivy, the problems encountered, and the solutions to these problems."[43] Moreover, Lookout Mountain's still pictures, developed and printed within days of the test, would give those back in Washington—Atomic Energy Commission commissioners, members of the National Security Council, and the president himself—a "firsthand" look at the test and its effects.[44]

And yet Lookout Mountain Laboratory clearly did more than document. If Joint Task Force 132 executed Operation Ivy, in important respects

Lookout Mountain *produced* Operation Ivy, and doubly so. They produced both a narrative film and an event. In the first place, the acute narrative affordances of motion pictures gave Lookout Mountain the opportunity to frame the meaning of America's entrance into a thermonuclear age in a way that no other medium could. Official written reports—and there were many of them—could document various phases and operations within the test, but they did not offer its story, nor did they attempt to do so. In the second place, cinema as technology and an art form could wrest the representation of the event from its analogical relationship to the represented and *become the event*. As Ariella Azoulay observes with respect to photography more generally, photographs are more than "the final product of an event"; they are events in and of themselves, having their own political ontology independent of their initial production.[45] As we will see, *Operation Ivy*, the film, was indeed itself an event within the state.

The studio began with a script, penned from February to July of 1952, months before the "Mike" detonation. The script was written in close consultation with scientists from Los Alamos, the same scientists who would oversee the test. Not surprisingly, therefore, *Operation Ivy* was scripted first as a story about the march of science, and second as a story about the authority of what David Henry has called the Cold War "technological priesthood": the caste of US scientific experts given a say over not only technical matters but political ones.[46] Lookout Mountain, however, immediately confronted a problem in planning for the production of the script. The unit was assigned, as it had been at past nuclear tests, to the Military Division of Joint Task Force 132, the task force responsible for the operational aspects of the thermonuclear test. This meant that they would be stationed with the military rather than the scientific team in the Marshall Islands, and consequently they would not be privy to the activities of the scientists, including the Los Alamos scientists with whom they had worked in writing the script.

Given the conflict between the story of science they would tell and their assignment within the Military Division, Lookout Mountain's head, Lt. Col. James Gaylord felt the 1352nd Photographic Squadron should be moved from the Military Division to the Science Division [thus reporting to the Atomic Energy Commission rather than the Department of Defense]. As Gaylord explained to his Air Force superiors, the Military Division "presents only the routine logistic support," and logistics was uninteresting narrative material: it "does not change, it does not present anything new to add to a documentary motion picture." Rather, he continued, "It is in the Scientific Program that the heart of the documentary story lies," and therefore it is to the Scientific Program that Lookout Mountain should be assigned.[47] Surprisingly, given that a reassignment would mean more independence from the chain of command for Lookout Mountain, the Air Force granted Gaylord's request and Lookout Mountain was allowed to transfer its operations to the Scientific Program.

The concept behind the script, as one Lookout Mountain report said, was to offer the story of the dawn of thermonuclear weapons "through the 'eyes' of an impartial observer."[48] There was, to be sure, a bit of irony here, for no outside observers were allowed to witness Operation Ivy. Instead, the outside, impartial observer had to be invented on film. At the same time, the appeal to an "impartial observer" was consistent with the recommendations of the Department of Defense's Ad Hoc Committee on Chemical, Biological, and Radiological Warfare that weapons of mass destruction should be addressed in film and other media in a matter-of-fact, even "deadpan," manner.[49]

For the part of the "impartial observer," Lookout Mountain chose a Hollywood actor as "the strength of the part had to be maintained throughout the entire picture."[50] The actor was Reed Hadley, who came to Lookout Mountain having worked for the First Motion Picture Unit in World War II [including narrating the First Motion Picture Unit's 1945 *The Last Bomb*] and

then having earned modest fame in the late 1940s and early 1950s in westerns and crime shows, as Hollywood was turning out a western every half-moon and crime stories nearly as frequently. Among his cowboy spots in 1950 alone, Hadley played the part of a saloon owner in *Riders of the Ridge*, Wild Bill Hickok in *Dallas* [starring Gary Cooper], and Frank James in *The Return of Jesse James*. In 1951 he became the regular host of *Racket Squad*, a "real-life" television crime show that featured Hadley exposing frauds and grifters who tried to milk people of their money.[51]

In Hadley himself the sensibilities of the military-industrial complex, the culture industry, and science intersected. Indeed, Hadley's on-screen introductions to *Racket Squad* episodes echoed the script of *Operation Ivy*. Both appealed to the authority, trustworthiness, and competence of the state and science from a position of the present, outside the diegesis, before viewers were swept into the story. Hadley would introduce a *Racket Squad* episode with a pitch for Philip Morris: "What you are about to see is a *real-life* story taken from the *official* files of the police racket and bunko squads, business protective associations, and similar sources by Philip Morris, a company whose product deserves your support and patronage. I smoke Philip Morris myself. I have for a long time because I know the Philip Morris manufacturing process and I am convinced that this cigarette is as fine as *human care* and *scientific skill* can make it."[52] So too, in Hadley's work for Lookout Mountain Laboratory, of which *Operation Ivy* was but one assignment, the actor would play the part of an impartial narrator highlighting the necessary, official, human, and scientific dimensions of the government's atomic adventures.

The sixty-three-minute original version of *Operation Ivy*, classified top secret, began not with Hadley's narration, however, but at the "desk"—fabricated on a Lookout Mountain set—of Major General Clarkson, commander of Joint Task Force 132. Clarkson, much like Hadley on *Racket Squad*, introduced the story of the thermonuclear test, telling viewers that the account which followed was the official report on Operation Ivy "in film form." The movie then cuts away from Clarkson to the opening credits, displayed against a backdrop of waves gently rolling up on an empty beach and accompanied by orchestral music.

Viewers are then taken to the USS *Estes*, the command ship for the operation, where sailors are shown busily at work preparing for the test. Viewers then meet Hadley, clad in a plain brown uniform, standing alone in a quiet space on the deck, sea in the backdrop. "Welcome aboard the USS *Estes*," Hadley begins. "We have minutes to go before the first blast, 'Mike' shot of Operation Ivy," he explains, stopping to light his pipe. "As you can image, feeling is running pretty high about now, and there's reason for it. If everything goes according to plan, we'll soon see the largest explosion ever set off on the face of the earth—that is, the largest that we know of." Hadley then previews the narrative structure of the film, pipe in hand, by explaining that he would like to take the time before the detonation, scripted as some fifty-nine minutes away, to "show you around . . . and introduce you to some of the people connected with this operation, and in general piece together the events which have brought us to this point." And so as the movie begins, the countdown begins; the movie's length matches almost minute for minute the scripted countdown's length of fifty-nine minutes [though the detonation comes two-thirds of the way into the film].

In the early parts of the film, Hadley introduces the operation by moving through the ship and talking to various key personnel, who are also shown eagerly waiting for the final countdown. They explain to Hadley, and by extension to the film's audience, the test's set-up, its innovative technologies, and the various precautions taken to prevent mishaps. In this "real-time" scenario, Hadley not only stands in for the viewer as witness, but invites viewers into the diegetic world over which he exercises knowledge and power. The spectator's time collapses into the film's time, and thus the time of the test.

Yet the film does not fully rest in the present. The script also sends Hadley, via montage, back to the past, to the early planning meetings at Los Alamos and to the early stages of test preparations on the Eniwetok island of Elugelab. Even on board the *Estes* in "real time," viewers hear appeals from a perspective outside of the present time altogether, as Hadley reminds audiences that the "Mike" detonation will be "one of the most momentous events in the history of science" and "the most powerful explosion ever witnessed by human eyes." But the logic of the present reasserts itself, inviting viewers to identity with the countdown as their own immanent and imminent time. Indeed, near the end of the film, viewers are summoned to the cinematic present of the dropping of the bomb itself, as the film cuts to a bomb falling ever closer to the ground: "Watch the air over Runit [Island]!" a narrator hails viewers. Then a bang and a mushroom cloud fills the screen to the sound of soaring orchestral music.

In this way, Lookout Mountain put the manipulability of cinematic time to work in support of "candor." Viewers were given a "real-time" account of the historic thermonuclear event. Still, the film shifted between assuring the viewers that what they were witnessing was but a candid state operation playing out as planned and presenting the "Mike" event as momentous, dangerous, and world-historical. In the middle of the film, Los Alamos scientist Robert Graves appears on board the USS *Estes* and explains to Hadley that the United States "must take risks" if it is to achieve "great gains." Hadley soberly replies, "But then the uneasy state of the world puts everything on a gam-

bling basis, I guess." In this way *Operation Ivy* scripted state science in the languages of not only historical necessity and scientific progress, but also the character type of the political adventurist—at least of a kind, for *Operation Ivy* squarely addresses the gamble of nuclear testing by pointing, literally, to the personage of the nuclear technician.[53] "Yes," Graves responds to Hadley, "but not as much [of] a gamble as you might think." He then points to an engineer standing upon the deck: "Take that man over there, he and his company have put a great deal of thought into the engineering and design of 'Mike.'"[54] The narrative of *Operation Ivy* was directed precisely to this point: while the politics of nations in a nuclear age is one big gamble, the science-and-technology competency of the United States means that even as the state pursues dangerous techno-military adventures, it does so fully in control of itself and its environment. The gamble, really, lies in the unpredictability of the Soviet response. The story of Operation Ivy, as scripted in *Operation Ivy*, was the story of America's scientific adventures in the hands of competent operators in an uncertain world.

Operation Ivy reaches its narrative high point as the countdown approached one minute. Military men with protective glasses assume the posture of spectators upon the deck of the ship, and other men hunched over consoles measure every gauge and dial on a second-by-second basis. When the detonation comes, *Operation Ivy* features a montage of mushroom clouds, followed by an extended account by an unnamed, offscreen narrator describing the effects

Operation Ivy

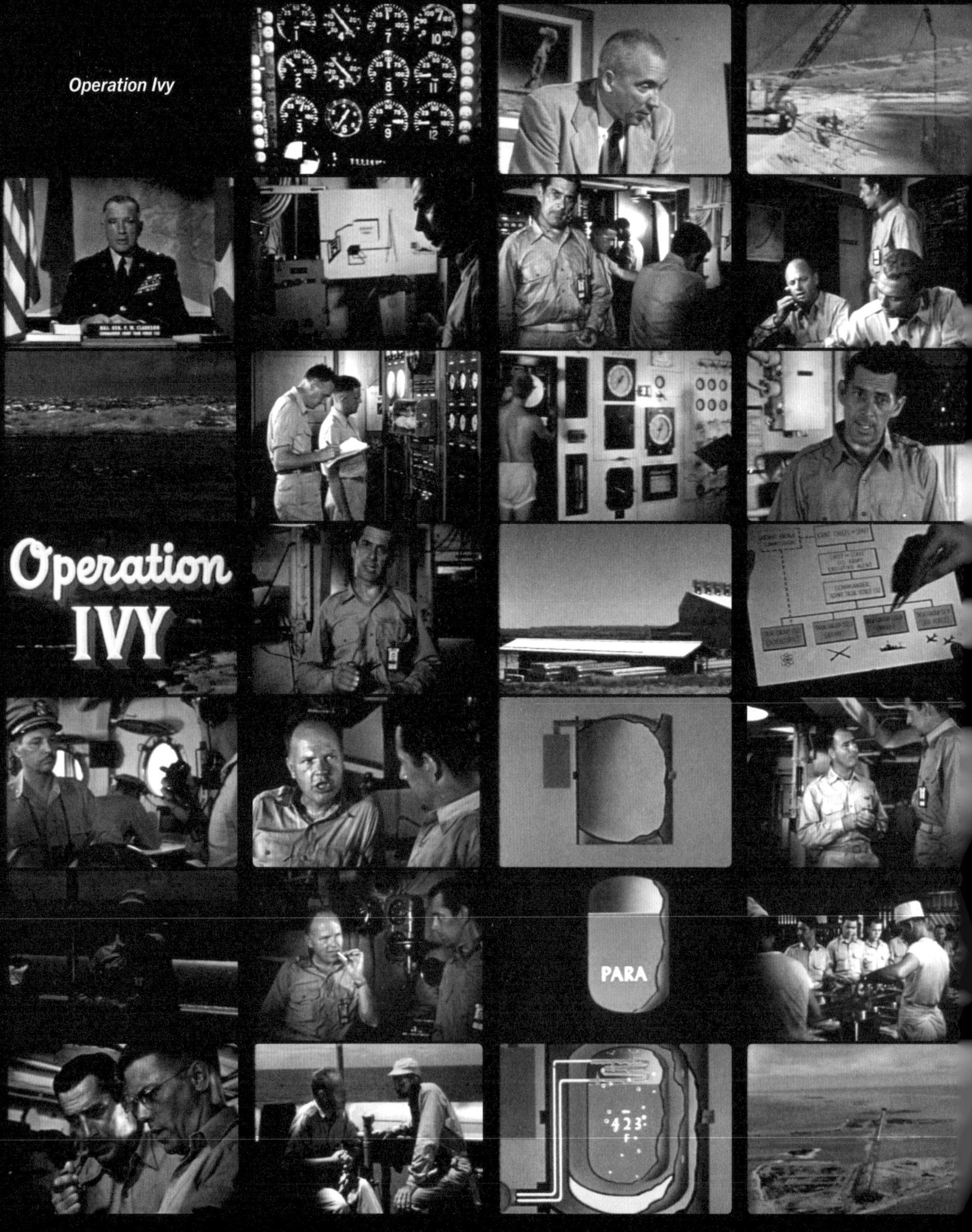

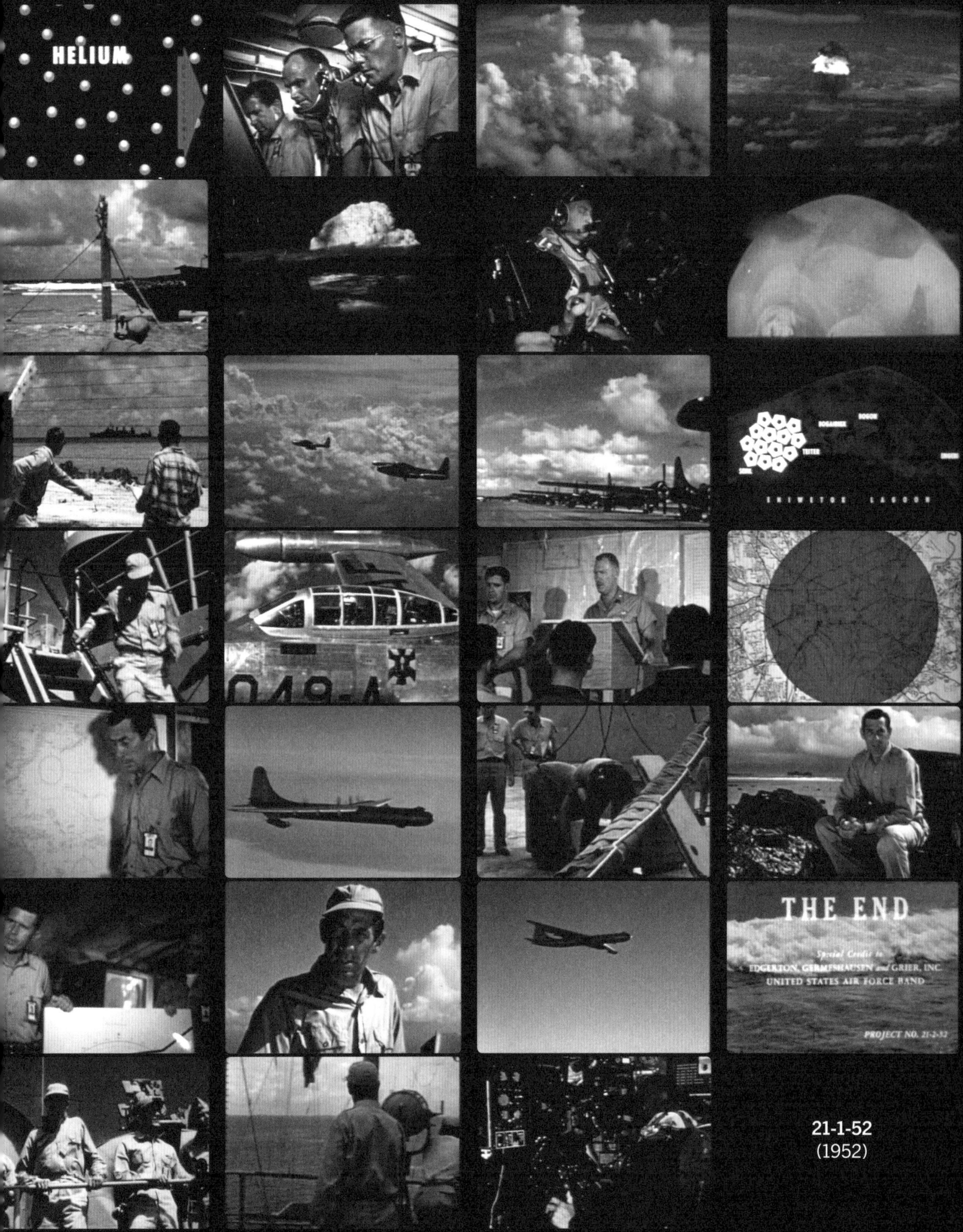
HELIUM
ENIWETOK LAGOON
THE END
Special Credit to
EDGERTON, GERMESHAUSEN and GRIER, INC.
UNITED STATES AIR FORCE BAND

21-1-52
(1952)

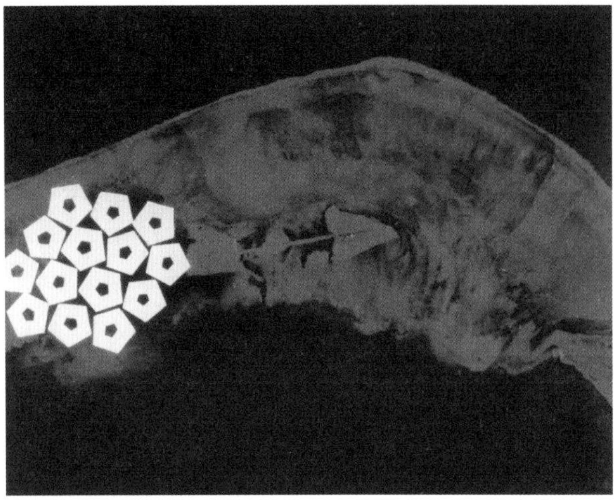

of the blast: maps and charts are used, the blast hole is superimposed onto Washington, DC, and "Mike's" effects are described in terms of the destruction it would do to New York City. The film then concludes with Hadley, now by himself on an empty beach, telling the viewers that although "it's been a pleasure to bring you the story of Operation Ivy," he nevertheless has "sort of an inadequate feeling." "There's so much more that could have been said," he explains. Moreover, he continues, "You get a feeling that even now nothing is really over, that this is a breathing spell, like a lull in battle before the next attack." *Operation Ivy* thus ominously concludes by portending a coming war.

Only 177 persons were authorized to see the original version of *Operation Ivy*; the sixty-three-minute film was designated Top Secret Restricted Data. Indeed, Lookout Mountain Laboratory made only three prints of the film. General Clarkson reviewed the first cut of the film on March 9, 1953, and a final version on April 6; with his approval, senior scientists at Los Alamos gave the nod to the final version on April 9.[55] On May 19, about six months after the November 1952 test, *Operation Ivy* was screened for the Atomic Energy Commission commissioners and the Joint Chiefs of Staff in Washington, DC.[56] It did not, apparently, make a major impression, presumably because the AEC commissioners and the Joint Chiefs were already thoroughly familiar with the test and quite familiar with its imagery, having been forwarded photo books of the "Mike" shot within days of the detonation.[57]

Instead, it would take President Eisenhower to generate enthusiasm about *Operation Ivy*. In June of 1953 the president and members of his cabinet would see the film. Eisenhower reacted strongly. He was apparently so impressed with the film that he exclaimed that every American should see it.[58] While concerned about keeping its scientific and technical secrets, the president requested that a new, "secret" version of the film be cut for a broader audience, including some members of Congress.[59] Lookout Mountain Laboratory went to work and would remain busy with various cuts and edits to *Operation Ivy* for most of the next nine months.

The Eisenhower administration was still caught up in debates over the meaning of "candor," and was slowly working its way toward what would become the "Atoms for Peace" campaign. *Operation Ivy*, as things turned out, ended up being at the center of various debates within the administration in 1953 and 1954 regarding the nature and limits of "candor." Indeed, the film would be instrumental in a larger debate within the Eisenhower administration about the meaning of such rich and complex topics as democracy, responsibility, and authority within a nuclear age.

Broadly speaking, *Operation Ivy* produced three different responses within the Eisenhower administration, each representing not only distinct lines of debate, but distinct institutional interests, and as important, distinct rhetorical forms and political sensibilities. To begin with, the Atomic Energy Commission, under the chairmanship of Lewis Strauss, would see in the film a state secret to be closely guarded. Strauss succeeded Gordon Dean on July 1, 1953. The two men had clashed amid the McCarthyist furor over Robert Oppenheimer, with Strauss [angry at Oppenheimer for a variety of reasons, including Oppenheimer's opposition to the thermonuclear bomb] leading the attack against Oppenheimer and Dean coming to his defense.[60] Moreover, whereas Dean had inherited Truman's commitment to the "civilian" stewardship of atomic energy, under Strauss's leadership the Atomic Energy Commission's institutional interests were framed in terms of the arms race with the Soviets. Strauss's primary concern was to safeguard American atomic superiority by keeping the Soviets in the dark.[61] The Atomic Energy Commission thus worked within the rhetorical forms of secrecy and disclosure and developed a political sensibility centered on control.[62]

The Federal Civil Defense Administration, however, was most immediately concerned with mobilizing citizens and their local leaders on behalf of civil defense. For them, *Operation Ivy* represented a means of "candor" with the American public about the effects of nuclear weapons, and thus ultimately represented a means of activating new forms of citizenship and federalism for a nuclear age. As we will see, the film also represented for the Federal Civil Defense Administration a means of thinking about the democratic responsibilities of a nuclear state. They worked between the rhetorical forms of "free speech" and "emotion management," seeing public speech as a means of engendering public action. The political sensibility of the Federal Civil Defense Administration centered on the inculcation of dispersed, "democratic" action on behalf of the nation.

Finally, Eisenhower's Operations Coordinating Board, his chief "public information" clearinghouse and the de facto ultimate arbitrator of *Operation Ivy*'s distribution, would work closely with the CIA in approaching the film as a means of massaging public and world opinion regarding America's nuclear pursuits. For the Operations Coordinating Board, *Operation Ivy* was a means not just of "emotion management" through propaganda, but of orchestrating support for the United States at home and abroad through the careful management of "information." The Operations Coordinating Board mediated between the Atomic Energy Commission's concern with secrecy and disclosure and Civil Defense's concern with "free speech" and "emotion management," always looking to strike a balance between the competing impulses of the nuclearized state. The political sensibility of the Operations Coordinating Board, therefore, centered on the ideological and ideational, especially the orchestration of an ideology of freedom and an idea of a free and powerful America.

But these rhetorical forms and political sensibilities did not appear in an a priori fashion. Rather, they had to be developed and worked through as the various agencies discussed, debated, and worried about common objects. The

Operation Ivy:
18 months to the public eye

Operation Ivy tests conclude

DEC

1953

Lookout Mountain begins Top Secret film of Ivy tests

FEB

MAR

Top Secret film completed

APR

Approval by Joint Task Force Commander

Approval by scientists at Los Alamos

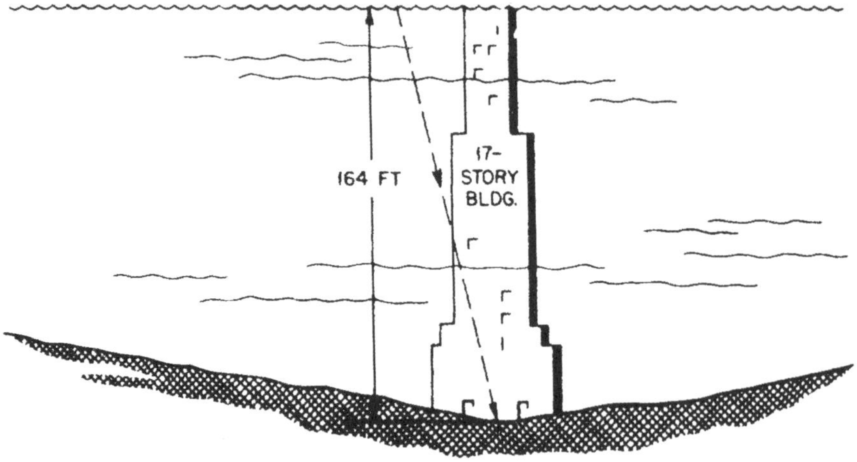

Fig. 7—Graphic presentation of Mike crater.

thermonuclear bomb certainly had been one such object; but by the fall of 1953, it was not the device itself, but rather its rhetorical representation in *Operation Ivy*, that became the common object around and through which these agencies approached the sensibility of the state. In the remainder of this section we offer an account of the lines of debates surrounding *Operation Ivy* by tracing the history of its screening from the summer of 1953 to the spring of 1954, paying special attention to implicit rhetorical forms and developing political sensibilities.

Eisenhower's enthusiasm about *Operation Ivy* set in motion a series of discussions between the Atomic Energy Commission and the Federal Civil Defense Administration through the summer of 1953. Meanwhile, Lookout Mountain Laboratory quickly set to work on a secret-rated version of the film, in accordance with Eisenhower's request, having it ready in a matter of days. On June 17, Dean, who would come to the end of his chairmanship of the Atomic Energy Commission two weeks later [succeeded by Strauss], notified Eisenhower that the secret version was ready for presentation "to any groups you may direct to see it."[63] Things seemed to be moving in the Federal Civil Defense Administration's direction, with Eisenhower apparently leaning toward mobilizing the nation for a thermonuclear age over and against closely guarding America's thermonuclear secrets.

In September, however, the Atomic Energy Commission put a temporary stop to "candor." When the secret version of *Operation Ivy* arrived in Washington, DC, for screening, Strauss informed Civil Defense's head, Val Peterson, that no one could view the film without a "Q" clearance, all but defeating the purpose of the secret version.[64] Civil Defense was frustrated, for it had been hoping that a public version of *Operation Ivy* would be next in line, and had not anticipated such Atomic Energy Commission opposition to screenings even of the secret version. The Federal Civil Defense Administration appealed directly to the White House. The acting administrator of Civil Defense, Katherine Howard, wrote a four-page memorandum in September 1953 to Eisenhower's special assistant for psychological warfare and Operations Coordinating Board head C. D. Jackson, about the differences between the Federal Civil Defense Administration and the Atomic Energy Commission. More than reasoning that it would be good for Americans to see the film in order to motivate them to take civil defense seriously—the argumentative course Civil Defense had adopted since the summer—Howard enumerated an argument for the state's democratic responsibility for releasing at least some version of *Operation Ivy* to the public.[65] In doing so, she both extended and modified the argument Oppenheimer had made for "candor" and suggested an alternative political sensibility.

Howard began by reminding Jackson of the visceral reaction Eisenhower had to the film. "For the past several weeks the Administrator, Admiral Strauss and the members of the FCDA and AEC staffs have had under discussion the possible declassification for public showing of portions of the film on thermonuclear tests at Eniwetok [*sic*] last year. This grew out of a remark by the President, after he had witnessed the picture, to the effect that every American should see it." Howard then explained that the Atomic Energy Commission and Civil Defense had been debating the release of a public version of *Operation Ivy*, but were stuck on the question of the "declassification of hitherto restricted data" [at minimum, the government would have to publicly admit the extent of their thermonuclear efforts]. "Basically," Howard continued, "it gets down to how much information should be given to the American people. Should it be as much as possible or as little as possible?" Indirectly referring to the Atomic Energy Commission, she noted that one "school of thought" holds that "nothing should be released unless there is a real necessity for making it public." To this position she opposed another, clearly her own and that of the Federal Civil Defense Administration, arguing first of all that "in a democracy, the people are entitled to an accounting by their government." "The burden of proof," she continued, "should be on those who wish to suppress the facts." If the release of information would endanger American citizens, then it should be kept secret. Otherwise, Howard argued, it should be made public.

Operation Ivy, Howard argued, represented an opportunity for the federal government to present "the facts." The current policies of the government, however, risked engendering two adverse psychological reactions among the people: panic and escapism. "The ability to reason or to take corrective action," Howard wrote, "becomes paralyzed" among all the speculation, misinformation, and rumor. The H-bomb, she claimed, would do horrible damage, but it is "not the absolute weapon. Its effects would be devastating, but they need not be catastrophic—*if* we have an informed public. . . . What is needed now, in our view, is a calm, unemotional and *authoritative* exposition of the essential facts about thermonuclear weapons, their probable effects, and civil defense measures to minimize these effects upon life, property, and national morale" [emphasis in original].

Screening for AEC and Joint Chiefs of Staff

JUN

President orders a less restricted Secret version

Lookout Mountain completes Secret version

JUL

AUG

Secret version delivered to Washington

SEP

AEC restricts access to Secret version

Debate ensues between agencies

OCT

NOV

White House orders an Unclassified version

Lookout Mountain plans for public Castle test films

Howard concluded her memo by arguing for a new set of criteria when thinking about the release of public information on nuclear weapons, asking the White House to weigh the real risks of secrecy. She asked that the president take such factors into account and "enunciate the fundamental policy to be followed by all departments of government."[66] Howard thus argued for a coherent and consistent democratic sensibility for the thermonuclear state, one that operated, as a matter of assumption, according to the principle that publicity was necessary for both public safety and a democratic society.

In one respect, at least, the Federal Civil Defense Administration would get its way. In October, the Operations Coordinating Board began discussing screening an unclassified cut of *Operation Ivy* at the US Conference of Mayors to be held at the White House in December. The Federal Civil Defense Administration argued that *Operation Ivy* was needed in order to communicate to the mayors the need for "new concepts of civilian defense" in light of megaton weapons. In November of 1953, Lookout Mountain completed a version of the film for the conference. They were more than prepared to do so; for as far back as the spring of 1953, Lookout Mountain, ignoring Atomic Energy Commission orders, began work on an unclassified version of *Operation Ivy*. Their head, Lt. Colonel Gaylord, "was certain that demands would be made for a 'public release' picture," Lookout Mountain reported later.[67] It was as if for them the existence of a well-crafted motion picture demanded a public screening: *Operation Ivy* drew on the cinematic conventions of Hollywood, and perhaps Lookout Mountain's Gaylord thought it deserved a Hollywood-size audience. Or it may have been the specter of the "Super": Gaylord may have felt that *Operation Ivy*, like the thermonuclear device itself, deserved to be seen, heard, and felt. In either case, he allowed the studio to move forward with the editing of an unclassified version of the film despite explicit instructions from above not to do so.

When considering the presentation of *Operation Ivy* to the mayors that fall, Eisenhower's National Security Council worried that even news of the film, let alone the film itself, "would be likely to create anxiety and disturbance" among the American public. The CIA's Allen Dulles added that the film could stir "neutralist feelings" abroad. However, Special Assistant to the President for National Security Affairs Robert Cutler echoed Civil Defense chairman Val Peterson in arguing that Americans needed to be alerted out of their indifference, even scared, in order to meet the challenges of civil defense. Eisenhower shot back at Cutler, arguing that no progress could be made at all by "scaring people to death." Rather, the people of the United States needed "real and substantial knowledge."[68]

The Atomic Energy Commission saw the writing on the wall. Though they had wanted to closely guard all images of the "Mike" test, they saw in the unclassified "For Official Use Only" version of the film Lookout Mountain cut for the US Conference of Mayors the beginning of a legitimation crisis. The Atomic Energy Commission forecasted that upon seeing *Operation Ivy* the mayors would spread the word to the press, despite orders not to, at which point "the Government's reputation with the media of mass communications and the public for not withholding unclassified material from publication is likely to be impaired." The "pressure for public showing of the declassified film will become very strong," the Atomic Energy Commission continued.[69]

Therefore, the Atomic Energy Commission and Federal Civil Defense Administration reached something of a détente. If the mayors were going to see the film, the best thing to do, the Atomic Energy Commission concluded, would be to go ahead and release the film shortly after the mayors' conference, perhaps with a message appended to the front of the film from the president or Civil Defense's Peterson.[70] Indeed, in January 1954, the month after the mayors' conference, Peterson recorded an introduction at the Lookout Mountain studios under the direction of MGM Studio head George Sidney. Eventually, the final public version of the film would also include a clip of Eisenhower delivering his "Atoms for Peace" speech.

That speech, delivered on December 8, 1953, came but a week before the mayors' conference at the White House; and Eisenhower's Operations Coordinating Board, under the leadership of Jackson, would use the mayors' conference as the first instance of their broader "Atoms for Peace" propaganda campaign, diffusing responsibility for a nation living under thermonuclear peril away from the federal govern-

Unclassified Ivy film delivered to Washington

Unclassified Ivy film shown at Mayors Conference

1954

Lookout Mountain shoots new introduction for public Ivy film

FEB

Public version of *Operation Ivy* screened for Congress

MAR

Castle Bravo detonation

Lookout Mountain completes Secret version of Castle film

APR

National broadcast of public version of *Operation Ivy*

MAY

JUN

AEC cancels production of Unclassified Castle film

ment. After welcoming the mayors, Eisenhower showed them the unclassified "For Official Use Only" version of *Operation Ivy*, finalized at Lookout Mountain the month before.[71] The mayors were told to watch the film closely, but they were ordered to remain hush-hush before their constituents about its contents. Eisenhower made his goal in showing the film explicit to the mayors: "I know of no other time when the President of the United States felt it necessary to invite to a conference the mayors of our cities, in order that they might together discuss . . . national security."[72] He thus offered in *Operation Ivy* the "facts," echoing the position of Oppenheimer and the Federal Civil Defense Administration. Eisenhower told the mayors, "Ordered haste will save you, and panic will destroy you. So it is, first of all, against the incidence of panic that we must be prepared. In other words, there must be understanding produced by leadership, inspired leadership—leadership that is unafraid."[73] The mayors of the cities of America, the administration therefore argued, had to come to see and feel themselves as at the front lines of civil defense. As Jackson told the mayors, "It does not make a bit of difference how much military brass there is in this town, or how many planning groups there are solemnly grinding out mimeographed sheets. If trouble comes—and trouble may very well come—the pay-off is how the people will behave. And how the people will behave is not something that can be ordered from Washington. There is too big a gap between the man in the street in your cities and towns and the White House or Capitol Hill. . . . After the bomb has gone off, those who are left will not turn to some anonymous and mysterious 'they' in Washington; you will be the first person to whom they will turn."[74]

The animated maps in *Operation Ivy* made this same case, demonstrating just how extensive the damage would be if the Soviets dropped thermonuclear bombs on New York and Washington, DC. The mayors watched the images as the offscreen narrator, working from estimates the scriptwriters had obtained from Los Alamos scientists, warned of unheard of destruction to major American cities. *Operation Ivy*, the film, was *the* event the mayors of America sensed and by which they were introduced to the new "common sense" of the thermonuclear state.

The Atomic Energy Commission, however, was right about the mayors' reactions. Rather than marching to the administration's orders, Houston mayor Roy Hofheinz, a Democrat, soon appeared on television to declare that the Eisenhower administration, and not just the Atomic Energy Commission, was being too secretive, and indeed was not doing "all it should do to inform the American people." Moreover, he argued that the Republican government was expecting far too much from local mayors in the way of civil defense coordination.[75] Meanwhile, the *Daily Boston Globe* ran a story on December 19 on a secretive "H-bomb" movie shown to the mayors, which read in full:

> Two Mayors tonight said they were shown a classified movie of a hydrogen "device or bomb" explosion while at a Mayors' conference in Washington this week. Mayor Clyde Fant of Shreveport first said he "understood" the explosion shown in the film was of an "H-bomb," but later denied he was certain. He then said he was told not to give out information on the movie, and asked not to be quoted. In Atlanta, Mayor William Hartsfield said the movie was of an explosion caused by some type of hydrogen device, but said there was no indication whether the object exploded was a portable bomb or some permanent structure. Although President Eisenhower has indicated the United States has a whole family of hydrogen weapons, it has never been officially confirmed that a workable hydrogen device was small enough to be carried by airplanes as a bomb.[76]

Word about the film having thus gotten out, various members of Congress desired to see the "For Official Use Only" declassified version of *Operation Ivy* shown to the mayors. In early February 1954, members of Congress viewed the film. They in turn began to push the Eisenhower administration to release the film to the public.[77] Consequently, the Operations Coordi-

The Family of Man

In spring of 1954, two years after the events of Operation Ivy, Americans saw their first images of the historic thermonuclear explosion in Lookout Mountain–shot images featured in *Life* magazine and in the heavily edited version of Lookout Mountain's feature film of the test, *Operation Ivy*, screened in movie houses.

The next winter, in January of 1955, visitors to the *Family of Man* photography exhibit at New York's Museum of Modern Art would pass through a dark gallery dedicated to a large-scale color image of the test, the same one featured in *Life* the prior spring. The light in the room seemed to come from the image itself, printed on a transparency and lit from behind so as to appear as an apparition. It was the sole image in the exhibition displayed alone in a gallery, and the sole image credited to a government agency, the Atomic Energy Commission, rather than a named photographer.

To enter the gallery, visitors had to pass by an image of the body of an American World War II soldier killed at Eniwetok, the very site of Operation Ivy. They left the gallery to enter a room of concerned faces and an image of the United Nations General Assembly.

The exhibition's curator, Edward Steichen, hoped to awaken concerns about the threat nuclear weapons presented to the "dignity of man." A former war photographer for the United States Navy, Steichen seemed to place his faith in the power of the orange fireball and mushroom cloud to awaken a new antinuclear consciousness. As scholar John O'Brien points out, Steichen could have done more by featuring images of victims from Hiroshima or Nagasaki, but instead he stopped with the stunning image of the thermonuclear explosion itself.

As the exhibition traveled, the darkened room disappeared and different images from Operation Ivy were used, save for the exhibition's stop in Japan, where the nuclear images disappeared altogether.

See also

O'Brian, "The Nuclear Family of Man"; Sandeen, *Picturing an Exhibition*.

nating Board began considering the nature and timing of a public version of the film. Citing the aesthetic quality of the film, they ultimately decided that only a twenty-eight-minute black-and-white version of the original color film would be released, that the timing of the release would be delayed until the spring [after the Berlin Conference summit between the United States and the Soviet Union], and that foreign release of the film would be as restricted as possible.[78] Thus, after nearly nine months of debate, the public release of *Operation Ivy* would quite literally be muted.

The short, unclassified black-and-white version of the film was finally screened to the public in April 1954, both on television and in movie theaters. The film was also widely distributed among the armed forces. Lookout Mountain Laboratory claimed the film "was in greater demand than any picture produced by Lookout Mountain and was given wider distribution than any service film produced since World War II." They claimed that it garnered "considerable praise," especially since "it gave the general public a chance to see the vast preparations and scope inherent in an atomic test."[79] As we will see, however, praise for the film was not universal.

Significantly, the unclassified version of *Operation Ivy* appeared just as the Eisenhower administration was wrestling with a new major thermonuclear crisis, the "Castle Bravo" disaster of March 1, 1954. The shot—including its radioactive contamination of twenty-nine Japanese fishermen—was making news around the world.[80] America's thermonuclear cat was out of the bag. Indeed, the Eisenhower administration now had moved beyond the fantastic image of the "Super" and had a real weapon in hand.

As such, it likely did not bother the Eisenhower administration that the public version of *Operation Ivy* included some technological and scientific matters that had seemed sensitive to the Atomic Energy Commission months before, such as the yield of the explosion and the fact that the device was not yet weaponized. The government was quickly moving beyond such concerns. In fact, the president may have been especially glad for its release. In a March 31, 1954, press conference with Atomic Energy Commission Chairman Lewis Strauss, Eisenhower interrupted Strauss just as the latter was beginning to suggest the yield of "Bravo" to journalists. When a reporter asked Strauss to "describe the area of the blast, the effectiveness of the blast, and give a general description of what actually happened when the H-bomb went off," the chairman began his response, "The area of the blast, would be about—." However, Eisenhower interrupted: "Why not depend on these pictures they are all going to see?" Strauss quickly got the message, continuing, "I understand you are going to see a film, a picture, of the 1952 shot. The area, if I were to describe it specifically, would be translatable into the number of megatons involved, which is a matter of military secrecy."[81]

The "Bravo" crisis meant as well that it probably did not bother the administration that *Operation Ivy* was, in the eyes of some cultural elites at least, an unimpressive production. In a somewhat anticlimactic conclusion to the nearly two-year story of *Operation Ivy*, the *New York Times* reviewed the film negatively on April 2, 1954. Reviewer Jack Gould described the film as overly theatrical and emotional, and found its explanation of the complex installation of the device in the Pacific "bewildering." Still, Gould was not strictly negative. "The truly effective part of *Operation Ivy*," he admitted, "came in those few moments when the scope and size of the destruction wrought by the explosion were explained by maps, pictures and charts."[82] And so, after all this, it was the legibility of the state that Operation Ivy made sensible.

Operation Ivy, the film, would make Operation Ivy, the nuclear tests, an object of sense and sensibility—not only to Atomic Energy Commission Chairman Dean, the Joint Chiefs of Staff, and President Eisenhower and his cabinet, but to congressmen, mayors of major urban areas, and eventually American and global publics. The story of the circulation of *Operation Ivy* begins, and could well have ended, with the president and his closest advisers, who watched the film in June 1953. The president, however, apparently felt others must see the film as well. Though Atomic Energy Commission plans had called for all pictures of Operation Ivy to remain strictly classified, and though the United States had not yet even officially admitted possession of a thermonuclear device, the president, coaxed on by Civil Defense, pushed the film forward into various cuts and classifications for several cleared audiences right up to December 14, 1953, when he opened the US Conference of Mayors at the White House by warning America's mayors of thermonuclear attacks on their cities.

Indeed, Operation Ivy, the test, did not remain an official secret beyond the spring of 1954, in part because the president and Civil Defense felt that *Operation Ivy*, the film, should not remain a secret. We might say that as a set of institutions the state was trying to feel its way into the thermonuclear age, concerned on the one hand with maintaining the legitimacy of state activities, and on the other with rendering a thermonuclear world not only legible but also sensible. The state, that is, was trying in various ways to construct a political sensibility for a nuclear age. That a motion-picture film would, even more than the Bomb itself, become the object around which this effort would take form may seem odd. But here we must recall that the "Super" was both an image and a story before it was a practical technology.

Operation Ivy, the film, rhetorically negotiated the very crises it would perpetuate. By offering the story of the thermonuclear age through "the 'eyes' of an impartial observer," *Operation Ivy* drew on the capacity of motion-picture film not only to address subjects and form subjectivities, but to negotiate sensibilities. In the way stage actors have to overplay the part in order to be seen playing it at all, so Lookout Mountain dramatized "objectivity" in order to render to the state its own sensibility before the drama of the thermonuclear bomb. But playing the part was not limited to the subjects of the film. As Edwin Black has noted, when we go to the theater we are invited to become "a special, social being with a special, social set of sensibilities and constraints." Audiences too, that is, are invited to be "an actor playing the part."[83] That *Operation Ivy* was obviously stylized was an index of the way in which it was trying to get audiences to also play their parts in the drama of the thermonuclear age.

On the one hand, that the *New York Times* panned *Operation Ivy* as being overly theatrical suggests just how indeterminate the sensibility of the new thermonuclear state was in the 1950s. To the scriptwriters and producers of *Operation Ivy* at Lookout Mountain, "impartiality" had to be dramatized in terms of scientific progress, technological competence, and political-historical adventure. To the *New York Times* reviewer, on the other hand, the advent of the thermonuclear age—while no less "objective"—appeared more as a brute fact than an epochal story. Before this brute fact the technologies of legibility—maps, charts, diagrams, and so on—felt a more appropriate medium than the theatrical technologies so obviously aimed at appealing to and forming sensibilities.

The film and its various receptions would anticipate the course and contradictions of the thermonuclear state in the decade to come. Over and over, thermonuclear weapons would appear variously as fantastic images of an apocalyptic history, as products of historical necessity, or as tools of a Cold War calculus. What would be missing from this spectrum of appearances and their corresponding sensibilities, however, would be anything approximating the "common sense" that the Federal Civil Defense Administration's Howard had argued for: a democratic sensibility.

no one can ever fully
make you realize what you'll

SEE AND FEEL

en you
perience an
ATOMIC WEAPON

Chapter Five

ROUTINE REPORTS

The Nevada Films

"Thirteen minutes from now, this airplane is going to drop an atomic bomb on *your* country."[1] For Americans in 1952, there could hardly have been more ominous words. Anxieties about atomic destruction were growing nearly as fast as the destructive power of new nuclear bombs. The Soviet Union had entered the nuclear arena three years earlier, and speculation was abuzz with talk of the new "Super" bombs that were, as we saw in the previous chapter, being tested at Operation Ivy. Meanwhile, the toxic power of fallout was becoming ever more apparent, forcing strategists and citizens alike to put atomic bombs in a special category reserved for "the End," or something like it. Hence, an official announcement like this of an imminent atomic bomb drop would have sent Americans into panic-stricken flight, had it not come from Reed Hadley on the big screen. The "thirteen minutes" was but a filmic conceit, measured in movie time—it was thirteen minutes of spectators sitting in their seats, anticipating a big cinematic bang.

"Thirteen minutes from now, this airplane is going to drop an atomic bomb on *your* country." The words, of course, were meant to sound like a threat, but not actually be one. Such was the magical power of film: creating believable fictions, illusions. However, as things turned out, this was as real a threat as there could be. For the bomb to be dropped was not a fictional bomb, and the country hit was not a make-believe country. The bomb belonged to the 1951 Buster-Jangle series of tests carried out in the Nevada desert. Together with the Ranger tests performed in Nevada earlier that year, the Buster-Jangle tests would inaugurate a domestic nuclear testing program that transformed the continental United States into, in the words of Joseph Masco, "the most nuclear-bombed country on earth."[2] "Thirteen minutes from now, this airplane is going to drop an atomic bomb on *your* country." So a secret film, *Military Participation on Buster-Jangle*, announced to rooms full of military men, many of whom were themselves preparing to depart for the Nevada Test

Site to help drop more atomic bombs, the beginning of large-scale continental nuclear bombing. "*You* will see it happen," Hadley continued in the film, and "*you* will know why."

If the Oceanic tests established for America a global atomic empire, in the Nevada tests the empire turned in on itself, subjugating the homeland to repeated atomic bombing. Some 928 nuclear detonations took place at the Nevada Test Site between 1951 and 1992, transforming 1,375 square miles of the Great Basin into the world's busiest atomic proving ground.[3] Of course, the area had been subjected to the empire's demands for many years before that. Home to the Western Shoshone for centuries, and still theirs by treaty in the 1950s, the Nevada desert had been pilfered by prospectors in the nineteenth century before it became America's most used theater of atomic operations in the middle of the twentieth century.[4] Nevertheless, in turning to Nevada the US nuclear testing regime overtly and explicitly turned in on itself: "Thirteen minutes from now, this airplane is going to drop an atomic bomb on your country."

Lookout Mountain Laboratory was founded as a Pacific operation, and it remained one throughout the course of its twenty-year history. Nevertheless, with the creation of the Nevada Test Site in 1951 the laboratory began a trek eastward. As of 1950, Lookout Mountain's work spanned the California coast westward. By the middle of the 1950s, if Lookout Mountain's activities were represented on a heat map, the hottest spots would have been the Marshall Islands and the Nevada Test Site, with Los Angeles neatly placed in the middle. By 1960 its work spanned not only the Pacific and Nevada, but most of the western half of the continental United States and assignments in Florida, stretches of Central America, and remote regions in Alaska and the Arctic.[5]

While Lookout Mountain took many of their Pacific techniques and technologies to their Nevada operations, there were substantive differences. Operationally, whereas Lookout Mountain had to be repeatedly deployed to the Pacific, Nevada was more or less a permanent base for them in the 1950s. The Nevada Test Site was about a seven-hour drive from Los Angeles, and Lookout Mountain crews were fixtures there, deployed on "TDY," or temporary duty basis, for months at a time. But the even more significant difference between the Pacific and Nevada operations was that in Nevada the Atomic Energy Commission and Department of Defense were atomic bombing "*your* country."

Rebecca Solnit, among others, has discussed the ways in which nuclear testing on what the Shoshone called "Newe Sogobia" represented a continuation of centuries-old Indian wars.[6] As such, it did not differ much from the Pacific tests with respect to the sovereignty and humanity of indigenous peoples. Still, the detonation of nuclear weapons within the boundaries of the continental United States presented a radically different rhetorical challenge than the Pacific tests. Officials needed to persuade publics and their representatives not only that the Nevada tests were necessary, but also that they posed no serious threat to the health or well-being of American citizens and military personnel [the well-being of indigenous peoples was far less of a concern]. Thus, whereas the Pacific afforded stories of civilizational expansion and technological triumph, all contained within the rhetoric of a bounded, if vast, space, tests at the Nevada Test Site called forth stories of tightly controlled, and above all "safe," scientific experimentation. Whereas the perceived remoteness of the Pacific testing sites afforded an opportunity to focus on the containment of "distant" or abstract problems—science growing beyond human understanding, a weapon's unpredictable effects, loose-lipped sailors spilling secrets—the desert afforded a chance for supposedly controlled scientific experimentation in America's "outdoor laboratories." Just as philosophical empiricists once imagined the mind as a "blank slate" on which should be written only experimentally verifiable knowledge, so too, as Tom Vanderbilt writes, in the eyes of cold warriors the great deserts of the western United States, above all Nevada, were represented as a "blank slate" on which the theories of atomic science could be verified and nuclear knowledge compiled.[7]

For Lookout Mountain, however, the Nevada Test Site was not so much a blank slate as it was an empty stage waiting to be filled with the performances and props of the national security state. As Trevor Paglen notes, the Nevada desert is a space of remarkable "illusions, deceptions, and redirections," such that "it's almost impossible to tell the difference between what's really there and one of the desert's cruel tricks."[8] So too, Lookout Mountain approached the Nevada desert as a space for national theatrics where the line dividing illusion and reality was more than fuzzy; it was movable and manipulable. Where, they might have asked, could there be a better staging ground for the theater of the state of operations, for what Solnit referred to as "rehearsals" for nuclear war, than this vast "empty" stage?[9]

In this chapter, we follow Lookout Mountain as it traveled eastward into the Nevada desert. Given its Hollywood location, the trek was familiar enough: whereas Americans have historically looked westward, Hollywood, by virtue of not only its geographical location but also its cultural position, had always looked eastward. The structures, styles, and ideologies of what David Bordwell and his colleagues have termed "classical Hollywood cinema" could be, and indeed were, put on Pacific as well as European settings.[10] But their typical provinces were the cities, neighborhoods, plains, and mountains of the continental United States. From 1917 to 1960, the period associated with classical Hollywood cinema, movies looked eastward, remaking the West, Midwest, South, and East according to Hollywood's own particular structures, styles, and ideologies.

So from 1950 to 1960 Lookout Mountain Laboratory looked eastward, especially to Nevada, portraying the newly formed national security state in images, assumptions, and narratives drawn from classical Hollywood cinema and the popular western genre films. It also eventually unmade these representations in order

to reframe America's nuclear operations in the idioms of a bureaucratic, documentary realism. Conventions of Hollywood westerns meant that Nevada, and the desert in particular, represented not only an empty stage for nuclear tests, but an available "screen West" already associated with national possibility and American exceptionalism.[11] Both as a geography and a set of cinematic conventions, Nevada offered a space for both utopian reimaginings and realistic acceptance of harsher fates—in this case, the nuclear bombardment of America.

Even though it would be viewed on countless screens, the Nevada Test Site was purposely screened *from* view. As early as 1947, the Armed Forces Special Weapons Project, the Department of Defense organization charged with developing nuclear weapons, sought to establish a continental nuclear test site. It was kept from pursuing the project further by the Atomic Energy Commission, which was concerned about the adverse publicity effects of fallout. The Soviet test of an atomic bomb in August 1949, together with the outbreak of the Korean War in 1950, changed that. The Soviet test, of course, alarmed Americans and their allies, kick-starting the Truman administration into new phases of nuclear-weapons development. Still, the Korean War threatened to halt these renewed efforts, as naval vessels and other personnel needed for Pacific tests were suddenly scarce. Scientists at Los Alamos, fearing the loss of the Pacific test sites because of international hostilities, began to push hard for a continental base from which to perform weapons experiments; and the Atomic Energy Commission obliged, arguing for a continental test site as an "emergency" measure, in keeping with Truman's exercise of emergency powers in the Korean War. Though several different sites were considered, Los Alamos pushed for the Nevada site for intertwined fallout and "public relations" reasons: the area, it was felt, was far enough from population centers to keep from having to execute economically and reputationally costly measures to protect citizens from radiation, and it offered natural barriers that "screened viewing from public roads."[12]

Given the desire to keep the tests in Nevada from public view, Operation Ranger—the first series of nuclear tests at the new Nevada Test Site, held in the winter of 1951—could not have been more different from Operation Crossroads. Hastily convened after President Truman gave formal authorization, with no public announcement, Los Alamos proceeded with the secret tests without the joint participation of the Department of Defense, let alone the involvement of the press.[13] When the Ranger blasts lit up the sky, only the cameras of Los Alamos Graphic Arts Division and their contractor, EG&G, took pictures, making Operation Ranger among the least photographed of America's 216 aboveground nuclear tests.[14] Nevertheless, Ranger's blasts could not fully be screened from public view. Knowing of the planned tests and seeing an opportunity for the new medium of television, a television station manager in Los Angeles sent a crew of cameramen to Las Vegas, where on February 1, 1952, they broadcast live the "Easy" shot of Ranger from atop a hotel.

Indeed, it was obvious enough to all officials involved that word would get out as soon as the Nevada sky first flashed with atomic light. Therefore, the Atomic Energy Commission conceived of a public relations campaign to emphasize radiological safety, using what would become the watchword of Nevada testing, the "routine" nature of atomic operations. As a Department of Energy historian writes, the Atomic Energy Commission wanted to "make the atom routine in the continental United States and make the public feel at home with atomic blasts and radiation hazards."[15] How was feeling "at home" consistent with a high level of state secrecy? It was a tricky question. Los Alamos scientists saw the Nevada Test Site as their new backyard outdoor laboratory and wanted to be able to work there free from the encumbrances of publicity. Moreover, they saw themselves, with their Atomic Energy Commission superiors, as the protectors of state secrets in a world of nuclear espionage. Making the atom "routine"

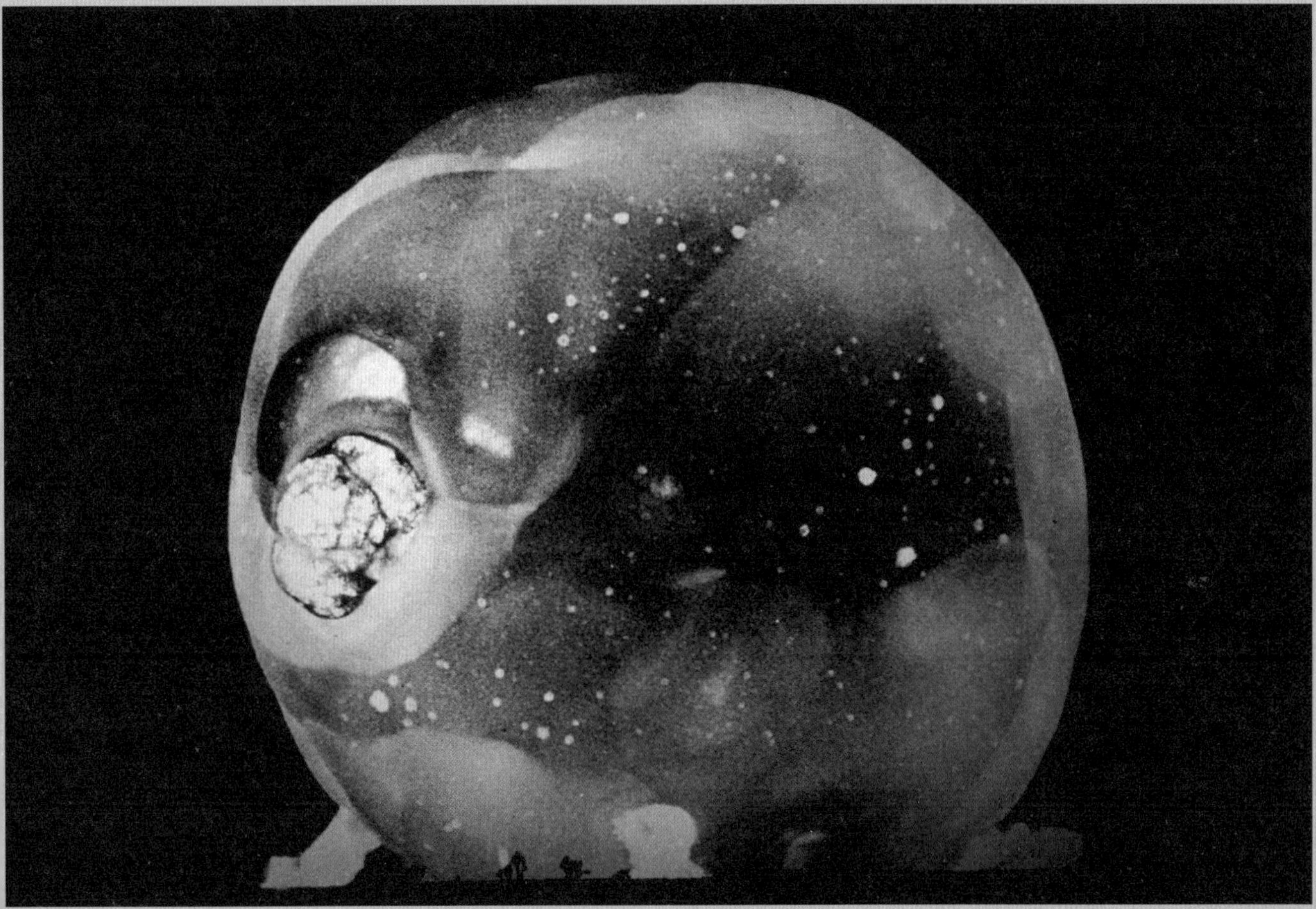

Edgerton, Germeshausen, and Grier

Edgerton, Germeshausen, and Grier, or EG&G, is one of the most important but least-known government contractors of America's Cold War. It served the Department of Defense, the Atomic Energy Commission (later renamed the Department of Energy), NASA, and other government agencies. The company's most iconic work was produced by its highly specialized scientific imaging instruments that documented nuclear tests, resulting in fireball pictures captured at microsecond speeds that no other cameras could match. EG&G's work on nuclear tests, however, extended well beyond imaging: they designed and typically operated the timing and firing mechanisms that ran the tests.

EG&G was a product of the Massachusetts Institute of Technology, where the company's figurehead, Harold Edgerton, invented electronic strobe photography as a way of "freezing time" to study irregularities in industrial motors. Edgerton's high-speed photographic techniques and technologies captured the popular imagination in the 1930s and 1940s, when his photographs of bullets passing through apples, drops of milk frozen in the act of splashing, and tennis rackets swinging in surreal sequences circulated in publications such as *Life* magazine. Less known is the way in which Edgerton's work—with that of his graduate students Herbert Grier and Kenneth Germeshausen—was behind the instrumentation of firing and timing mechanisms installed inside the "Fat Man" atomic bomb that fell on Hiroshima.

EG&G worked alongside Lookout Mountain Laboratory throughout the latter's two-decade history. Typically, EG&G and Lookout Mountain worked in a complementary fashion at weapons tests, with EG&G performing technically difficult high-speed photography and Lookout Mountain doing the bulk of the day-to-day documentary work. Sometimes EG&G consulted Lookout Mountain; other times Lookout Mountain helped out EG&G. Together, they are responsible for the overwhelming majority of America's nuclear test footage.

See also

O'Gorman and Hamilton, "EG&G and the Deep Media of Timing, Firing, and Exposing."

at home would mean convincing citizens that despite the dangerous and secret nature of their work, everything was under control.

Nine months after Ranger and five months after Greenhouse, the Atomic Energy Commission and the Department of Defense performed a second series of continental nuclear tests in Nevada under the code name Buster-Jangle. Like Ranger, the Los Alamos–run tests were closed to the press, but now open to over five thousand military personnel who were brought in for battlefield training purposes.[16] And for the first time, Lookout Mountain Laboratory was summoned to the Nevada Test Site. Still, they were but one of several photographic groups at Buster-Jangle: Los Alamos, the Navy, and other Air Force photographic units were also there. The small group of photographers arrived from Lookout Mountain to do technical and documentary photography for "indirect bomb damage assessment" on the air-dropped bombs.[17]

By the next test series, Operation Tumbler-Snapper, held from April 1 to June 5, 1952, Lookout Mountain's role would expand to incorporate the preponderance of documentary and technical photography work. Indeed, 1952 marked a critical year in Lookout Mountain's history: just as they were pushed to the center of the photographic operations at Greenhouse, so too they moved to the center of photographic operations at Nevada. A crew of thirteen Lookout Mountain personnel spent the spring and summer encamped at Nevada, even as crews worked back at the Wonderland Avenue facility constructing stage sets and art designs for what would become *Military Participation on Tumbler/Snapper*.[18]

Lookout Mountain's rise to the center of American nuclear visuality in 1952 grew out of the strange conjunction of state secrecy and Hollywood art. As we have seen, from Lookout Mountain's inception the Atomic Energy Commission saw the studio as a processing and storage facility for top secret film footage and photographs of America's nuclear tests. They had sunk close to $25,000 into the Wonderland Avenue facility in 1948 for, among other things, the construction of five film vaults that together could hold 3.5 million feet of 35 mm film, and soon after they would help pay for the expansion of Lookout Mountain's film processing laboratories.[19] Such investments could keep classified footage out of commercial processing facilities (even if those commercial facilities had the requisite security clearances), and thus lessen chances of espionage. The Air Force, to which of course Lookout Mountain belonged, was more than willing to oblige. Indeed, as we saw in chapter 2, in 1952 the "exceedingly strict security requirements established by the Atomic Energy Commission" pushed the Air Force to grant operational independence for Lookout Mountain Laboratory, such that they could work directly with Defense's Armed Forces Special Weapons Project and the Atomic Energy Commission without having to run everything through the Air Force chain of command.[20]

Yet at the same time Lookout Mountain was being asked to produce films for military personnel and broader publics that had all the trappings of a very public art, Hollywood cinema. The conjunction of state secrecy and Hollywood art came to a head around the 1952 Tumbler-Snapper series of Nevada tests. By 1952 significant pressure was being put on the Atomic Energy Commission to ease the secrecy restrictions around continental atomic testing. In November 1951, for example, Gene Sherman of the *Los Angeles Times* wrote that the Atomic Energy Commission's "security policy" was "both inconsistent and obstructive." Five thousand troops had witnessed Buster-Jangle, Sherman complained, but no members of the press were allowed to see it. Not even in wartime, he complained, had the press faced such strict security restrictions. "Newsmen," he argued in a kind of journalistic syllogism, are "representatives of the public." The public is paying for atomic testing. Therefore, the public is "entitled to know."[21]

Pressure for public access to Nevada's atomic tests came from elsewhere too. After Buster-Jangle, both the Federal Civil Defense Admin-

16mm Film Processing at Lookout Mountain

A picture of demand

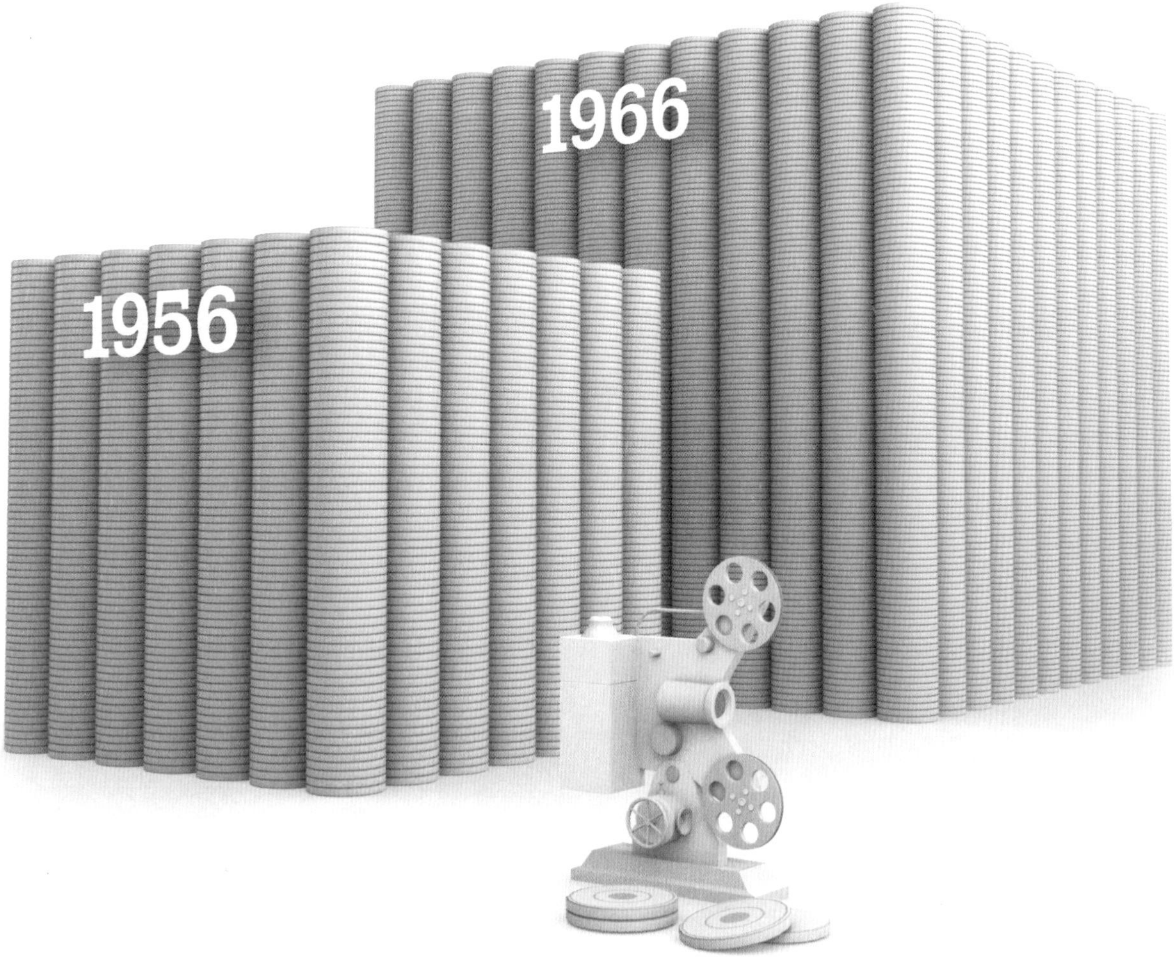

3,327 REELS
2.7 MILLION FEET
1,232 HOURS

ONE REEL
800 FEET
22 MINUTES
(at 24 fps)

16,171 REELS
12.9 MILLION FEET
5,989 HOURS

Civil Defense Films

On learning of Lookout Mountain Laboratory, most with some familiarity with Cold War America think of the films connected with the Federal Civil Defense Administration, an agency launched in the 1950s to manage the effects of impending nuclear war among the nation's populace. Through screenings, television broadcasts, and circulation libraries, film played a large role in the Federal Civil Defense Administration's efforts.

Leaders of civil defense paid frequent visits to Lookout Mountain's Hollywood facility as part of test preparations, working in more or less harmony with other federal organizations in the planning of publicity around each nuclear test operation. Moreover, sometimes civil defense leaders appeared in Lookout Mountain films, sitting behind desks on the soundstage to deliver messages of assurance and urgency to the American people. From time to time, the Federal Civil Defense Administration advised Lookout Mountain on how to approach the imagery of nuclear blasts. For example, for Operation Redwing (1956) they urged Lookout Mountain to consider the best way to show the scale of a nuclear blast, writing, "From the point of visual impact, magnitude of detonation as seen on the screen is a function of camera distance as well as shot yield. Therefore, a great need is for detonation shots that provide a proper frame of reference." Not surprisingly, footage shot by Lookout Mountain cameras made its way regularly into civil defense films.

Surprisingly, however, Lookout Mountain did not directly produce many films for civil defense. Indeed, they may have produced only one such film, 1954's *Let's Face It!* That project entailed two years of labored wrangling and changes in direction over the script, style, and message of the film. Given the difficulty of producing *Let's Face It!*, there is little wonder that Lookout Mountain ended up limiting their contributions to civil defense films to stock footage.

LA 97-INP SOUNDPHOTO-LAS VEGAS, NEV., 3/20/53 "LIVING OCCUPANTS" OF HOUSE NO. 1 AFTER A-BLAST WERE IN SIMPLY CONSTRUCTED, INEXPENSIVE BASEMENT SHELTERS. FALLING DEBRIS SLID DOWN INCLINE "LEAN-TO" SHELTER LEAVING MANEQUIN UNSCATHED. (USAF LOOKOUT MOUNTAIN LAB. PHOTO FOR FCDA FROM INTERNATIONAL NEWS PHOTOS.

istration, created in 1950, and the Department of Defense argued that coverage by journalists would benefit the atomic weapons program. To motivate publics to take civil defense seriously, the Federal Civil Defense Administration wanted the tests open to not only the press but also local and state government officials. Similarly, the military was having to deal with the growing fears of servicemen about atomic warfare, and they began to see value in demonstrating to the nation the survivability of atomic warfare.[22] In light of such pressures, the Atomic Energy Commission permitted selected press and other observers to witness the Tumbler-Snapper tests, and even to bring cameras.[23]

As we saw in chapter 4, the respective positions of the Atomic Energy Commission, Federal Civil Defense Administration, and Department of Defense suggested important differences within the government about atomic publicity. The Atomic Energy Commission consistently wanted to keep a tight lid on not just atomic publicity but atomic "information" of any kind. Meanwhile, Civil Defense advocated for relative openness to motivate the American public to take their civil defense responsibilities seriously. And perhaps most surprisingly, the armed forces, especially the Air Force, wanted to publicly promote atomic power: it could "prove" to Americans and the world the force of American military might, and it could help American servicemen understand the whys and hows of nuclear operations.

Lookout Mountain could seemingly meet all of these exigencies. Operationally speaking, they could process and store America's nuclear film secrets in a government-owned secure facility. Yet at the same time they could make Hollywood-style movies that could satisfy the desire of both the Federal Civil Defense Administration and the Department of Defense for compelling and motivating film stories about America's new nuclear operations. But even more, Lookout Mountain Laboratory could move nimbly among various cinematic styles and carefully match style to substance for the needs of each client or application. Most of their films were made for the Department of Defense. When commanders wanted official "film reports" for those up the chain of command, Lookout Mountain could oblige with bland bureaucratic documentary productions, typically using on-site documentary footage narrated by an unnamed offscreen narrator. Such film reports had very little in the way of cinematic frills. Yet when Defense wanted motivational orientation or training films for the rank and file, Lookout Mountain could oblige with films that drew on standard Hollywood conventions, featuring, for example, well-known stars as narrators, making heavy use of vivid animations, or telling Hollywood-style stories of conflict and resolution.

So too, when Civil Defense wanted a film meant to dramatize the challenges of the atomic citizenry, Lookout Mountain could oblige with music, mise-en-scène, and on-screen characters with which publics could identify. Yet in the very same production period, Lookout Mountain could—and did—generate for the Atomic Energy Commission toned-down "informational" films focused on "just the facts." Lookout Mountain's writers, producers, and editors, that is, had facility with a range of film styles, and could tailor their productions accordingly. This stylistic facility, as much as their ability to operate within the walls of strict state secrecy, put Lookout Mountain at the center of America's nuclear visuality. In Lookout Mountain films such as *Target Nevada*, *Military Participation on Buster-Jangle*, *Military Participation on Tumbler/Snapper*, *Atomic Tests in Nevada*, and *Let's Face It*, we see the studio wielding its expertise in cinematic styles to match style with rhetorical purpose. Lookout Mountain was not only a Hollywood studio in its composition, location, and aspirations; it also proved to be a capable wielder of Hollywood art, working to tell the right story in the right way for each client and audience.

Lookout Mountain's first Nevada productions focused on the how and why of continental testing. The Buster-Jangle series of tests were conducted not to develop new weapons, but to

help better understand the effects of nuclear weapons on terrain, structures, animals, and humans. Documentary photography at the tests was accomplished by personnel from Los Alamos and EG&G.[24] The only Lookout Mountain photographers at Buster-Jangle were aboard planes, busy creating film records of the scopes on scientific instruments for later review by scientists. Given that Lookout Mountain photographers had a relatively minor role in the tests, the unit had to rely more on actors and studio sets for their public-release *Target Nevada* and their classified *Military Participation on Buster-Jangle*, both produced at the Wonderland Avenue facility soon after the Operation Greenhouse films were made. Of course, the studio, numbering some seventy-five civilian employees and over a dozen Air Force personnel in the spring of 1952, had ample resources to put their mark on the production: narration, music, and numerous scenes shot on and off set.

Target Nevada was Lookout Mountain's first attempt at convincing American publics that continental atomic testing was safe and atomic warfare survivable. The short fifteen-minute color film, designated "Special Film Project 281" by the Air Force, was produced in 1952 and released to American movie theaters and television studios in 1953. It begins with an image of an Air Force bomber flying high over the Nevada desert. Like so many of Lookout Mountain's Hollywood-inspired films, the opening shot established a theme, in this case the new atomic connection between the Air Force and the Nevada desert. As orchestral music crescendos and the bomber fills the screen, the title screen flashes "Target Nevada," followed by "The Story of the United States Air Force Support to the Atomic Energy Commission on Continental Atomic Tests." Credits follow before viewers are brought to a panorama of the Nevada desert. Carey Wilson, the offscreen narrator, addresses the audience, "Nevada, USA. This is the valley where the giant mushrooms grow. More atom bombs have been exploded on these few hundred square miles of desert than on any other spot on the globe." A series of blast shots from the 1951 Buster-Jangle series of tests follows, each shot culminating in an image of a mushroom cloud. Wilson goes on to explain that the Nevada desert, though now the United States' most active atomic proving ground, is reserved for relatively small, if frequent, nuclear tests, affording the scientists of Los Alamos a site within their own "backyard" for better understanding atomic power.

But *Target Nevada* is less interested in justifying nuclear tests in Nevada than in convincing Americans that atomic operations can be controlled, contained, survived, and even made "safe." Here the Air Force, not the Los Alamos scientists or civil defense experts, is the most important actor in the film. The Air Force, *Target Nevada* explicitly argues, assures the safety of continental nuclear testing through the precise work of its pilots, navigators, and bombardiers—those responsible for the bomb drops over the Nevada desert—and through its expertise in, of all things, weather science. Why is meteorology so central? Mushroom clouds. The Air Force, *Target Nevada* suggests, knows something about clouds, and now they know something about the mushroom cloud—how to track it, how to measure its scope and substance, and even how to "fly through the cloud without harm" and "stay in it for a while." Against a shot of an Air Force plane flying through a mushroom cloud, Wilson explains to viewers that the Air Force has learned how take "proper precautions" to make the dangers of atomic radiation manageable, and that what the Air Force has learned is being passed on to the Atomic Energy Commission and the Federal Civil Defense Administration. The Air Force, Wilson concludes, knows better than anyone how to deal safely with "the real thing," as Wilson calls it, and can lead America in safe continental nuclear testing and in preparations not only for fighting, but for surviving, atomic warfare.

Military Participation on Buster-Jangle, also produced in 1952, is less reassuring about the prospects for surviving the atomic age, at least initially so. Narrated by Lookout Mountain regular Reed Hadley, whose career we considered in the previous chapter, this is the film that begins with, "Thirteen minutes from now, this airplane is going to drop an atomic bomb on *your* country." [This line is more than a little ironic, though certainly not meant to be, given that it was Hadley who had announced the atomic bombing of Japan in the First Motion Picture Unit's 1945 *The Last Bomb*.] Hadley's announcement sounded like a threat, creating more than a little narrative tension, and this for good rhetorical reasons: *Military Participation on Buster-Jangle* was aimed at military men readying for deployment to the Nevada Test Site, or at the very least, asking what the new atomic arsenals might mean for war fighting. The atomic bombing of America formed the basis of the narration's crisis as well as that of an imaginary American atomic apocalypse. In *Military Participation on Buster-Jangle*, as in so many of the Lookout Mountain Nevada test films, the resolution of that crisis came by means of "routine."

Military Participation on Buster-Jangle was broken into seven segments, resulting in an unwieldy episodic structure that did not cohere as well as other films produced by the unit. Each section ended with a countdown to the footage of one of Buster-Jangle's six successful nuclear blasts, accompanied by a recurring dramatic score. [Buster-Jangle had seven planned blasts; however, the first shot was a fizzle, a fact the

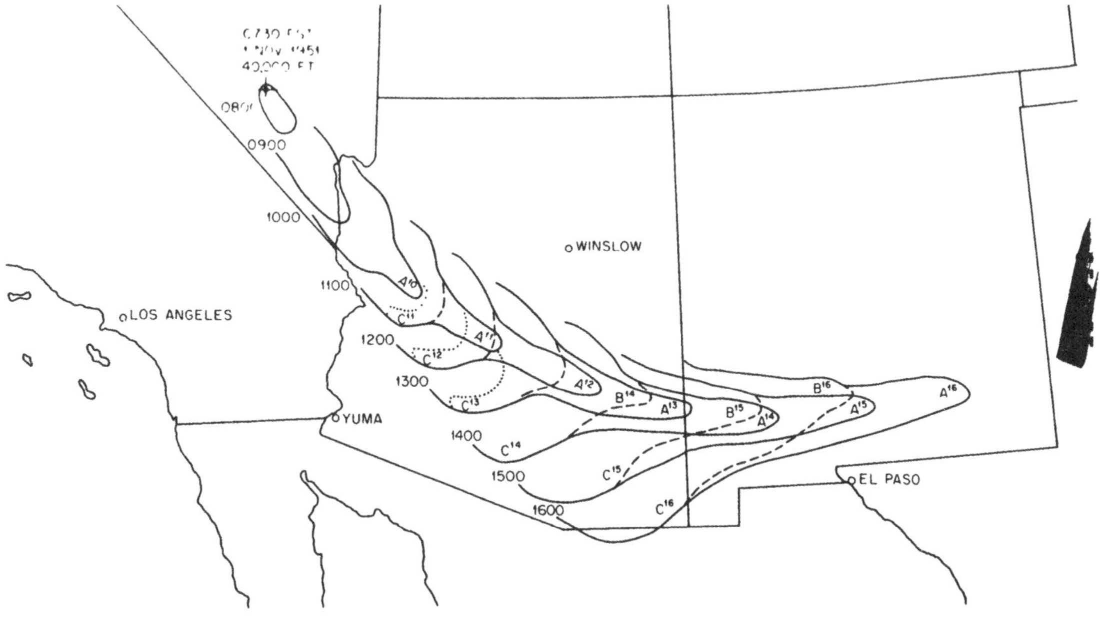

Fig. B.3—Outline of Buster Dog cloud at 1-hr intervals. ——, leading edge of all activity. – – –, leading edge at 18,000 to 25,000 ft. · · · ·, trailing edge. A^{14}, 40,000-ft debris at 1400 PST. B^{14}, 30,000-ft debris at 1400 PST. C^{14}, 20,000-ft debris at 1400 PST. Data by SWC and AWS; analysis by HQ, USAF (AFOAT-1).

Target Nevada

4025th
TEST GROUP
(ATOMIC)
THE END
Produced By
UNITED STATES AIR FORCE
AIR PHOTOGRAPHIC & CHARTING SERVICE
LOOKOUT MOUNTAIN LABORATORY
HOLLYWOOD, CALIFORNIA

SFP-281
(1964)

film does not even mention, let alone display.] The first segment of the film announces the beginning of continental nuclear testing and declares that from here on out every military man in America is in the "business" of atomic warfare; the second segment focuses on overall test operations; the third on allaying fears about radiation among test personnel; the fourth on effects on animals and on atomic cloud tracking and analysis; the fifth on the need for security and secrecy in atomic testing operations; the sixth on crater analysis, fallout tracking, and effects on structures; and the concluding segment on the need for ongoing nuclear testing. The film thus served as an introduction to nuclear testing operations at Nevada. Though tempo rally it is positioned as a documentary—it looks back on a testing operation—it functioned as a means of orienting future test site personnel to the nature of continental atomic testing. The past was to be a preface to future nuclear-testing routines.

Although narrator Hadley doesn't appear on-screen, as he did in *Operation Ivy*, his role in *Military Participation on Buster-Jangle* implicates viewers, addressing them directly from the very first scene. "Wherever you go," he begins, "you are a part of atomic warfare. It involves you personally." Hadley, and the film more broadly, stand in for a military commander briefing servicemen for the work they will soon be supporting or conducting. The film seems intent on addressing its military audience as personally as possible, as it is scaled to the individual human form. On-screen, instead of the massive cables laid by heavy machinery and scores of shirtless men featured in the Pacific films, we see a collection of uniformed individuals setting up a variety of human-scale instruments and objects to be subjected to atomic blast. One instrumented object, we are told, stands in for a human torso; we also see a human-sized foxhole fitted with instruments. Thus, far more than asking viewers to see the Bomb dropped on their country, the film invites its military viewers to imagine their own bodies in the spaces of these atomic bomb drops.

If directness of address and attention to individual vulnerability brought fears to light, *Military Participation on Buster-Jangle* answered such fears through an emphasis not on a big America engaged in "big science," but on a mode of discipline available to individuals and organizations alike—that of "routine." The film emphasizes routine in two principle ways. First, the testing operation is presented as a well-organized "machine." Throughout the film, operational order and efficiency is stressed: Buster-Jangle is presented as a coordinated collective effort making use of both the best in science and technology and the best in scientific minds and military men. Throughout the film viewers see staged military and scientific briefings, where military and scientific men—or men playing military and scientific men—act out official meetings for the camera. Second, Hadley stresses the "ongoing" nature of continental nuclear testing. We hear that "for the first time, we in the military have a full-scale program" of regular ongoing tests and not just one-offs. "This is a continuing job, this business of atomic testing," Hadley concludes. "The scientist never stops in his search for more efficient use of our stockpile material." So too, "We must never stop in our work for more complete knowledge about the effects of atomic weapons. We don't dare." Of course, military men would have been quite familiar with routine as an answer to disorder and danger. The effect of *Military Participation on Buster-Jangle* was to show that these new threats could still be met using traditional military methods and discipline. To see a soldier going to a nuclear war on-screen in the same familiar fatigues, responding to new threats with the same routines, all on a familiar "homeland," is to see a dangerous technology neutralized.

But even if the future means routine atomic testing, danger still lurks. However, danger in the film comes not from America's atomic testing operation itself, at least not directly so. Rather, danger comes from two forms of border crossing. The first is the weather: though fallout is never overtly presented as a great danger in the film, *Military Participation on Buster-Jangle* does pay special attention to the importance of monitoring wind and weather patterns. Meteorologists have a special screen presence in the film, capable, as they are presented, not of controlling the weather but of judging it so as to assure "controlled" atomic experiments, such that fallout did not cross borders into populated areas. [In fact, it did.]

Another form of border crossing gets even more screen attention: espionage. The segment of the film devoted to security and secrecy features two men in a military office [actors or actual military men, it is not clear—Lookout Mountain films rarely credited the on-screen personalities] reviewing the security procedures in place for Buster-Jangle. The officer reports to his commander that he has checked with the FBI:

> OFFICER: There are still five known members of the Communist Party operating in our area, Zone 1, at the present time. They are the same five we had for quite some time. They are still underground and still no indication of any organized meetings.
>
> COMMANDER [*pointing to a map on his wall*]: Along the Mexican border there doesn't appear to be any movement of subversive elements into the country.

Still, the commander concludes, there are two members of the Communist Party at a hotel in Las Vegas, and they could represent a threat to national security. He assures his subordinate that they have been placed under "twenty-four-hour surveillance." So the segment replaces fear of nuclear technology with fear that the technology will fall into the wrong hands. By making espionage a greater threat than the bomb itself, the script makes a strong case for keeping such toxic tests on the homeland. In addition, by reasserting the role of the border in defining territory and homeland, the script implicitly achieves further distance from any possibility that others, such as the Shoshone, might have legal claims over the land being wrecked by the national security state.

Indeed, *Military Participation on Buster-Jangle* makes sovereignty a means of assuaging the soldier's fear of bodily harm, while displacing worry about testing in such proximity to civilian populations. Style is key to this effort. Where *Military Participation on Buster-Jangle* falters through a less-unified script or lackluster acting, the national dramas of nuclear danger and foreign espionage compensate. The mock briefings, which offer a dramatic look into the inner workings of the nuclearized national security state, function as causal mechanisms in the plot—the plot is essentially bureaucratic, rooted in the rhetoric of institutional procedures—and as didactic mechanisms: *this is how a nuclear test works*.[25] Meanwhile, the strong if drawn-out "deadline" structure of the film [a term borrowed from Bordwell's analysis of classical Hollywood cinema] functions to provide a punctuated and linear temporal structure for the plot, one built around a series of cinematic crescendos, blast shots. If atomic testing is to be routine, suggests *Military Participation on Buster-Jangle*, at least the routines are full of climaxes. Lookout Mountain thus met the needs of a newly routine military practice with routine stylistic elements of Hollywood cinema.

The next Lookout Mountain Nevada film could have been titled "How I Learned to Stop Worrying and Love the Bomb." As part of ongoing nuclear tests in Nevada, the Defense Department instituted a series of troop exercises and maneuvers meant to refine tactics for the nuclear battlefield. Beginning with Buster-Jangle, these so-called Desert Rock exercises meant that thousands of military men would be directly involved in and exposed to continental nuclear testing during the 1950s. More than a few were nervous: Would they be blinded? Deafened? Would their testicles be irradiated and their semen poisoned? Such were the concerns radiating through the military barracks in and around the Nevada Proving Grounds.

These were the questions Lookout Mountain's 1952 *Military Participation on Tumbler/Snapper* sought to answer for military personnel. Even as the atomic testing program in Nevada became more "routine," the official organizers of the tests remained reactive, constantly trying to assuage not just public anxieties, but those of test-site workers. *Military Participation on Tumbler/Snapper* works extra hard to try to convince its audience that "The Nevada Proving Ground is beginning to be an old stomping ground for a lot of us in the services." As Hadley, again the narrator, says, "The armed forces machine for atomic testing was better oiled than ever before." As in the film for Buster-Jangle, the Tumbler-Snapper film still assumes a military audience, and the narrator's script addresses the viewer directly. But here the narrative approach is less dramatic and more documentary: we see few scenes filmed on set with actors; there is no scripted dialogue; and the test events are explicitly presented as having already concluded, with information on the effects already gathered. The implied viewers of *Military Participation on Tumbler/Snapper* are military men being brought up to speed on Nevada's nuclear tests in order to not only participate in future tests, but be brought into what the film describes as "the order of the mushroom." As with the Buster-Jangle film, *Military Participation on Tumbler/Snapper* strives to assuage fears—indeed, where the former film only showed proxies for humans exposed to atomic effects, here we see actual living soldiers hunkered down to endure the blasts. But again the message is that there is nothing to worry about. We have not only routines to keep us steady, but knowledge.

In *Military Participation on Tumbler/Snapper*, Lookout Mountain returned to the bookish prop they had used in *Operation Sandstone*, beginning with the image of a man in a white starched shirt and blue tie pulling a book off the shelf with the same name as the film. There are two significant differences, however, between the book in *Operation Sandstone* and that in *Military Participation on Tumbler/Snapper*. First, the book in the former looks very much like a picture book, whereas the book in the latter looks like a large bound volume of documents. Second, *Military Participation on Tumbler/Snapper* takes great care to show that the book is locked in a large vault—the door to which is no doubt the door to one of the film vaults at the Wonderland Avenue facility—labeled, for the purposes of the film, "Restricted Area: Document Vault."

These two differences indeed are thick with significance: at Sandstone, set as it was against the backdrop of Crossroads, images were at the heart of the basic documentary logic of American nuclear testing, and secrecy essentially a means of regulating their production. With the "routine" Nevada tests, however, bureaucratic actors took center stage, complete with their volumes upon volumes of written documents, and secrecy shifted from the regulation of production—bureaucracies thrive on the production of texts—to the regulation of circulation. The vault thus becomes a door to the secretive new world of perpetual "routine" nuclear testing for the original, cleared audiences of *Military Participation on Tumbler/Snapper*.

Whereas the Buster-Jangle film turned on images of fireballs and mushroom clouds, *Military Participation on Tumbler/Snapper* relies for its basic structure on the book, bound and illustrated, to document the tests viewers are watching unfold on-screen. At transition points in the film, a bureaucrat, standing in the secure vault, is shown leafing through the book. The book structures the film's reporting, as each return to a hand turning pages advances the film's narrative on a linear path. As a chronicle of the past, the book also reassures viewers that all went

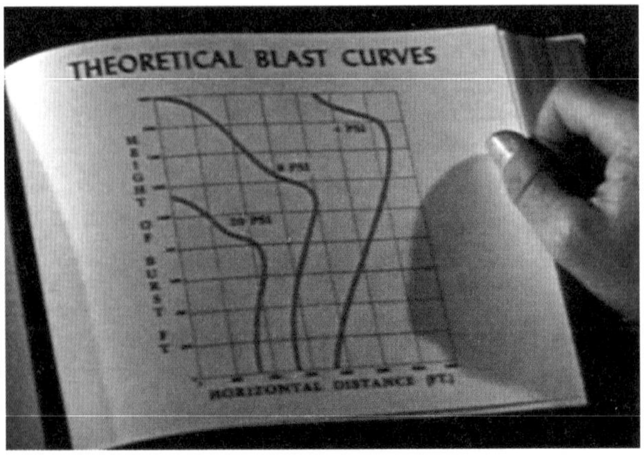

Film Indexing and Cataloguing

Lookout Mountain Laboratory's Laurel Canyon facility was not just a film production site, it was a storage site. Storage of classified film and photographs of nuclear tests formed a core part of the outfit's mission from the beginning. It served as a clearinghouse, indeed for many *the* clearinghouse, for atomic imagery.

In the early years of its operation, cataloging and indexing photographs and film footage was the responsibility of the "depository" branch of the unit, the staff of which spent each working day reviewing, classifying, and storing visual material according to its proper security clearance and subject matter. As the quantity of photographs and film footage grew, the task became increasingly unwieldy. Lookout Mountain therefore developed new routines and protocols that shifted some of the burden for the work of identification and classification to its cameramen. Cameramen were given ever more detailed caption sheets to complete while in the field. Whereas in 1948 they took with them caption sheets with eight fields for information about each reel they shot, by 1962 the caption sheets contained seventeen such fields, such that Lookout Mountain photographers reported spending as much time typing up caption sheets as shooting images.

These caption sheets were made the basis of a cataloging system at Lookout Mountain that helped the unit fulfill "utilization" requests from industry and government production houses who wanted to draw on Lookout Mountain's vast storehouse of images for everything from Department of Defense technical briefings to Hollywood feature films. Indeed, in the 1960s the "depository" branch was renamed the "utilization" branch, which could fulfill upward of 450 requests each month.

The utilization branch's efficient cataloging and storage processes made Lookout Mountain all the more valuable to the Department of Defense during the Vietnam War, when thousands of feet of combat photography were processed each month. During the busiest years of the war, nearly the entire staff at the Laurel Canyon facility was devoted to the task of intake, review, storage, and distribution of Vietnam film footage.

well with the test series. It assures viewers of a kind of safety by eliminating suspense. For if the book is safely bound and shelved, must not the tests have been a success?

The book prop and structure also emphasize the importance of the tests for producing *information*, shelved among other books in a vault, compiling the inscription of data. A heavy reliance in the film on charts, graphs, technical illustrations, and maps drives this point home, with more time given to measurement and meteorology than to mushroom clouds. Testing in this new routinized regime, the film suggests, is less about the money shot, the big bang, the atomic spectacle everyone was hankering to see at Ranger and Buster-Jangle, and more about understanding and controlling atomic effects. Indeed, in a striking departure from any of Lookout Mountain's prior nuclear test films, the first fireball shot shown on-screen comes in a rapid four-square sequence. Four shots, rather than one single shot, fill the screen in succession. This and later detonations in the film take place without an orchestral score, playing instead against the sound of the explosion and the voice of Hadley relating the statistics of each yield.

"The problems with working with high levels of radioactivity are pretty well understood by this time," Hadley claims. But what is not well understood, he adds, is why atomic bursts are not always as destructive as predicted. *Military Participation on Tumbler/Snapper* devotes a great deal of screen time to outlining this mystery: "For unknown reasons nuclear weapons were producing in some cases only about one-third the blast pressure that we had expected. This raised some very sobering questions in the minds of military planners. We knew the energy was there. But something somewhere along the line was happening to lessen or cushion the full effect of the blast. . . . Getting the answers was our priority objective on Tumbler."

Hence, the film walks viewers through an elaborate narration focused on getting to the bottom of the problem of blast-pressure prediction. The on-screen bureaucrat turns the pages of the film's book prop to take viewers to graphs of "theoretical blast curves." An elaborate and colorful animation sequence is used to explain to audiences the nature of the "incident shock wave" and the "amplification" of blasts. Hypotheses are then offered, also in animated form, as to what might be happening to mitigate the force of the blasts. The Tumbler experiment is then described, focusing especially on the myriad of instruments that will be used to gauge blast pressure. Two atomic detonations are then shown, and the data from the blasts is discussed—again using graphs and animation. Hadley then announces a finding, the discovery of a "precursor pressure wave" that may account for the mitigation of blast effects. The precursor wave is visualized by means of animation. But, Hadley concludes, "We'll have to study, analyze, and cross-check and then return to our outdoor laboratory again to proof-test our findings."

This roughly twenty-minute segment of the film is a remarkable example of a kind of midcentury "scientific thinking," worthy of the classroom, and was clearly shaped by the Los Alamos scientists with whom Lookout Mountain was working so closely in crafting their scripts. But it is also notable for the way in which it shifts the focus of the dangers of atomic blasts away from fallout, a matter of the weather, and radioactivity, which was positioned as "pretty well understood." "Military effects" in the film are oriented away from radiation to the conventional military concern with ballistics and blast effects on personnel and equipment. Fighting an atomic war, the film subtly suggests, is really no different from fighting a conventional war, except for the scale of the bombs.

Therefore, the remainder of *Military Participation on Tumbler/Snapper* focuses on the effects of nuclear blasts on military equipment, structures, and even pine trees. [Military personnel could use trees as cover from the effects of nuclear blasts, or so the film suggests.] Through the tests, Hadley explains, "We set out to broaden the foundation of knowledge on which we can reliably base true participation

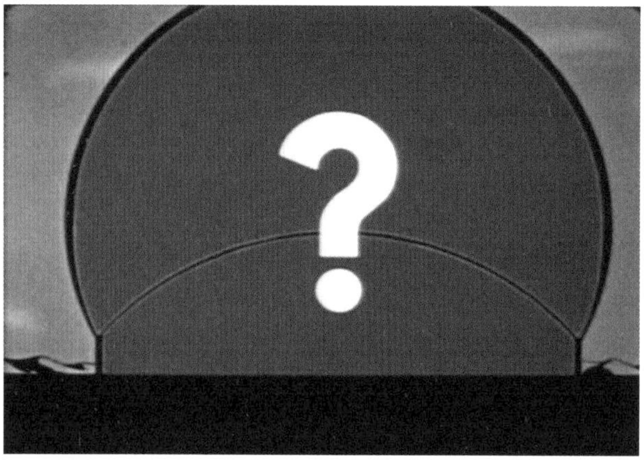

in atomic warfare." With that knowledge in hand and with an arsenal of atomic bombs, the United States military could go about fighting atomic war just as it had fought nonatomic war in the 1940s and was fighting, during the Tumbler-Snapper tests, in the not-yet-atomic war in Korea. Indeed, as the Korean War armistice was not signed until the summer of 1953, when *Military Participation on Tumbler/Snapper* was first screened, it was still within the realm of possibility that atomic weapons would be used in Korea.

Atomic warfare could be standard warfare, the film suggests, except for one barrier: a psychological one. "Throughout much of recorded military history," Hadley explains, as romantic orchestrated music starts to play quietly before scenes of footage of troops in maneuvers on shot day, "it's clear that the effectiveness of troops is geared to their psychological attitude toward the weapons used and situations encountered." The troops on-screen, Hadley explains, have been thoroughly trained on the hazards of atomic warfare and the means of protecting themselves against those hazards. "Like all too many people both in and out of the military, before these men got their assignment for this operation, they had many misconceptions about the bomb and its effects. Some of them thought they would never again be able to have families. Some of them expected to be deaf or blind. Some of them expected to glow for hours after the bomb went off. . . . They had never taken the time or invested the effort to learn the facts about what to do in case of atomic warfare. These men have been indoctrinated in what goes on and what to do."

Moreover, as Hadley goes on to explain, psychiatrists were on hand at the Tumbler-Snapper tests to help the military better understand how to adjust. For "no one can ever fully make you realize what you'll see and feel when you experience an atomic weapon detonated for the first time." In the film's final chapter, we see a screen filled with vulnerable military bodies being subjected to the test's blast. At this point, *Military Participation on Tumbler/Snapper* shifts from addressing "you" to "we." "We made it!" Hadley exclaims. "Three months ago, all the gold in Fort Knox wouldn't have made us want to do it. Now we wouldn't take anything for the experience. We've proved a lot to ourselves and to a lot of other people who need to know it can be done, and we're proud of it." Here the "blank slate" of the desert serves as a staging ground for the accomplishment of a contained mind. "We" stage danger in order to show that it does not affect us. The blast over, the men walk back into the blast zone, not only to collect tests and instruments, but to survey, to touch, to occupy. Two soldiers share a smoke in the shelter of a burned-out jeep. With the right knowledge, "we" can exercise ownership of our psyche the way we routinely exercise occupation of alien lands.

The Nevada Test Site thus appears in *Military Participation at Tumbler/Snapper* as a proving ground less for munitions and more for military and moral mettle. Indeed, in a way

Animation at Lookout Mountain Laboratory

Perched atop Lookout Mountain's Laurel Canyon facility sat a small room with windows on all four sides. Sometimes mistaken for a lookout tower, the space was built to house Lookout Mountain's animation department. Whereas much of Lookout Mountain's work avoided daylight, keeping light-sensitive materials out of the California sun, the animators and artists of Lookout Mountain needed all the light they could get.

Animation was used widely in Lookout Mountain's films, such that by 1954 the unit boasted as many animators as camera operators. With each incoming film project, producers would determine if animation was required, and often it was. Animation was regularly used to help illustrate and explain complex technical and scientific phenomena, from the inner workings of thermonuclear weapons, to the effects of nuclear fallout, to the unique challenges of stratospheric flight, none of which were ready subjects for photography. Far from mere technicians, the animators and artists of Lookout Mountain applied an array of experimental visual strategies to the complex tasks given them.

The department faced heavy work demands and was often behind in its work. At one point, it faced a six-month backlog. Driven by this demand, the department devised some clever ways of saving time, using transparencies, magnets, and models to create the cinematic illusion of motion without the need for animation.

Though not credited in Lookout Mountain films, the animation and art department included on its roster such Disney greats as Jules Engel, Cy Young, Howard Swift, Clifford Devirian Sarkis, and Dan Noonan, known from their work on films such as *Dumbo*, *Fantasia*, and *Snow White and the Seven Dwarfs*. The work of Lookout Mountain's animation department would have broad influence across the animation industry in Hollywood and beyond.

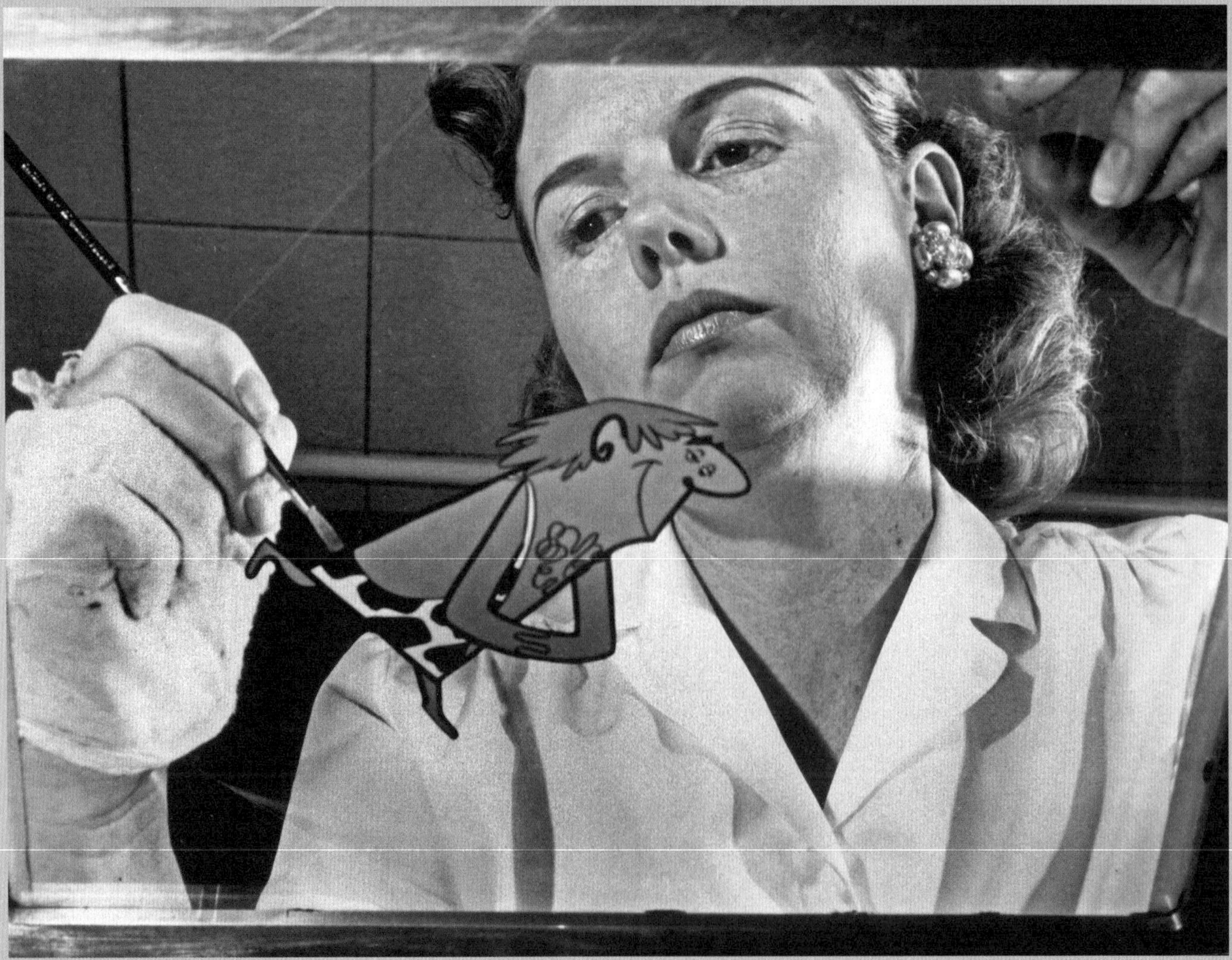

that the Pacific never would be, the Nevada Test Site was for the armed forces a stage for rehearsing the feasibility of atomic warfare as a mode of standard warfare. While deterrence was ascending to the status of grand strategy, attempts to imagine atomic warfare as conventional warfare were being made in Nevada, with Lookout Mountain enlisted in converting those images into stories of success. Whereas for Buster-Jangle, Lookout Mountain called on routine Hollywood styles, for Tumbler-Snapper the writers went to the diegetic style and voice of documentary, supporting this informational approach with rhetorics of scientific communication through animation. The substance of the Tumbler-Snapper test, which treated the bombing of the Nevada desert and Shoshone land as wholly routine, and the irradiation of soldiers as acceptable in the service of information, required a style that emphasized the work as already completed, managed carefully through measured risk, resulting in critical new knowledge that made the whole effort worthwhile.

Both *Military Participation on Buster-Jangle* and *Military Participation on Tumbler/Snapper* were written for the Armed Forces Special Weapons Project, the group charged by the Pentagon with overseeing the military's atomic weapons arsenal. The two films, as with almost all of Lookout Mountain's films, bear the marks of their commissioning agency, especially in their scripts, which were written in consultation with and ultimately approved by the Armed Forces Special Weapons Project. Lookout Mountain could not tell a story that the commissioning agencies did not want told. They *could*, however, amplify that story through the range of Hollywood techniques and styles they had at their disposal, from actors, to props, to sets, to music, to animation, to special effects. Deliberate decisions were made at the studio about staging, lights, and sound, as well as the range of visual effects. Though the two films are quite different, both reflect certain classical Hollywood conventions: strong narrative structures, or plots, built around crises and resolutions; characters with whom the audience members could identify, though the characters were types rather than distinct individuals; the strategic use of spectacle; heavy use of the "deadline," building cinematic tension, climax, and denouement by means of orienting the narration toward marked points in dramatic time; and narration by a well-known Hollywood voice.

Indeed, it was the military much more than the Atomic Energy Commission that wanted to infuse their films with Hollywood structures and styles. Military men, leaders of the Armed Forces Special Weapons Project seemed to believe, would find in the devices and props of Hollywood a means by which to identify with the new routines of continental nuclear testing. The Atomic Energy Commission, however, was much more circumspect about looking too "Hollywood." A "civilian" agency concerned not with assuaging the fears of servicemen but the concerns of citizens, the Atomic Energy Commission preferred, when possible, to avoid detailed discussions of America's nuclear weapons activities at all. But when they were forced to, they, like the Federal Civil Defense Administration, preferred "informational" films relatively free of Hollywood devices.

Still, the Atomic Energy Commission would give the Hollywood style one good shot. In 1953 the commission called on Lookout Mountain to make a film, *Why Nevada?*, eventually retitled before its release as *Atomic Tests in Nevada: The Story of AEC's Continental Proving Ground*. The Atomic Energy Commission wanted a twenty-eight-minute, color, "interesting documentary" to justify continental nuclear testing to American publics [something they had failed to do in any deliberate manner when the Nevada Test Site was commissioned in the first place], and to argue for the commission's priority on public safety.[26]

In April 1953, Lookout Mountain forwarded an initial script of *Why Nevada?* to Washington for approval. But the Atomic Energy Commission wanted to talk things over, sending Ned Trampell, the special assistant to the general manager of the commission, to Los Angeles to relate to Lookout Mountain's writers the "policy and feelings" of the commission about the project.[27] After Trampell left, a new shooting script was drafted, sent to Washington for review, and approved with minor changes. In the late summer of 1953, Lookout Mountain sent a camera crew to St. George, Utah, to shoot footage for the film. A picturesque and relatively well-off town, St. George was chosen by the scriptwriters, in consultation with the Atomic Energy Commission, as the basis for the film in order to feature the safety of continental testing for nearby communities. [In fact, as would become public a decade later, the residents of St. George suffered significant health consequences from the Nevada tests.] Lookout Mountain's crew took cameras, but no microphones, as they were there only to gather footage of the people of St. George out and about. They spent nearly three weeks in the community, returning to Los Angeles with ample film footage, which was quickly processed only to be put on the shelf while Atomic Energy Commission officials fretted further about what exactly they wanted the film to be about. In mid-November, another commission official, Edwin Wilber, visited Lookout Mountain to help oversee the film's production. But Alvin Graves, test director at Los Alamos, Morse Salisbury, information officer at the commission, and Ned Trampell could not fully settle on what they wanted to say in the film, so production was further delayed.[28]

In the winter of 1954, as the project approached its one-year anniversary, the Department of Defense grew interested in the film. They wanted Americans to understand how crucial the Nevada tests were to weapons development, and in turn, how crucial weapons development was to national security. Meanwhile, the Atomic Energy Commission asked that the topics addressed in the film be expanded to include not only weapons development and national security, but also fallout, the medical aspects of radiation, the effects of detonations on weather, and the relationship of one test series to the next. An exasperated writer at Lookout Mountain wrote that while the interest of Defense in the project was "gratifying," it had "presented a dilemma to LML." The original charge was more than enough to fill the designated twenty-eight-minute movie, he explained.[29] Lookout Mountain's directors and writers eventually persuaded Defense and the Atomic Energy Commission of the limits of the project, and they were permitted to proceed with the original project with only minimal modifications.[30]

The result was a twenty-five-minute color film, once again narrated offscreen by Hadley. The film outlined the whys and hows of Nevada nuclear testing, focusing especially on the questions of radiation and weapons development. The film was documentary in style in that it had a narrator and relatively little diegetic sound. Yet its opening and closing were strongly styled according to Hollywood idioms: the serif script title screens appear against the sonic backdrop of orchestrated dramatic music.

The opening scene features a quiet town, St. George, with townspeople going about their early-morning business; a flash is seen in the sky above a church steeple, and people return to their business. The narrator states, "That great flash in [the] western sky. An atomic bomb at the Nevada Test Site one-hundred-and-forty miles to the west. But it's old stuff to St. George. Routine. They've seen a lot of them ever since 1951. Nothing to get excited about anymore." Not even fallout is worth getting excited about: when a radio announcer breaks in with an emergency bulletin announcing that fallout from the Nevada Test Site is heading in the direction of St. George, the people simply obey what the radio announcer describes as "routine Atomic Energy Commission safety procedure" and go inside until the all-clear signal is given.

This vignette of life in an atomic city begs the question, at least in the film, why the hassle? Why continental testing in the first place? Why not limit it to the far-off Pacific? *Atomic Tests in Nevada* pushes hard at this point: "We need *both* testing areas," the narrator insists. While weapons of "tremendous strength" are tested in the Pacific, "smaller" weapons are tested in

Nevada. If these smaller weapons had to be proved in the Pacific, Hadley argues, it would add months to the whole process. However, in Nevada—but a "backyard workshop" and "some of the loneliest acres the world has ever seen"—scientists can "conduct a test on one day and return to their laboratories on the next to start evaluating results immediately." The speed and efficiency of continental testing, the film argues as it visually depicts and narratively explains basic operations at the test site, have put the United States in a position to have a "family of weapons": big bombs for bombers, small bombs for jet fighters, and atomic artillery shells for infantry (here the famous "Grable" artillery atomic shot at Nevada is shown).

But what of fallout? The most striking feature of *Atomic Tests in Nevada*, given that by the time of the production of the film the United States had compiled nearly ten years of data about fallout effects, is that the film goes to great lengths to minimize its dangers, arguing explicitly, "Radioactive fallout beyond several miles from the test site has not been known to be serious." Why were the people of St. George asked to take shelter, then, the narrator asks? "For a very simple reason: the Atomic Energy Commission doesn't take chances on safety." Whereas science, the film argues, conclusively shows that the effects of fallout are negligible for people more than several miles from a test shot, it is still good "common sense" to take precautions. Thus, *Atomic Tests in Nevada* culminates in an image of a mushroom cloud climbing its way up into the desert sky over Nevada, set to a romantic orchestral score. Far from a danger to the American people, the film asserts, "the towering cloud of the atomic age is a symbol of strength, of defense, of security for freedom loving people everywhere, people who want peace."

In her work on this and other desert test films, Susan Courtney not only reads *Atomic Tests in Nevada* as a direct response to concerns about real fallout events already experienced by citizens of St. George, but points to how the producers at Lookout Mountain turned to the cinematic conventions of the western to help mediate the controversial questions surrounding radiation. Indeed, as soon as the narrator voices the questions of St. George's residents about why testing on "their" landscape and backyard is necessary, we receive a visual answer in a scene remarkably reminiscent of the opening scene of *The Searchers*, filmed contemporaneously with *Atomic Tests in Nevada* by Lookout Mountain's friend and occasional collaborator John Ford.[31] In both films, a woman stands silhouetted in her doorway, looking out at the desert landscape beyond. And in both cases, Courtney argues, viewers are invited to identify with the woman and "to patiently stand by ['indoors'] and do their best to shield themselves from whatever dangers might threaten from without, while men off screen—somewhere out there in that exceptional landscape—do what they must in the name of larger causes."[32]

Atomic Tests in Nevada was made at the same time the Federal Civil Defense Administration commissioned Lookout Mountain Laboratory to make what turned out to be one

of Lookout Mountain's few civil defense productions, *Let's Face It!* That the two productions happened simultaneously indicates both the differences between the Atomic Energy Commission's and Civil Defense's respective aims, tones, and sensibilities, as well as their near conjunction for a brief period of time in 1953. Whereas *Atomic Tests in Nevada* minimized the effects of fallout, *Let's Face It!* dramatized it. *Let's Face It!*, a thirteen-minute color film, warns Americans of the profound dangers of the "thermonuclear age," especially fallout, and urges citizens to seriously study civil defense measures for the sake of national and personal survival. *Let's Face It!* rings with warning sirens, radio communications, and emergency police actions. It features disaster footage from Kansas tornadoes to Hiroshima and Nagasaki to America's nuclear test sites. It even goes so far as to suggest that the United States might begin "constructing a complete city at our Nevada proving ground" and then "exploding a nuclear bomb over it." Here Lookout Mountain superimposed the outlines of an American city on actual footage of a Nevada atomic blast, such that the mushroom cloud rises above it and the city disappears. However, such a full-scale project, *Let's Face It!* concedes, "is not possible"; hence makeshift, sample structures were built in Nevada, the narrator explains. *Let's Face It!* then picks up the footage used in *Military Participation on Tumbler/Snapper* and *Atomic Tests in Nevada* of the military and civil-effects tests at Tumbler-Snapper. Whereas the latter films took a studied approach to the effects tests, *Let's Face It!* breaks into a rapid sequence of the footage culminating in high-speed camera shots of domestic structures carried into nothingness by atomic fire.

Lookout Mountain would never again make such a staccato spectacle. Though it was the Nevada Test Site's main photographic operation, and though footage from its cameras would be used in numerous civil defense films, after *Let's Face It!* the studio did relatively little direct work for the Federal Civil Defense Administration. The Atomic Energy Commission and the

Department of Defense, via the Air Force, were its main clients, while Civil Defense couldn't seem to get a foothold in the Hollywood studio.

At the same time, Lookout Mountain would never again make such a dramatized film as *Atomic Tests in Nevada* for the Atomic Energy Commission. To the contrary, in subsequent years when the commission came knocking, they would ask for the opposite of drama, especially with their public films. For example, when the Atomic Energy Commission asked Lookout Mountain to make a film on an atomic reactor for display at the 1955 "Atoms for Peace" conference in Geneva, Lookout Mountain made the utmost effort to keep it from having anything in it that smacked of Hollywood. Simply called *Borax*, the film was projected in black and white as an unseen deadpan narrator explained the technical processes of nuclear reactors using what look like chalk diagrams rather than Lookout Mountain's typical vividly colored animations. "The picture was designed to be a technical program report rather than a smooth scientific propaganda tool," Lookout Mountain explained. "In a sense the [*sic*] LML had to underplay its production capability in order not to put the US in the position of putting out preplanned propaganda." Moreover, the Air Force, let alone Lookout Mountain, could not even claim credit on-screen for the film when it was shown in Geneva. The documentary, stripped of every Hollywood cinematic signature, was reported by Lookout Mountain to be "a complete success from the AEC–State Department viewpoint."[33]

Lookout Mountain did the same with subsequent films made for the Atomic Energy Commission on Nevada tests. Whereas both classified and public films made for defense agencies drew on Hollywood structures and styles to drive the message, Lookout Mountain's nuclear test films for the commission tended to stick closely to the unstylized documentary or report. This is not to say that they lacked strong rhetorical aims. To the contrary, the Atomic Energy Commission relied on Lookout Mountain to perpetuate the argument that the Nevada Test Site was essential to the progress of atomic science, and that dropping nuclear bombs on American soil posed no significant risk to the people of the nation.[34] Nor did these deadpan documentary films lack cinematic highlights: fireballs and mushroom clouds took up disproportionate screen time relative to their "informational" content. But with few exceptions, such as the unit's employment of CinemaScope technology at an early stage to capture imagery of breathtaking detail, no one watching the films Lookout Mountain made for the Atomic Energy Commission would mistake them for films of high production quality.

This was the way it was supposed to be. At Lookout Mountain, style was always strategic. Though embedded in Hollywood and able to achieve a production quality on par with neighboring studios, Lookout Mountain Laboratory had no economic motive, let alone an artistic one, to perpetuate Hollywood conventions. They could use them at will and then discard them if they did not serve the client. The film medium was for Lookout Mountain what the Nevada desert was for the national security state, a blank slate. Other industrial or "nontheatrical" film studios, we learn from film scholars, tended to rely on established and repeatable stylistic formulas in the interest of efficiency. Though Lookout Mountain certainly availed themselves of such routines in the interest of efficiency, they could, and did, dramatically adjust their filmmaking approaches according to rhetorical needs. We have seen how the desert offered not only a "nonplace" suitable for spoiling, but also a range of available aesthetic tropes and recognizable human conditions for reconfiguring in the staging of story. Likewise, film offered Lookout Mountain a medium for recording and a host of techniques and rhetorics for the strategic application of cinematic art. In the next chapter, we consider just how far Lookout Mountain took the cinematic art, not only deploying different cinematic styles at will toward various types of film production, but also inventing technologies and techniques for a new cinematic subject and purpose: tracking missiles.

we've got to understand just

WHAT WE'RE BUILDING

PHOTO

Chapter Six

THE VECTORS OF AMERICA

Missile Films

Lookout Mountain Laboratory was opened in Hollywood in 1948 to draw on the technical expertise and cultural capital of the greatest moviemaking industry in the world. But Hollywood was more than the capital of moviemaking. As we discussed in chapter 1, it stood in the middle of the world's greatest air-power center, Los Angeles. If World War II vaulted the Air Force into strategic preeminence, postwar independence, and ultimately Cold War supremacy among America's armed forces, then the war also launched Los Angeles into the lead of the "air age." By the end of the war, Los Angeles was home to the "Big Six" aircraft corporations [Douglas, Lockheed, Vultee, North America, Vega, and Northrop] as well as Caltech and its Jet Propulsion Laboratory. Moreover, just after the war Air Force Gen. "Hap" Arnold and Douglas Air Corporation collaborated to create Project RAND, which would go on to be the most significant military think tank in US history, drawing on operations research, systems theory, astrophysics, and a host of engineering schemas to propel the United States not just into the air age, but into the age of mutually assured destruction.

The consequences of this conjunction of postwar air power with Hollywood's cultural power would be more than a little ironic for Lookout Mountain Laboratory. While from its inception Lookout Mountain styled itself as a comprehensive, Hollywood-style film studio, its most lasting cultural legacy would come in the form of reel upon reel of documentary "footage" of not just nuclear detonations but air-age airplane exercises and missile tests. While Lookout Mountain's Hollywood-esque films such as *Operation Ivy* and *Military Participation on Buster-Jangle* sit today as relics from a distant cultural past, remote in time and also in style and sensibilities, the raw footage of mushroom clouds, fighter jet acrobatics, missile launches, and space techno-adventures continue not only to reappear but to reverberate in everything from images of North Korean nuclear tests to wars in the Middle East to SpaceX launches.

In other words, it was Lookout Mountain's "scientific" and "technical" photographic work more than its finished film productions that represent its most lasting and truly innovative contribution to Cold War visual culture and beyond.

In this chapter, we look at the operational side of Lookout Mountain's technical photographic work. In fact, the great majority of the work Lookout Mountain did was never destined for finished cinema productions. Rather, it was raw footage of Air Force activities, especially technical activities, that took up most of its energies: nuclear detonations, test flights, silo construction, high-speed vehicle tests, biological and chemical warfare exercises, and above all missile launches. Lookout Mountain played an indispensable engineering role in the missile-development programs of the late 1950s and 1960s, a role that would then help make possible America's outer space adventures. They learned to expertly track missile launches—no easy technical feat, as things turned out—providing engineers with what was often the only means of diagnosing missile mechanics and mishaps. This documentary and diagnostic work, in turn, provided the Air Force with vaults of film footage of technological spectacles, procedures, and performances that circulated not only among engineers, but among operators, airmen, and various decision makers in the form of training films and film reports that explained the what, how, and why of testing and experimentation. Some of this footage ended up on television or in Hollywood films, creating a repertoire of Air Force–born visual tropes for the air age in Cold War culture.

The air age was more than a fact of flight. It was an idea, and even a conviction, profoundly reorienting America's relationship to the world. For the Air Force and its strategic advisers at MIT, RAND, and elsewhere, the air atomic age called for two complementary projects: a "defensive" project meant to detect and, if possible, shoot down enemy invaders, and an "offensive" project meant to ensure a devastating and massive retaliatory attack on the enemy. With regard to the former, beginning in the early 1950s the Air Force led a large-scale attempt to engineer the Arctic and parts of the Pacific and Atlantic Oceans to form a defensive, radar-based "electronic fence." At the cost of billions of dollars, they built and ran a network of manned radar stations that spanned from the Aleutian Islands to Greenland to parts of England, and then down the Atlantic and Pacific coasts of the United States. The Distant Early Warning Line [DEW Line], the ocean-based "Texas Towers," and eventually the Ballistic Missile Early Warning System [BMEWS] formed the fence. Wired into the SAGE [Semi-Automatic Ground Environment] system and into NORAD [North American Aerospace Defense Command], the system was less a fence and more a trip wire, meant to trigger a highly automated retaliation system. [See the next chapter for our discussion of radar-defense films.]

But as much as the Air Force invested in detection systems, it also invested in retaliatory technologies, which it justified as deterrent technologies. At first, retaliatory plans consisted exclusively of long-range or medium-long-range bombers dropping megatons of atomic weapons on the Soviet Union, the German Democratic Republic, and other countries within the Soviet orbit. But by the middle of the 1950s, Air Force brass, to the chagrin and objections of bombardiers, began to push intercontinental ballistic missiles [ICBMs] as retaliatory vehicles. By 1960 the United States was moving headlong toward a three-part nuclear deterrent program consisting of bombers, missiles, and submarine-based warheads.

Lookout Mountain documented the rise of the nuclear triad, but missiles took center stage. Their first missile film came as early as 1953. An official report on their work that year obliquely mentions "Project 30-19-53: Secret Film on Guided Missiles."[1] To be sure, in 1953 the Navy, Army, and Air Force were each pursuing missile projects, but in a "confused and confusing array."[2] Missiles, especially long-range ones, presented all sorts of technological challenges, some of which seemed insurmountable in the middle of the 1950s. Moreover, in the Air Force at least, bombers reigned supreme. While some Air Force leadership imagined a future missile-based Air Force, Gen. Curtis Lemay's Strategic Air Command was in full charge of Air Force power and strategy, and for him a nuclear force needed to be a piloted force.[3]

Hence, when not at nuclear tests, Lookout Mountain's photographers spent much of their time in the first half of the 1950s at airfields filming flight tests. The planes more than the pilots were the subjects of their footage, but the footage itself was often edited into short film reports or training films for pilots and their commanders—*here's what plane X can do*, etc. Lookout Mountain's official reports would not mention missiles again until 1956 when they described new work with the Western Development Division of the Air Force's Air Research and Development Command, a project run by Bernard Schriever, the Air Force officer in charge of missile development. Schriever called upon Lookout Mountain to produce "technical reports, engineering in nature," and even invited Lookout Mountain representatives to a conference in the Los Angeles area to demonstrate to defense contractors and armed forces representatives what could be done with different kinds of film and cameras in filming missile launches.[4] Schriever in this sense picked up where Arnold left off. If in World War II Arnold employed Hollywood to project air power, a decade later Schriever turned to Lookout Mountain to fit missiles to the big screen.

But a more important moment in Lookout Mountain's missile work came in the fall of 1956, when a crew from the studio was sent out to film the Air Force's Thunderbird flying troupe. Tracking the Thunderbirds' acrobatics presented severe challenges to the camera operator. To solve the problem, Lookout Mountain's Harold "Hal" Albert repurposed a wartime antiaircraft mount for camerawork. An M-45 gunsight mount was rigged with a camera,

The M-45 Camera Mount

Among Lookout Mountain's most lasting and influential contributions to the nuclear age was the redesign and modification of an M-45 antiaircraft gun turret to serve as a mobile camera tracking mount. Developed to support filming the Air Force Thunderbirds jet demonstration team, the M-45 camera mount would become the workhorse of missile and rocket tracking at Florida's Cape Canaveral and California's Vandenberg Air Force Base.

The M-45 was effective as a camera tracking mount for the same reasons it was effective as a gun mount: observing a subject through mounted binoculars, a gunner or photographer used an electric drive to allow them to rotate and tilt while firing as many as four simultaneous guns or cameras. For Lookout Mountain, the M-45, for example, could be mounted with a 16 mm camera with a wide-angle lens and a 35 mm camera with a telephoto lens. The footage from the former might be used for press releases, while footage from the latter might capture a close-up view of the filmic subject for later technical observation.

The M-45 camera mount was the product of Lookout Mountain's Photo Engineering division, headed by Chief of Operations Hal Albert. Albert first proved the M-45's usefulness beyond Thunderbird exhibitions at Cape Canaveral in 1956. By 1958 it was being used heavily at Vandenberg on missile tests.

For the photographer, the work of keeping the M-45 trained on a missile in flight at great distances was not easy. Indeed, it was downright risky. When a missile blew midair, the cameraman would track the largest fragments all the way down to the ground, even as they sometimes seemed to be headed for his own head!

enabling ground-based camera operators to track the Thunderbird acrobatics through the air.[5] The resulting footage was so striking that Warner Brothers' Mervyn LeRoy got wind of it and requested footage for his 1956 film *Toward the Unknown*. Lookout Mountain in turn made a short film out of the footage and forwarded it to Air Photographic and Charting Service headquarters, where it was passed on to Air Force headquarters in Washington, DC. Headquarters was so impressed with the film that they forwarded it to the Academy of Motion Picture Arts and Sciences, where it earned a nomination, but not a final laurel, in that year's Academy Awards.[6] The film also set the stage for a much bigger prize, one in the annals of missile development. For in these images of Thunderbird airplanes in flight, Air Force brass would see future missiles in flight.

On January 25, 1957, the Air Force was set to launch its first intermediate-range ballistic missile, Thor 101, on a hastily constructed launchpad at Cape Canaveral. Thor 101 was a short-lived missile, but its design was the basis for the Thor missiles stationed in the United Kingdom in 1958 and for a range of subsequent military and space rockets. Much was riding on Thor—in fact, the entire Air Force missile program. In the run-up to launch day, worries were understandably high, especially as the liquid oxygen used to help fuel the rocket was known to be very volatile. Neil Sheehan, in his account of incident, writes:

> But on this day, the fueling process went off without incident. The final steps in the countdown were completed. [Lead engineers] Mettler and Thiel and everyone else in the blockhouse felt their year of toil under unremitting pressure was soon to be rewarded with a ballistic missile sailing downrange across the islands of the Caribbean. "Everything looked just perfect," Mettler remembered. He turned loose the simple computer of the day that controlled the electrical firing sequence to ignite the engine. Roaring flames enveloped the launch pad, thrust built to the lifting point, the steel latch mechanisms holding down the missile were thrown open, and the Thor 101 began to rise. It rose about eighteen inches and then suddenly fell back on the pad. With a deafening blast and shock wave that was felt in the blockhouse, the missile blew up.[7]

The Air Force, of course, wanted answers. So did Douglas Aircraft Company, the primary defense contractor for the Thor missile. For weeks, the engineers struggled to offer them: they combed through wreckage, dug through instrumentation data, rechecked checklists, and reviewed records, but nothing. "Finally," as Sheehan writes, "they turned to examining every photograph and every bit of film that had been taken of the launch." While watching a Douglas Aircraft Company film about the launch, they saw two technicians pulling the knob of the fueling hose through the sand on their way to fuel the rocket. A grain of sand, as things turned out, was enough to cause the liquid oxygen to explode. In an apparent piece of superfluous film footage, the engineers found the answer that had eluded them.[8]

Lookout Mountain had shot the footage in the Douglas Aircraft Company film, having been summoned to Cape Canaveral in the fall of 1956 and told that—despite the Plumbbob nuclear tests in Nevada—the missile program needed top priority. Their mandate was "engineering photography," training their cameras on every technical process, procedure, and phenomenon from the time of mounting the missile on the launchpad to the launch of the missile hundreds of miles into the Caribbean sky. As such, they brought an array of photographic equipment, including their M-45 gun-mount camera bearing a forty-eight-inch focal lens to track the missile far into the sky. Just as they did at the Pacific and Nevada nuclear tests, Lookout Mountain set up several manned camera stations, as well as a network of remotely controlled cameras, allowing them to create a comprehensive visual record of the operation.

Within days of the Thor disaster, Lookout Mountain processed the footage they had shot of the operation and produced a set of film reports, including the promotional film for Douglas Aircraft that the engineers eventually ended up keying in on.[9] In but a week or two, Lookout Mountain had sent the Thor footage and films to the ballistic missile development group. After a bit of a wait, they were notified that their footage had been "extremely valuable" for identifying "equipment failures."[10] That was the end of their missile mission, or so they thought. In fact, the Thor 101 disaster taught engineers far more than the power of a grain of sand: they learned that footage of launches might be the only means of figuring out what went wrong in the case of failure. Film therefore became instrumental to missile development. Lookout Mountain had learned something too: in certain cases, raw footage could do more for the Air Force than finely produced films.

Moreover, Lookout Mountain learned something that must have been unexpected given their experience with nuclear testing. At nuclear tests a fizzle was a fizzle, a dud, and a rather uninteresting photographic subject. But at missile tests the "best" shots, the "money shots" of missile testing, would be of *failures*. If everything went right with the missile, the only parties interested in the footage were Air Force leadership and defense contractors who wanted to promote their achievements. But if things went wrong, as they often did, a whole army of engineers and operators would converge on the film footage.

Lookout Mountain had been sent to Cape Canaveral for the Thor 101 test because they were the most capable of the Air Force's Air Photographic and Charting Service film units. Though the command had a number of other photographic units, Lookout Mountain proved itself over and over again to be the most reliable, flexible, and capacious of the bunch. Nobody could match them, and by the middle of the 1950s, Lookout Mountain started to think none of the Hollywood studios could match them either. Their cameramen, they boasted, were Hollywood veterans and every bit as able as anyone at Warner Brothers or MGM. Their set builders

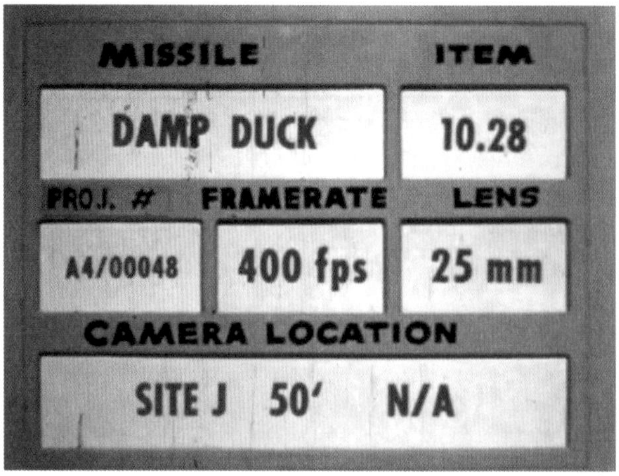

were drawn from the big studios and every bit as skillful. Their animators were drawn from Disney and every bit as artistic.

But in the middle of the 1950s, it was Lookout Mountain's engineering division that began to take center stage at the studio. Though Hollywood-style productions were central to the unit's brand, technical and scientific photography, which had been part of its mission from the early days of Operation Sandstone, took on more and more prominence as films presented as "engineering reports" became a regular part of Lookout Mountain's products. Initially, Lookout Mountain's technical work was focused, quite literally, on instrumentation. Cameras trained on instruments could provide records of gauges, dials, meters, and so on for later review. For more advanced high-speed photography, Lookout Mountain partnered with Los Alamos photographers, or more frequently, with the government contractor EG&G. Founded by MIT's Harold Edgerton and his graduate students, EG&G would provide high-speed photographic documentation of nuclear tests, designing cameras with rates of two to three millionths of a second. Moreover, in the 1950s EG&G would not only shoot pictures; they would design and run the timing and firing systems that detonated the bombs themselves.[11] In the 1950s, Lookout Mountain worked alongside EG&G to photographically instrument America's nuclear testing landscapes and seascapes. [For more on EG&G, see chapter 9].

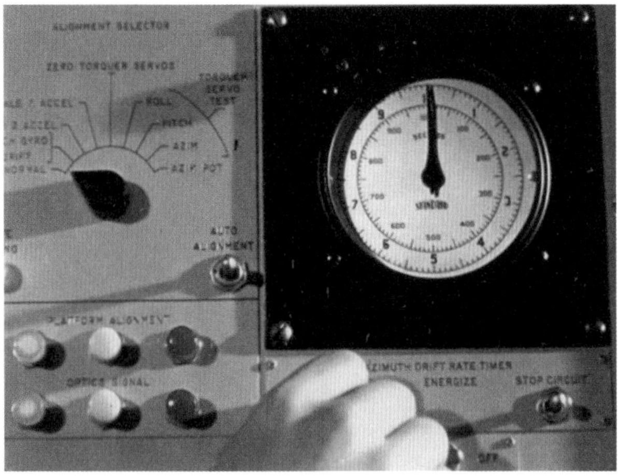

Still, Lookout Mountain Laboratory had to consistently advocate for their engineering and technical missions, faced with an Air Force command that had grown accustomed to seeing them primarily as a Hollywood cinema operation. As we saw in chapter 4, Lookout Mountain had to argue to be stationed with the scientific division of Operation Ivy. In 1954 Lookout Mountain initiated a new "Special Engineering Projects Branch" to help fulfill duties typically carried out by EG&G or Los Alamos. The new group took a lead scientific photography role at the 1954 Operation Wigwam test in the Pacific, designing a remotely controlled system of cameras operating simultaneously in both air and sea. Lookout Mountain's engineering group garnered accolades not only for its Wigwam work, but for special effects innovations, including a device built in the studio to simulate low-level high-speed flight over photographic mosaic models.[12] Nevertheless, in 1955 the Air Force, apparently seeing such work as redundant, removed "instrumentation and analysis photography and time and motion studies" from the unit's stated mission; and the studio was discouraged from pursuing engineering and special effects innovations further. Lookout Mountain's commanders, needless to say, were frustrated. In typically understated fashion, unit commander James P. Warndorf wrote in 1955 of this change, "Thus, an acquired capability that demonstrated its full value . . . was subordinated to a pure documentary effort."[13] Lookout Mountain, it seemed, was destined to be seen as nothing but a Hollywood studio.

The missile race, beginning with that grain of sand at Cape Canaveral, would save Lookout Mountain from such a pure documentary destiny and in fact throw them, more than any other photographic unit in the United States, into engineering photography. On November 16, 1956, as Lookout Mountain photographers were preparing for their voyage to Cape Canaveral for the Thor 101 launch, Eisenhower's defense secretary Charles Wilson transferred 64,000 acres of land at the Army's Camp Cooke to Schriever's Western Development Division for missile testing. Camp Cooke was located on the California coast, about a three-hour drive from Hollywood. Renamed Vandenberg Air Force Base on October 4, 1958, the site would be, along with Cape Canaveral, the preeminent launching pad for America's missiles and space rockets in the years to come.[14] The south-facing Purisma Point at Vandenberg afforded the government two big advantages over Cape Canaveral: it allowed rockets to go into space without crossing land until Antarctica, thus absolving the United States from worries about sovereign airspace; and it was an ideal location for launching objects southward into polar orbit, an orbit that provides worldwide coverage every twenty-four hours, a capacity critical for satellite-based surveillance.[15]

In 1958 Vandenberg would become the operational site of Lookout Mountain's "Operational Location 1," redesignated "Detachment 1" in 1959, and eventually designated the 1369th Photographic Squadron in 1962. The 1369th Photographic Squadron would be the largest of Lookout Mountain's numerous detachments for most of the 1960s, as well as its most transformative. For in the rise of the 1369th, the technical and scientific work at Lookout Mountain Laboratory came to surpass that of its cinematic work in both scale and reputation.

In September 1958 Lookout Mountain sent two officers and thirty-two airmen up the California coast to Vandenberg. The group was put under

the charge of Maj. Daniel A. McGovern, a storied Air Force photographer who had, among other things, served as one of two American combat cameramen to document the effects of the Hiroshima and Nagasaki bombs in the devastated cities.[16] Lookout Mountain was assigned to be the photographic detail to Strategic Air Command's First Missile Division (redesignated First Strategic Aerospace Division on July 21, 1961), which functioned both as an operational missile squadron and the nexus of missile testing and missileer training at Vandenberg. Working alongside America's new missileers, Lookout Mountain's plate was immediately full. "The mission of the unit," they detailed, "includes motion picture coverage of static firings and launches, production of operational film reports, training and safety films and still photography for 1st Missile Division, also technical photography, i.e., engineering sequential, surveillance, documentary motion-picture and still photography of research and development missile launches and documentation of construction progress of systems and equipment installations for the Air Force Ballistic Missile Division and its contractors."[17] They soon wrote of the "unprecedented scale" of their Vandenberg operations, which was saying something given the size of the Pacific tests. The new Vandenberg work was "undoubtedly the most significant in the history of Lookout Mountain Air Force Station," they claimed.[18]

The missile program was indeed gargantuan. Schriever would claim in a Lookout Mountain film that the degree of military, science, university, and industry collaboration in the missile program had "never before [been] equaled in any single program" in US history.[19] Whereas the Manhattan Project at its peak employed around 125,000 people, the missile and space programs would soar into hundreds of thousands of employees, permanently transforming not only the armed forces but also American research universities and defense contractors. That Lookout Mountain felt the effects of this momentous shift in the military-industrial-university complex is therefore no surprise: from 1958 to middle of the 1960s (when the effects of Vietnam kicked in) the unit's time, money, equipment, and energy were increasingly dominated by the work of the First Missile Division at Vandenberg.

On December 16, 1958, the First Missile Division successfully launched a Thor missile.[20] Under the technical supervision of Harold Albert, creator of the M-45 camera mount, Lookout Mountain used fifteen cameras for documentation of the Thor test, and another thirty for technical photography, generating over forty-five thousand feet of color footage of the liftoff. Shortly after the launch, selections from the footage were distributed nationwide for publicity. The rest was stored for the engineers to review on demand. "The success of our technical

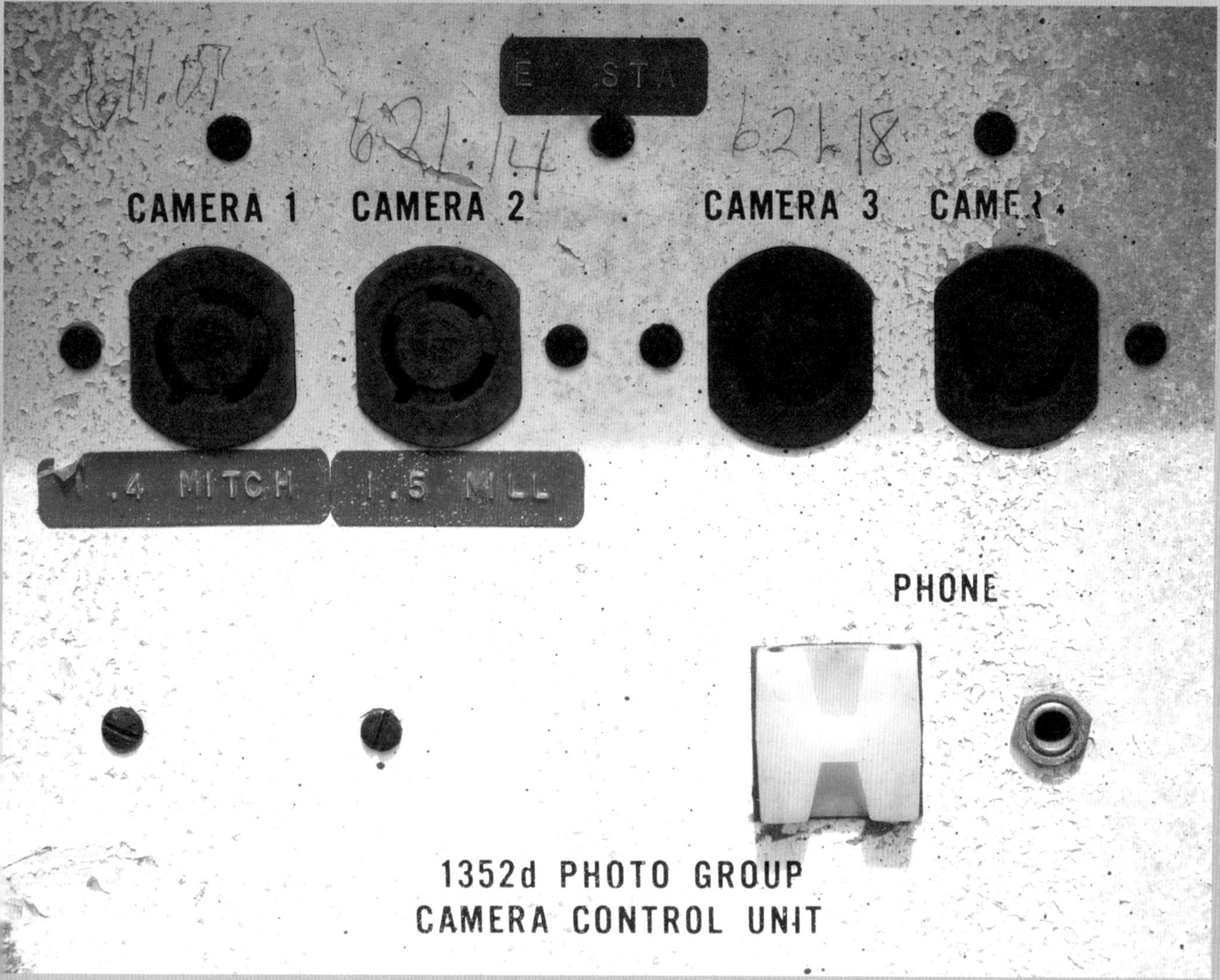

Camera Systems at Vandenberg Air Force Base

The demands of the missile age pushed Lookout Mountain's technicians deep into systems engineering. In the late 1950s and early 1960s, Lookout Mountain's Photo Engineering Division worked on designing and constructing what they described as "complete camera control systems" for missile launchpads. At Vandenberg Air Force Base, the primary test facility for the Western [Missile] Development Division, Lookout Mountain designed and built complex photographic systems that would allow missile engineers to see in fractions of a second each launch, and especially each failed launch, from virtually every visual angle imaginable.

Missile launchpads were rigged with multiple film cameras, several at distances too close for human operators, and others farther off in towers or on M 45 mounts. Operating all these cameras simultaneously required not only networked and centralized control from a blockhouse, but also precise synchronization so that missile technicians could later reconstruct launch events from multiple angles at precise time points.

To make this possible, Lookout Mountain's Photo Engineering Division, led by Charles Bradley, designed a sprawling communication and control system. At the core of this network was a unified timing signal—a regular pulse, amplified across Vandenberg's twenty-two-square-mile facility through underground cables, to which cameras could connect via control boxes distributed across the coastal landscape. Cameras would record this signal on the soundtrack portion of 16 mm, 35 mm, or even 70 mm films of missile launches to aid in later synchronization. These and other ambitious projects led to the redesignation of the Photo Engineering Division of Lookout Mountain as the Photographic Plans and Systems Division in 1964.

Ballistic Missile Development: Program Highlights

THE END
Produced by
UNITED STATES AIR FORCE
Air Photographic and Charting Service
(MATS)
FR-26
1958

FR-26
(1958)

and documentary photography," Lookout Mountain gleefully reported, "established the fact that OL 1 at Vandenberg AFB is there to stay."[21]

In subsequent operations, Lookout Mountain's Vandenberg detachment used up to fifty cameras per launch, capturing each event in a variety of film speeds and formats, ranging from remotely operated pad cameras triggered from bunkers to the M-45 mounts, which typically contained several high-speed scientific cameras as well as a conventional newsreel camera. The operators of these M-45-based tracking cameras had an especially tough job. Not only did they have to track missiles from the launchpad high into the air, but when a missile went bad, they had to track the largest piece of the falling rocket, following it all the way down to when it hit sea or land. (Such tracking shots would give engineers the best chance of figuring out what went wrong.) Sometimes these cameramen found themselves in the path of the fiery danger itself, such that while other missile testing personnel were running for cover, the camera operators were left out in the open, sitting on their M-45 seats like ground-based gunners under aerial attack.[22] Lookout Mountain's cameras also circled launches from the air in planes and surveyed the pad from distant towers or mountain peaks. Finally, there were remote control cameras linked together on a single timing circuit designed by Lookout Mountain's engineering branch. As the launch took place, the circuit emitted a pulse that was recorded on the soundtrack of the film to aid in later synchronization of simultaneous reels shot from different angles.

Work at Vandenberg was hectic, to say the least. In the winter of 1959 demand grew at a rate of over 600 percent in a six-month period.[23] Detachment 1, as they were now called, complained of being "deluged." They had to borrow equipment and personnel from Lookout Mountain's Hollywood facility and appeal to other Air Force photographic groups for help.[24] Meanwhile, the construction of new missile launchpads at Vandenberg was moving at such

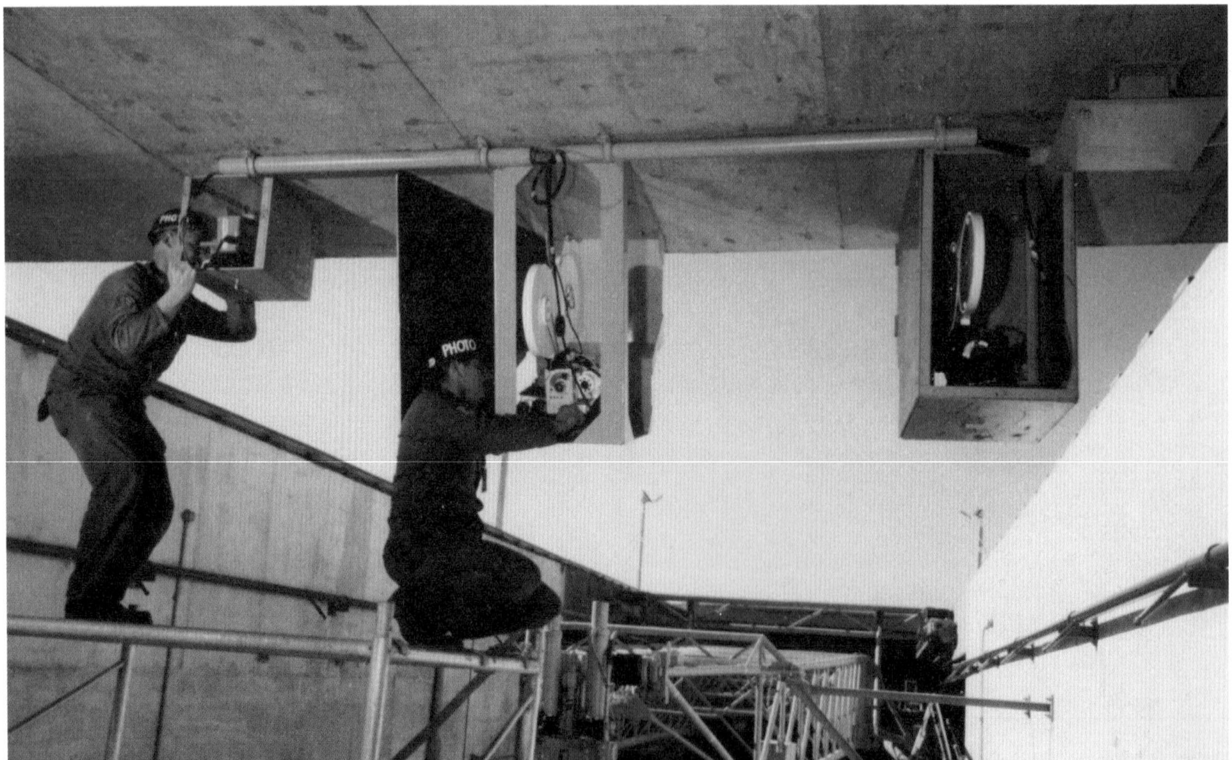

a pace that construction engineers bypassed photographic considerations: consequently, Detachment 1 crews had to string their own cables "along the rolling sand dunes, under culverts, over obstacles of assorted sizes and shape," in order to properly rig their elaborate camera systems.[25] By 1959 Detachment 1 personnel were working fourteen to sixteen hours per day, seven days a week.[26] From July to December 1959 they covered thirteen launches at Vandenberg, processing tens of thousands of feet of footage on-site at Vandenberg and sending select reels down to Lookout Mountain for the rapid production of film reports and film training aids.[27]

In 1960, in order to address their labor shortage, Detachment 1 established a Motion Picture Camera School at Vandenberg, consisting of a twelve-week curriculum to "cross-train" new "teletype operators, jet engine mechanics, personnel specialists, etc." who came to fill staff positions without a background in photography.[28] By the end of 1960, Detachment 1 had nearly two hundred people working as part of its operation, more than the Wonderland Avenue facility ever had.[29] The unit was still "swamped." "The rapid and large changes in requirements," Detachment 1 wrote to their headquarters, "continues to create havoc in the allocation of assigned personnel, equipment, and the requisitioning of supplies. Officers and non-commissioned officers, have had to continue working many additional hours each week to accomplish assigned tasks."[30] Subsequently, talk started about making Detachment 1 its own photographic squadron separate in command, if not in operations, from Lookout Mountain Laboratory. In 1962 Detachment 1 became the 1369th Photographic Squadron, and the unit was authorized to add a hundred more personnel to its staff.[31] That year the unit would cover one hundred launches of Atlas, Thor, and Titan missiles, in addition to a host of other assignments ranging from the "Huntley-Brinkley Report" news footage on the Minuteman missile, to a base visit from President Kennedy, to Cuban Missile Crisis coverage for Strategic Air Command.[32] When 1962 was all

said and done, the 1369th had completed 4,670 still photography projects and 1,915 motion-picture projects, taking three hundred thousand still photos and shooting 2.5 million feet of film.[33]

In the early 1960s, the Vietnam War slowly began to encroach on the 1369th's work. In 1962 a few men were sent from the unit to Vietnam, where they helped a small Lookout Mountain detachment document the US air war there [see chapter 8].[34] But Vietnam's effects were not fully felt until five years later. While in 1967 the 1369th had over four hundred personnel, including 174 civilians, by the end of 1968 its numbers had dwindled to 218 airmen and 154 civilians. The rest had moved to Vietnam.[35]

As in the nuclear tests, cameras served multiple purposes at Vandenberg. They provided data for specialists to process and interpret. They also provided "money shots" for display at Air Force briefings or on the nightly news. But more subtly, the 1369th's cameras helped situate the emerging missile program within a new regime of vision and reason characterized by networked media designed to assure officials and publics alike that even with the missile program's repeated mishaps nothing was being wasted, as even the failures—indeed, especially the failures—were means of progress. As such, the missile program became not only the largest military-industrial complex operation of the Cold War, it became the most productive of visual data.

Two Lookout Mountain films about its Vandenberg activities stress the different ways in which camerawork constituted a guarantee of data plentitude. *Air Force Photographic Highlights*, a Lookout Mountain film produced in the early days of missile testing at Vandenberg, concerns camerawork at one of the first launches at the base. Edited in the style of a report, with little narration or diegetic sound, it shows viewers not only a variety of cameras and cameramen, but a striking sequence within the blockhouse where technicians initiate and monitor the launch. The thirty-second scene features quick cuts that take viewers from operator to operator, with each man monitoring and manipulating his controls, adjusting his glasses, and stealing a quick glance at a countdown clock. Looks of concern and concentration dominate their faces as the launch approaches. In the final seconds, viewers see pairs of eyes filling the screen, askew so as not to be looking at them. But while viewers are led to anticipate an imminent fiery launch, the eyes of the operators are not watching the launchpad at all. Rather, they are watching mediated representations of the rocket's activity conveyed through telemetry and rendered as visual data. Here the camera watches the watchers, so to speak, in order to create the appearance of a comprehensive visual field.

A few years later, in a film called *The Bird Watchers*, Lookout Mountain produced a feature documentary dedicated to Air Force instrumentation and launch photography at Vandenberg. The unnamed narrator of the film explains that missiles—the "birds"—are "so complex that no human could possibly observe every detail of launch and flight." As if to drive home the point, the narrator introduces a nearly two-minute unedited clip of high-speed footage from a camera trained on the engines of a launching missile. As the ignition turns catastrophic, a confusing fire overwhelms the field of vision. Here Lookout Mountain's filmmakers illustrate the inadequacy of the human eye by overwhelming it, much like the fireballs and mushroom clouds of atomic denotations. However, while power and force are as much in play in missile launches as in nuclear explosions, in missile launches it is not the scale of the explosive force that dwarfs the human form as much as the scale of visual information overwhelms human capacities. Indeed, *The Bird Watchers* argues that not even sophisticated telemetry data devices can handle all the data packed into a missile launch. "Sensing devices in the missile send back data to a ground station where it is recorded and analyzed," viewers are told over footage of spinning magnetic tape reels. "But telemetry can only supply part of the necessary evidence. The sharp eye of the camera is needed to complete the record." Hence, cameras come to comprehend the missile event, *The Bird Watchers* claims.

As we have seen, the storage and retrieval of unedited film had always been part of Lookout Mountain's mission, if a quieter part. By 1955 the unit already had a backlog of 17 million feet of film, among which lay countless reels of film no longer needed but that could not be disposed of until someone reviewed it and determined its proper classification. Lookout Mountain struggled with this problem throughout its history. In the middle of the 1950s, they began to add to their staff personnel whose sole job it was to inspect and properly classify the millions of feet of footage sitting in their vaults, but the review-

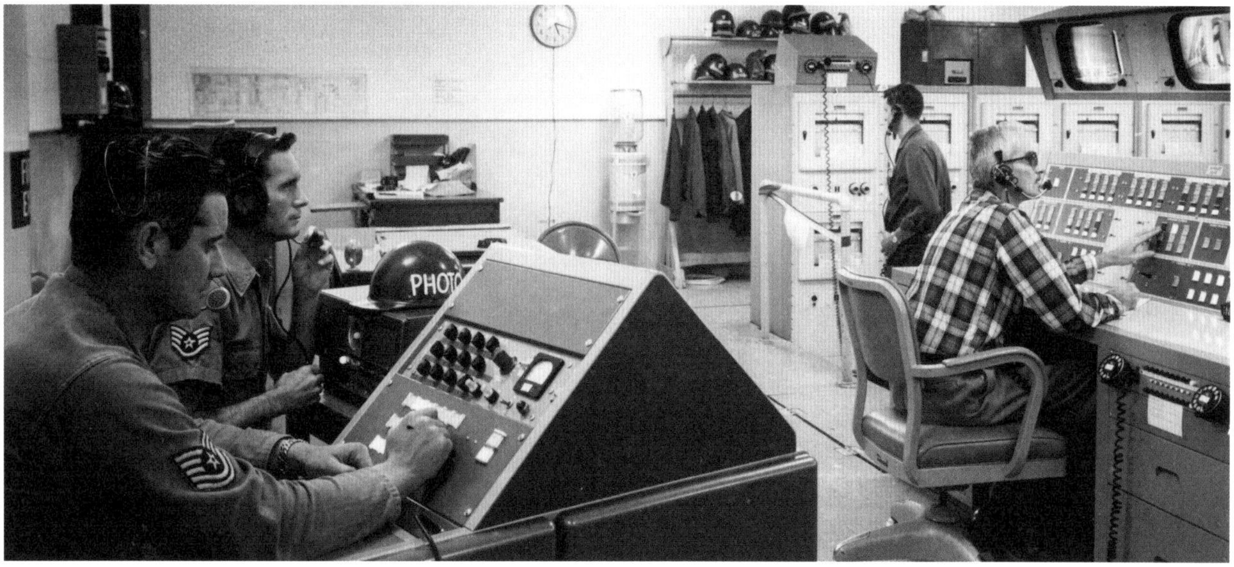

ers never came close to getting through it all. In fact, as we will discuss in chapter 8, when Vietnam heated up, Lookout Mountain was overwhelmed by footage emanating from the air war over Southeast Asia that needed immediate review, leaving years' worth of nuclear and missile test footage stuck in their vaults.

It was the 1369th's work at Vandenberg, before Vietnam, that transformed Lookout Mountain Laboratory into a large-scale information system for the generation, storage, and retrieval of "footage" used in support of military operations. A proliferation of Lookout Mountain detachments followed the establishment of the 1369th, most of which would help cover the United States' expansive missile operations: 1961 saw the establishment of a new Detachment 1, this time at Elmendorf Air Force Base in Alaska, where crews documented Arctic engineering efforts aimed at missile defense (see the following chapter); a Detachment 2 was begun in Colorado Springs in 1959, and by 1964 it was shooting over 250,000 feet of motion-picture film per year for over 125 projects on subjects ranging from NORAD operations to Air Force Academy football games to missile silo construction in the upper plains; Detachment 3 at Hickam Air Force Base in Hawaii, begun in 1961, tracked missiles and documented the recovery of payloads; Detachment 3-1, at Tan Son Nhut Air Base in Vietnam (redesignated Detachment 5 in July 1964), could barely keep up with America's growing Vietnam operations, shooting some 150 productions in 1964 and outfitting fighter planes with automatic cameras to record bombardment footage (see chapter 8); Detachment 3-2 (redesignated Detachment 6 in July 1964) at Yamato Air Station in Japan, a small unit that covered US operations in Japan and Korea, worked on some sixty films per year in the mid-1960s; Detachment 4, based in Los Angeles, was commissioned in 1964 to handle primarily closed-circuit television and video work, most of it covering the missile program; and Detachment 7 at March Air Force Base in California, begun in 1966, was charged with covering Strategic Air Command operations.[36]

Other than the 1369th, Detachment 2 in Colorado Springs and Detachment 3 at Hickam Air Force Base were Lookout Mountain's next biggest missile operations. Detachment 2 was initially established to cover Air Force Academy events, but in 1959 it began documenting the construction and operation of Atlas and Titan missile bases in the western United States. In 1959 alone, they would work in some ten different states, driving approximately 15,000 miles per month.[37] Their work expanded into the central and southwestern United States in

1960. While their workload began to subside in 1961—the construction of missile sites was becoming more standardized to the point that the Air Force determined that only "representative complexes" needed filming—Detachment 2's responsibilities were expanded at some missile sites to include the installation of "photographic optical instrumentation in various launch areas in which power cables, camera positions, and permanent mounting pads for camera stands were required."[38] In fact, Detachment 2 was documenting the transformation of the American West and Midwest into the operational heartland of the strategy of deterrence.

Meanwhile, Detachment 3, located at Hawaii's Hickam Air Force Base, led Lookout Mountain's Oceanic operations into the missile and space age. In addition to missile recovery operations, Detachment 3 handled most of the documentary and news photography work for the Pacific Air Forces, doing work in places such as New Guinea, Indonesia, Thailand, and Vietnam and overseeing subsidiary units at Clark Air Base in the Philippines, Yamato Air Station in Japan, and Tan Son Nhut Air Base in Vietnam. [The latter two units would become stand-alone units by the middle of the 1960s.] While Detachment 3, like the 1369th, specialized in footage used for analysis by engineers and other military personnel, especially footage of missile reentries and recoveries, their most iconic work focused on the water landings of America's astronauts, which was rapidly processed at one of Detachment 3's photo labs in Hawaii, the Philippines, or Japan and sent by air to Los Angeles and New York for broadcasts to national television audiences.[39]

To be sure, "footage" was not all that was being shot in the late 1950s and 1960s by Lookout Mountain and its detachments. Personnel at the Wonderland Avenue facility in Hollywood continued to produce scripted and edited films, dutifully striving to meet the requests of their clients. Yet by the end of 1950s, the cinematically styled nuclear test films of the early 1950s no longer represented the ideal type of filmic production for Lookout Mountain. Rather, the studio tended to adopt a "report" approach nearer to the no-frills documentary style we looked at when discussing the Dominic films in chapter 4. In *Ballistic Missile Development: 1 January 1959*, for example, Maj. Gen. Bernard Schriever is featured at his desk explaining the doctrine of nuclear deterrence: "Our job is to help our country and the whole free world to build deterrent power sufficiently persuasive to prevent outbreaks which would lead to global war, to buy the time for working out conditions of peace."[40] After Schriever's introduction, the film cuts to a footage-filled history of missile development and then to animations describing how missiles work, before cutting back to Vandenberg's and Cape Canaveral's most recent satellite launch, all crowned by President Eisenhower's famous December 18, 1958, Christmas message beamed from a US satellite lifted into space by an Atlas rocket. "For the ballistic missile story there is no end," an offscreen narrator concludes with modest flourish as an image of a rocket ascending into the sky is projected on the screen, "but only a series of new beginnings." *Ballistic Missile Development: 1 January 1959* represents a typical film report made by Lookout Mountain in the late 1950s and early 1960s: introduced by a VIP, heavy in footage, strategically using colorful animation to explain technologies, and narrated by an offscreen voice using a crafted script.

Yet Lookout Mountain still got its fair share of "money shots." Most noteworthy in this regard was their work documenting the activities of NASA. Even as Lookout Mountain was overwhelmed by Vandenberg missile work, its personnel went to Florida, Arizona, Texas, remote parts of California, and the South Pacific on various NASA projects. Lookout Mountain's two most famous subjects during this time were NASA's space monkeys and the Mercury Six astronauts, both of which became part of the new Cold War star system in the 1960s.[41] As significant, if not as iconic, Lookout Mountain built camera pods (see chapter 8) to mount onto Gemini's spacecraft for in-flight photography at speeds exceeding Mach 1.[42] Lookout Mountain shot reels and reels of footage of NASA control-center operations, the raw footage of many NASA film reports and the cinematic inspiration for many subsequent Hollywood films.[43]

Indeed, Lookout Mountain could still pull off highly crafted narrative film productions. Representative here is *The Air Force Missile Mission*, produced in 1959. The film features Jimmy Stewart in what Lookout Mountain's set designers made to look like his home. As the film opens against the music of violins, we see the façade of a Tudor-style home beneath the night sky. All windows are dark except one. The film then cuts to a shot of a bespectacled Stewart, wearing a brown wool sport coat and a matching tie, sitting at his wood desk, book in hand. As the camera pans closer, Stewart looks up and into it, and in a moment of recognition (as if to acknowledge the entrance of a visitor) he exclaims, "Good evening!" "I hope you'll excuse all this," he says, pointing to various papers strewn across his desk, "but I've been taking some time off from my job to look into something important to all of us that seems to be pretty well confused." He continues, "What I mean is missiles, high-performance airplanes: why do we have so many? Why do we need both? Where are we going with all of this? A fellow asked me that question in London not very long ago. You know, it's not a simple question, and I couldn't give him a simple answer. That's the reason for all this (*he looks across his desk*) 'homework' (*he puts his book down*). It seems to me that we've got to understand just what we're building, how each of these missiles and airplanes add to our deterrent strength, and why we've developed them and what they do. Now I'd like to tell you what I wish I had been able to tell that fellow in London not very long ago."

Stewart then turns from his desk to a shelf behind him, on which sits an Oscar award together with models of military airplanes. (Stewart was in fact an avid builder of model airplanes.) He pulls a model of the B-24 bomber off the shelf. ("The kids make them out of plastic nowadays," he says, chagrined. "This is the old-fashioned wood type.") Stewart begins to reminisce about his days flying B-24s in World War II. Footage from World War II bombings cuts in as he explains how fighter pilots and bombardiers worked together in the war. "Working together," we soon learn, is the one lesson from World War II that is still current in the Cold War, only now it is unmanned missiles and manned aircraft that must work in tandem.

Still, the sheer proliferation of missile and airplane types in 1959 is a problem. Stewart reads out the alphabet soup of Air Force aircraft,

Brigadier General James "Jimmy" Stewart

The iconic Jimmy Stewart needs no introduction, except perhaps as an airman and actor in military films. Stewart was a squadron commander in the 445th Bombardment Group of the Army Air Forces in World War II, and he appeared regularly in recruitment and training films shot by the First Motion Picture Unit, Lookout Mountain's Hollywood predecessor. In the 1950s Col. Jimmy Stewart (promoted to brigadier general in 1959) of the Air Force Reserve hosted or narrated a number of training and promotional films shot by Lookout Mountain, even as he was working with Alfred Hitchcock on such films as *Rear Window* (1954), *The Man Who Knew Too Much* (1956), and *Vertigo* (1958).

As a highly visible member first of the Army Air Forces and then of the newly independent Air Force, Stewart provided a face, a physique, and a character for a military branch in search of a style and brand. Across his roles, we see men tested and formed as much in mind as in body, with psychological well-being and visual acuity often emphasized over physical strength. He could move easily from playing an injured photographer in *Rear Window* (with a Lookout Mountain photograph of a Desert Rock nuclear test among those on his character's shelf of accomplishments) to a late-career pilot struggling to meet the physical and mental requirements of the Cold War's long global missions in *Strategic Air Command* (1955).

Work at Lookout Mountain found Stewart playing himself as narrator, typically in uniform. The Air Force called on him to explain on screen everything from new communication technologies and command structures, to experimental aircraft, to deterrence to the dangers of brainwashing.

See also

Eliot, *Jimmy Stewart: A Biography*; Smith, *Jimmy Stewart*.

as footage of each missile or airplane is synced with his words. "Why so much? What's it all for? How do all these weapons work together to defend the United States and deter an enemy attack?" Stewart asks, bewildered. "Well, I'll tell you—that is, I'll *try* to tell you," he says as the camera cuts back to a table full of missile and airplane models. For several minutes, Stewart walks viewers through the roles of ICBMs, bombers, and fighter jets in relation to each other, using his models as props, while the film breaks on and off to footage of America's aeronautical wonders.

Like so many of Lookout Mountain's films, in addition to footage and narration *The Air Force Missile Mission* relies on animation to envision unrealized scenarios [e.g., a retaliatory nuclear strike] and to efficiently tell stories. In the case of *The Air Force Missile Mission*, the most elaborate animation sequence comes as Stewart tells the story of America's literal rise to higher and higher altitudes. We see animated fighter pilots start to don oxygen masks, and then full flight suits. "Not slowly, but almost by leaps and bounds," Stewart explains meditatively, "aircraft has been evolving toward a true spacecraft." As the animation shifts from a picture of a jet ascending into the sky to a scene of planets and stars, Stewart asks, "Because what is space, or what's the difference between air and space?" After all, he continues, "As far as flight is concerned, Air Force crews have been making space or space equivalent flights ever since they left their natural habitat back in 1942, '43." *The Air Force Missile Mission* moves toward a cinematic crescendo dedicated to the future of space travel: "Because space," Stewart says, speaking into the camera, "is for us what the unknown land was, the uncharted sea, a place into which all of man's history, everything he is and all that he's ever been and done compels him to move. He has no choice. And like the explorers of the past, he may have to fight up there. And that's why the Air Force has to do what it has always had to do: get up higher and go faster than the other fella. Because war, if it comes, cannot confine itself to air, but it will expand into the billions of space miles surrounding us." "*That's*," Stewart concludes, "the only way it all makes sense!" Here, among other things, Stewart made explicit Lookout Mountain's sense-making mission.

Whereas the Schriever-hosted *Ballistic Missile Development* was targeted at political and military decision makers, *The Air Force Missile Mission* was directed to Air Force personnel, especially those skeptical about the need for bombers in an age of missiles, or vice versa. *The Air Force Missile Mission* also differs from the more bureaucratic film reports in that it features Stewart, who really is more than a Hollywood star in the film. A member of the Air Force Reserves himself [in other Air Force films shot by Lookout Mountain, he appears onscreen in uniform], he brought not only a bona fide Air Force identity to Lookout Mountain films, but also the exceptionally rare capacity to break from the script. He was undoubtedly the most "natural" cinematic figure Lookout Mountain's cameras ever laid eyes on. An aim of *The Air Force Missile Mission* is to convert Stewart's ease before the camera into a form of filmic authority so as to bring a kind of "aw-shucks," commonsense realism to the fantastic prospect of fighting war in "billions of space miles," and the film comes close to achieving this aim.

Indeed, Lookout Mountain could have used Stewart more often. For as we will see in the next chapter, their narrative tasks became more and more daunting as the Air Force ascended higher and higher into thin, or just plain cold, air. As if nuclear extinction could be evaded through planetary evacuation, the Arctic and outer space became the futures before which the Air Force sought to realize human destiny, and Lookout Mountain found itself having to convince airmen, congressmen, and the public alike that Air Force engineering for life among the stars was not just plausible, but inevitable, and that it wouldn't be so bad.

THIS LAND

OF

OURS

Chapter Seven

ENGINEERING GEOGRAPHIES

Arctic and Space Films

It was the air age. Pearl Harbor had convinced many Americans that the measurements of space and time would now structure America's relation to the world more than treasure and territory, and that the hemispheric hegemony of the Monroe Doctrine, let alone isolationism, was a thing of the past.[1] As one American geographer, Walt Ristow, wrote in 1944, "The implications of present and future air routes over hitherto barren and inaccessible lands are comparable, and, in some ways, even more revolutionary, than the changes in geographical thinking which resulted from the discoveries of Columbus or the invention of the steamboat."[2] As Ristow indicated, the air age did not simply shrink the world. It opened it up: "All geography becomes *home* geography when the most distant point on earth is less than sixty hours from your local airport. Air Age geography thus is *world* geography, with the world greatly reduced in size as measured by the fourth dimension of *time*."[3] Indeed, from the standpoint of "aeriality," mapping, charting, and vision from the air became a matter not only of spatial perspective, but of compressed temporalities: the air age would be measured in hours, minutes, seconds, and microseconds rather than years, months, or days.[4] In turn, land gave way to space, and geopolitics became a matter of "sudden" possibilities.

Especially one sudden possibility: that of a surprise atomic attack on North America from the air. It is hard to underestimate just how much this possibility structured the strategic thinking of America's strategists in the decade after World War II. The next war, General Eisenhower cautioned after the war, "may come in a multitude of ways, over many routes, from many directions. Scarcely any form of attack can be written off as obsolete or so fantastic in conception as to remain forever impossible. No frontier or inland city can be considered immune."[5] Hoyt Vandenberg, Air Force chief of staff, warned in 1949, "Almost any number of Soviet bombers could cross our borders and fly to most of the targets in the United States without a shot being fired at them and without even being challenged in any way."[6] And George M. Humphrey, Eisenhower's secretary of the treasury, decried to Congress in 1953, "The danger of an atomic Pearl Harbor is real."[7]

If there were to be an atomic Pearl Harbor, many believed that it would come from the north. As Air Force Gen. Hap Arnold stated bluntly in 1950, "If there is a Third World War the strategic center of it will be the North Pole."[8] A year later, an MIT-led government panel concluded that the United States was "highly vulnerable" to surprise attack from the Soviet Union by means of Arctic airspace.[9] NSC 68, the formative Cold War policy statement of the Truman administration in the early 1950s, declared that the Soviet Union had the capability "to attack selected targets with atomic weapons, now including the likelihood of such attacks against targets in Alaska, Canada, and the United States."[10] The Arctic was seen as an "exposed flank," especially once the Soviets developed a hydrogen bomb.[11] The strategic frontier was now oriented northward. The air atomic age was the Arctic age.

In the 1950s the United States Air Force led a large-scale attempt to engineer the Arctic frontier in the name of US national security. They built and ran a network of manned radar stations that spanned from the Aleutian Islands to Greenland to parts of England. The goal was an "electronic fence," as it was frequently called, so as to bring about a kind of closing of the strategic world that the air age had opened. The Distant Early Warning Line [DEW Line] and the Ballistic Missile Early Warning System [BMEWS] were built to detect Soviet bomber and missile incursions into Arctic air space, providing the Air Force with not only early warning of an atomic Pearl Harbor, but also what was supposed to be a highly automated retaliation system [eventually designed as the SAGE system]. The projects were largely invisible: shrouded in secrecy, remote from population centers, and harnessing the barely understood radio properties of the Earth's upper atmosphere. The Air Force realized the systems with little publicity and without public supervision.

They did document the projects on film, however. Lookout Mountain photographers were on hand to capture the work. And in the 1960s, Lookout Mountain shot or produced a series of films that explained to military personnel, government officials, and on occasion, broader publics the operations and intentions of the Arctic radar-defense systems. Films such as *Eyes and Ears of the Arctic: The DEW System* [ca. 1960], *The Reins of Command* [1961], *Aleutian Skywatch* [1961], *Shield of Freedom* [1963], and *Eyes of the North* [1966] offered important records, rhetorics, and rationalizations of Air Force Arctic engineering efforts and adventures.[12] As records, these films narrated America's engineering incursions into Arctic land and air space. As rhetorics, they represented the Arctic not as the habitable home of humans and other species for millennia, nor even as the bounded land of a sovereign nation-state, but as space, empty space, geometric space, and indeed even as a form of outer space. And as rationalizations these films not only justified a project fraught with contested and even contradictory claims and defended America's military incursions into foreign lands, but as significantly, propagated the Air Force's fantasy of re-closing, by means of automated technical systems, the world the air age had so suddenly opened. As such, the Air Force's Arctic documentaries did by means of representation what the air age did by means of technological force, showing that abstract *time-space relations* more than history and territory structured America's new relation to the world. The entire Earth, and indeed the space beyond the Earth, became space for the engineering of American security strategy.[13]

In this chapter we consider these films, first by recounting the evolution of air defense from World War II to the Cold War, and then by looking at the Air Force's documentary accounts of the expansion of air defense into the Arctic by means of the DEW Line and the BMEWS. The North American Arctic has long served imperial interests as a *terra nullius*, or nobody's land, as had the islands of Oceania.[14] The Air Force's Cold War efforts brought this imperial practice into a new age, where not only land but *space* in its geometrical sense and *outer space* as a space of fantastic projections, played critical roles in the enactment of imperial power. In Air Force arctic films shot and sometimes produced by Lookout Mountain Laboratory, space and outer space converged to produce not only a new geography but a new temporality, referred to in these films simply as the "future." The "future" was presented as that which displaces history, tradition, and nature, but also as that which needs to be engineered, transforming the state of operations into a boundless deterrent state.

The postwar history of automated defenses against air attack began with a nightmare and led to a dream. The nightmare was that of the German V-1 rocket.[15] A weapon of terror as well as physical destruction, the V-1 autonomously veered into British cities during World War II with stunning speed. The V-1 made the basic problem of antiaircraft artillery central to British research and development during the war, and central to the mission of the US National Defense Research Committee (later the Office of Scientific Research and Development), created in 1940 under the leadership of Vannevar Bush to spearhead military research and development to aid the British in fending off the German manned and unmanned air assaults. During the course of the war, Bush and his colleagues, with the help of private firms such as Bell Labs and Western Electric, made significant advances in air defense, including the development by Bell Labs of systems that could

calculate missile curves and direct antiaircraft guns with significant accuracy.

Ten years after the war, the nightmare was amplified a hundredfold. An atomic version of Pearl Harbor on the North American continent by way of Arctic airspace would likely mean the total destruction of the United States. Bell Labs and Western Electric engineers again were summoned to work on air defense, alongside a scientific team rivaling the scope of the Manhattan Project.[16] Together they designed a large-scale and largely automatic antiaircraft system that could intercept Soviet bombers as they attacked the United States. Western Electric won the contract for building the system, constructing the first section of the Distant Early Warning Line in 1957. When completed, the project would stretch along the 69th parallel from Alaska to Greenland. The design called for DEW Line stations to detect airplanes crossing the Arctic, registering them on radars at North American Aerospace Defense Command (NORAD) in Colorado. Ideally, the blips would then be identified as Soviet bombers—*if* they indeed were Soviet bombers—so as to be intercepted and destroyed. Or so was the dream.

This was no antiaircraft gun writ large, however. Despite the dream, even if bombers could be accurately detected (a dodgy proposition), the air space over the Arctic and Canada was so vast as to make intercepting enemy aircraft in time a crapshoot. Moreover, the DEW Line radars could not detect missiles. In the late 1950s, a supplemental radar system was constructed, the Ballistic Missile Early Warning System (BMEWS). But even then, missiles could not be reliably intercepted and destroyed. In short, the "shield" was incomplete at best.[17] DEW Line and BMEWS merely offered overlapping electronic projections—radar signals—that, like a trip wire, could alert NORAD of an incoming threat, but could not reliably prevent it.

In fact, DEW Line and BMEWS were articulations not of antiaircraft protection but of something new and profoundly different: the nuclear deterrence system. Though built from some of the same technologies as World War II radar defense, and by some of the same engineers, this deterrence system was qualitatively different from its antecedent. *It was above all an idea*. Unlike World War II antiaircraft guns, nuclear deterrence could never be materialized and manufactured in complex servomechanisms, not at least *as deterrence*—for the basic idea of deterrence was the "credible threat," and no automatic system could be contrived that could reliably produce it.[18] The "credible threat" was not a projectile. It could not vector. It could only be *believed*. But if it were to be believed, it had to first be rhetorically constructed.

To be sure, nuclear deterrence was hardwired into technical networks, ballistics, bombers, missiles, and routines of action and reaction, but these large-scale technological systems cohered in only policy and rhetoric. Its constitutional and thus legal status remained suspect at best.[19] The result was a technological and rhetorical "fantasyland of reality," a phrase the Lookout Mountain film *Shield of Freedom* used to describe the DEW Line project in the Arctic. Indeed, the Arctic as depicted by Air Force photographers was emblematic of nuclear deterrence, at once an "empty space" of geographic and human engineering and an image of an apocalyptic future. It portended the idea, the imaginary, of technological necessities and engineered futures. The Arctic, like the air age, was pictured as vast and boundless. Moreover, its polar quality wrested it from traditional hemispheric geographies of east and west, allying it instead with the topsy-turvy perspectivism of the air age. Finally, the strangeness and harshness of its environment—its long winter's night and perpetual summer's day, its cold, its wind, its glaciers and permafrost—made the Arctic a projection of the apocalyptic future the deterrent system both sanctioned and sought to defer. The Arctic, as such, was all but another planet, a "new frontier" in a qualitative as well as chronological sense.

Building a radar-defense system in the Arctic demanded that a range of new technologies and techniques be developed to operate in the harsh conditions. It was an extended venture

NORAD and the Cheyenne Mountain Operations Center

in the middle of the 1950s, Colorado Springs emerged as a new center of activity for not only the Air Force but also nuclear defense more broadly. Accordingly, Lookout Mountain established a subunit, Detachment 2, there in spring of 1959, charged with documenting Air Force activities in Colorado and across the region. In the late 1950s and early 1960s, Detachment 2 photographers documented the construction and operation of new missile complexes in Kansas, Wyoming, South Dakota, Nebraska, Texas, Oklahoma, New Mexico, Arizona, Montana, and Idaho. Closer to home, they covered the formation of the new Air Force Academy, from its last days at Lowry Field in Denver to its first days at a new facility in Colorado Springs, and the construction of a new home for the North American Air Defense Command (NORAD) deep inside Cheyenne Mountain.

NORAD was a joint Canadian-US effort. At the core of the project was a unified early warning and response system for detection of airborne attacks; radar stations and planes across the Arctic and the Atlantic provided a network of signals for automated analysis at supercomputing centers. Monitoring this network from a single location, NORAD leaders could then collect data, make judgments, and decide on appropriate responses. This central command was initially housed at Ent Air Force Base in Colorado Springs, but a RAND Corporation study in 1958 recommended that a hardened location be constructed inside the granite Cheyenne Mountain, so that NORAD could be protected from a direct thermonuclear blast. In May 1961 the massive construction project began, taking five years to complete. Lookout Mountain's Detachment 2 was charged with documenting the construction progress.

As early as 1960, before construction began, a tenth of Lookout Mountain's budget went to supporting documentation of NORAD's operations at Ent Air Force Base. That same year, Detachment 2 documented the construction of three hundred Titan and Minuteman missile sites across the Midwest. Photographers working underground, whether in Cheyenne Mountain or in underground missile sites, faced challenging conditions, shooting not only in inadequate lighting, but also amid dangerous construction conditions.

in geographical engineering.[20] It also demanded that military personnel be sent for extended periods of time to tours of duty under the harshest of conditions: no sunlight, no outdoor recreation, and little contact with family and friends. As such, the DEW Line and BMEWS sites also meant human engineering.[21] Last but not least, the projects meant incursions upon land outside of the sovereign territory of the United States, entailing not simply cooperation with Canada, but entrance into the diplomatically fraught territory of Arctic colonization. To accomplish the "idea" of deterrence through a northern shield meant establishing American-occupied posts on land claimed by Canada, but in many cases, not yet fully mapped by Canada.[22] These outposts would require careful positioning to avoid both the appearance of Soviet-style expansion and, for the United States and Canada, nagging questions surrounding indigenous sovereignty. The task called for new formations of imperialism, engineered through both the DEW Line networks and their portrayals on film.[23]

It began with engineering. If the dawn of the air age entailed a new geographic imaginary, one where space was collapsed into time and revisable perspectives took precedence over fixed axes, the dawn of the Arctic age in the Cold War entailed what Matthew Farish, citing Edward Teller, calls "geographical engineering," or "the physical shaping of the earth to reflect human needs," specifically the needs of national security.[24] For next to its new strategic centrality, the most obvious thing about the Arctic to military planners was that its climate was unsuitable for normal operations. The Arctic was an environment of extremes, and extreme measures would have to be taken to operate permanently there. Geographical engineering in the Arctic would mean constructing above- and below-ground structures that could withstand subzero temperatures and high winds, buttressing equipment against the elements, and creating systems of long-term self-sufficiency for crews: means of electrical power, food provisions, protection from the cold and wind, and so on. As such, the cameras of the Air Force, among them Lookout Mountain's, would frame the aesthetic counterpart to geographical engineering, what might be called "engineering geographies," representations of the Earth that foreground systematic human technical and technological dominion.

The 1961 Air Force film *Aleutian Skywatch*—photographed by Lookout Mountain but produced for Western Electric, Bell System, and the Air Force by the educational and industrial film producer Audio Productions of New York, and distributed by the Air Photographic and Charting Service[25]—tells the story of the extension of the DEW Line into the Aleutian Islands off the coast of western Alaska. The film's rhetorical exigencies appear divergent. Its most pressing concern seems to be addressing the dread Air Force men felt at the prospect of being stationed far off in "the Arctic" (in this case, the Aleutian Islands, which sit well outside the Arctic Circle, but were still associated with the Arctic). However, the film explicitly promoted the engineering work of Bell System and Western Electric on behalf of the Air Force. In fact, the two exigencies converged at the point of engineering geographies, for the story, and by implication the argument, of *Aleutian Skywatch* is that engineering can transform "nowhere" into somewhere and "nothing" into something. The engineered Arctic, that is, is not the same as the Arctic.

But first engineering has to create reasons to transform nowhere into somewhere. Hence, after flashing the Bell System logo, *Aleutian Skywatch* begins at a switchboard, where the feminine hand of a Bell Telephone operator fields calls and makes connections. A male caller is heard but not seen: he asks the operator to be connected to Bell's film library, where viewers see a young, white-gloved woman organizing film canisters. The connection is made, and the film librarian picks up the phone to hear the caller request a copy of *Aleutian Skywatch*. Having been granted the request, the unseen caller asks the film librarian a further question: "How come the telephone company is involved in this? Wasn't it an Air Force project?" Smiling, she explains to the caller that the DEW

Line was the work of Bell System and Western Electric, and "We're sort of proud of the whole thing."

It is hard to overstate the importance communications played in the incursion of the US national security state into the Arctic and beyond. The massive radar-defense networks built by Bell System, Western Electric, and many other government contractors were premised on the power of "communications," understood technically, metaphorically, and even ideologically. Using the design of the DEW Line's Semi-Automatic Ground Environment [SAGE] computer system as a case study, Paul Edwards has argued that demand for efficient capacities for "communications" and "control" lay at the heart of many tools, metaphors, and discourses surrounding Cold War computers and computing.[26] In the Air Force it was widely assumed that of the three "Cs"—command, control, and communications—the last was the condition of possibility for the former two. In this way, the Bell System prologue provided the first of several justifications that *Aleutian Skywatch* offered for Air Force incursions into the Arctic: the antidote to enemy air power is the power of communications.

When the narrative of *Aleutian Skywatch* begins, viewers meet the film's main character and narrator, Captain Huntley, boarding a plane headed for the Aleutians, where he is to begin a new tour of duty. Huntley's journey is the film's journey: his flight introduces viewers to the Aleutian "nowhere," his arrival at the Cold Bay DEW Line station occasions an account of the design and creation of the DEW Line system, and his settling into his new assignment offers viewers a sense of what the "daily routine" of DEW Line work looks like.

As viewers see Captain Huntley sitting in the airplane transporting him northward, his voice is heard [nondiegetically], as if he is looking back on his journey, telling his story. He's been sent on a new tour of duty, he explains, "what they call a remote-site tour." He's not very excited, but acknowledges, "The ball can't always bounce right for everyone." Drawing near to his destination and looking out on the Aleutian panorama from the air [long shots of the landscape fill the screen], he muses, "No one ever mistook the Aleutians for a Shangri-La. You don't make a lost paradise out of tundra and volcanic dust, marshy lakes, and dead volcanoes covered with snow and ice, even if they are pretty to look at. Man, we were really heading out to nowhere, and we were getting there fast."

Upon landing, Huntley boards an Air Force vehicle for transport by dirt roads to the remote DEW Line station at Cold Bay. The camera assumes Huntley's perspective, looking out through a damp windshield onto a gray, barren, and apparently "uninhabited" scene. And so, as Huntley moves through the bleak landscape, a sense of despair at the *human* prospects of Arctic life grows.

Until the captain sees an engineered marvel: "deep in the heart of nowhere, *there it was*." Against the barren backdrop *Aleutian Skywatch* establishes, appears, framed in a long shot, a radar tower capped in a geodesic dome and flanked by a set of antennas designed in such a way that they look like wings protruding from the ground reaching for the sky.[27] Through Huntley's windshield, the architectural arrangement appears as a sign of civilization, an icon of technological triumph, and as Huntley's new home. Reflecting on first seeing the site, Huntley relates, "The way it loomed up suddenly out of that desolation, solid and efficient looking . . . I don't mind admitting it gave me a real charge." There is a "somewhere" in the middle of "nowhere" after all.

But why this spot of civilization? What is it all about? Why a somewhere in the middle of nowhere? *Aleutian Skywatch* takes up these questions as Huntley enters the station—but oddly, ironically, and only as the film leaves the scene of the station altogether and enters an animated world of sensing signals, red-arrow attacks, and shielded space. An extended animated sequence in *Aleutian Skywatch* charts an imagined polar strike from the Soviets as they approach America's DEW Line radar net, which shoots warning signals southward

Detachment 1 at Elmendorf Air Force Base

Located near Anchorage, Alaska, Elmendorf was an active base for the Army Air Forces during World War II. After World War II, it became a headquarters for US military operations in the Arctic. In 1946 President Truman and Congress divided the globe into a new unified command structure comprising seven regions, with the Alaskan Command based at Elmendorf. The specter of Soviet attack from the north put intense pressure on the command. Accordingly, Lookout Mountain established a small but busy subsidiary unit at Elmendorf in 1961, a unit that would go on to outlast Lookout Mountain itself, operating well past 1969.

The detachment documented, in still and motion-picture photography, the construction and supply of the DEW Line radar locations and other tracking stations associated with NORAD's detection systems. They also documented large-scale military activities in the polar north, such as Exercise Polar Siege in 1964, meant to test US military capabilities in extreme artic environments. Finally, Detachment 1 served as a kind of public relations wing of the Alaskan Command, regularly creating materials for news outlets testifying to the command's strength as the northern arm of American military power.

As such, Lookout Mountain photographers traveled extensively around and across the North Pole, documenting runways and radar stations as well as ceremonial activities at remote locations. The arctic conditions were challenging for them, to say the least, as they had to keep their equipment from freezing, their camera batteries humming along, and their fingers agile in the extreme cold.

to command centers in the United States. By illustrating the purported "complete" protective power of the deterrent system, animation gave vision to what could not be seen by the naked eye, both because of the invisibility of the system's electronic signals and because the DEW Line, as we explained previously, was at best an "incomplete shield."[28] Whereas older maps tended to treat the north as a cartographic limit, a nontraversable, apolitical boundary, animation in *Aleutian Skywatch*, as with other Air Force Arctic radar-defense films, presented the Arctic as a traversable space, a sort of new Pacific. Taking aesthetic cues, and likely an animator or two, from the popular wartime film *Victory through Airpower* produced by Disney, these animated sequences borrow air-age understandings of the Pacific to help conjure a new image of the Arctic. Animation also offered to viewers images of an imaginary boundary around the North American continent, giving solidity and surety to a precarious and problematic system.

Having seen what the DEW Line is all about, Captain Huntley responds with wonder, even awe. We find him imaginatively surveying the radomes, the antennas, the control rooms, the shelters. "I looked around," he reminisces, "from the impressive installations to the wild terrain and wondered how this line was ever built." A Western Electric engineer stationed at Cold Bay does the explaining for Huntley and the viewers of the film, starting scripturally: "In the beginning, of course, there was nothing." To the contrary, of course, there was plenty in the Aleutians before Western Electric showed up: millennia worth of movements, peoples, histories, and ecologies, as well as a recent World War II history. But from the distinct engineering perspective of *Aleutian Skywatch*, prior to the construction of these DEW Line stations there was "nothing": this is a story of creation *in nihilo*. *Aleutian Skywatch* walks viewers through the entire story of this engineering act of creation *in nihilo*, climaxing in a gesture that both reflects back on the Bell System prologue

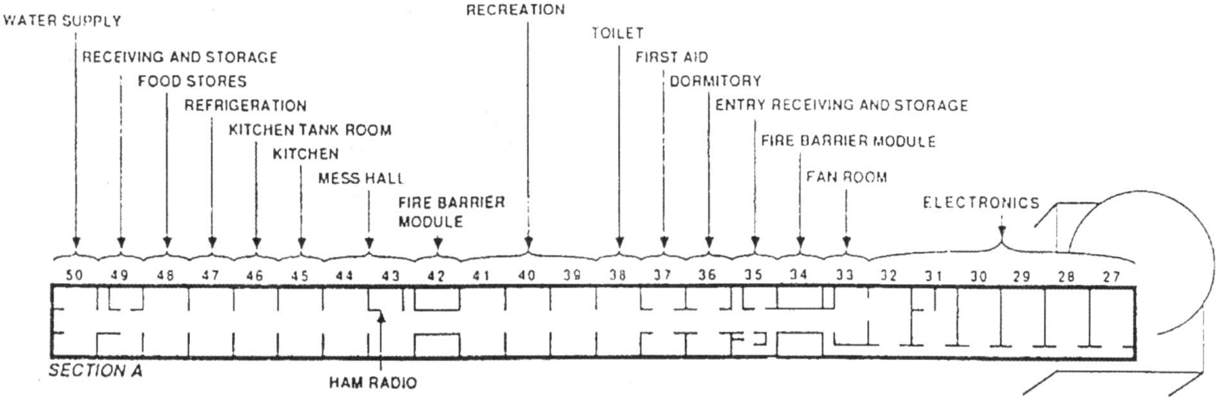

to the film and anticipates a later science fiction filmic trope: phoning home. At the end of the creation sequence, an engineer at the Cold Bay DEW Line station sits down at a phone and dials project headquarters in New York. An Air Force commander is shown picking up the call on the other end. It is "the proof of success," as the film puts it: communications.

Aleutian Skywatch's penultimate scene puts Captain Huntley [as well as the film's viewers] back on an airplane. But this time, rather than a journey to nowhere, the air ride consists of a flyover, a tour, of what is now "somewhere," an engineering geography. Viewers see the DEW Line system from the air: an empty, open space, the technological mastery of which supposedly necessitated its construction in the first place. Seen from high up in the air, the radomes lose their angularity and resolve into spheres. The effect is geometric and idealistic: from the perspective of the air, the radomes resemble a platonic solid rather than an iterative, modular, reconfigurable mesh. Viewers also, strikingly, are allowed to see the Aleutians for the first time as something other than an engineering geography, as a space of natural wonders. Huntley's flyover takes him by the Cathedral Peaks mountain range and the erupting Pavlof volcano. Back on the ground, now thoroughly established in the routines of "good system management," Huntley and *Aleutian Skywatch*'s viewers are also allowed to see the past, the history of the Arctic, by means of an image of an Inuit mother with her children [the only such image the film shows] posed in a photogenic manner before a frontier church dating back to the days of Russian settlers. The scene is for Huntley what he describes as "a touch of history." It is as if it is only when "nowhere" becomes "somewhere" by means of technological dominion that nature and history are allowed to appear in engineering geographies at all.

So too the human. Engineering geographies, in fact, are filled with humans, either as their imprint is seen on the architecture and artifacts of technological systems, or as they are functionally integrated into those systems. Farish, in reflecting on the Arctic as a frontier for engineering, notes that the counterpart to Cold War "geographical engineering" was "human engineering": "The management of life at DEW stations according to certain rituals and techniques of design, or *human engineering*, was a singularly important subject. From the planning phase of the 1952 MIT summer study onwards, advocates of the DEW Line were concerned with the behaviour of personnel posted to the high Arctic, if only because human alertness was still the ultimate factor determining the Line's potential efficacy."[29]

However, humans, nearly universally white men, were pictured in America's nuclear deterrence system not only as functional compo nents of technological systems—ideally interchangeable with the nonhuman components of the system—but as *legitimating subjects*, "operators," whose performance of technical mastery and control represented systematic human technical and technological dominion of earth, sea, sky, and even the Arctic.[30] As such, engineering geographies called not only for human engineering but also for "engineering humans," representations of figures functionally and existentially "at home" in the architecture and artifacts of large-scale technological systems. Indeed, it was crucial for political reasons, among others, that these humans be portrayed as more "at home" in their artificial habitats than in the landscape. Like the platonic spheres under which they toiled, DEW Line operators needed to be seen as on, but not of, the landscape, for fear of representing a threat to the sovereignty of Canada, who laid claim to much of the land on which the DEW Line stations sat.

In *Eyes of the North*, another film photographed by Lookout Mountain photographers, though likely scripted and produced elsewhere, we find these engineering humans forming an international Arctic techno-political alliance of Americans, Canadians, Greenlanders, Danes, Icelanders, and Englishmen, together rendered "at home" in the American architecture and artifacts of the DEW Line and BMEWS systems. Unlike *Aleutian Skywatch*, which was aimed at making airmen feel better about their DEW Line assignment, *Eyes of the North* bears all the marks of being aimed at making decision makers—above all, US congressmen—feel better about the enormous economic and geopolitical investment of Cold War radar defense in the Arctic.[31] It also bears a subtle but profound message: technology has made necessary the transfer of responsibility for America's defense to "operators." Produced in 1966 at the height of not only Vietnam and the doctrine of mutually assured destruction but also the space race, *Eyes of the North* argues for the urgency, but also the possibility, of America's political leaders being "at home" in high-speed technological systems, even massively destructive ones.

Eyes of the North, like *Aleutian Skywatch*, begins with a prologue. A shot of two sharp-suited men, presumably congressmen, begins the film. They are shown leaving the Capitol building. As they do, one of the men turns to his watch, using his index finger to point to the time, and the film cuts to a close-up of the watch. "In the minds of men and nations," an offscreen narrator begins, "one-quarter of one hour, fifteen minutes, is a tiny span of time." And yet, "To those responsible for the defense of our civilization, fifteen minutes could be the priceless interim between the first alarm of approaching enemy missiles and the counterstrike of our own forces." Whereas *Aleutian Skywatch* begins with "communications," the coverage of vast space by means of electronic signals, *Eyes of the North* compresses space into time. As such, the Arctic is introduced as a point in the rapid passage of time. *Eyes of the North*, the film's narrator explains, concerns "a partnership that guards the transpolar route against air attack." As the second hand on a watch passes by its northern "null" point to start a new minute, so the Arctic is rendered as the northern starting point, the trigger, the beginning of the "fifteen-minutes" the film features as the time necessary to launch a counterstrike against the Soviets.

Rendering the Arctic as a trigger point in a large-scale, high-speed technological system entails not only a massive engineering project, but also the de facto submission of humans to the structures and exigencies of technological systems. In the narrative of *Eyes of the North*, neither engineering systems nor humans submitting to them are "natural." Yet both are "necessary." In this film the Arctic becomes a scene against which to explore a space-time paradox of modern life. On the one hand, the artificiality of modern life has rendered harsh natural climates such as the Arctic uninhabitable for modern people. To be modern is to vacate the space of nature's extremity; it is suitable for only "primitive" forms of life. On the other hand, the temporal artificiality of modern life has made a return to the extreme natural space necessary. Space, again, is compressed into time.

After a short sequence of opening credits, *Eyes of the North* continues with images of the bleak landscape of the Arctic. However, it is not the extreme harshness of the Arctic that the film's narrator stresses; it is the fact that humans have long lived there. "Startling as it may be," he continues, "men have been living in the Arctic, fighting the cold, the winds, the darkness for thousands of years." The film's camera makes the point explicitly by focusing on an Eskimo driving a dog sled through the snow. The scene then quickly shifts to an image of men exiting from an Air Force plane sitting on an icy Arctic surface. The shift in scene sets up a contrast: "And now to guard us from possible attack over the pole, modern men, men from cities like Dallas and Atlanta, men from states like Oregon and New York, men from Denmark and the United States have learned also to live in the Arctic." The basic contrast between primitive and modern forms of life is as old as Rousseau, even older, but *Eyes of the North* offers something new in the form of a problem and a solution. The problem, as the film renders it, is how modern men might come to dwell in a climate and context suitable for only primitive men. For modern men, the Arctic is uninhabitable—indeed, it is from *only* the perspective of the modern that the Arctic is "uninhabitable." The solution is engineering. For "modern men" the Arctic is inhabitable as only an engineering geography.

Indeed, the question before *Eyes of the North* is not how the BMEWS and DEW Line systems work, but how "modern men" can "survive" at the sites. "Survival," the narrator states, "is an iron discipline. One mistake, and man dies"—that is, a *modern* man. Indeed, the challenge to the survival of modern men in the Arctic is not only physical; it is also psychic: "The men fight boredom as well as the cold." The keys to survival, as the film presents it, are architecture and logistics: the former provides shelter, warmth, and work, and the latter supplies and provisions. Together they represent a

thoroughly engineered form of existence: these modern men, no less than the astronauts of the space program, survive only within artificial systems.

And so do the nations of the "free world." *Eyes of the North* culminates in a turn from the Arctic to the underground, artificial life of commanders at NORAD in Colorado. "If a missile threat occurs," the narrator explains, "automatic transmission circuits take over," consisting of "information racing with an electronic speed of light from BMEWS sites . . . to the North American Air Defense Command." At NORAD, "military decisions are made." If an enemy attack is identified, "the entire free world could be instantly alerted," giving the United States and NATO nations "the precious warning time" they need to "prepare for the attack and the counter-attack." Thus, in the space of an imagined future, and yet still thoroughly engineered in the present, in fifteen minutes, an international alliance is formed: "Americans, Canadians, Greenlanders, Danes, Icelanders, and Englishmen, in tactical operation rooms, on the flight line, in generator rooms, in kitchens, fight the cold and the boredom, manning the eyes of the north, to give us maximum warning time, time to prepare, time to retaliate, minutes of priceless time." International space is compressed into time as high-speed, large-scale technological systems forge a Cold War alliance that leaves, in fact, *no place* for political deliberation in a moment of emergency, *because there is no time*. The temporality of political deliberation has been eradicated by the speed-of-light temporality of artificial technical systems. In the words of James Der Derian, "space" is displaced by "pace."[32] For the commanders at NORAD, immediate "military decisions" represent the only feasible moment of judgment, but it is clear from *Eyes of the North* that even this judgment is as pre-scripted as a computer program. The commanders and captains of nations, not just the operators at consoles, are the integrated subjects of engineering, subject to its logic not by law or ideology but by the sheer speed of electronic systems.

In the hands of Lookout Mountain's photographers, the Arctic was an emblem. In its transformation from a place of "uninhabitable" remoteness to the trigger point in a minutely measured all-out nuclear war, the Arctic was not only subject to the power of a space-time compression, it was representative of it. It represented a rationale for a new American imperialism rooted in the logics of technological systems rather than territory or treasure. Far from "nowhere," the DEW Line and BMEWS sites were often built near indigenous communities, significantly disrupting the lives and livelihoods of Inuit.[33] And the majority of these sites sat on the sovereign land of other nations, especially Canada and Greenland. As such, these distant stations were not only sites of "radar defense" but also of rhetorics and rationalizations for an American presence in spaces outside US sovereign territory—anticipating America's movement into outer space.

Lookout Mountain photographers, as we have discussed, were regularly on temporary duty in Alaska and across the Arctic recording the activity of the Air Force and its contractors. Long before the scripting of edited films, the camera already participates in the rhetorical projects outlined previously, through choices of framing and composition that guide us away from the Arctic as a thriving, inhabited land and toward the DEW Line outposts as victorious against the region's climatological and diplomatic perils. In the hands of writers and producers, however, such footage performs new work. It is hardly surprising that of all the Air Force's scripted Arctic radar-defense films, the most ambitious is one for which Lookout Mountain could claim full authorship. In 1963 Lookout Mountain produced *Shield of Freedom*, a bold argument for northern nuclear defense in the explicit terms of colonialism and empire. The nearly thirty-minute film bluntly articulates a new imperialism, an engineering imperialism, by drawing the air atomic–Arctic age into filmic dialogue with the longer history of American colonialism from the Puritans to the age of Manifest Destiny. *Shield of Freedom* presents America's Cold War colonial efforts in the Arctic as continuous with these older colonial adventures, all the while arguing for an utterly different rationale for them than the Puritan "errand into the wilderness" or the Manifest Destiny of westward expansion.[34] This new Cold War expansion of American geographical power, *Shield of Freedom* argues, is rooted not in the sense of moral mission or historical destiny, but in technological necessity: following the logic of *Aleutian Skywatch* and anticipating that of *Eyes of the North*, "land" is rendered as "space," ideologically indistinguishable from "air." But more than these other films, "history" is the subject of *Shield of Freedom*, and history, the film implies, *has ended*. It has been compressed into the time-space "future" of engineering systems whose purpose is to secure an interminable future against the prospect of nuclear annihilation.

Lookout Mountain produced *Shield of Freedom* as what they described as a "public relations" film for the Air Force's Air Defense Command. Shown in movie theaters and on television, the film included an original score and a theme song, "This Land of Ours"—written by Lookout Mountain staff composers and recorded at Capitol Recording Studio in Hollywood—and was narrated by Canadian actor and Lookout Mountain regular Raymond Massey.[35] Relative to not only *Aleutian Skywatch* and *Eyes of the North*, but other Air Force radar-defense films such as Lookout Mountain's *The Reins of Command* [1961] and *Polar Strike* [1965], *Shield of Freedom* is conspicuously "theatrical." Nevertheless, for all its affectation, it is, in filmic terms, the most comprehensive and complex of the Air Force's radar-defense films.

It, too, starts with a prologue, this one shot from the air: scenes of antelope running through grassy fields start the film, as the anthem "This Land of Ours" begins. The scene bleeds into a visual anthem, a montage: a lake, a mountain peak, bears bathing, kids playing, Mount Rushmore, a busy intersection, boys playing football, a cowboy on horseback, a teenage couple leaving school, a church, and a pan of an open western plain. The title screen flashes, giving way to a cartoon rendering of the Pilgrim story: the cartoon moves from the Pilgrims to the early colonists, culminating in Massey quoting, unacknowledged, a line from the 1942 Warner Brothers film *Yankee Doodle Dandy*—"thirteen sisters by the sea who built their home and called it 'liberty'"—and then Lincoln's "government of the people" line. The film then cuts to a medium close-up shot of a NORAD commander, who explains to the audience that as "the threat against us is changing in scope and degree" so "our aerospace defense capability must therefore change continuously."

Shield of Freedom then turns, somewhat surprisingly, to a call-and-response. Massey speaks and a chorus of male voices responds, reminiscent of Hollywood depictions of "Indians" reciting war chants. This ritualistic call-and-response reoccurs throughout the film and is the central means by which the film is narrated. *Shield of Freedom* uses the chant to offer an overall justification for the deterrence system, before taking viewers to the Sioux City Air Defense Sector of the SAGE system. There, during a brief visit to the campus of the University of South Dakota, viewers meet Oscar Howe, an art professor who is introduced as Sioux and designer of the emblem for the Sioux City Air Defense Sector.[36] A second animated sequence soon begins: this time of stereotypically depicted Native American war councils. America's deterrence efforts are explicitly compared to Native American war practices: "It's the same performance, with a different cast," the chorus chants. As the animation comes to an end, NORAD commanders are shown at work in a command room and are compared to Native Americans.

> MASSEY: The battle staff as it is known today includes the intelligence officer.
>
> CHORUS: Formerly known as the medicine man.
>
> MASSEY: The communications electronics officer.
>
> CHORUS: Chief Thunderbolt.

And so on. NORAD's functions, Massey and the chorus explain, are fourfold: detect and identify, and if need be, intercept and destroy. Canadians, Massey explains, have joined America in the NORAD effort, bound as they are by "their historic creed."

Shield of Freedom then shifts to long shots of the Arctic, scenes that, like *Aleutian Skywatch* and *Eyes of the North*, feature a barren and unforgiving expanse. The camera cuts to an image of a black-and-white photograph taped to the inside of a portable record player case, featuring a young woman posing in a grass skirt and wearing a lei. Next to the photograph is a mirror, and in the mirror viewers see the face of a young man who we are led to believe is a Pacific islander. The man is playing "tropical" music on his record player. He stops his record player, puts on his coat, and heads out the door into the dark and cold of Thule Air Force Base, a site of "readiness."

Soon viewers again meet a NORAD commander, who explains that while the air age has advanced at a remarkable rate, "just around the

Shield of Freedom

SFP-1099
(1963)

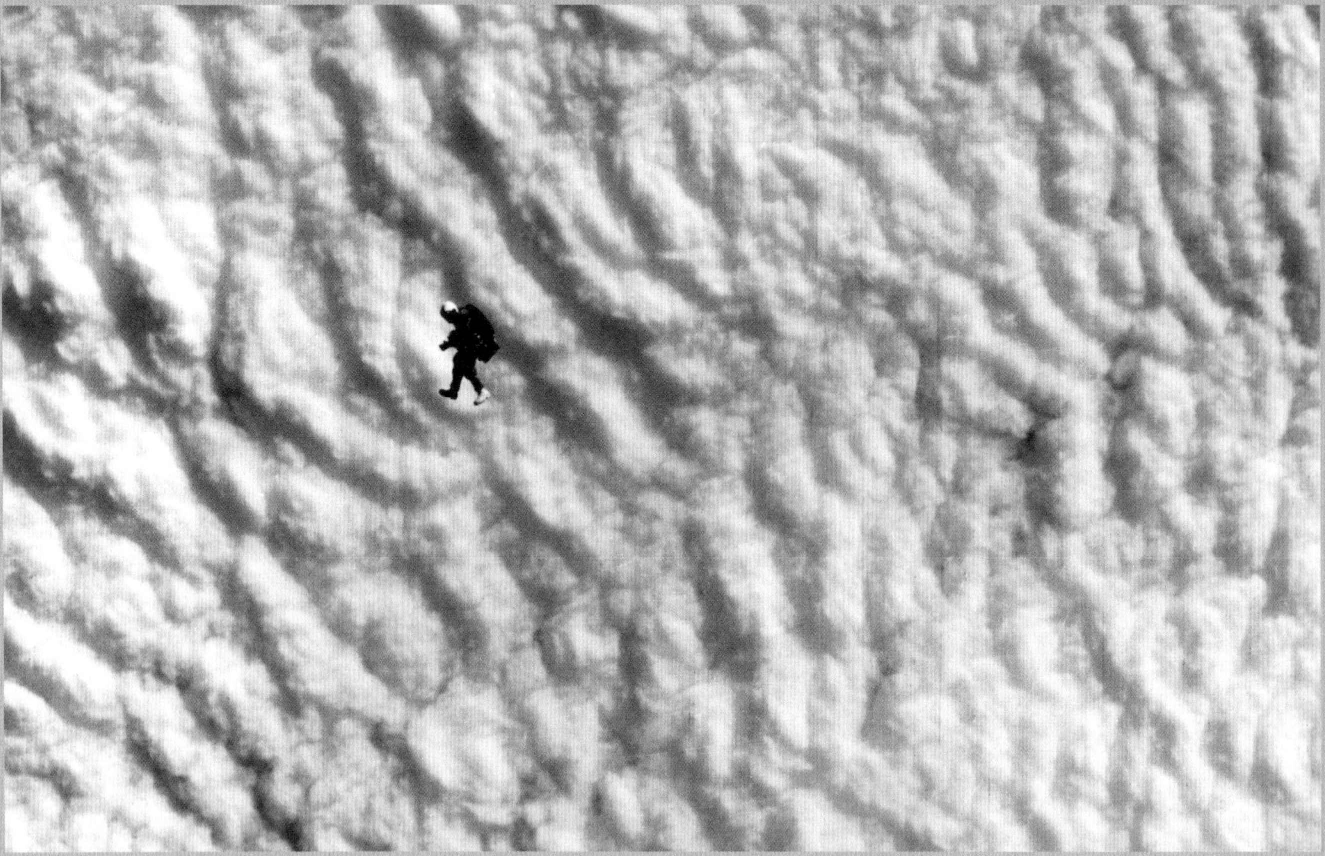

Colonel Joseph W. Kittinger II

The weekly Universal Newsreel in the middle of August 1960 featured a story on downed American pilot Gary Powers's trial in the Soviet Union, followed by a segment on Project Excelsior, Air Force test pilot Capt. Joseph Kittinger's "daring ascent into the stratosphere." Showing footage shot by Lookout Mountain, the newsreel pictured Kittinger borne aloft in a specially designed gondola suspended under a balloon. At the stratospheric height of 102,800 feet, Kittinger jumps, beginning a long descent to a parachute landing in New Mexico's White Sands Missile Range and setting three world records along the way.

Here, as elsewhere, Lookout Mountain's cameras were doing double duty. On the one hand, they were doing "technical" work. Lookout Mountain was called on to do specialized photography for Col. John Paul Stapp's group at Holloman Air Force Base in New Mexico, where the physical and mental limits of airmen operating cutting-edge aerospace technologies were aggressively tested. On the other hand, Lookout Mountain's photography of Kittinger's jump was used to prove to potential pilots the viability of surviving catastrophe in the stratosphere—helpful for recruiting top airmen—and provided American audiences with yet another image of military "techno spectacle" and air-based heroism. The jump also spoke to Powers's trial, as it demonstrated it was indeed possible for airmen to survive high-altitude jet mishaps, the kind Gary Powers had experienced over the Soviet Union.

Photography for Excelsior included onboard cameras that recorded instrument readings in the gondola; cameras on Lookout Mountain's ground-based M-45 tracking mounts; and a camera on loan from National Geographic, in an arrangement secured by Kittinger himself, which was rigged to produce picture-perfect images for the photo magazines that dominated print media in the 1950s and 1960s. The most iconic images of Kittinger's leap came from this National Geographic camera: in these we see a man falling into the clouds, his puny body set against an expanse, both a sign of human vulnerability and human triumph. In this and other respects, Kittinger's leap presaged the iconography of the astronaut that was to come in the 1960s.

See also

Kittinger and Ryan, *Come Up and Get Me*.

corner lays the most challenging era of all time, landing on the moon, the exploration of space, and eventually interplanetary travel." *Shield of Freedom* shifts to a third animation sequence, this of ships and astronauts on the moon. Space, the NORAD commander explains, might bring "men closer together"; but in the meantime, "We must have the capability to counter any threat which any aggressor may impose in space." *Shield of Freedom* turns to images of Air Force "space track" stations and their personnel at work, describing the latter as an "aerospace yardmaster." BMEWS sites then become the focus, "all-seeing watchtowers of defense, scanning, searching, probing, penetrating the cosmic reaches of outer space from the top of the world." Viewers are taken through a relatively lengthy, slow-paced tour of a BMEWS site to a backdrop of electronic, organ-like music. Indeed, the BMEWS site is compared to "a giant pipe organ, through which surges a concerto of sensitized chords, chords broken into minute parts and concentrated to form a central sounding board capable of capturing the relay of movement from the boundless lanes of infinity." The men of the BMEWS sites, Massey explains, live "like moles in an underground domain of ice and snow."

The film comes to a close by returning to NORAD, where a military man interacts with an electronic map in the darkened control room. "As we stand today," Massey concludes, "we are somewhat in the same position that we were in the fifteenth century when the explorations of Marco Polo, Magellan, and Columbus opened up new vistas of man's world." An image of the title page of a book by Erasmus cuts in; as the camera draws back, we see a young Air Force officer reading it intently. "So exciting," Massey continues, "became the hopes of the future that the great scholar, Erasmus, in the closing years of his life, expressed his reluctance to die with this vast new world opening up before him. Today man on the threshold of century twenty-one continues to delve into the laws of nature and is coming closer to solving the mysteries of the boundless universe. And with the promise of this bright and enlightening era, the importance of defending our hard-earned freedom has increased enormously."

In closing, viewers see an animated image of the Milky Way, then an animated image of the Earth, then an image of the Air Defense Command shield, and finally the closing credits, all to the choral anthem "This Land of Ours."

As this summary suggests, *Shield of Freedom* throws together into twenty-nine minutes what seems to be a hodgepodge of themes and arguments. And yet there is a basic rhetorical coherence which runs throughout the film that ends up asserting itself with relentless discipline: "history" has been compressed into the interminable "future" of national security. The NORAD commander that the film first introduces describes this "future" as demanding continuous change and adaptation in the name of deterring the aggressor, putting off, interminably, an apocalyptic end to American history. From the standpoint of this interminable "future," all that is past or "history," be it Pilgrims or Native Americans or Erasmus, is available for the "symbolic" legitimacy of the deterrent system.

Deterrence was, to be sure, a White Man's story, but one *Aleutian Skywatch*, *Eyes of the North*, and *Shield of Freedom* reach to make the cosmos's story. In *Aleutian Skywatch*, Captain Huntley finds not only himself but history incorporated into the deterrent system, made visible and meaningful within only large-scale, high-speed technological systems. In *Eyes of the North*, men—White Men—remain in control, but are at home only within the deterrent system. And in *Shield of Freedom*, man the maker rather than man the conqueror sits on top of Earth and stares into space, a new frontier as boundless in scope as the deterrent project itself. Indeed, the voracious aesthetic appetite of *Shield of Freedom*, which gives the film both a quality of camp and art, mirrors the voracious appetite of the deterrent system, which carried at once the urgency of "future" and "necessity," and at every step promised far more than it could deliver.

United States Air Force Academy

The creation of the Air Force Academy was a decidedly image-conscious affair. The Air Force recruited renowned landscape photographer Ansel Adams to shoot starkly beautiful images of the mountain home of the academy; its architecture was designed by the vanguard firm of Skidmore, Owings, and Merrill; and even the cadet uniforms were carefully designed, by renowned filmmaker Cecil B. DeMille no less. The United States Air Force Academy would not only be devoted to symbolism and iconography; in itself it was a symbol and an icon. And in the cameras of Lookout Mountain Laboratory, it would be a stage.

Lookout Mountain produced a number of films promoting the Air Force Academy: *Wings of Tomorrow* (1955), *Creation of a Monument* (1956), *School of the Sky* (1958), and *At the Ramparts* (1966). The unit also produced recruitment films to encourage young men to apply to the academy, including one featuring musician Tennessee Ernie Ford. These short recruitment pieces were broadcast on television nationwide. Film and visual materials also played a large role in the education of cadets at the academy, with Lookout Mountain doing a fair share of the work. And Lookout Mountain filmmakers were regularly on campus to document notable academy events, from graduations to football games to visits from dignitaries.

In many ways, the Air Force Academy was an ideal subject for Lookout Mountain's ongoing efforts to further Air Force identity. A gleaming jewel of modern design perched against a landscape long identified with the sublime, the Air Force Academy provided Lookout Mountain with a ready stage for projecting a majestic Air Force in an age when much of the world feared the annihilating destruction that Air Force power could bring.

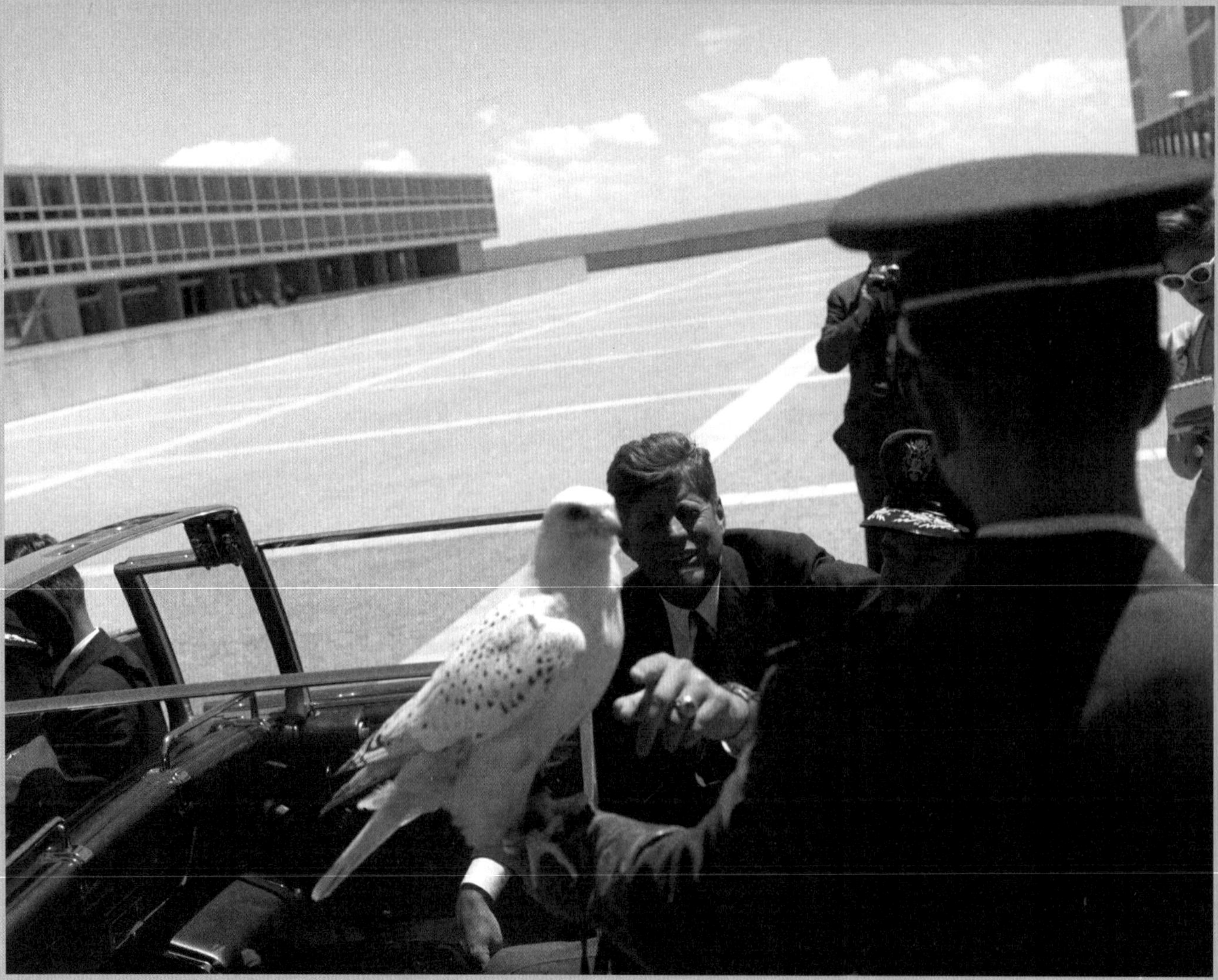

Two cinematic acmes in *Shield of Freedom* illustrate this. First, there are the remarkable moon-landing animation and space-travel montages, imaging and imagining what would be in but a half-decade's time. The Earth sits high in the sky, taking the place the sun normally holds in similar terrestrial vistas. An elegant spaceship comes to land softly on the wide-open barren plain of the moon. Men in snug white space suits exit the spaceship from the top, as if descending from a tower, dropping supplies to the surface. A space station is seen orbiting the Earth, cumulous clouds at ease far below, lightly covering the sea. Men in space suits sit erectly at the controls of their space vessels, rocketing this way and that. The second highpoint comes but a minute after the space-travel sequence. Cameras pan slowly across the inner workings of a BMEWS station: cylinders, struts, beams, pipes, and braces weave together in a complex but symmetrical architecture, composing a modernist marvel.

In both scenes *Shield of Freedom* approached the status of art: the scenes were as powerful as anything being produced in Hollywood science fiction in the early 1960s. Yet here *Shield of Freedom*'s voracious aesthetic appetite also comes into view. Its rhetorical point was that technological necessities have surpassed old imperial justifications, pushing America into frontiers that are "new," less in the sense that they are as yet unconquered and more in the sense that their possession is a matter of technological imperatives rather than economic or overtly political ones. The Arctic was paradigmatic here: remapped as a boundary between the Soviet Union and North America, its transformation into an engineering geography was justified by the air-atomic-age threat of surprise nuclear attack, just as the DEW Line system depended on a new understanding of the atmosphere as an ionosphere, a space of transmission for remote communication across unprecedented distances.[37] That the reimagining of the Arctic would give way to reimagining outer space as a new frontier for technological dominion was entirely in keeping with this new imperial rationalization. Or was it? What deterrent purpose could a moon landing have? What's the air-defense point of the interplanetary travel that *Shield of Freedom* forecasted? What "shield" could be built for the nation when the Earth is but a planetary ball on another planet's horizon? Neither *Shield of Freedom* nor any of the other Air Force Arctic documentaries had answers; the questions were not even posed. Productions such as *Shield of Freedom* were thin on argument but big on symbolism. Indeed, as these films were being made, the Cold War's "symbolic" dimensions were in high gear. Kennedy had ridden to the presidency on the power of the image [his own above all], promising a closing of the "missile gap" and the engineering-enabled exploration of space as the next great techno-symbolic achievements of American liberalism, "new frontiers."[38] Lookout Mountain's missile-defense films went right along with Kennedy, producing an extravaganza of images and associations, a voracious artifact of symbolic conquests.

And the Arctic was the stage. First "discovered" by the engineers of the Cold War as an opportune space for triggering massive retaliation in case of a Soviet nuclear attack from the north, the Arctic became a test site for both large-scale, systems-based technological systems *and* the tight-quartered remote living of men in "uninhabitable" climates: the two spectacular poles of the US space program in the 1960s. By 1963, with Soviet nuclear attack technologies accelerating at a pace in proportion to, if not in keeping with, US capabilities, the dream of radar defense, a "shield of freedom," was very difficult to sell. The easier sell, as Kennedy knew, was the symbolism of American technological adventures in outer space. *Shield of Freedom* suggests that the Air Force knew this too.

PHOTOGRAPHY is

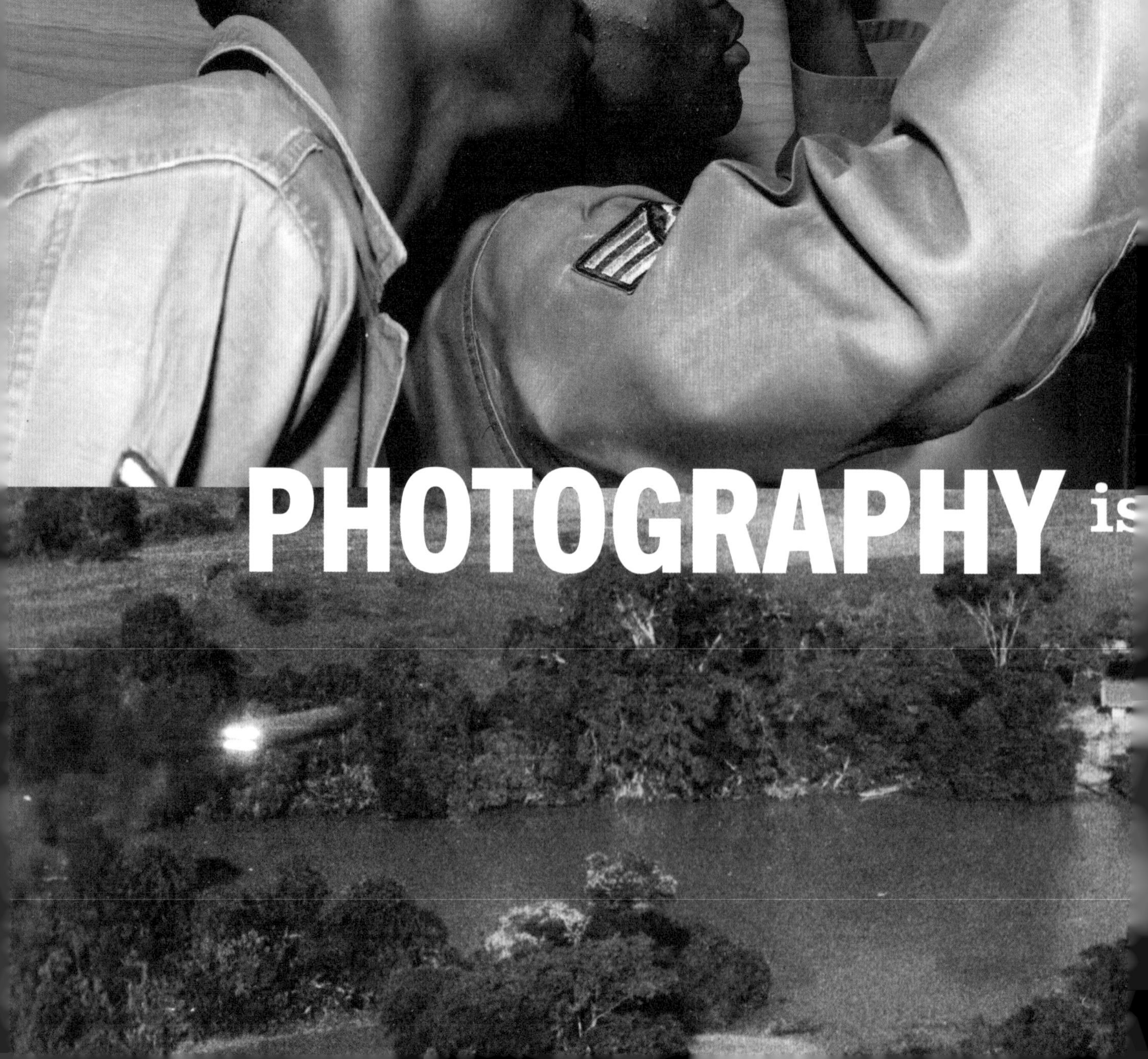

he RAW MATERIAL

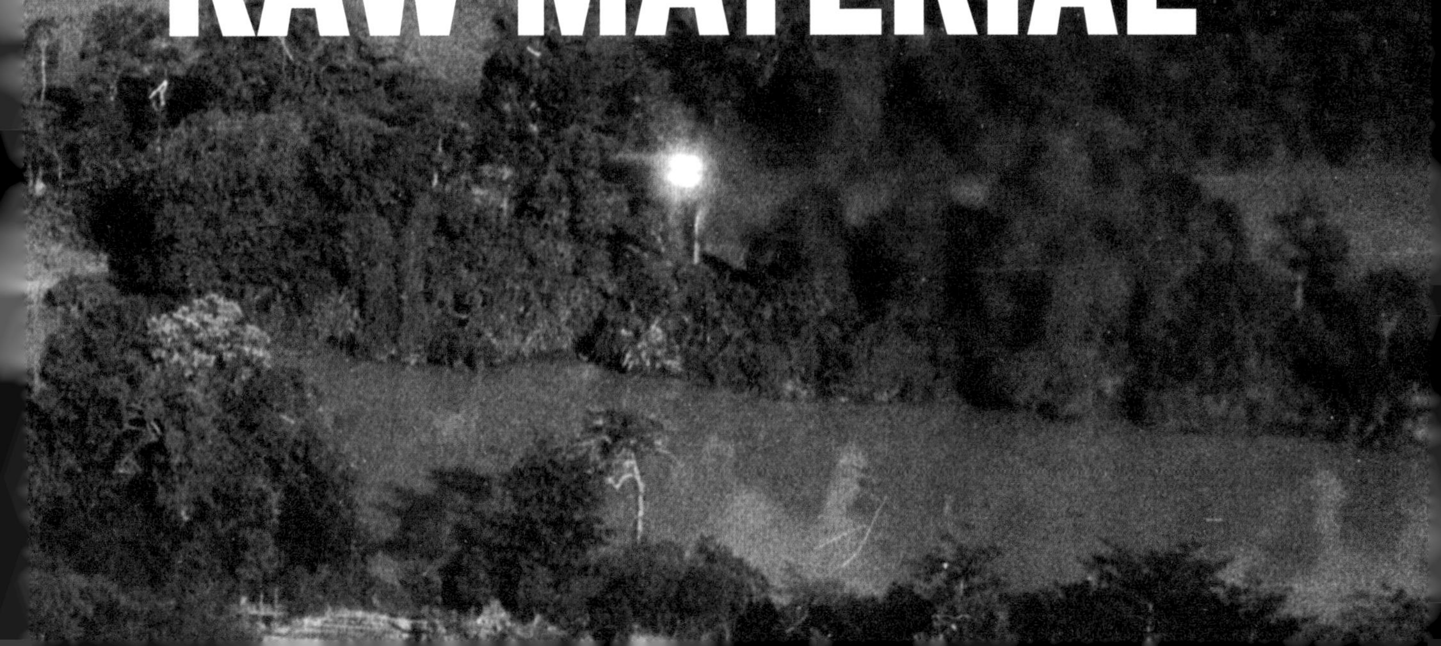

Chapter Eight

THE VIETNAMIZATION OF THE COLD WAR CAMERA

One. B-29s scramble; atomic bombs are dropped, one on Hiroshima, the other on Nagasaki. Two. Winston Churchill, at an outpost in rural Missouri, describes "an iron curtain." Three. George Kennan's "Long Telegram," followed by his "X" article, establishes a strategy of containment. Four. Andrei Zhdanov describes a "crusade against Communism" originating in America, one that uses "diverse means" such as "the cinema, the radio, the church, and the press." Five. A thermonuclear device ignites in the Pacific; word gets out by means of errant radio signals. Six. A coup d'état in Guatemala is led by the CIA, for President Eisenhower against President Árbenz. Seven. Sputnik. Eight. Mao Zedong launches the Great Leap Forward. Nine. A fizzle at Novaya Zemlya, an archipelago in the north of Russia where, in 1958, twenty-four nuclear weapons tests took place, twenty-three successfully. Ten. A wall is built in Berlin; people cry. Eleven. U-2 photos show missiles in Cuba. The world scrambles.

And so the Cold War tick-tocked, year by year, right up to an end. But this end, the End, was too horrible to contemplate, as Kennedy saw with Cuba. And so the United States got into the business of "safeguarding credibility" by sending combat troops and warplanes to deter Communist aggression in what Kennedy's secretary of state, Dean Rusk, referred to uneasily as the "periphery."[1] "If you don't pay attention to the periphery," Rusk warned, "the periphery changes. And the first thing you know the periphery is the center. . . . What happens in one place cannot help but affect what happens in another."[2] In the ensuing war in Vietnam, it was as if the strategic scriptwriters had reached a bargain: instead of a cataclysmic end, let's make the real surreal, history a loop rather than a dead end, and war an ad hoc exercise in new operational idioms and management techniques aimed at saving face, rather than the means of global annihilation. Therefore, innumerable sorties flew daily from airfields called

Udorn, Ubon, Bien Hoa, Nha Trang, Tan Son Nhut, and other transliterations of names otherwise exotic and illegible to the American ear. The sorties dropped explosives, chemicals, and chemical explosives on the dense wood of the jungle, and took pictures as they did—the cameras often triggered by the same device that triggered the arms. The pictures were still and in motion: pilots reviewed them with professional interest; Air Force commanders watched them with cynical impatience; and the public periodically saw them on the nightly news. Meanwhile, virtually everyone paying attention agreed that Vietnam was an "unwinnable" war (one must never stop asking, what does it mean to "win" a war?), but this did not keep it from being the most thoroughly filmed and photographed war the United States had ever fought.

In this chapter, we follow Lookout Mountain Laboratory into Vietnam, the war that would end up wresting "cinema" from the outfit's grasp and knocking it headlong into new visualities and emerging technologies. Television and computers, the televisual and the cybernetic: these were not, as we might think, successive stages in the evolution of a technologically determined networked "globalism," but rather synchronized parts in the development of the global project we know as the Cold War. That war, which became so horribly hot in Vietnam, gave up on the heroics of the big screen as soon as it became apparent, all too apparent, that although the Cold War was an ideological war, it was one which the United States could not ideologically "win" by means of nuclear deterrence, let alone nuclear war. For as Joseph Masco has written, "Nuclear war is ultimately beyond the power of cinematic representation," which also meant it is beyond the range of ideology planning.[3] "Cold war" by means of the threat of nuclear war was self-defeating. Instead the Cold War was reorganized in the 1960s around combat operations in the "periphery" that were factored into the calibrations of "systems analysis." For the airmen of Lookout Mountain, this peripheral Cold War was rife with inputs and outputs, calibrations, metrics, data, processing, processes, chemicals, bombs, and nervous breakdowns.

And so the Vietnam War pushed Lookout Mountain out of the business of big productions featuring scripts, scores, rocket launches, and big bangs into the rhetorics and rhythms of small screens: the pulsing screens of television, made regnant in America by Kennedy's graphic death, and the graphical displays of computers.[4] The unit and its Vietnam-era spin-offs worked overtime during the war shooting, distributing, and processing millions of feet of film footage, most of it shot from the air. The aerial footage was intended for pilots and their commanders to analyze and quantify, supposedly to better calibrate aerial bombings. And highlights from the same footage were clipped and repurposed for the television screen, supposedly to better inform the American public of the Air Force's successes. In fact, neither effort was very successful, but this did not keep the Air Force from being utterly preoccupied with the processes of processing film footage: new systems, new temporalities, and indeed new technologies were developed to command, communicate, and control what later came to be called the "bright shining lie."[5]

This then is the story of the emergence of a cybernetic sensibility within the American Cold War state. It culminates not only in the end of Lookout Mountain Laboratory, but in the beginning of a new audiovisual regime, one premised on an ideal of communication and control that is noise free and embedded in self-regulating systems. This new audiovisual regime, we argue, was realized institutionally not only in the Air Force (via the establishment of the Aerospace Audio-Visual Service, or AAVS) but more broadly in America's Cold War. Indeed, at the heart of the story we tell, and of the distinction we draw between the cinematic and the cybernetic, are two visual cultures of America's Cold War. On the one hand, America's strategists cast the nation as a *sight to see* in the context of its war on communism. More than "a city on a hill," America was envisioned as a global

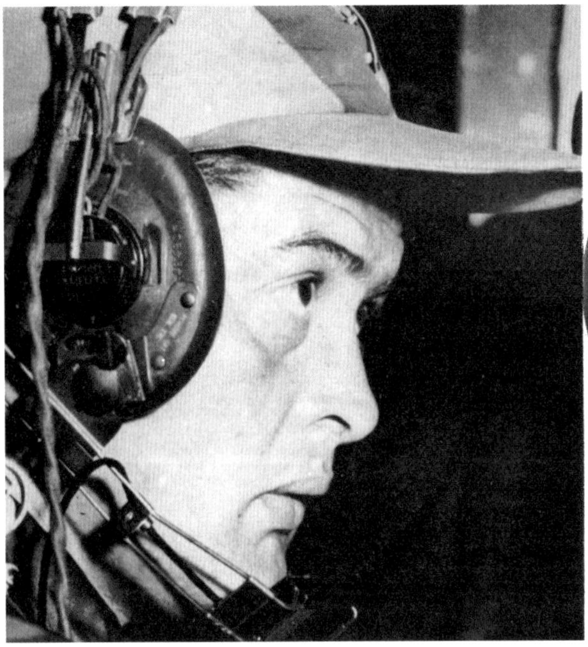

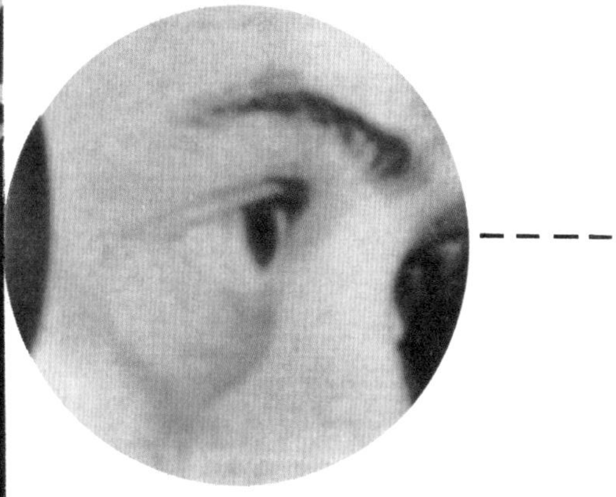

Your eye is like a camera, having a shutter, diaphragm, lens, and light-sensitive film.

force with which to reckon, a power that could purportedly, as President Kennedy declared in 1961, "deter all wars, general or limited, nuclear or conventional, large or small."[6] American power, as the strategists said using a cinematic metaphor, could be *projected* onto the world so as to manage international affairs. America was here an "image." On the other hand, America's Cold War gave rise to an insatiable American appetite *to see*, to monitor and survey the world over and render all actions and events as "data" or "information" to be processed. Here both television and computation, more than cinematic projection, were the central strategic metaphors, as America became a global monitor of world events. These two visual cultures, the cinematic and cybernetic, constituted a Cold War visual alliance that was also a Cold War visual contest, and cameras were situated at the heart of the contest.

In a seminal essay in visual studies, Hal Foster presents "visuality" as the social, historical, and discursive dimensions of the visual, as distinguished from its "physical operation" or what Foster refers to as "vision."[7] In a more recent work, Nicholas Mirzoeff, drawing from the work of Thomas Carlyle, recounts visuality as "the making of the process of 'history' perceptible to authority."[8] Visuality therefore entails the social construction of perception *and* power. But as Foster stresses, visuality and vision "are not opposed as nature to culture: vision is social and historical too, and visuality involves the body and the psyche."[9] Indeed, visuality is both configured with and within the physical mechanisms of sight. Hence, we can learn a great deal about the visual by attending the *visuality of vision*: that is, the relative visibility or invisibility of technologies of vision within a given way of seeing, as well as how these technologies are seen or not seen to be seeing.

Cameras play a central role in the visuality of vision. Cameras make images appear to spectators who sit at a spatial and temporal remove from the events filmed or photographed, and they authorize by means of their mechanical, electrical, and chemical bases the significance of the image as variously "authentic," "real," "artistic," "staged," "candid," "spectacular," and so on. Cameras here are instruments of representation and appear to possess an immediate relationship to their subjects, a relationship

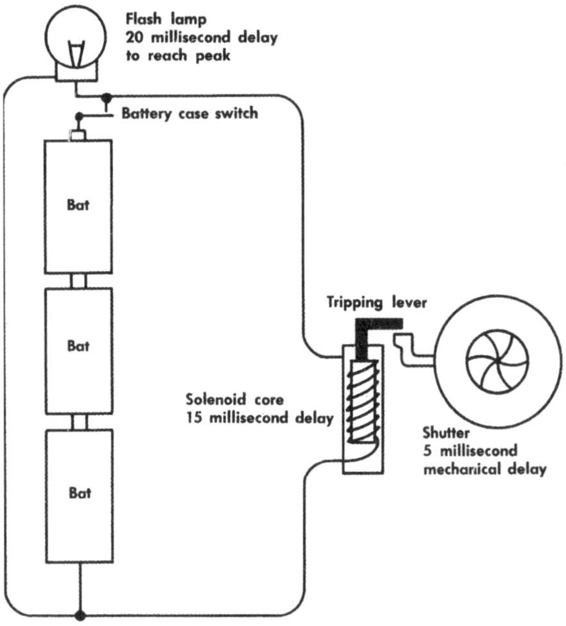

Fig. 70. Wiring and Schematic Diagram of a Typical Solenoid-operated Synchronizer

that brings new intensities to the representation of fantasy and reality alike. Significantly, within the field of representation cameras do not themselves typically appear to the viewers of images. Rather, they stand in a transcendental relationship to the image, constituting the condition of its possibility and forming the assumed basis of its authority. [Thus, Christian Metz writes of the spectator's "identification with the camera."][10] Here the visuality of vision consists of the presumption of both the power and prestige of cameras to frame a scene, record an event, shoot a portrait, tell a story, or construct an image, even as the camera is *not to be seen*—it is "invisible." As we have suggested in previous chapters, both the "big-screen" productions of Hollywood in the 1940s and 1950s and the spectacle of nuclear deterrence put cameras in a transcendental position and participated in what we call a cinematic strategic visuality. We will discuss further in this chapter how "big-screen" film and nuclear deterrence collaborated together to help constitute the US national security state of the 1950s as a nuclear-deterrent state.

Cameras, however, can appear in a very different manner as they give way to the flow of images. Surveillance images, for example, often lack visibility altogether, seen by few or none, except when representing the record of extraordinary, exceptional events. Even so, surveillance cameras exist *to be seen*—their physical operations are themselves, we might say, representations. Here the visuality of vision is centered less on *what* the camera sees and more on *that* it always sees and that it is *seen as always seeing*. Hence, while still participating in a representational regime, surveillance approaches the status of statistics, becoming one of the state's tools "for rendering the invisible visible, for making that which one could formerly only imagine into something factual and manageable."[11] Here cameras are less transcendental, a condition of possibility for the image, and more tools of *transcendence*, offering a "god's eye" view of a realm, a "panoramic *tour d'horizon* of a world far too vast for mortal eyes."[12] Indeed, as we will discuss, cameras were used widely in the Vietnam War as a means of surveillance, statistics, and analysis; and they helped give rise to what we refer to as a *cybernetic* strategic visuality, and with it a diffuse deterrent state in which the strategy of deterrence functioned apart from the "nuclear."

As we have seen in earlier chapters, as a script nuclear deterrence spawned new forms of routine action and reaction in the national security state: testing, operations, command and control, and a constant attention to the "psychological" effects of American Cold War activities. The rationalization of human labor amid the nuclear deterrent state also gave rise to new visualities of vision, new ways of seeing the operations of sight. Most significantly, two older visualities were combined into one system, spectacle and surveillance.[13] The spectacle of nuclear destruction, so widely circulated in still photographs and motion pictures, not to mention in the cultural imagination, represented both the threat—the sign of an intention to destroy if provoked by the Soviets or another adversary—and the fantasy of national survival amid a nuclear holocaust.[14] Surveillance, conducted by means of aerial photography, radar, seismology, and other forms of electrified vision, was a means of gauging provocations and of constructing the fantasy of a shield around the homeland. Amid the national preoccupation with nuclear deterrence in the 1950s, both spectacle and surveillance drew on cameras as representative tools of "vision."

Hence, images of nuclear tests shot by the photographers of Lookout Mountain Laboratory took on major strategic significance, quite apart from any technical or scientific data they might offer, for deterrence made the display of American power central to its exercise of power. Such display was not mere propaganda. Rather, display was integral to the structure and direction of the script of nuclear deterrence. Tests were means of establishing the credibility of the overwhelming nuclear threat before the adversary and of communicating before the same adversary American competence and control. And these displays of American nuclear power were not for America's adversaries alone: throughout the advent of the nuclear age, nuclear tests were used to quiet the worries of US government officials, America's geopolitical allies, and citizens in the United States and abroad about the capacity of the United States to control its daunting new atomic arsenal. Nuclear tests were intended to "prove" such control, and as Masco has argued, summon the sorts of affective states among the citizenry that would be "politically useful."[15]

In an essential and not merely propagandistic manner, therefore, nuclear tests were scripted *for and by cameras* as tools of both spectacle and surveillance. Not only was every nuclear test that America staged in the 1940s and 1950s enveloped by electrified image machines, but so were the myriad of instruments and exercises that comprised the nuclear deterrent state. Cameras were part of broader political and cultural networks of image and story production. In the context of the strategic script of nuclear deterrence, cameras functioned as the transcendental condition of strategic possibility. Cameras did not come to nuclear deterrence from the "outside" so to speak, merely to "document." Rather, they were a condition of its possibility.

In the 1940s and 1950s, Lookout Mountain served the nuclear deterrent state. As we have

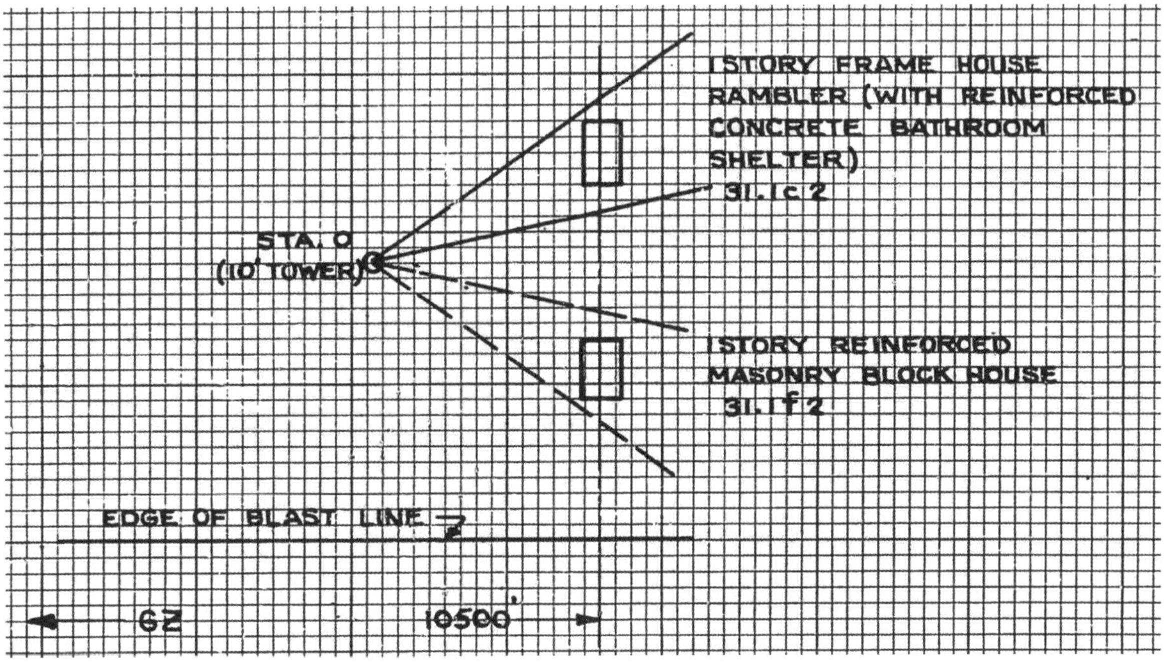

seen, in 1947 the Air Force established it to provide "specialized photographic documentation of atomic weapons tests."[16] Lookout Mountain thus began primarily as a film production unit, taking film footage shot by their own photographers and other government units at nuclear tests and producing from it "documentary" films about these operations. However, within a short time, as we saw, its mission expanded to include more and more on-site photographic shooting of nuclear tests. It became at once a full-scale, Hollywood-style film studio and a global camera operation. As such, Lookout Mountain was integrated into the logics of spectacle and surveillance that were themselves so integral to the nascent strategy of nuclear deterrence.

As we saw in chapter 4, *Operation Ivy* put into the form of narrative film the emergent script of nuclear deterrence. Even more, in certain respects the film *performed* the script of nuclear deterrence: by covering through hundreds of cameras hidden from the screen's view the full scene of a massive state operation and by offering, in turn, the image of a future End in the form of the "the largest explosion ever set off on the face of the earth," *Operation Ivy* performed both surveillance and spectacle, and produced in cinematic form the convoluted rhetoric of dissuasion that typifies nuclear deterrence. Indeed, American nuclear deterrence, as it developed in the 1950s, rested not only on the visualities of surveillance and spectacle, but also on the ability of the United States to control the story, and to do so indefinitely. For deterrence was a script in need of production.[17] Formally speaking, the major motion documentary picture, produced in the idiom of the Hollywood spectacle, enclosed into a singular aesthetic system each of these components: surveillance, spectacle, story, and epochal temporalities. Nuclear deterrence, we might say, was a "big-picture" strategy that found an aesthetic counterpart in the big-picture cameras and screens of Hollywood, and had found its place within a cinematic visuality.

By the late 1950s, the United States, with the Air Force at the lead, was fully organized around the script of nuclear deterrence. Strategic Air Command, under the command of General Lemay, stood at the center of an overwhelming nuclear striking force, ready to act upon the president's command [and even, quite possibly, apart from that command]. Meanwhile, aboveground nuclear tests, which a few years earlier had been the most complex and spectacular of state operations, were increasingly routine. Though nuclear scientists and other engineers of the Cold War saw nuclear tests as indispensable to the further advancement of these weapons of mass destruction, Eisenhower became willing to dispense with them if a testing moratorium could be used as a bargaining chip in diplomatic negotiations with the Soviets. Conditions were ripe, it seemed, for nuclear weapons development to stabilize, and for nuclear deterrence to become the economical basis for the "long-haul" approach to national security that Eisenhower had desired since taking office in 1953.[18]

But it would not be so: far from stabilizing, deterrence would undergo significant transformations in the next decade. First, America's nuclear weapons capabilities would continue to grow. Both the United States and the USSR were building ever-growing "triad" nuclear forces, combining land-based strategic bombers with intercontinental missile forces and submarine-based nuclear arsenals. The result was a combined nuclear striking force capable of forever exterminating most species on Earth, all in the name of national security. The expansion of nuclear forces under the auspices of deterrence would eventually be codified as Mutual Assured Destruction, or MAD. It "guaranteed" reciprocal destruction if either side launched a first strike. According to the theory of Nash's equilibrium, the "guarantee" would prevent either nation from precipitating a nuclear attack upon the other.[19] And so the world was left looking at an apocalyptic End to keep the peace.

The second transformation in deterrence was far less dramatic, but just as consequential: *deterrence* supplanted *nuclear* deterrence to frame a subtler but more generalized American approach to the Cold War, and indeed to the horrible "counterinsurgency" war in Vietnam. The idea of coercion by means of threat became an overarching script for American war, as in the 1960s not only the Cold War but the more notorious "hot war" in Vietnam were made in the image of deterrence. For the explicit goal in Vietnam for Presidents Kennedy and Johnson, with their secretary of defense Robert McNamara, was not to conquer the adversary, but rather to compel them to behave amenably toward US interests. War, especially aerial bombing, was seen as a *communicative* means by which to do this.

McNamara's approach to Vietnam was premised on the idea of "flexible response" and the methods of "systems analysis" to calibrate responses.[20] Rather than commit to one or several courses of action, McNamara, acting in the vein of the corporate executive he had been with Ford Motor Company, used weekly meetings in the Pentagon and White House to gauge and adjust the progress of the war in Southeast Asia, right down to selecting particular bombing targets. Throughout, McNamara and his advisers approached warfare as a form of message sending not only to their immediate adversaries, the North Vietnamese and Vietcong, but also to the broader world. US offensives in Vietnam were understood as essentially communicative, a means of asserting American prestige, compelling compliance, and above all deterring enemy aggression and expansion through the display of American military force.

As John Lewis Gaddis writes of the relationship between "flexible response" and America's humiliating defeat in Vietnam, "Rarely have accomplishments turned out so totally at variance with intended objectives."[21] While many factors contributed to the futility, and indeed absurdity, of the US war on Vietnam, Gaddis explains it in terms of a curious fixation on the part of McNamara and his team with "process." They assumed "that the defense of Southeast Asia was crucial to the maintenance of world order; that force could be applied in Vietnam with precision and discrimination; that means existed to evaluate performance accurately; and

that success would enhance American power, prestige, and credibility in the world. These assumptions in turn reflected a curiously myopic preoccupation with process—a disproportionate fascination with means at the expense of ends—so that a strategy designed to produce a precise correspondence between intentions and accomplishments in fact produced just the opposite."[22]

A preoccupation with process was a major feature of the US war in Vietnam, at least as it was operationalized from above. But Gaddis too hastily concludes that this was at the expense of ends, for it is clear that the goal of the war for the White House was to coerce the North Vietnamese, and secondarily the Vietcong, into a particular behavior pattern for rhetorical reasons, namely, the maintenance on a global scale of US prestige and credibility. As Gaddis writes of the assumptions guiding the Kennedy and Johnson administrations in Vietnam and elsewhere, "Power, they believed, was as much a function of perceptions as hardware, position, or will; minute shifts in distribution—or even the appearance of such shifts—could cause [they believed] chain reactions to sweep the world, with potentially devastating consequences."[23] Indeed, when it came to the US war in Vietnam, *perception* was the end in sight, and the preoccupation with *process* became the means by which to structure perception.

Again, there is both an Air Force bombing and an Air Force camera story to be told here. Throughout the war in Vietnam, the Air Force and McNamara incessantly argued over the nature and extent of the air attack. The Air Force pushed for an aggressive assault on North Vietnam, meant to utterly disable and destroy the enemy. McNamara, however, insisted on restraint. From McNamara's perspective, as the infamous *Pentagon Papers* summarize:

> The air war against the North was launched in the hope that it would strengthen GVN [South Vietnam] confidence and cohesion, and that it would deter or restrain the DRV [North Vietnam] from continuing its support of the revolutionary war in the South. There was hope also that a quite modest bombing effort would be sufficient; that the demonstration of US determination and the potential risks and costs to the North implicit in the early air strikes would provide the US with substantial bargaining leverage; and that it would redress the "equation of advantage" so that a political settlement might be negotiated on acceptable terms.[24]

In McNamara's thinking, the air campaign "should be structured to capitalize on fear of future attacks. At any time, 'pressure' on the DRV [North Vietnam] depends not upon the *current* level of bombing but rather upon the credible threat of *future* destruction which can be avoided by agreeing to negotiate."[25] Warfare had thus become not only a form of instrumental communication, or message sending, but also the fine-tuning of messages: just as McNamara sought to calibrate nuclear deterrence through the imposition of "systems analysis" and game theory, culminating in MAD, so too he sought to calibrate his deterrent "messages" to the North Vietnamese via the air war, and it was here that he butted heads with the Air Force.

Even so, both the Air Force and McNamara saw air war as a means of demonstrating to the adversary American power and resolve, and both conceived of the air war as always entailing a *threat of future attack*, on not only the North Vietnamese but also other adversaries in the world. The Air Force simply wanted to do the threatening by means of big bangs, shock and awe, and spectacle. General Lemay "called for an end to the policy of sending 'messages' in the form of the low-level military actions, in the hope that Hanoi would change its policy . . . . It was time to convey a 'message' sharply and directly."[26] Habituated to the "money shot," the Air Force wanted to go big, but McNamara and his civilian advisers held tightly to the reins of the air war [especially early on], pursuing "perceptions" that better fit small rather than big screens.

For the Air Force, the detachment of "nuclear" from "deterrence" in Vietnam was correlated with a shift in photographic labor, technologies, and circulation patterns. A small crew of photographers—numbering fewer than ten—was sent from Lookout Mountain Laboratory to Vietnam in 1962. This seemingly minor episode would represent the beginning of the dramatic transformation of Lookout Mountain's activities and a transformation in Cold War visuality with implications across the armed forces. While the camera in service of *nuclear* deterrence borrowed from cinematic techniques to establish authority for the image as *witness*, deterrence in Vietnam required a different sort of camera, a cybernetic camera. This new camera did not serve the spectacle of potential massive destruction, but the calculus of measured threat; it served not as a transcendental condition for witness, but as a node in the system of state power. If the cinematic camera in nuclear deterrence lent authority, in transcendental fashion, to the image, the cybernetic camera lent the authority of transcendent vision to its impersonal, institutional bearer. Indeed, the human bearers of these cybernetic cameras became hard to see. Within the older regime of nuclear deterrence, the camera operator was a craftsperson and a *flaneur*. As a valued, if often silent, expert, the photographer under nuclear deterrence was cast as an adventurer in the construction of the image of America. Under the regime of supranuclear deterrence, however, the engineer and the manager surpassed the photographer in importance. The resulting images' ability to incriminate, demonstrate, or threaten was dependent not on the artistry of the camera, but on the analytic system of which the camera was but a part. In the context of this diffuse deterrent state, the cybernetic photographic system included not only the regimes and cycles by which the camera captured data, but also the labor that managed it, ensuring visual truth through the guarantee of regularity and precision. Spectacle lost primacy—indeed, the image itself did not speak in the cybernetic regime, but had meaning only as part of a larger set of nested systems processing inputs and outputs.

The organizational conditions for the Air Force transition from cinematic to cybernetic visualities were already stirring in the early 1950s, when managers began to weigh the inefficiencies of the decentralized, improvisational managerial style of cinematic labor at the squadron level against its benefits. The year 1951 saw the creation of the Air Pictorial Service (APS), given a mission to "control and supervise all Air Force activities in the fields of photography and television."[27] By all accounts, however, the Air Pictorial Service (later named the Air Photographic and Charting Service after the addition of charting and aerial mapping to its mission, and still later absorbed into the new Aerospace Audio-Visual Service) assumed little of its mission in the first decade of operations. Rather, photographic squadrons could take a decentralized, improvisational approach with relatively little interference from upper management. Meanwhile, nonphotographic units in the Air Force—which were often tightly managed—hardly noticed the relative freedom of the photographic and motion-picture units. Though cinema was central to the Air Force's public identity, nonphotographic units in the Air Force saw photography as a mere material or logistical concern that could be procured and employed as needed, and thus not in need of centralized supervision.[28] Thus despite the establishment of the Air Pictorial Service, in the 1950s specialized photographic units continued to rely on improvisational techniques that did not translate particularly well into centralized, hierarchical systems. Lookout Mountain was a case in point. In serving the nuclear testing regime in the 1950s, the 1352nd had drawn from whatever film production and photography techniques and technologies were available; and when no suitable techniques and technologies were to be found, they invented new ones. When the first Lookout Mountain personnel arrived in Vietnam in 1962, it was this ethos of expertise, adventure, and improvisation that they self-consciously brought with them. They shot and produced "Fact Finder" films meant to orient Air Force headquarters back in the United States on Air Force "ordnance, personnel, and training needs" in Vietnam, and built and ran experimental, mobile, trailer-based film-developing labs to process aerial footage of potential targets, landing spots, and strike damage photographed by pilots. In the first half of 1962, the small detachment managed to cobble together sixty-one thousand feet of camera footage while working on the fly.[29]

Film footage of strike damage, however, would become more and more central to Lookout Mountain's work in Southeast Asia, and thus their work would become more and more systematized. On January 1, 1963, Lookout Mountain spawned a formal detachment in Vietnam, Detachment 3-1, which was assigned to work with the Second Air Division of the Air Force [later in the Vietnam War known as the Seventh Air Force], which had been providing air support to the armed forces of the Republic of Vietnam. The still small crew of Detachment 3-1—one officer and nine airmen—spent much of their energies in 1963 working on equipping American-made aircraft with Republic of Vietnam markings [in fact, sometimes flown by American pilots] with camera devices to record defoliation and bombardment successes and failures. The footage was developed in the mobile darkrooms Detachment 3-1 had built and sent back to the wings for review. With it, pilots could, among other things, calculate their CEP, or "circular error probable," the diameter of the circle encompassing 50 percent of the weapons delivered on a bombing run.[30]

As in their work on mobile darkrooms, this new combat aerial camera project started as a deviation from standard practice—fighter wings had in the past taken care of their own aerial photography. Detachment 3-1 stepped in to help the fighter wings by building a few different remote pod and wing-bracket camera assemblies for strike aircraft, using primarily 35 mm motion-picture cameras and 70 mm sequence cameras.[31] Pilots were to trigger the cameras remotely upon striking targets. However, the airmen of Detachment 3-1 quickly learned what they would relearn over and over again in Vietnam: pilots are not very good cameramen. They would sometimes forget to switch the cameras on, or—as frequently—they would accidentally run the cameras at the wrong time, wasting all the film stock on useless subjects.[32] Before long, Detachment 3-1 photographers—renamed Detachment 5 in 1964 to reflect their growing responsibilities—found themselves no longer following missiles off the California coast, or tracking bomb tests in the Nevada desert, but seated in the exceptionally uncomfortable confines of the backseats of fighter aircraft on low-altitude flights, taking snapshots of Vietcong targets and shooting airstrikes by hand with long-lensed cameras as pilots pulled away from their bomb drops. This footage, too, proved unsatisfactory: even these expert cameramen could not hold the camera steady amid the aerial convolutions of Vietnam.[33]

Detachment 5 struggled with airborne photography in Vietnam for nearly two years. Back in Hollywood, Lookout Mountain engineers and photographers hurriedly tried to problem solve. They eventually landed on a solution, designing and building from scratch camera "pods" that would be mounted on an airplane's wing or belly [where ordnance would usually be] and wired such that the 16 mm Milliken high-speed cameras inside—typically stocked with color film—would be automatically triggered upon the pilot firing ordinance. As of March 1965—after testing the devices at Nellis and Eglin Air Force Bases—the 1352nd had installed ten of these Type IV camera pods, as they called them, on propeller-driven aircraft, all of which operated smoothly.[34]

Indeed, the Type IV camera pods returned footage of strikes that the Air Force described as "spectacular."[35] The success of the Type IV program created an insatiable appetite at all levels of the Air Force for more "spectacular" footage from the skies above Vietnam; and as the 1352nd was not just responsible for building and installing the pods, but also for processing, storing, and distributing their film footage, the pressures on the unit became extraordinary. Whereas at the beginning of 1964 Lookout Mountain considered its most significant work to still be missile- and other nuclear weapons–

Type IV Camera Pods

Among other firsts, the Vietnam War was the first large-scale war in which the United States relied heavily on jets for gunning and bombing. As with jet-based assaults today, the military very much wanted high-quality visual recordings so as to gauge the effectiveness of the assault, surveil the visual field below, and provide pilots, gunners, and bombardiers with ready training material.

Lookout Mountain personnel were first sent to Vietnam to help process film, yet before long they found themselves in the middle of new photo engineering feats. By the middle of the 1960s, Lookout Mountain's Photo Engineering Division, led by Hal Albert, was quite experienced at building specialized camera mounts, the M-45 tracking mount being the most successful. In Vietnam, the division would build an even more successful device, the Type IV camera pod, which helped transform American jets in Vietnam into mobile multidirectional photographic recording devices, providing footage of the Vietnam air war that would whet appetites in Washington and beyond.

Charles Bradley, a Lookout Mountain engineer at Vandenberg Air Force Base, first began working on prototypes for the camera pods in 1963. He and the shop back at the Wonderland Avenue facility began by modifying discarded fuel tanks and napalm canisters. With cameras mounted behind glass at one end, the pod could be installed on a plane's belly in spots where armaments or spare fuel tanks would normally go.

Over the next two years, engineers at Lookout Mountain worked to eliminate vibration at high speeds, to integrate operation with other onboard electrical systems, and to develop recommendations on installation procedures, lens focal lengths, camera speeds, and even flight patterns. Lookout Mountain engineers would take regular trips to Nellis Air Force Base to test their modifications and innovations. Soon, Lookout Mountain would design even more integrated camera systems, rigged on so-called "blister" mounts reminiscent of the portals constructed on the "flying cameras" used at Operation Crossroads in 1946.

USAF Participation in Southeast Asia July-December 1963

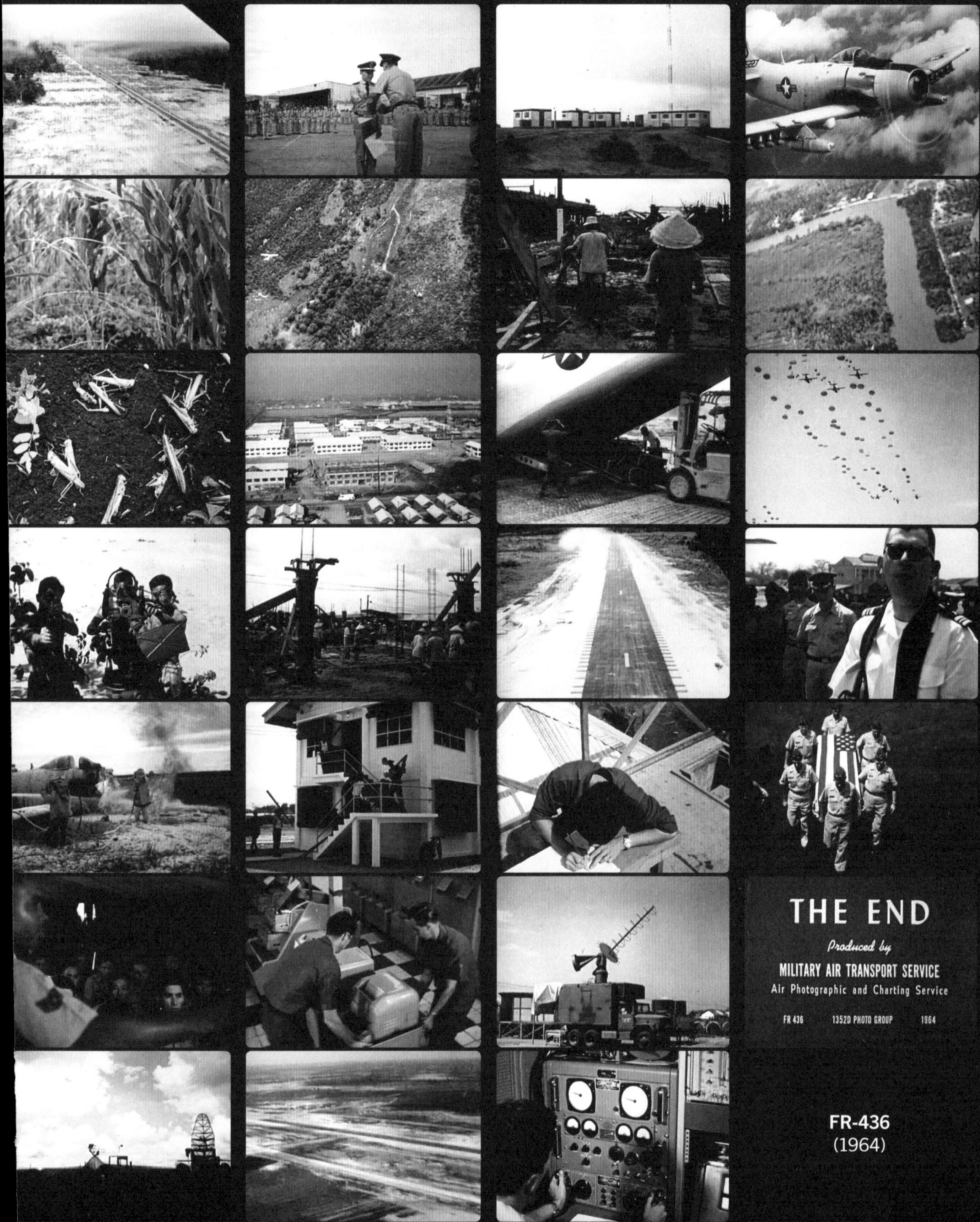
THE END
Produced by
MILITARY AIR TRANSPORT SERVICE
Air Photographic and Charting Service
FR 436
1352D PHOTO GROUP
1964

FR-436
(1964)

related activities [including space launches], by the beginning of 1965 the 1352nd would report that the air war in and around Vietnam was so taxing that the unit had to abandon or neglect these other significant projects. By the middle of 1965, the 1352nd reported that both its civilian and military personnel "expended thousands of hours of unpaid overtime to fulfill emergency requirements" of its Southeast Asia activities.[36] Over the first half of 1965, Detachment 5 of the 1352nd, based at Tan Son Nhut, exposed 82,855 feet of 16 mm color film, a staple of the new pods.[37] In the second half of that year, amid the rollout of the Rolling Thunder "calibrated" aerial bombardment campaign against North Vietnam, over double that amount was exposed, 204,644 feet.[38] Thus, whereas in 1963 Detachment 5 did not even exist, by 1965 it was the most significant and sizeable detachment in the 1352nd.

Meanwhile, Air Force command back in Washington, DC, began to worry that the Air Force was not getting enough airtime on television news. Hence, in August 1965 headquarters launched what they referred to as the "Skypoint" program. Among other things, this initiative required that the 1352nd begin to "receive, process, cull, print and ship to the USAF Command Post, Washington, DC, all pod motion-picture film within an 18-hour period from time of receipt to time of shipment."[39] Consequently, even as it was rapidly processing aerial bombardment photography, Lookout Mountain had to learn the new temporality of the televisual screen: whereas *Operation Ivy*, as we saw, was a two-year project, Vietnam footage for television was being demanded on a *daily* basis. The eighteen-hour schedule was made to do double duty as pilots, too, were demanding rapid turnaround of the pod footage, anxious to gauge their CEPs.[40] Lookout Mountain devised a system of processing and distribution that would turn out hundreds of feet of new footage some nine times a week. They made it their priority to get this footage back to the field in Vietnam as quickly as possible, sending additional copies to headquarters in Washington, DC, the office of Air Force information, the Pacific Air Force, and the headquarters of the Air Photographic and Charting Service.[41]

Thus by 1966, the use of cameras in Air Force Vietnam operations was becoming so ubiquitous as to render film footage the "raw material" of the war. "A great deal of emphasis has been placed on obtaining over-the-target motion picture coverage," Col. Frank R. Amend at Air Force Command Post wrote his subordinates in September 1965. "This type of photography is used in a number of ways and is the raw material from which a number of valuable end-products are produced." Henceforth, Amend ordered, it was essential that "a high degree of control, accessibility and identification" be established over the raw photographic material of the war.[42] Command wanted the film footage on demand, ready to do whatever bidding was deemed necessary, be it news, propaganda, instruction, or—as it seems the footage increasingly served—a means of constructing data for Pacific Air Command and the Pentagon to review in its ongoing efforts at calibrating this war of nonnuclear deterrence.

The demand for data from a centralized photographic service found institutional form in the redesignation of Detachment 5 as a full-blown squadron at the start of 1966.[43] As part of an effort called Operation Morepix, the new 600th Photographic Squadron, based at Tan Son Nhut and supervising nine detachments across Southeast Asia, would carry photography ever deeper into the technological and strategic mechanisms of aerial warfare. As the planners behind Rolling Thunder increased bombings in their calibrations, the 600th worked with the 1352nd to develop and install a whole new suite of cameras onboard planes. In the hands of Lookout Mountain's specialists, armament recording expanded to include not only pods mounted below the planes, but smaller "blister" pods integrated into the body of the plane fuselage, gun cameras to capture strafing and plane-to-plane combat, scope cameras to record the onboard radar throughout each mission, and strike cameras that captured 180-degree

Experiments in Aerial Imaging at Lookout Mountain

Camera locations on an
F-105 Thunderchief

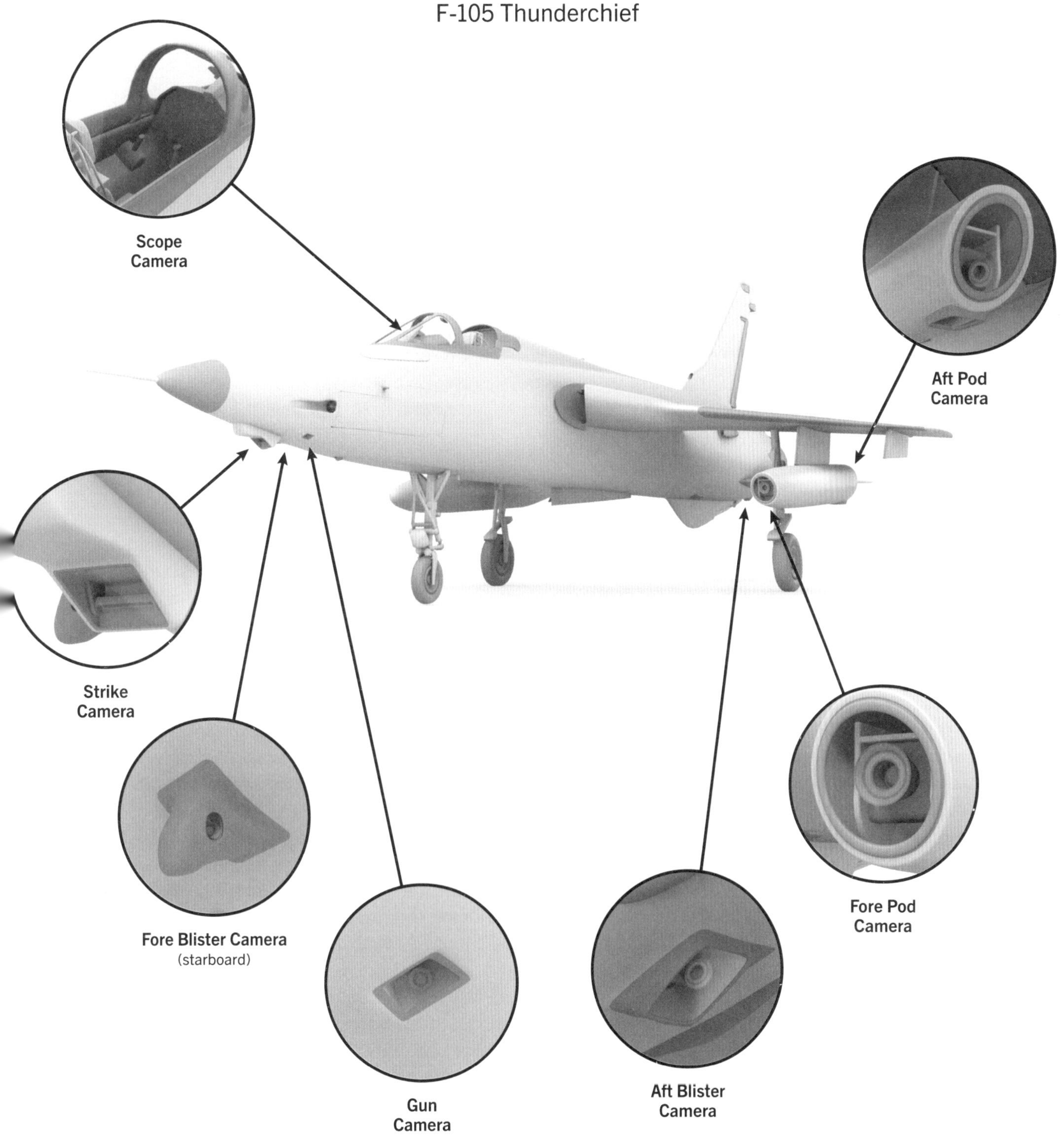

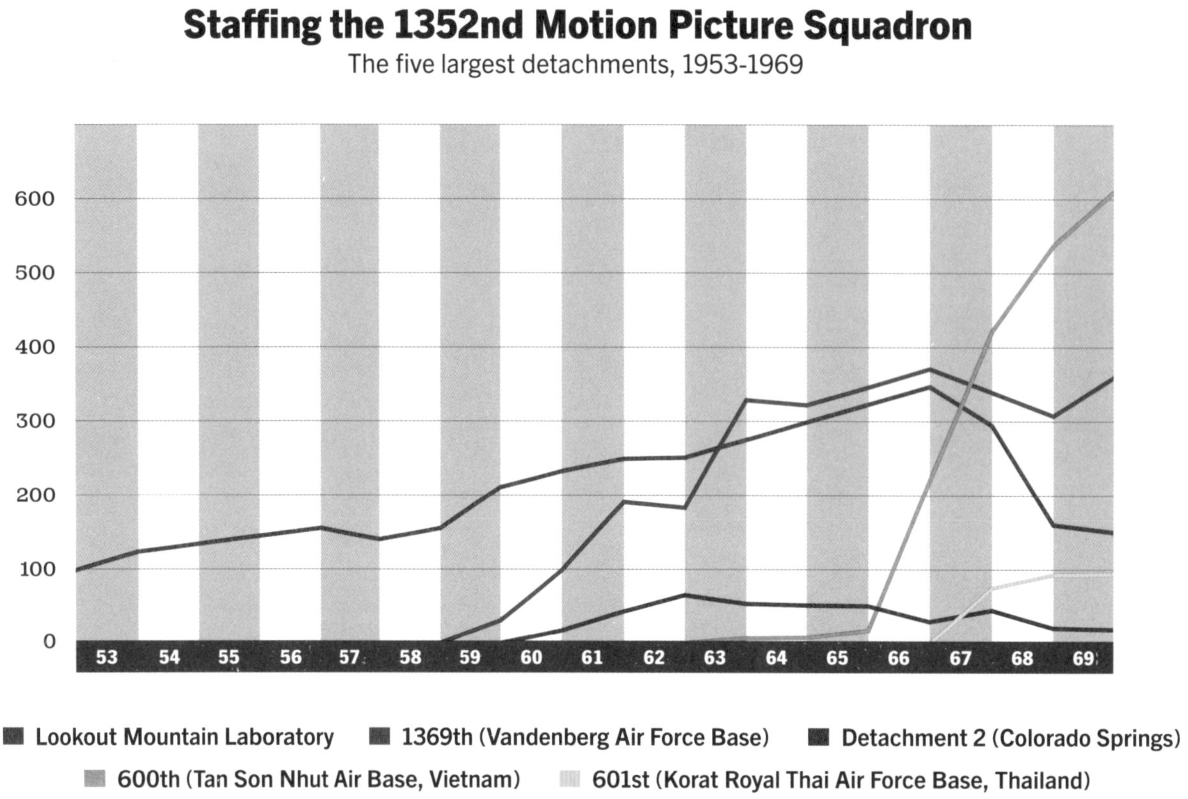

views of bombing targets before, during, and after attack.[44]

The 600th was formally inaugurated in January 1966 and assigned ten officers and 398 enlisted personnel, though the unit would still not have even half of the latter by midyear.[45] [Midyear also brought the loss of the first 600th cameraman—Airman Darryl G. Winters died when flying in the backseat of an F-100F on a combat mission.[46]] The Air Force placed one of their top photographic commanders in charge of the new squadron, Col. James P. Warndorf. Warndorf had led Lookout Mountain for six years during the height of nuclear testing in the 1950s, before being moved up to headquarters of the Air Photographic and Charting Service, where he became an advocate for consolidation of photographic responsibilities across the Air Force. [In 1965 the Department of Defense had charged him with leading a study of consolidating audiovisual needs across *all* the armed forces.]

Still, the 600th and 1352nd struggled to meet the demands of McNamara's efforts to make the national security state more streamlined, efficient, and flexible. Amid the continued Rolling Thunder campaign in 1966 and 1967, 600th personnel [now divided into fifteen detachments scattered throughout Vietnam and Thailand], especially those in photo labs, were worked to the maximum and were constantly understaffed.[47] Its photo labs operated on a twenty-four-hour basis, seven days a week. Some personnel did not get a day off for three or four months.[48] Whereas it had taken the 600th's predecessors three years to process their one-millionth foot of film, the second half of 1966 alone saw the total amount of film processed by the 600th exceed one million feet, a pace that held steady, and even increased, right up to the end of Rolling Thunder.[49] The workload meant that Colonel Warndorf found himself sending some of his men off to hospitals, suffering as they were from hallucinations and other

The Bob Hope Specials

Bob Hope, the multitalented star of radio and television, began his lifetime association with the US military during World War II, when he began touring bases to entertain troops, often bringing along fellow actors and musicians as part of the show. After the war, during the 1948 Berlin Airlift, the Secretary of the Air Force asked Hope to entertain the troops in Germany, leading to subsequent postwar tours of Korea, Alaska, and the South Pacific.

In 1954 the Air Force asked Hope to entertain airmen in Thule, Greenland. Hope agreed, but on the condition that the Air Force help him film the appearance for a Christmas television special. The Air Force gladly accepted, sending a Lookout Mountain film crew along with Hope's troupe. When the program hit the air, nearly 60 percent of the nation's viewers watched, Hope's largest audience ever. And so began his nearly twenty-year annual Christmas special and a new regular gig for Lookout Mountain crews.

The 1963 show from Korea earned Hope an Emmy and a Golden Globe award. The 1965 show from Vietnam saw a viewership of 24.5 million in the United States. Here, as always, Lookout Mountain was rarely publicly credited for their work, and their roles shifted over the years in accordance with the Air Force's agreements with Hope and the various demands of each annual show. Yet it is fair to say that in the Bob Hope Specials, Lookout Mountain Laboratory put its mark on the "golden age" of television.

See also

Faith, *Bob Hope: A Life in Comedy*.

"mental disorders." One of his men committed suicide.[50] To try to relieve his men of some of the burden, Warndorf mechanized approaches to film-processing as much as possible, creating less hands-on work. And in the fall of 1966, the Tan Son Nhut supply center of the 600th received a UNIVAC 1050-II computer to aid with logistics.[51] Still, the nervous breakdowns and suicides continued.[52]

But there was something more than new management techniques and metrics at work in the 1352nd's relentless push toward centralization, systematization, and processes: the *image* was also undergoing a profound change. Television was a major part of this change. The small screen, with its already incessant demand for content, meant visual power would be measured by the likes of Air Force brass less in terms of spectacle and more in terms of quantity of coverage. "Air time" was the new metric. Hence, the COMDOC [or Combat Documentation] division of the 600th, working without preset scripts or even specific assignments from above, set out each day to capture footage of the war and its environs that might make for good television.[53] The footage was sent by air back to Lookout Mountain in Hollywood, where it was reviewed, spliced, and edited into television-worthy clips that were sent to Washington, DC. Meanwhile, reviewers at Lookout Mountain and other units in the Aerospace Audio-Visual Service [which succeeded the Air Photographic and Charting Service in 1966] would regularly send critiques back to 600th cameramen in the theater of war instructing them how to better shoot footage for "good usable film stories" for television.[54]

This emphasis on ever-refined cycles of exposure, development, and distribution meant, as well, that unedited aerial footage, processed and prepared at great speed, was eventually available to pilots within as little as forty to sixty minutes of hitting the lab.[55] As Colonel Warndorf later recounted, "It got to the point where the pilot did not know what cameras he had aboard his aircraft, because everything worked automatically. When he [dropped his bombs], cameras started running. Consequently, we devised

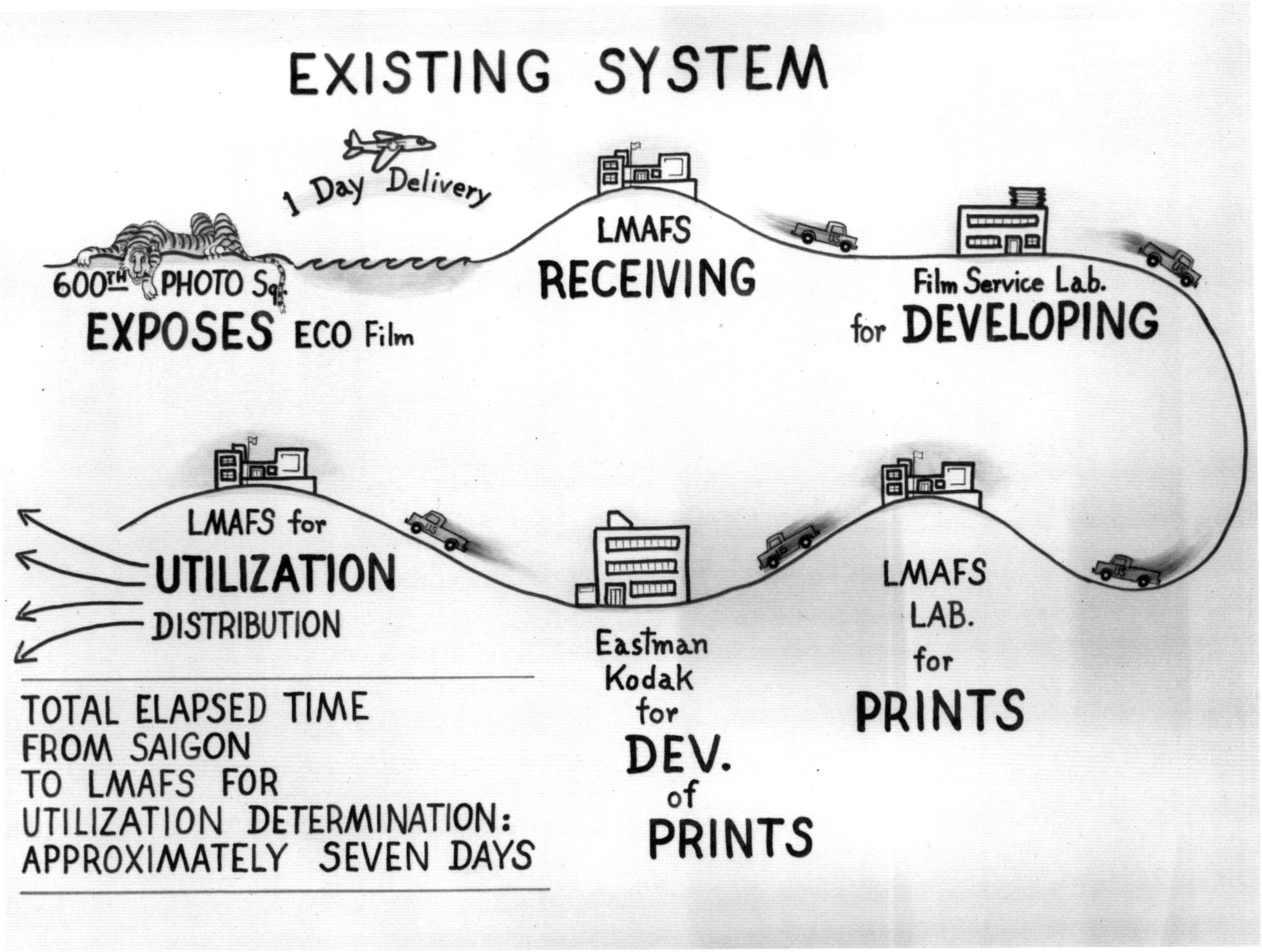
EXISTING SYSTEM
1 Day Delivery
600TH PHOTO Sq.
EXPOSES ECO Film
LMAFS
RECEIVING
Film Service Lab.
for DEVELOPING
LMAFS
LAB.
for
PRINTS
Eastman
Kodak
for
DEV.
of
PRINTS
LMAFS for
UTILIZATION
DISTRIBUTION
TOTAL ELAPSED TIME
FROM SAIGON
TO LMAFS FOR
UTILIZATION DETERMINATION:
APPROXIMATELY SEVEN DAYS

a form in Thailand that when the pilot landed we'd say, 'You exposed ninety-seven feet on your strike camera. It operated satisfactorily. You used your guns, and your gun camera magazines are empty, not empty.' We'd tell him what he had done photographically; and that form went into the debriefing; and the debriefing officers were aware that there was photographic evidence now being processed, in a lab, of what this particular aircraft had done on his mission."[56]

Indeed, the so-called single-manager approach to Air Force photography that Warndorf championed and helped to develop may have had as its chief achievement a situation in which neither the cameraman nor the cameras were visible to those up the chain of command: "There was photographic *evidence* . . . of what this particular *aircraft* had done on *his* mission." Here the image collapsed into process, the photographer into photographic structure, and the camera into a system of data collection. At the same time, the pilots themselves were integrated into a disciplinary regime made possible by the transformation—at the hands of the 600th—of their fighter planes into "flying cameras." At one point Pacific Air Command headquarters stepped in to take over postflight review from the pilots altogether, subjecting the footage from combat planes to analyses and analytics from above, and sending feedback to individual combat pilots regarding their CEPs and other efficiency measures. The pilots so resented the process that they worked to keep good footage of their missions from getting back to headquarters. Eventually, headquarters relented and returned the review process to the tactical wings.[57]

Whereas in the nuclear deterrence regime, an affectively potent still or moving image was often the end goal, this new deterrence regime—based on "flexible response" and "calibration"—treated affectless "information" as an end goal. The war's planners did not need images—they demanded information. As part of the management and training of pilots, affectless images served to ensure the precision needed for a calibrated deterrent war. To be sure, morale also remained an instrumental goal: aerial camera footage was regularly edited into "highlight" films screened for commanders in the field and at headquarters overseas. The Air Force Office of Information also tried to make effective use of these highlight shots, albeit to little effect. Ultimately, however, such highlight reels were peripheral to Vietnam—they often functioned as inputs with no clear outputs. Rather, the chain of nested systems that began with cameras in cockpits ended not with affective "money shots" on movie screens, but in a well-lit room in the White House, where the Johnson administration planned the war from week to week. On Tuesdays, a small group of men would convene for lunch in the president's dining room, the same room where Johnson's family ate their daily meals. At these "Tuesday Cabinet" meetings, as the gatherings came to be known, men would fine-tune the deterrent war in Vietnam.[58] Johnson, McNamara, and their advisers kept the future tense of the spectacle of nuclear deterrence in place; but now without the nuclear, they sought to stimulate the imagination of the North Vietnamese and Vietcong with respect to future destruction so as to steer them to the negotiating

table. But even more, the surveillance of deterrence took hold for McNamara and his advisers. They wanted their war games played with full information.

Official photographs of these deliberative sessions portray the group seated in a well-lit room before open windows, papers interspersed with the remnants of lunch. The Tuesday Cabinet meetings took place apart from any darkened visual-presentation space in a well-lit setting suitable for reading tables and charts, or watching television. Still, the setting for these critical conversations was seemingly epochs away from the screen-oriented operations centers that dominated depictions of decision-making bodies throughout the Cold War. Though images of potential bombing targets likely lay buried among other dossiers and papers full of statistics, there were no visible images of the war in Vietnam before this executive deliberative body. Rather, the dominant image in the room was a nineteenth-century panoramic landscape depicting Virginia's Natural Bridge and Revolutionary War scenes, put there by Jacqueline Kennedy. Thus, while Johnson and his men sat amid the images of war, it was war rendered nostalgic, pastoral, and pure.

It was as if the camera, so central to America's Cold War, had to become not only invisible by being integrated into a cybernetic system, but actively transcended. While Vietnam was on fire and the wider world preoccupied with rockets and nuclear fireballs, the White House constructed a stage for deliberation that was fitted to the eighteenth century. Here, amid paint and paper, decisions would be made that would leave many Americans, some of them for the first time, publicly asking not only *why?*—Why this horrible, senseless war?—but *what?* What had America become?

shutterstock
mushroom cloud
Photos
Popular
New
Best Match
Photos
Orientation
Color NEW
People NEW
Photos ×
Mushroom Cloud Stock Photos, Illustrations, and Vector Art (3,948)
Related: nuclear explosion, atomic bomb, explosion, mushroom, nuclear bomb, bomb, nuclear, atom bomb, apocalypse, atomic explos

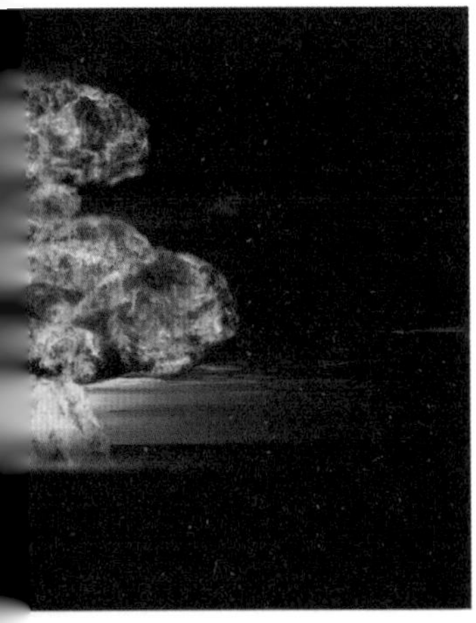

Chapter Nine

MUSHROOM CLOUD CAMERAS

In a widely cited journal article published in *American Literary History* in 1991, "The Nuclear Mushroom Cloud as Cultural Image," Peggy Rosenthal recalled visiting Albuquerque's National Atomic Testing Museum and seeing what she described as "a videotape cut from a 1954 television film of the first H-bomb test, 'Mike'": "As footage of the red fireball and rising mushroom cloud is played, replayed, then held still with a sketch of the Manhattan skyline inserted to demonstrate the extent of the damage, the narrative voice exults: 'An island completely erased. Mike was power. . . . Complete annihilation!' The voice sounds wild with delight, but without a trace of either hatred for a potentially annihilated enemy or concern that the erased island could be Manhattan."[1]

The "videotape" to which Rosenthal refers is, of course, Lookout Mountain Laboratory's *Operation Ivy*, which, as we saw in chapter 4, was at the center of an irresolvable debate within the national security state about who gets to see what and in what ways with respect to America's nuclear past, present, and future. *Operation Ivy*, that is, was far more than a "1954 television film," as Rosenthal describes it. It was an event in history of American visuality, statecraft, and politics.[2]

It was also an event in the history of the sensibility of the state. *Operation Ivy*'s musical orchestration; its plot; its dialogue; its maps, charts, and graphs; its Hollywood host: together they worked to make sense of America's nuclear operations and to incorporate them into a national, and indeed international, common sense. In the middle of the 1950s, nuclear visuality and sensibility were such twisted matters—tangled threads of sound, image, argument, and story—that, again as we saw in chapter 4, the very Hollywood styles and mechanisms meant to have their biggest impact on publics may have had their most powerful impact on President Eisenhower himself; and the scientific styles and mechanisms constructed for official audiences—maps, charts, graphs, and the like—may have had their most profound effects

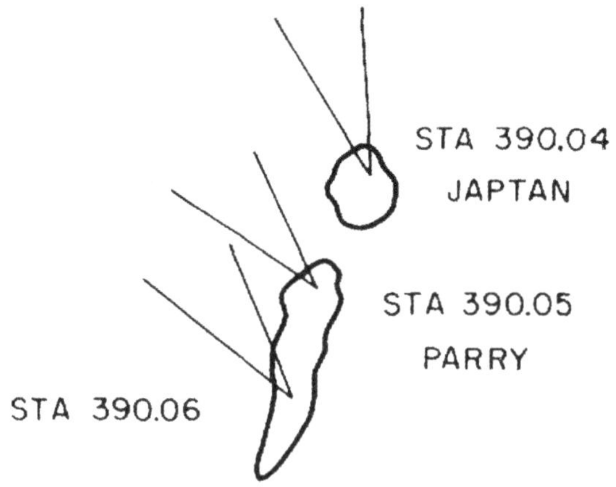

Fig. 2.13—Location of auto-remote camera stations for Mike Day.

on the public. Indeed, in the first half of the 1950s, there was no settled way of looking at the Bomb, let alone a common sense or sensibility about its historical significance.

Nevertheless, Rosenthal's identification of the film clip as "a videotape cut from a 1954 television film" [as if *Operation Ivy* were an arcane piece of 1950s nuclear melodrama] together with her concern at the lack of concern in the voice of the narrator, points to the eventual achievement of a common sense and sensibility in American culture around nuclear rhetoric, as well as a more settled set of the social and cultural visual practices suited to it. To Rosenthal in the 1990s and to us today, the narrative voices, the fireballs, and the mushroom clouds of Lookout Mountain's films are jarring at best, silly at worst. They speak to us as from another era, another age, a now distant past of geopolitical drama and big-screen spectacle, when the likes of Marilyn Monroe and Humphrey Bogart could capture the mass imagination and presidents could campaign on formulas as simple as "I like Ike!"

But this past is not distant. The bombs and missiles that Lookout Mountain filmed, the fallout that their film could register only in traces, the silos and the sites of strategic gaming, the test areas, and the logics of nuclear deterrence and rhetorics of nuclear annihilation are all still with us, even if Ike's eventual successor to the seat of nuclear sovereignty, President Donald Trump, weekly makes a mockery of them in ridiculous tweets. Scholars, critics, and even everyday citizens would do well to problematize, rather than normalize, the way the nuclear past seems to come out of a strange Nowhere to surprise, shock, or amuse us. To render Lookout Mountain films and images morally reprehensible, or just plain odd, kitsch, or camp, is to transform the nuclear past into a cultural and political *terra nullius* with respect to our own present cultural and political life.

More than any other type of image, the image of the mushroom cloud articulates the distance we have put between our nuclear past and present. The nuclear mushroom cloud is "dated," not in the sense of "old"—though to many it is that—but in the sense of a *particular time and place*. In fact, every photograph or motion picture of a nuclear mushroom cloud has its historical provenance in a particular state operation. These images are, more so than most photographic subjects [a kiss, a skyline, or a flower], intensely of a time and place: like snowflakes, no two nuclear mushroom cloud images are alike. Indeed, the ubiquity of cameras at nuclear tests in the 1940s, 1950s, and 1960s was an indication of the unique importance of each and every particular nuclear detonation to the national security state. Yet as Robert Hariman and John Lucaites have argued, the mushroom cloud is an *icon*, "not any one photograph but a composite image that remains in the mind's eye after seeing hundreds of versions of the same." Indeed, critics, scholars, artists, and publics habitually approach the image of the mushroom cloud as indexing what Hariman and Lucaites characterize as "a general condition rather than a specific event."[3] Hence, we pull our nuclear past—our particular, historical, and dated nuclear past—out of history and make it akin to a spiritual condition that comes to us out of nowhere to appear in our fantasies, nightmares, exhibits, and uncovered archives. This, to make matters more challenging, is what the state producers of the mushroom cloud could be said to have intended: as we saw with *Operation Ivy*, the mushroom cloud was scripted as signifying an epochal or liminal event, such that it was not to be comprehended within the frame of "history" in any mundane sense at all. It was to be, as we saw with *Operation Sandstone*, otherworldly. That the archives of the particular state operations which generated particular mushroom-cloud images have been, and still are, subject to intense state secrecy furthers this otherworldliness, as state secrets often seem to come to us as from another world.

Rosenthal's encounter with *Operation Ivy* in Albuquerque's National Atomic Testing Museum is illustrative here. Had she, as we later did, wished to know the provenance of the "television film" she saw in 1991, she would have not gotten very far, not without security clearances. The Department of Energy's Openness Initiative during the Clinton administration, which largely made possible the book before you, had not yet been enacted. That it took an act of the state to disclose the archives necessary for historicizing the state operations responsible for the generation of the mushroom cloud as a record of particular state operations, as well as a cultural image and icon, is itself a commentary on overreaching state secrecy. It raises fundamental questions about the relationship of the state to the conditions necessary for historical perspec-

tives. "Always historicize!" cultural critic Fredric Jameson famously declared.[4] Yet in a kind of Foucauldian rejoinder, we have been repeatedly reminded in the course of writing this book that it is not always structurally possible to historicize, and moreover, to historicize by means of the archive is to participate in the very same state structures that are responsible for nuclear violence.

Indeed, there is one population for whom the nuclear past is always present, and for whom historicizing nuclear images matters in intimate ways: either the people who have suffered the effects of these bombs, or whose family members have suffered such effects. For the soldiers, test workers, neighbors, and residents of test sites—the "downwinders" who experienced radiation sickness or cancer as a result of these tests, or whose livelihoods were affected by relocation or contamination—the bombs themselves, as well as their clouds, have always been painfully present and historical. For decades, state secrecy about these tests had the very material effect of keeping the stories of irradiated downwinders and test workers out of the courts, where proof might result in restitution. In fact, the Clinton-era Openness Initiative was primarily aimed at serving these people, focused as it was on fallout studies and radiation measurement. Indeed, the iconic life of mushroom cloud imagery could be said to work against the cause of downwinders and test-site workers not only as it removes the Bomb from history but as it propagates a notion of the bomb as relatively contained, wherein visible force and light are its greatest effects. But these clouds dispersed, and radiation at its most dangerous is invisible, not iconic.

Given this, what does it mean to approach the mushroom cloud as present history? What else can we add to the work of those who have worked so hard to rescue these events from iconicity and secrecy, wresting them back into histories that aspire to pass muster in court settings? What does it mean to look for other stories in the documents released to serve juridical work? Such are the questions lurking throughout this entire book, but they come into focus in this penultimate chapter. As we proceed, we will not so much try to untangle the twisted threads of sensibility, visuality, cinema, and cybernetics in the official production of nuclear images as follow the threads, turning this way and that to show how science and spectacle, culture and the state, image and icon, and diagnostics and judgment intertwine throughout this history right up to the present.

To historicize the mushroom cloud would be to restore the frozen or bracketed cinematic sequence to its place within a longer reel. The most straightforward thing we can say is that the long reels of Lookout Mountain Laboratory had a pivotal role in the production of the mushroom cloud as a cultural image and icon. It was Lookout Mountain Laboratory, together with its government contractor partner EG&G, that solidified the iconicity of the mushroom cloud; for with the partial exception of Operation Crossroads and a few Nevada tests, images of mushroom clouds came in and through official state cameras, and these cameras were by and large either those of Lookout Mountain or EG&G.

What about *how* to look? Perhaps a treatment such as Bruce Conner's 1976 experimental film CROSSROADS is in order, wherein viewers see original footage of that early Pacific detonation played back repeatedly, and in real time, from different angles—often allowed to play long past the cloud's dissolution into mist and air. Projected in an art gallery, the footage [some of it shot, we'll remind you, by the group that would become Lookout Mountain Laboratory] invites contemplation of the cloud's aesthetics as a tem-

poral and even sculptural event. Diegetic sound abruptly comes in and out through the first half of the film, allowing viewers to briefly experience the projected horizon as their own and to project themselves into this historical event. On one occasion, Conner's edit even allows a clip to play out until the camera swung down away from its subject, reminding viewers of the human operator, peering out a lens-shaped hole in a modified C-54 "flying camera" plane. On another occasion, before cutting at the film's midpoint to the large white cross shape that starts and ends the film, viewers see a mushroom sequence shot from the atoll; and for almost a minute it is unclear whether they are watching a still, a slowed clip, or a real-time view. The icon in Conner's CROSSROADS becomes visually and temporally unstable; the film never lets the audience rest for long in any one approach to image or time.

So too, we do not want to rest too long in any one way of looking at Lookout Mountain Laboratory and the mushroom clouds it produced. We have argued throughout this book that Lookout Mountain was caught up in two sensibilities, the cinematic and cybernetic. Likewise, the mushroom cloud was the product of cinematic and cybernetic visualities. These sensibilities and visualities were sometimes complementary and other times in competition with each other. But never did one work independently from the other. They were coproduced. Sensibilities structured visualities, even as visualities informed sensibilities. The cybernetic animated and coursed through the cinematic even as the cinematic informed, framed, and otherwise influenced the state's cybernetic sensibilities and visualities. The mushroom cloud appeared in the cameras of Lookout Mountain and EG&G as both the subject of story and spectacle and as the subject of diagnostics, surveillance, control, and cognition. These cinematic and cybernetic modes of sensing and ways of seeing represented two simultaneous aspirations of the nuclear deterrent state, aspirations that could appear, depending on the particular historical situation, as harmonies or as antinomies.

Thus, while the overall argument of this book is that through the cameras of Lookout Mountain we see the American Cold War state graduate from a cinematic sensibility [think story, spectacle, actors, props, and imagination] to a cybernetic sensibility [think data, signals, processes, operators, consoles, and cognition], we also mean to complicate the evolution of the Cold War state, which is now the twenty-first-century national security state, by showing how the cinematic framed the cybernetic, and vice versa. And nowhere do we see the simultaneity and reciprocity of the cinematic and cybernetic better than in the historical emergence of the "mushroom cloud" as a subject of the camera's aesthetic and analytic framings.

While "Trinity," Hiroshima, and Nagasaki each produced a mushroom cloud, it was Crossroads that transformed it into an object of fascination and anxiety, as well as something of a cultural image and icon. These tests offered to the world a virtual picture book of black-and-white images of glistening, if imposing, mushroom clouds.[5] Still, other images were not as extraordinary. After the tests, the Navy's Vice Adm. William H. Blandy, who oversaw the operation [including having to fend off public anxieties that the blasts would blow a hole in the bottom of the ocean, draining the sea], was pictured at a celebratory gala event in Washington, DC, together with his wife cutting a puffy white mushroom-cloud-shaped cake, his wife wearing a white hat that looked like a cumulus cloud.[6] Indeed, early on a significant aspect of the image of the mushroom cloud, in addition to its size and explosiveness, was that it looked like a *cloud*, and in 1946 most Americans had little reason to fear clouds. That many of the Crossroads photographs were shot by Colonel Cullen's "flying cameras" from the air only strengthened the association between atomic power and milky clouds. In these aerial shots, the mushroom cloud seems to gently rise upward to join a chorus of cumulus floating cotton. One scholar has observed of these photographs, "Photographed from above, the rising cloud looks like a blossoming rose," hardly a terrifying scene.[7] Even the ground-based shots told a story of cloud power, offering its object as a giant white canopy set against a Pacific horizon of sturdy palm trees and quiet waters.[8]

To be sure, these same photographs would soon become the focus of worries about the toxic power of nuclear explosions. In the aftermath of Crossroads, citizens, journalists, and experts sharply contested the dangers of atomic radiation. Historian Paul Boyer writes, "Bikini became a kind of ideological battleground, as its symbolism was appropriated for different polemical purposes. While some saw it as a useful antidote for imaginations overheated by fears of the bomb, others tried to use it to sustain such fears."[9] Reports started to appear that suggested the Crossroads bombs had emitted lethal quantities of deadly radioactive material into the sea and sky, and the cry of contamination competed with the military's celebratory cheers.[10] The image of the mushroom cloud already contained within itself the contradictions of the new nuclear age.

Hence, controlling images of mushroom clouds, with the hope of controlling their meanings, rose to be among the most significant problems of the national security state. Beginning with the next test series, Operation Sandstone in 1948, the Atomic Energy Commission and the Department of Defense attempted to take hold of the unstable significance of nuclear weapons by strictly limiting photography of nuclear tests. Official cameras thus became means of official spectacle and surveillance in an official and permanent nuclear state. At the same time, the notion of nuclear deterrence grew in power and persuasiveness within the national security state, becoming official doctrine during the Eisenhower administration. Within the logic of nuclear deterrence, the mushroom-clouded spectacle of nuclear destruction, widely circulated in still photographs and motion pictures, not to mention in the cultural imagination, represented both the threat—the sign of an intention to destroy if provoked by the Soviets or another adversary—and the fantasy of national survival amid a nuclear holocaust. Surveillance, conducted by means of aerial photography, radar, seismology, and other forms of electrified vision, was a means of gauging provocations and of constructing the fantasy of a shield around the homeland. Amid the national preoccupation with nuclear deterrence in the 1950s, both spectacle and surveillance drew on cameras as representative tools of official vision.

From "Trinity" in 1945 to "Dominic" in 1962, photographic technologies and techniques, including motion-picture photography, were also a means of establishing a different kind of control over nuclear weapons by assuring, at least in theory, a comprehensive visual record for scientific analysis. Indeed, even the mushroom cloud was subject to the visual tracking of cameras and visual analysis. Time-lapse photography was used to chart the course of the atomic blast from its inception to its dispersion. The language used by Lookout Mountain Laboratory to describe the process was patently cybernetic, rooted as it was in the metaphor of a living system: "Cloud growth studies were made throughout the Teapot series. The life history of each atomic cloud [was] recorded by time-lapsed photography from birth to eventual dissipation by winds at altitude. Analysis was made of the influence of weather patterns on cloud evolution."[11]

More commonly, high-speed cameras were used for fireball photography: they afforded engineers and scientists means by which to detect physical phenomena that the unaided human eye simply could not discern because of the scale, brilliance, rapidity, heat, and debris-ridden nature of the nuclear blast, not to mention its radiochemical toxicity. Such vision was integral to building bigger, more efficient bombs, as well as for offensive and defensive planning for a nuclear war. For example, through high-speed photography, Los Alamos scientists were able to solve a puzzle that had been perplexing them for some time: some weapons were only producing a third of the predicted blast pressure. Cameras were able to detect a "precursor wave" that accounted for the loss of blast pressure.[12]

These very same diagnostic images, however, were also used toward the end, again, of controlling the meaning of the Bomb. The mushroom cloud became, in the words of one Lookout Mountain film, "the symbol of nuclear power."[13] This sort of control—what was thought of in the Cold War deterrent state as a form of "psychological effects"—was of course more elusive for state operators to achieve than control of the physical processes [imperfect as the latter was]. But aspirations toward such control were always there, as well as a belief that such control was feasible, at least at the level of meaning production and management. Such aspirations were nowhere more clearly articulated in the annals of the American Cold War state than in an unsigned paper circulated in Truman's National Security Council in the early 1950s:

> It is a remarkable fact—one which might lose any next war for the United States—that while we Americans have spent billions on the so-called terror weapons, we have spent almost nothing on the study of the principal effect: terror itself. We have stockpiled atomic bombs. We have manufactured "nerve" and other poison gases. We have experimented with agents for "bacteriological" and "biological" warfare. We know that our potential foe has followed the same course. We know from theory and observation that all such instruments are rightly called "terror weapons" because they do more mental than physical damage even though they do enormous amounts of the latter.[14]

Such thinking was paramount in civil defense efforts, as well as the training of military personnel, both of which were focused on the subjective "psychological" states of individuals amid a nuclear attack.[15] It was also, as we have seen, integral to the form of psychological warfare known as nuclear deterrence. Cameras, working in their cinematic and cybernetic modalities, were essential for all this operational, scientific, psychological, and geopolitical work.

Not surprisingly, therefore, it was cameras themselves that were the subject of many Lookout Mountain films. Cameras circumscribed a self-conscious panoptic field of vision. Nothing, the camera's attention to cameras implied, would be permitted to escape the visual record, for the camera always sees, creating not just an archive but a comprehensive view, a god's eye view, of every nuclear detonation. With respect to knowledge, nothing will be lost to oblivion. With respect to witness, nothing will escape view. And with respect to judgment [be it scientific or political], no evidence will be missed. Hence, Lookout Mountain's nuclear testing films habitually turned the viewer's gaze on cameras, lenses, and other optical instrumentation.

This concern with what we called in the last chapter "the visuality of vision"—the way cameras were staged to be unseen or seen—was unique to not only Lookout Mountain's nuclear test films [including missile tests] but the American Cold War state more broadly. Cold warriors overwhelmingly wanted an opaque visuality of vision: they wanted, metaphorically speaking, cameras to see but to not be seen, projectors to project but not be seen as projecting. America's cold warriors were often preoccupied with naturalizing the state's operations, making them seem less than staged, the antithesis of propaganda. "The way to carry out good propaganda is never to appear to be carrying it out at all," declared Richard Crossman, a Cold War propagandist.[16] As Time-Life executive and Eisenhower psychological warfare adviser C. D. Jackson, once mused, "There is a basic dilemma which throws the problem [of propaganda] into the area of taste and intuition, rather than into a book of rules." Reflecting on his experience launching *Time* and *Life* magazines in Europe after World War II, Jackson continued, "By that I mean that these American publications, particularly Time and Life International, become immediately suspect if the overseas reader gets the impression that they are being carefully edited to or for him. Their entire usefulness, propaganda-wise, depends on their credibility, and they achieve maximum credibility if the foreign reader thinks that he is simply looking over the shoulder of an American reader, seeing the news of the world and of the US freely presented with no punches pulled, instead of seeing what is 'good for him.'"[17] No matter how the agents of the Cold War American state might have wanted to make the state appear to publics, they did not want the state to seem like it was staging itself to be seen. They therefore overwhelmingly used covert, indirect, or official means of propagation—anything to hide the deliberate state organs of message production, management,

and manipulation. The illiberal word "propaganda" was the last word American cold warriors wanted associated with their Cold War communication campaigns.

At nuclear tests, by contrast, the national security state went to great lengths to appear to be *staging* nuclear tests. This staging went well beyond the practices of laboratory experimentation to include national spectacle, civil defense rehearsals, military exercises, and the "theatrical display of resolve for the Soviets."[18] Here cameras not only circumscribed but constituted the stage; they offered not only the assurance of surveillance and statistics, but also the authorized production of images. Cameras represented, that is, not only means of diagnostics and data, but the technological conditions for the staging and publicizing of secretive national security operations. It was the cameras that announced this, not the remote test sites, not the official announcements of tests, not even the public relations officers of the Atomic Energy Commission. The state wanted the capacity for its secret nuclear test operations to appear as staged spectacles, and cameras were the condition of that possibility.

But the cameras did not even need to be seen on-screen for this visuality of vision to be manifest. Some of the most "staged" footage of nuclear tests was shot by means of high-speed cameras, most of them run by, and often manufactured by, EG&G. As we have seen, EG&G had been part of the nuclear weapons development program from the beginning, providing both timing and firing mechanisms for nuclear detonations as well as specialized photographic documentation. With respect to the latter, "technical" photography was their hallmark: EG&G's Rapatronic [Rapid Action Electronic] cameras, which were first used at the 1951 Greenhouse tests, could shoot an exposure rate of two to three microseconds [or millionths of a second]. The photographs from these cameras were used to measure the "yields" of bombs: knowing the distance of the camera from ground zero as well as the rate and time point of the exposed film, scientists could calculate bomb yield by tracing the growth of the fireball in microseconds.[19] But EG&G's cameras also could yield what Hollywood would recognize as "special effects": their otherworldly images of mushrooming fireballs and seemingly slow motion renderings of structures being flattened by winds of fire would transform the visual iconography of nuclear detonations.[20]

Yet the subject of these images was the camera as much as the fireballs or structures. They announced the technological spectacle of high-speed photography itself, indexing in their surreal images the presence of a camera.[21] Far from documentary realism, these photographs grasped for the "aesthetic." Rosenthal argues that such photographs—what she calls *the aesthetic mushroom cloud*—"deliberately deny everything about the reality they're drawn from except what they need to show off their artistic medium."[22] To the contrary, in the historical moment of their production these images *announced* the reality they were drawn from: militarized state science. They spoke of the laboratory, not just through their hermetic staging but because they offered "proof," glimpses of the unseen to publics that purportedly needed to be convinced less of the mysteries of nature and more the powers of science and engineering in the hands of the national security state. And they spoke the legitimating discourse of deterrence: *terror*, or as the case may be, *awe*—the affective ingredients of the deterrent threat—required an aesthetic perspective, not a "realistic" one.

At Lookout Mountain Laboratory, images served such reflexive purposes as well, announcing their own staging in a variety of ways. Diagnostic photography called attention to itself through the capture of unlikely, elusive, or dangerous images. Footage from pad cameras brought viewers uncomfortably close to the fires of ignited rocket engines, while pod cameras under tactical fighters in Vietnam produced spectacular images in frightening proximity to the hellish flames below. Such informational imagery served the cybernetic needs of self-improving

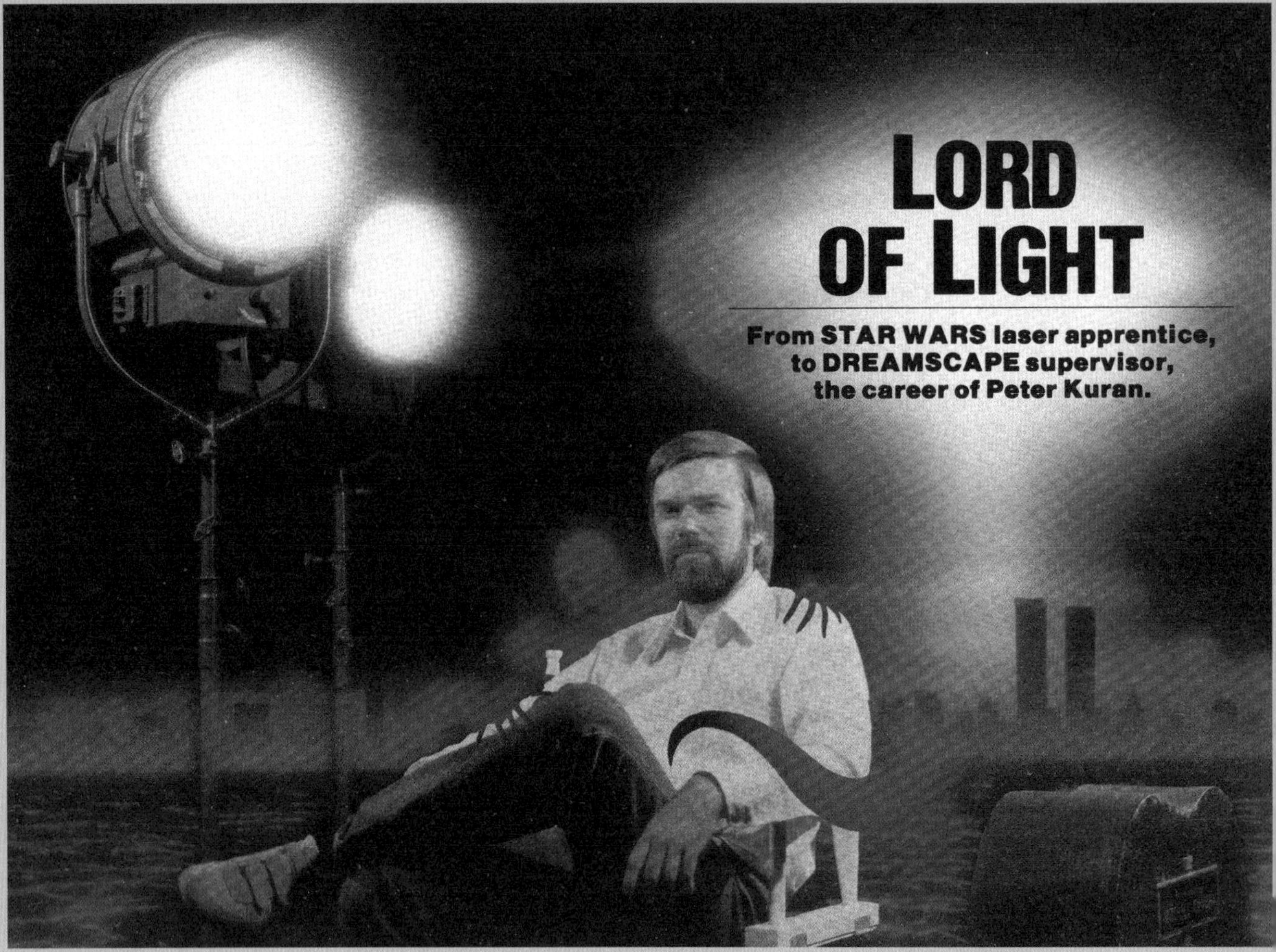
LORD OF LIGHT
From STAR WARS laser apprentice, to DREAMSCAPE supervisor, the career of Peter Kuran.

Peter Kuran

Peter Kuran, a special effects artist, animator, and filmmaker, has been critical to the legacy of Lookout Mountain Laboratory. He began his successful motion-picture career at the age of eighteen, when he joined the production crew of the first *Star Wars* film as an animator and rotoscope artist. From there, on his own or with his award-winning company Visual Concepts Entertainment, Kuran has worked on over three hundred films, including *The Empire Strikes Back* and *Return of the Jedi*, the *Robocop* films, *Men in Black*, and *The Thing*.

Kuran began devoting attention to nuclear test films in the 1990s, initially in support of his award-winning documentary film *Trinity and Beyond* (1995), which recounts the history of nuclear testing based on footage that had been little seen at the time. Through four more edited documentaries (including one on Lookout Mountain itself), a book, an iPad app, and licensing of restored versions of nuclear test films, Kuran has brought popular attention to Lookout Mountain's work and significance.

Kuran continues to work with the Department of Energy on the restoration of films from Lookout Mountain and EG&G, granting periodic views into the process through his YouTube channel. As such, Kuran and his company have become the primary access point to the clearest, most spectacular versions of these government-produced films. It is also more than fair to see in his special effects work, and that of others, a lasting legacy of Lookout Mountain Laboratory. Kuran is a student and steward of spectacular cinematic explosion shots, having learned from Lookout Mountain, as he writes in the introduction to his *How to Photograph an Atomic Bomb*, "the techniques and procedures for photographing an atomic or nuclear explosion."

See also

Stover, "Peter Kuran: Bringing Hollywood to History"; Kuran, *How to Photograph an Atomic Bomb*.

and self-correcting human-machine systems. On television or cinema screens, however, these same images proclaimed their own making in cinematic ways, anticipating the influential "smart-bomb" footage American viewers would see during Operation Desert Storm.

Meanwhile, imagery that emerged from Lookout Mountain with a more cinematic mandate also at times called attention to its own staging. Typically, this took place in a straightforward way, through photography of cameramen on the job. Lookout Mountain's photographers were rarely formally credited for their work in Lookout Mountain films. Hence, they turned themselves into occasional cinematic and photographic subjects, reminding spectators that the images of missiles, mushroom clouds, and sundry military operations came from somewhere and were shot by someone. Indeed, much of Lookout Mountain's twenty-first-century legacy has focused on the cameramen. In the work of Peter Kuran, the pages of the *Huffington Post*, the analyses of scholars such as Julia Bryan-Wilson, and the film work of César Pesquera, Lookout Mountain cameramen have served as indexes of nuclear awe, artistry, dilemmas, and danger.[23]

As we have seen, however, much of the cinematic work scripted and edited at Lookout Mountain avoided reflexivity, instead depending on the traditional seaming of diegetic time and viewer time common to classical Hollywood cinema, toward the end of implicating viewers in stories of the inevitable advance of nuclear weapons. Still, within the Air Force and the armed forces more broadly, the unit had a brand to manage and a reputation to maintain, much of which was based on exclusive expertise gleaned from not only experience but also proximity to the Hollywood film industry. Hence, in support of building credibility and brand, on occasion the unit would emphasize its cinematic imprimatur at the expense of seamlessly transporting viewers into the narrative. This took place most boldly in the unit's experiments with alternative wide-screen formats.

These included experiments in the unwieldy Cinerama format, which utilized multiple lenses for filming and playback to create a more panoramic view.[24] Circarama, a 360-degree version of Cinerama, was also used by Lookout Mountain. Disney loaned the unit an eleven-camera Circarama rig to film the newly completed Air Force Academy in action.[25] The resulting short film ran for a limited time in the Circarama theater at Disneyland, and some of its footage was spliced into an "America the Beautiful" attraction that would run at Disneyland for many more years. Lookout Mountain's work with such experimental formats, the products of which were circulated more through fairs and festivals than movie theaters, tended to emphasize spectacle over narrative, foregrounding technology over story.[26]

CinemaScope, a more technically manageable and therefore more widely adopted format, employed a combination of specialized anamorphic lenses and wide-format film stock to achieve a similar panoramic effect. Work in CinemaScope tended to emphasize narrative over reflexive attention to the media staging of spectacle, but still brought opportunities for the festival-like staging of enhanced visuality in marketing and branding.[27] Lookout Mountain was one of the earliest adopters of CinemaScope, working with developer Twentieth Century Fox studios to discover early applications. In 1953, eight months before the release of Fox's first feature Cinemascope film, Lookout Mountain used the technology at the Nevada Test Site to record the famous atomic cannon shot "Grable," part of the Upshot-Knothole series of tests.[28] "Grable," the first and only atomic artillery test conducted by the United States, was part of the Army's efforts to introduce atomic weaponry into its ground artillery arsenal, such that atomic weapons could be used in the field against enemy armies. The Army Signal Corps commissioned Lookout Mountain Laboratory to do motion-picture documentation of the "Grable" test in both 35 mm color and 35 mm black and white. Lookout Mountain fitted two of the 35 mm color cameras with CinemaScope lenses. The result was one of the more iconic mushroom-cloud motion pictures of the era, and a very satisfied Army Signal Corps. Two years later in 1955, Lookout Mountain not only filmed the "Met" shot of the Teapot series in CinemaScope, but scored and narrated a short featurette on the shot.[29]

CinemaScope footage of the "Grable" shot made it into the Fox-produced feature *Hell and High Water* in 1954, and featured prominently in the marketing of that film, highly touted as part of the CinemaScope brand. Lookout Mountain worked just as closely with Fox rival Paramount, utilizing CinemaScope's competitor in the new wide-format business, Vistavision. [It is notable that the first feature film to take advantage of Vistavision's wide-projection format was *Strategic Air Command*, starring Jimmy Stewart and produced with the cooperation of the Air Force.] Lookout Mountain also bragged about having produced a short 3-D film almost a year before *Bwana Devil*, the first full-length 3-D film to premiere in Hollywood in 1952.[30] Clearly, Lookout Mountain not only participated in the industry's newfound appreciation for the staging of photography as a technical act, but helped pioneer it. In the cases of the Nevada tests at least, the testing of new weapons technology also seemed a ripe case for the testing of a new cinematic technology.

The story of Lookout Mountain's application of experimental cinematic technologies suggests an appetite among its clients—the armed forces, Civil Defense, and to a lesser degree the Atomic Energy Commission—for the imprint of the camera on atomic spectacle, even as atomic bombs offered ready test subjects for Hollywood's newest technologies. CinemaScope, high-speed photography, and other visual innovations rendered the mushroom cloud an aesthetic object, but in the historical moment of their production there was no chance that such "aestheticization" would result in the removal of the event from reality, as commentators on the iconography of the mushroom cloud have since claimed.[31] Rather, cameras performed functions key to the construction of history at nuclear tests. They lent scientific authority through specialized aesthetics, state authority through the inclusion of photographers in shots of detonations, and even gendered and racialized authority through the prominence of these mostly white men with their cameras, boldly confronting dangerous blasts. And by employing the new supravisual wide-format technologies of the 1950s, Lookout Mountain identified nuclear history with the histories of commerce and technology. Nuclear test footage, even at its most aesthetically marvelous on the panoramic screen, borrowed new historical import from the innovative photographic technology it employed—even as, in reciprocal fashion, the movie industry borrowed gravitas for its innovations from such tests.

Cameras were therefore the subject of cameras and of the broader discourse of official nuclear weapons testing because in this case, as in few others, the American Cold War state wanted to be seen as seeing and producing: they wanted *to be seen as staging*. The only Cold War state operation that would match nuclear testing in this regard was the space program, with which Lookout Mountain was, of course, also involved—as the space program was part of the same nuclear deterrent state, relying on not only the same camera operations, but more generally, the same sensibilities and visualities.

Because cameras were performing multiple functions, the mushroom cloud could never be a stable signifier. For just as cameras were doing double duty as diagnostic and diegetic devices, so the mushroom cloud was projected as an object of controlled scientific experimentation and, simultaneously, an object of "psychological" terror or reassurance. Just as cameras stood in both a transcendental and a transcendent position in nuclear testing, so the mushroom cloud functioned as a cybernetic subject of information and a cinematic subject of spectacle. In the language of test planners and state strategists, the mushroom cloud was always approached in terms of "effects," but effects were approached dualistically as psychological and physical.

It is straightforward enough to see how cinematic visualities could be summoned to assert psychological control over the mushroom cloud: cinema [and, it should be clear by now, we use the term with all of its cultural resonance] could assert control of the situation by means of the control of story and spectacle. It is also apparent that such control is elusive, as it depends on not only message management but also the interpretive or "hermeneutic" capacities of audiences. In its most aggressive version, such official state ideology management of the mushroom cloud and all it represented would have to be *tailored* to audiences, and the audiences themselves would have to be *conditioned* to receive the messages in a certain manner, or within a particular affective and cognitive framework.

It is also easy enough to see how cybernetic visualities could be deployed toward the end of controlling the physical effects of nuclear detonations. Cameras and other diagnostic devices could record or otherwise measure physical phenomena and convert them directly or indirectly into visual information in the form of marks, graphs, numbers, or images. Cybernetic systems of communication and control aspired to omnipresence [presence everywhere], which promised to lead to omniscience [total knowledge], which would result in omnipotence, or complete power over the physical dynamics and effects of the nuclear detonation.

Perhaps less straightforward, but critical nevertheless, are the ways in which cinematic visualities could be deployed as a means toward the physical control of the Bomb, and likewise the ways in which cybernetic visualities could be a means toward psychological control. With respect to the former, cinema afforded weapons operators a crucial means by which to document operational processes so that they could be replicated in the future. Everything from how to operate equipment to how to assemble a weapon was documented. Moreover, cinema set apart the test sites themselves as sets and

stages, sites of visual performance not just for a select few, but for future anonymous state actors. The test site comprised a site for the display of technical performances or military maneuvers caught on film so that future technicians or soldiers could replicate them.

Additionally, cinema provided a means by which to determine the status of the test site with respect to publics. Deliberations over if and when to release Lookout Mountain's films to publics, like those about whether or not to allow journalists access to nuclear test sites, were not just about state secrecy—indeed, there was hardly a question of secrecy. There were plenty of mechanisms in place by which the state could maintain secrecy even when going public. The crux, rather, was the nature and degree of the state's control of the physical space of test sites: releasing films, let alone allowing photojournalists on-site, would transform the test site into a semipublic space—a physical, and not merely a "symbolic," transformation. This point is more apparent if we recall that there were hundreds of national security sites at that time for which the question of public presence vis-à-vis cameras was never an issue.

The cybernetic control of the psyche, too, was imagined. "Information" campaigns were premised not on theories of the irrational apprehension of citizens, but rather on their rational cognitive capacities (at least of the citizens who seemed to matter so much to the state in the 1950s: white middle-class citizens). A cybernetic sense of "information" was crucial to official understandings of social and individual psychological processes. As Paul Edwards has shown, "cognitive science" itself grew out of the conjunction of state-supported science with cybernetic theories—the mind was conceived of as an "information machine."[32] As such, the "information" offered by test-site systems of communication and control was conceived of as the basis for "programming" publics with the information it was felt they needed to live with the Bomb.

The "Apple-2" shot of Operation Cue illustrates the ways in which cinematic and cybernetic visualities were coproduced, as well as a certain disconnect between Lookout Mountain's operations and America's Cold War culture in the mid-1950s. Operation Cue was a civil defense exercise held at the Nevada Test Site as part of Operation Teapot, a series of fourteen shots staged at the Nevada Test Site from February 18 to May 15, 1955. Operation Cue involved well over one hundred corporate and industrial association sponsors and about two thousand journalist and civilian "participants," who functioned as proxies for a white, middle-class public.[33]

As was standard practice by the middle of the 1950s, Lookout Mountain was responsible for all documentary photography at Teapot, while EG&G handled all specialized high-speed "technical" photography. (This division of labor, which we hope is clear by now, followed the logic of Lookout Mountain's and EG&G's respective sets of technical expertise rather than the use of the footage they shot, let alone its dissemination.) EG&G photographers came equipped with an array of high-speed, remotely operated cameras, as well as the means for tying them together into a single, integrated system designed to automatically fire upon detonation. Most of EG&G's cameras were installed in towers and were tied directly into the timing and firing circuits for the bombs. Lookout Mountain sent three mobile film crews together with a team of reinforcements to the Nevada Test Site on January 12, a month before the Teapot tests commenced. Lookout Mountain was formally charged with producing a film report and an orientation film for the Atomic Energy Commission and Department of Defense. They were to efficiently "document" the test too, leaving for later reviewers a shelf of stock footage and still pictures.

In addition to an array of cameras, film, and lighting equipment, Lookout Mountain showed up with an RC-47 aircraft and several trucks and boom trailers. They not only fulfilled their declared mission, but improvised to fulfill several other major projects, from picking up an Army motion-picture project to shooting the

Defense Threat Reduction Information Analysis Center

Given that Lookout Mountain Laboratory was not only a film-production site, but also a major storehouse for highly classified films and still photographs, the facility's closure in 1969 presented a major security challenge. It is surprising, therefore, that there is little documentary evidence of where the contents of Lookout Mountain's vast film vault went or how they were distributed. Not even the stewards of the contemporary nuclear state really know.

The evidence we have suggests that while some of Lookout Mountain's images went to Atomic Energy Commission laboratories, a large swath went to Norton Air Force base near San Bernardino, California, the site of the newly centralized Air Force audiovisual operations. When Norton was closed in 1994, the collection was dispersed. Some items were disposed of; some items went to the National Archives in College Park, Maryland. The most sensitive and technical items were transferred first to Travis Air Force Base and then to the Defense Atomic Support Information Analysis Center (DASIAC), a facility in Santa Barbara, California.

And that is where Byron Risvet, a geologist and weapons expert for the Defense Threat Reduction Agency (which was once the Armed Forces Special Weapons Project, a chief Lookout Mountain client), rescued these sensitive materials from obscurity. In 1995 Risvet moved over twenty thousand mostly unedited films, comprising over 10 million linear feet, as well as thousands of photographs and archival accessories such as logbooks, caption sheets, and memos to a new facility at Kirtland Air Force Base in Albuquerque, New Mexico, the Defense Threat Reduction Information Analysis Center (DTRIAC).

Today, these holdings are still used by Department of Energy scientists and military personnel with the requisite security clearances. Well protected in temperature-regulated and highly secure rooms, the DTRIAC collection is one of the most important present-day material legacies of Lookout Mountain's work, a massive vault of images whose chief function is as technical and scientific information.

See also

Chavez, "DTRIAC Celebrates 50th Anniversary."

Cinemascope Featurette:
Shot Number 12
(2003)

Restored and reconstructed by Peter Kuran
from historical footage.

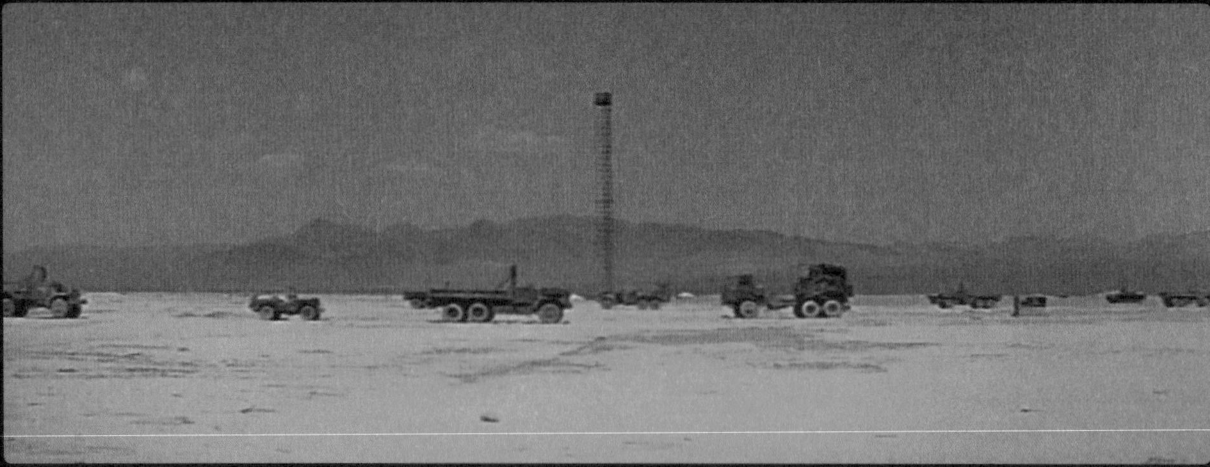

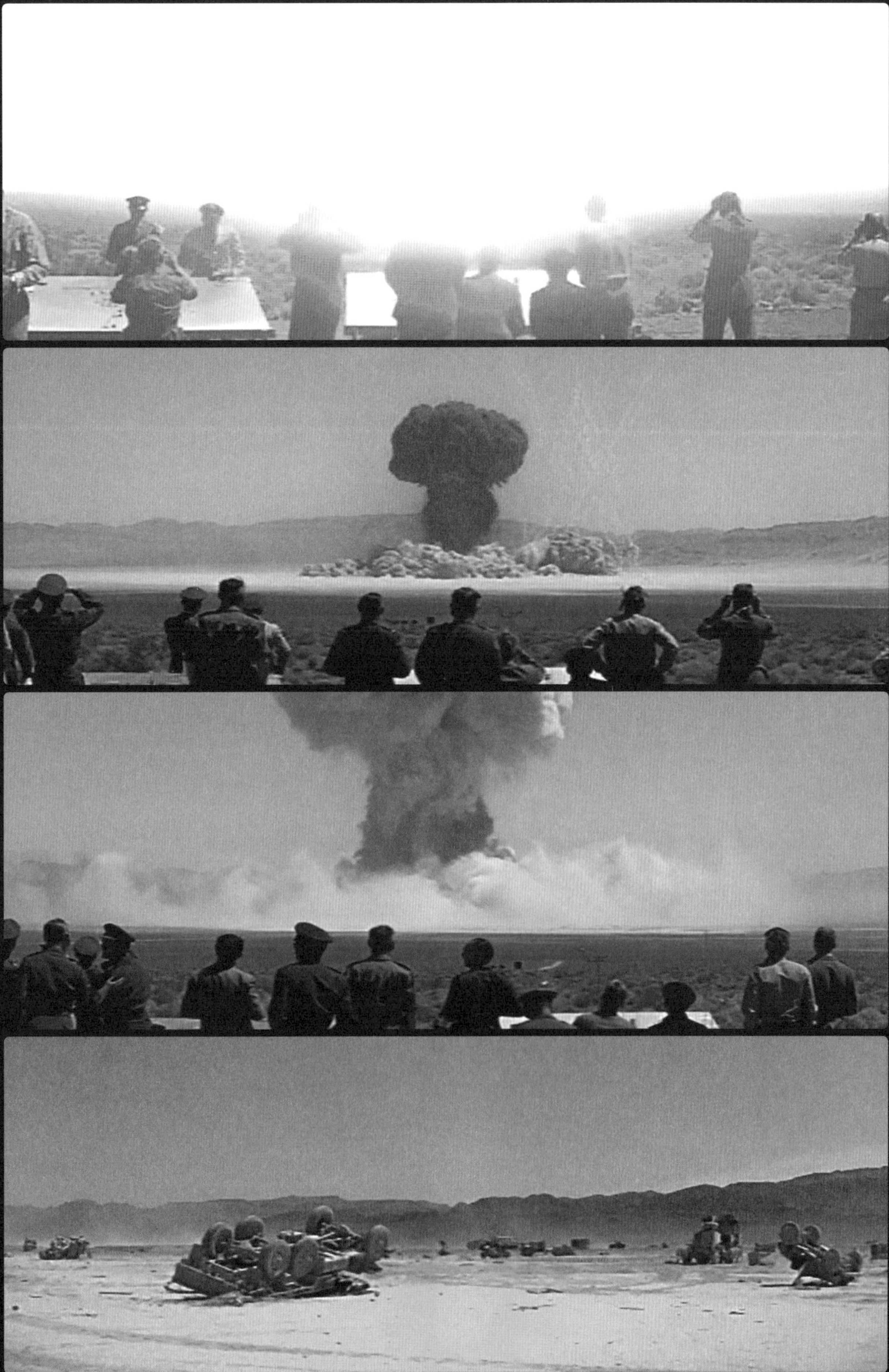

twelfth shot of the series, MET [for "military effects tests"], using CinemaScope. When Teapot was all said and done, Lookout Mountain had shot more than eight thousand feet of 35 mm motion-picture film and over eighty thousand feet of 16 mm motion-picture film [totaling some forty hours], and had taken thousands of still photos from both the ground and the air. Lookout Mountain, indeed, was virtually omnipresent: they claimed to have "more technicians present, and closer to all the blasts, than any other service agency."[34]

"Apple-2," a May 5 shot that went off at ten minutes after five in the morning, was the centerpiece of Operation Cue. It yielded a twenty-nine-kiloton blast, nearly twice as big as the Hiroshima bomb, and nearly a third bigger than the Nagasaki weapon. The shot sent a nuclear cloud protruding fifty-one thousand feet into the sky, where it carried northward. Dust from the blast continued to swirl in and around ground zero for nearly four hours after the detonation.[35]

At the center of Operation Cue was "Survival City," a makeshift civil defense village staged to demonstrate civil defense protocols. Survival City consisted of ten buildings, ranging from homes to a firehouse, and a range of "typical American" props: utility infrastructure, cars, furniture, appliances, food, and mannequins "dressed as family members." The village, especially the houses, was instrumented by EG&G and other units with equipment "to measure the blast, thermal, and radiation effects of the detonation on the structures, furnishings, food, and mannequins positioned in various locations throughout the community."[36] For the shot, EG&G operated fifty-six specialized cameras for "technical" photography that produced, among other things, some of the most well-known footage of atomic blasts ever made.[37] Meanwhile, Lookout Mountain documented the construction of Survival City and, after the test, its ruins. At the moment of the detonation itself, millions across the United States watched live on tele-

vision. Coverage showed thousands of civilian witnesses, observing the blast from afar, "surviving" the blast—as if to say to suburbanites across America, "If the Bomb hits your urban centers, you can survive by virtue of your distance from those centers." And this visual spectacle took a more permanent form by means of film and photography. Photographs of the test were distributed to the press, and a civil defense contractor was commissioned to produce a film, *Operation Cue*, hosted by Joan Collins.[38] Virtually all the photography and film that ended up in the public venues came from the cameras of Lookout Mountain and EG&G.

Operation Cue was a national spectacle, seemingly ready-made for historic, iconic status. *And yet it barely registered within the larger nuclear testing regime.* "Apple-2" was but one of fourteen shots at Teapot over three months, and Operation Cue was but one aspect of the "Apple-2" test, and not the primary one. The main objective of the shot was to further test weapon designs: "Apple-2" was, in the official parlance of nuclear testing, a "weapons development" test rather than an "effects" test. The secondary goal of the "Apple-2" shot was military effects and training: combat troops practiced maneuvers, and military equipment was subjected to the blast's effects. Finally, "Apple-2" functioned as an occasion for Operation Cue.

Moreover, Operation Cue barely registers in the official reports of Lookout Mountain and EG&G. Indeed, it is not even mentioned in Lookout Mountain's account of Teapot; and EG&G, in their relatively brief technical report of the operation, notes only that they provided "photographic footage . . . useful for imparting to the American public the message of Civil Defense."[39] For both Lookout Mountain Laboratory and EG&G, Operation Cue was but a small blip on the screen of their operations.

What are we to make of the relative operational insignificance of Operation Cue for Lookout Mountain and EG&G? What are we to make of the fact that its "mushroom cloud," so to speak, was but a part of much longer reels? By the time of Teapot, what would now be seen as atomic icons were acute objects of public desires and anxieties, yet they were for Lookout Mountain mere products of "routine"—this even as atomic spectacles were front-page news. After each of the fourteen shots at Operation Teapot, the Atomic Energy Commission would release photographs of the mushroom cloud shot by Lookout Mountain to the press.[40] Yet as much as the press had an appetite for mushroom clouds, anxieties about fallout resulting from the clouds were more intense. The 1954 Castle disaster in the Pacific caused many in the United States, especially in the Southwest, to worry about America's atomic recklessness. State officials in turn worried about public anxieties. Operation Teapot generated an especially severe level of activity among the Atomic Energy Commission and Department of Defense staff with respect to addressing public fears. Lookout Mountain's *Atomic Tests in Nevada* film, discussed in chapter 5, was central to "public information" discussions about how to quell potential public panic. Officials debated questions such as, What should the film say? What should it portray? Should it be released prior to, during, or after Teapot? Should it be circulated nationwide, or just in the southwestern United States where fallout anxieties were most acute?[41]

Such crises would seem to be more than enough to earn Operation Cue front-page attention in Lookout Mountain reports to commanders, had there not been so much else going on. For Lookout Mountain, the period of January through June of 1955 was an extraordinary six months. It was the period of Operation Castle's literal and rhetorical cleanup. At the same time, the unit had to cover two major American nuclear tests simultaneously, Operation Teapot and Operation Wigwam. Teapot, as we saw, demanded months of Lookout Mountain's time and a significant portion of its personnel and equipment. Wigwam was even more demanding: as the United States' first deep underwater nuclear blast, Wigwam was a totally new operational and technical undertaking. Since EG&G was tied up in Nevada, Lookout Mountain was saddled with both documentary and technical

Lawrence Livermore Laboratories Nuclear Film Scanning and Reanalysis Project

In 2017 historic footage of nuclear explosions began finding its way back into the public eye through publicity surrounding an ambitious digitization and declassification project under way at Lawrence Livermore Laboratories. The California facility, historically associated with the development of thermonuclear technology, today houses a large collection of EG&G films that are being digitized.

In the 2010s, a team at Livermore, headed by physicist Greg Spriggs, located about seven thousand EG&G films, digitizing over 4,200 of them. Advised by Peter Kuran, who has scanned and color corrected a number of Lookout Mountain films, and Jim Moye, who helped digitize the Zapruder film of President Kennedy's assassination for the Smithsonian, the team began posting declassified excerpts of EG&G films to YouTube in 2017, at a point when, perhaps not coincidentally, the threat of nuclear weapons was being thrown back into the collective imagination via North Korea's ongoing feud with the Trump administration.

Nevertheless, the Livermore project is driven primarily by science, not geopolitics. Spriggs's team began to embark on the digitization of these films so as to conduct new analyses of their content. They found that the official records of yield and performance of nuclear bombs and devices from the 1950s and 1960s were not always accurate. Therefore, thanks to the films of EG&G, the official scientific annals of America's midcentury nuclear testing program are being rewritten in the twenty-first century.

See also

O'Brien, "Physicist Declassifies Rescued Nuclear Films"; Zhang, "Movies of Cold War Bomb Tests Hold Nuclear Secrets."

photography responsibilities at Wigwam. And yet, with all this and more, Lookout Mountain could report halfway through 1955, "A review of the past six months of work in regard to motion picture projects accomplished and specific problems overcome would appear fantastic to one unfamiliar with the work conducted at LML, but in comparison to the previous histories of LML, [the] work of the six months was strictly routine."[42]

What are we to make of the relative operational insignificance of Operation Cue? Some of the most iconic images of the aboveground nuclear-testing era were products of established organizational and technical routines, including, and perhaps above all, images of mushroom clouds. The "routine" nature of atomic image production does not in and of itself tell us much about the images' cultural functions among publics. It does, however, situate these images within particular historical institutions and practices.

What made Lookout Mountain's atomic image production "routine" was not regular hours or even streamlined processes and practices. To the contrary, Lookout Mountain reported that at Wigwam and Teapot some "photography demanded the use of equipment not yet manufactured—let alone designed." Lookout Mountain's engineering branch "conceived, designed, and engineered" new technologies and techniques to meet the ever-changing demands of the nuclear testing regime.[43] No, the "routine" was not in the processes. Rather, it was in the institutional culture, a culture where, as in Hollywood more broadly, the production of spectacle was a matter-of-fact function of work routines, and where, as in scientific laboratories more generally, the production of scientific or technical representations was usual business. To call this work "mundane" would be misleading. It was not mundane or ordinary. Rather, the history of the production of the mushroom cloud and other iconic American nuclear images entailed the paradoxical normalization of the extraordinary, the routinization of the "fantastic." For nearly fifteen years, from 1948 to 1963, Lookout Mountain Laboratory not only developed the means and modes of producing the science and spectacle of the mushroom cloud and its attendant visual artifacts, but also institutionalized them, transforming them into operational, technical, and cultural routines.

Cameras are typically seen as producing images that index their referents. You take a snapshot of New Year's Eve fireworks to both mark the moment and capture the event; enough snapshots over the years by enough people will lead to a generalized image of fireworks—*another fireworks picture*. So too appear images of nuclear mushroom clouds: they stand before us as icons, *another nuclear mushroom cloud*, to become "a general condition rather than a specific event."[44] Generalizing the particular is the essence of the ideological work of the image of the mushroom cloud. It can be resisted only so long as images of mushroom clouds are seen for what they also are: indexes of particular cameras. Here the indexicality of the photographic image is reversed as the photograph indexes the camera [rather than the camera, through film, indexing an event]. And those cameras are themselves indexes of particular state operations. Therefore, it is not enough—it cannot be enough—to render images of mushroom clouds as cultural images, even icons, though they certainly appear as such and must be examined as such. Images of nuclear mushroom clouds—each particular image of each particular nuclear mushroom cloud—must also be approached in terms of particular histories of particular operations, state operations, violent state operations that, by extension of the geographic scale and temporal durations of their violence, must be exercised upon "friends" and "enemies" alike. Each image of a nuclear mushroom cloud indexes that total, indiscriminate state violence as it was repeated over and over again in institutional and organizational routines that themselves became, through their entrenchment and entanglement, barely sensible, let alone commonsensical.

AIR COMBAT CAMERA SERVICE
24B

Chapter Ten

CLOSURE

When Lookout Mountain closed in July of 1969, the flagship facility at Wonderland Avenue had lost much of its technical capability for seeing and recording the United States' massive Cold War operations, even as it supervised a massive structure for global vision. By 1967 Lookout Mountain had only three 16 mm movie cameras in its Laurel Canyon inventory and was barely able to assemble a single production crew without resorting to equipment rentals.[1] A year later, equipment inventory was at "an all-time low."[2] At the very same time, the unit saw its largest ever year for processing 16 mm color film, as assignments to its detachments had soared; for example, over six hundred airmen were deployed to the 600th Photographic Squadron at Tan Son Nhut Air Base, and almost four hundred were stationed at Vandenberg Air Force Base. At the end of the 1960s, Lookout Mountain encompassed some twenty-five subsidiary units.

In this way, by its final year of operations, Lookout Mountain's inventories and institutional structures came to resemble the Cold War national security state itself, which, far from being concentrated in a single location or small set of locations, was distributed in a diffuse network across the globe in a professed effort to contain communist danger wherever it might appear. The base facility on Wonderland Avenue in Los Angeles, which in the early 1950s had been the largest self-contained film studio in Hollywood, became by the end of the 1960s the brain of a new technical and managerial machine, daily receiving new footage from all over the planet for developing, viewing, critiquing, storage, and circulation as part of a large-scale information system.

In 1969 that brain would be moved north to Norton Air Force Base in San Bernardino, California, the new headquarters of the Aerospace Audio-Visual Service, bringing an end to the illustrious history of Lookout Mountain Laboratory. Centralization, efficiency, and reorganization were the watchwords of the Pentagon, forcing Lookout Mountain to close shop and be consolidated into a larger Air Force photographic operation. To be sure, a number of other factors also contributed to Lookout Mountain's closing. Representatives from the motion-picture industry had long been urging the US government to get out of the motion-picture production business and send such work to contractors instead.[3] The backlog of work at Wonderland Avenue meant that the Aerospace Audio-Visual Service started to seriously consider ways to limit Lookout Mountain's work to "unusual" projects, leaving contractors to do the rest of the work.[4] One of Lookout Mountain's final commanders even wondered whether they had contributed to their own demise by failing to get enough produced material into the public eye.[5] By and large, however, it was the push toward centralization that brought Lookout Mountain Laboratory to a close.

In this, our own closing chapter, we consider the legacy of Lookout Mountain Laboratory in both military approaches to what would soon be called "audiovisual production" and "information management" and in the larger structures of American Cold War and post–Cold War culture. For Lookout Mountain Laboratory, though closed in 1969, would live on in the institutions of government and culture alike. More than any other site on Earth, Lookout Mountain visually chronicled the activities of the US Cold War state. As G. E. Hayes, the official historian of the 1352nd Photographic Group in 1969, wrote in what would be the final report to come from Lookout Mountain Laboratory, "To enumerate their [Lookout Mountain's] involvement would virtually duplicate the chronology of major achievements of the United States Air Force in the fields of aerospace and nuclear development. Among the many activities photographed were every United States atomic test except the first; unmanned and manned space programs such as Mercury, Gemini, and Apollo; the development of missiles such as Atlas, Thor and Titan; and operations in Korea and Viet Nam."[6]

Indeed, if we were to somehow strip from public circulation all the photographs and film footage that Lookout Mountain shot over its two-decade history, the majority of Cold War iconography as we know it would be in the dark. But Lookout Mountain's legacy is not only its images; it is the work its images did for the national security state, as well as in the practices, organizational structures, and ambitions it helped institutionalize in the Air Force and the Department of Defense more generally.

From its earliest postwar beginning, the Air Force faced questions about how to best manage the production of photographic and motion-picture images. As we saw in chapters 1 and 2, photography had been central to the rise of the Air Force, offering a means of not only navigation, targeting, and bombardment assessment, but also training, publicity, and propagation. Photographic images, both still and moving, would thus play a broad, vital, and contested range of roles in the Air Force's rise to power. Could motion-picture and still photography be managed using the same structures and approaches used for managing mapping and aerial surveillance? Was photography a tool that any airman should learn, or was it a specialized technical skill requiring careful training and the centralized management of labor and technology to ensure quality and consistency? What should be done in-house and what by contractors? Should every camera-equipped unit also carry its own darkroom? And if the material was classified, how could a film unit efficiently ensure that only the right eyes saw the film at each stage in the production process? Finally, what storage and retrieval processes could possibly deal with the ever-growing amount of film footage and productions resulting from all these imaging efforts? The Air Force faced such questions even as it wrestled with its own larger mission, structure, and support in response to institutional, technological, and geopolitical changes.

Gen. Hoyt Vandenberg first tried to consolidate all of the Air Force's "nontactical" photographic services in 1951, forming the Air Photographic and Charting Service.[7] The Air Photographic and Charting Service was charged with all major photographic needs for the Air

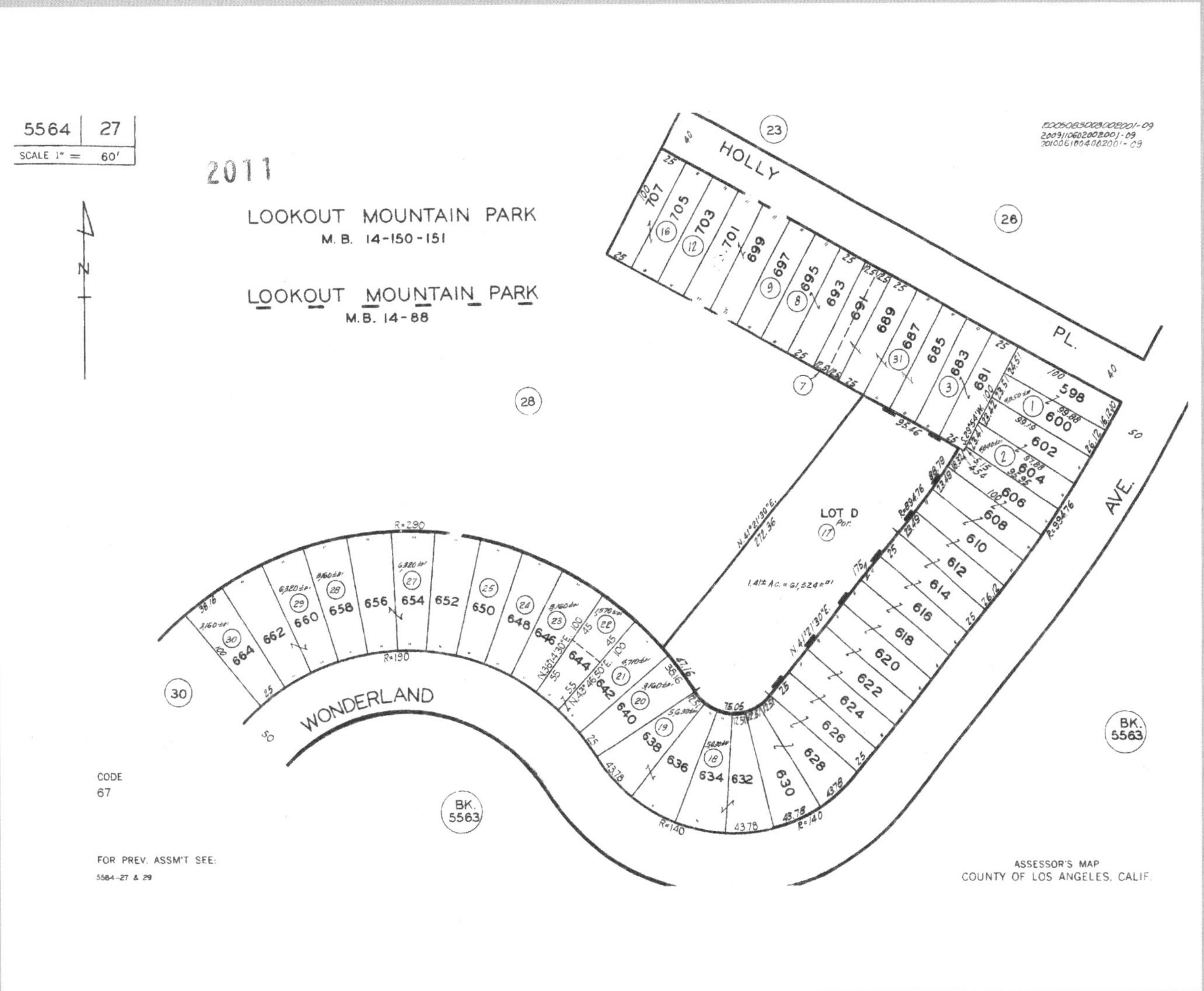

8935 Wonderland Avenue

When Lookout Mountain finally vacated their Laurel Canyon facility at 8935 Wonderland Avenue in 1969—some five years after Secretary of Defense Robert McNamara included the facility on a list of planned base closures—the building passed into obscurity, at least for a time.

As early as 1967, Gregory Peck visited the facility to explore purchasing it for the American Film Institute, a plan that never came to fruition. Dehl Berti, a Chiricahua Apache actor known for playing American Indian roles on television and film, owned the place for a few years in the late 1970s. Indeed, he appears in photographs of a Lookout Mountain reunion on the property in 1979. In the early 1980s, the facility appears in the little-known science fiction film *Wavelength*, released in 1983, in which the visibly neglected structure is staged as the site of a secret military experiment involving aliens. Property records indicate at least one foreclosure in the 1980s.

In 1994 John Ladner, a judge, and Mark Lipscomb, a painter, bought the property at auction. The two lived there for a number of years, where Lipscomb used the soundstage as an artist's studio and many of the larger rooms as galleries for displaying his work. Ladner and Lipscomb unsuccessfully tried to sell the facility in 2010, and they subsequently rented it out.

In 2015 the property was purchased by actor and musician Jared Leto, even as it was designated as a Historic-Cultural Monument by the City of Los Angeles. The former brought new attention to the facility and its history; the latter will make future renovations subject to review according to national standards, and demolition subject to a review by the Cultural Heritage Commission.

Force other than reconnaissance, but in the eyes of many Air Force brass it never effectively met its mission.[8] As early as 1953, one Air Force study cast doubt on the effectiveness of consolidation, recommending that the Air Force make heavier use of contractors and discouraging [unsuccessfully] the proposed establishment of an Air Photographic and Charting Service headquarters in Orlando, Florida.[9] The challenges of the Air Photographic and Charting Service were seen in its relationship to Lookout Mountain in the 1950s. On the one hand, Lookout Mountain was the star unit within organization, and at least two of the unit's leaders would move up into senior leadership roles in Orlando. On the other hand, Lookout Mountain's successes seemed proportionate to its relative autonomy from the Air Photographic and Charting Service, as the unit operated with far more independence from Orlando than any of the other Air Photographic and Charting Service units.

In 1964 the Air Force had another go at consolidation. An Air Force–wide program for achieving "greater operating efficiency and economy" included a formal study of Air Force photographic requirements that would lead to a new plan, announced by Defense Secretary McNamara himself on November 19, 1964, to consolidate all Air Force photographic functions at Norton Air Force Base, promising to save the Air Force over $11 million annually.[10] The plan included the closure of Lookout Mountain Laboratory and the sale of the Laurel Canyon facility.[11] Lookout Mountain could do little to protest. Senior Air Photographic and Charting Service leaders, who had struggled for a decade to live up to their mission, saw in the move toward greater centralization a chance to finally get the Air Force's photographic operations under control, arguing to the Pentagon that the plan would improve quality control and operations management.[12]

The move to Norton, however, was met with ongoing delays. The most immediate hurdle was a $6 million renovation of a former SAGE radar facility at Norton into a working film lab, archives, and production facility, a kind of next-generation Lookout Mountain facility. But the growing war in Vietnam also played a major role in the delay, draining blood and money from the Pentagon despite McNamara's managerial efforts to limit its effects. At one point, the move to Norton seemed at risk of collapse, as the congressional Government Accountability Office launched an investigation into why so much money was to be spent on renovating the facilities at Norton when the Army Pictorial Center on Long Island, New York, lay largely dormant.[13]

Meanwhile, after years of debate within the Air Force about the relationship between photography and mapping, the Air Force decided to separate the two functions, resulting in the renaming of the Air Photographic and Charting Service as the Aerospace Audio-Visual Service [AAVS].[14] One report described the rise of the AAVS as being "freed" from the mapping responsibilities of the old Air Photographic and Charting Service, and also in terms of the rise of "an audio-visual, rather than a merely photographic organization."[15] There was, however, one major hitch in the move to the "audiovisual": few in the Air Force seemed to want it. A 1968 AAVS report bemoaned the fact that though the Air Force may have given it a new and renewed charge, it had placed "no obligation on other USAF commands and agencies to utilize AAVS capabilities," resulting in a "degraded" function and the ugly burden of having to "'sell' its products and services to its USAF 'customers.'"[16]

Lookout Mountain Laboratory, or the 1352nd Motion Picture Squadron [later the 1352nd Photographic Group], had been instrumental in demarcating the "audiovisual" as more expansive than mere photography. Lt. Col. James P. Warndorf had been the second, and longest serving, commander of the 1352nd, serving from 1954 to 1960 during a period of tremendous growth for the unit, with ongoing work in the Pacific and Nevada and the founding of the 1369th at Vandenberg. In 1960 Warndorf was transferred to Air Photographic and Charting Service headquarters in Orlando, where he was promoted to full colonel. He was made deputy chief of staff for photography for all of the Air Photographic and Charting Service.[17] Warndorf became a champion for consolidation and for a move beyond photography toward the "audiovisual." In 1965 he embarked on a thirteen-month stint as director of the Department of Defense Audiovisual Study Group, producing a study that led to the new plan to centralize audiovisual operations at Norton. In 1966 Warndorf was sent to Vietnam to serve as commander over Air Force photographic operations there, providing him with the opportunity to test and prove theories he had refined as director of the study group.

We saw in chapter 8 how the demand for images in Vietnam arose from multiple sources, ranging from the aim of pilots and their supervisors to assess bombing efficacy and accuracy to desires in Washington for more images of Vietnam "successes" for television broadcast. The rise of the 600th Photographic Squadron under Warndorf's leadership reflected not only an exercise in meeting such demands, but a successful struggle to convince the Pentagon that audiovisual work was best left to the experts to be managed through a centralized network of geographically distributed audiovisual units. Many Air Force units in Vietnam would have preferred to procure and operate their own cameras, perhaps only relying on the 600th to provide and manage portable darkroom trailers. But Warndorf made sure that the 600th would serve as a comprehensive, "single-manager" audiovisual operation in Vietnam. His approach, in which over twenty newly numbered and formal detachments sprang up across Vietnam and

Thailand, highlighted not only the photographic prowess of the 600th and Lookout Mountain, but the organizational strength of managing that many units in the context of an ever-increasing demand for efficiency in the global circulation of imagery and film.

The success of Warndorf's "single-manager" approach in Vietnam was enough to convince skeptics of its merits back home. A 1968 Aerospace Audio-Visual Service report described the approach in Southeast Asia as a model for the entire Air Force. Comparing audiovisual needs to medical, rescue, or communication services, the report argued that managerial consolidation could lead to not only greater efficiency but greater tactical strength. The report even compared the Air Force's failure to move more quickly in this regard to Hitler's failure to utilize Germany's powerful tank division in a counterattack on Normandy.[18]

The single-manager approach would mean, among other things, that photography's role would become more efficient and tactical even as it became more invisible. Whereas during the 1950s Lookout Mountain had promoted its acclaimed documentation of nuclear tests with a surplus of images of photographers and their technologies at work, this new era of Air Force photography lauded the relative invisibility of the photographers and their technologies.[19] Seemingly light years away from the "flying cameras" of Operation Crossroads, Warndorf described with pride how in Vietnam pilots barely knew the cameras on their planes were there at all.[20] Photography was everywhere it needed to be without getting in the way or stealing the show. The single-manager concept prioritized efficient and largely invisible photographic systems over the artful production of images.[21]

Over the course of Lookout Mountain's history, photography moved from geographic centralization to managerial centralization, and from the production of spectacular cinematic footage, sometimes taking years to produce, catalog, and distribute, to the production of constant images flowing efficiently through the war machine's daily routines and processes.

Whereas in the Pacific and Nevada nuclear tests, "logistics" served as a means of mobilizing the men and tools of vision to cover a grand event, the new Air Force regimes of the "audiovisual" and "single management" made perception itself a matter of logistics, culminating in a new logistics of perception.[22]

All the while, the very definition and value of photography in the Air Force moved ever more toward both the informational and the economical. In 1972 the "Audio-Visual" in Aerospace Audio-Visual Service lost its hyphen to become "audiovisual," even as the mission of the Aerospace Audiovisual Service systematically replaced mentions of "motion picture and television" and "photographic and television" with "audiovisual" or "audiovisual products."[23] In the second half of the 1970s, under the Carter administration, the Aerospace Audiovisual Service itself was absorbed into a new and even larger Pentagon-wide organization called the Defense Audiovisual Agency, ultimately stripping audiovisual central management responsibilities from the Air Force altogether.

If in the eyes of the Air Force and the Pentagon, this move represented a further streamlining of operations in the service of a consistent and reliable flow of information, others saw the move in precisely the opposite way, worrying instead about administrative bloat, inefficiency, and economic waste. The *Lissit Report*, a high-profile study of federal audiovisual production commissioned by President Carter in 1977 and led by broadcast journalist Robert Lissit, reported millions of dollars of waste, resulting in a pair of congressional hearings held in Washington, DC, and Los Angeles. At the hearings, leaders of the film and television industries blamed the military for sloppiness and substandard products, turning the postwar relationship between Hollywood and the military on its head. Leaders from the military found themselves on the defensive, answering accusations of waste and inefficiency. Staff from a House subcommittee even visited Norton to investigate reports of excessive space and deliberate conversion of film to videotape to evade federal regulations that required more reliance on subcontractors for film. The *Lissit Report* resulted in new policies and regulations that would end up with much of the audiovisual work of the military being passed on to contractors. Under the new regulations, motion-picture processing by federal labs was to be avoided; films promoting the producing unit were prohibited; and actors needed to come from union labor, not the enlisted ranks or government employees. A new board was also set up to review requests for films so as to evaluate their usefulness and appropriateness as government productions.

The new regulations, however, proved difficult to apply. "The government is an audiovisual monster," Lissit quipped in an article for the *Boston Globe* a few years later, admitting the failure of reforms.[24] Daniel McGovern, an Air Force filmmaker who went from filming at Hiroshima to a post at Lookout Mountain to leadership at Vandenberg, described the new post-Lissit Defense Audiovisual Agency as a "boondoggle."[25] Even Harold Brown, Carter's secretary of defense and a proponent of decreasing military spending, later conceded that the Defense Department just can't be run "as a business."[26] There were just too many expenditure contingencies, Brown argued, from changes in technology to changes in foreign policy. The "business" of the Air Force or any other armed

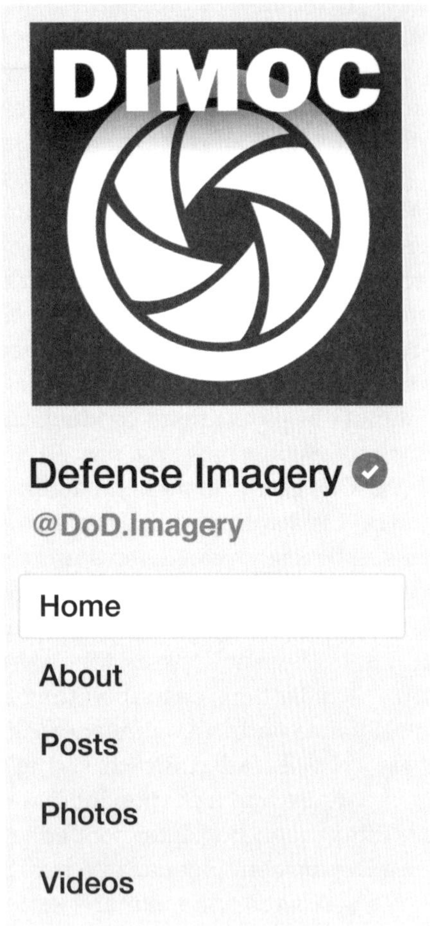

force would need to include support for basic operations, but also the flexibility for responding to deep and unexpected challenges.

As such, the Defense Audiovisual Agency, successor to the Aerospace Audiovisual Service, which was itself a successor to Lookout Mountain and its parent organization the Air Photographic and Charting Service, would after a few short years close in 1985, dispersing into a combination of more narrowly defined military photography units and government contractors.[27] The only centralized entity that remained was the Defense Visual Information Center, established at March Air Force Base in 1994 primarily as a repository for armed forces imagery for use by commercial industry.[28] The Defense Imagery Management Operations Center (DIMOC), today's "operational arm" of the Defense Visual Information Center, serves industry and government imagery needs through a combination of services that include both federal agencies and private contractors. (The distinction can be difficult to discern.)

Department of Defense Instruction 5040.02, issued on October 27, 2011, concerns "Visual Information." Still active as we write, Instruction 5040.02 defines "visual information" as "Information in the form of visual or pictorial representation of person(s), place(s), or thing(s), either with or without sound."[29] "It is DoD policy," the document states, "that V[isual] I[nformation] shall be viewed and used as an essential information resource and a supporting capability for strategic communication."[30] Such information, the policy makes clear, is essential for a variety of internal and external functions that include educating the public about Department of Defense operations, furthering "public diplomacy" objectives, influencing or disrupting the "decision making of adversaries and potential adversaries," aiding in "operational planning and decision making," providing a "historical and evidentiary record" for the work of the DoD, and supporting "business operations" and "other critical DoD functions."[31] Instruction 5040.02 structures the collection, processing, storage, and distribution of imagery across the armed forces, establishing not only the functions of imagery in the military, but processes for department-wide oversight, standards for the management of materials over time, protocols for digital file naming and numbering, prohibitions against alteration, and more.

Whereas Instruction 5040.02 mandates that military agencies maintain an "Information Dissemination Management System" to make "visual information" available to publics where and when deemed appropriate, two pages of the document are dedicated to instances in which the policy is not to apply.[32] These include photocopies, maps, "mixed media packages with a predominance of text," and "weapons, reconnaissance, and unmanned vehicle system imagery."

Also excluded from the policy are "command and control imagery created as a function of weapons system operations"; imagery obtained from "test programs that reflect capabilities and limitations of weapon system performance"; imagery related to "military morale, welfare, and recreation programs"; and anything related to reconnaissance or geospatial intelligence, helmet cameras, video surveillance systems, or training simulations.[33]

The reorganization of military photography around an epistemology of "information" represents the fulfillment of a direction begun in the automated, centrally managed processes established by Lookout Mountain in Vietnam, but with two significant differences. First, the management of images as "information" makes possible a more ready and steady delineation between public and secret material, driving a great deal of military image production wholly out of the public eye. Contrast this with the imagery from Operation Ivy, where, as we saw in chapter 4, there were long and vigorous *arguments* in the meeting rooms and hallways of the government about what to release to the public, when to release it, and how to release it. Today's approach to the production and management of imagery in the Pentagon largely precludes such debate. Contemporary information management protocols, applied to the creation of images at the very moment of generation through such banal matters as a schema for file naming, govern the flow of images as information through private or public domains.[34] It's no wonder then that contemporary analogs to debates over the proper publicity for Operation Ivy have taken place largely over "leaked" imagery, as in the horrific footage of aerial assassinations discovered and released by information analyst Bradley [now Chelsea] Manning. Today's information-oriented approach to generating, processing, and distributing images in the military has addressed older debates over affective control not just through secrecy, but through the wholesale exclusion of vast numbers of spectacular and banal images from subjection to any public eye.

Second, the spectacular cinematic work for which Lookout Mountain achieved the most renown is today absent from the military's "visual information" mission. The eclipse of state-produced nuclear spectacle would seem to be more than an artifact of concerns about nuclear fallout. It indicates a certain fatigue with images of nuclear annihilation as well as, paradoxically, the normalization of the nuclear. Nuclear bombs, as we have reminded readers, are still very much with us. Now, as much as at any point in the last seventy years, we live with the ongoing threat of nuclear terror. However, images of nuclear destruction today belong exclusively to the archives of the state or the occasional Hollywood blockbuster. The Bomb exists in the present, but its public images reference a distant past. Today over fifteen thousand nuclear weapons dot the globe, and President Trump is calling for a new, aggressive phase of nuclear weapons production. Yet images of the Bomb circulate as if it were a relic from yesteryear: as postage stamp–sized animated gifs, as background for fan-made music videos on YouTube, or in historical documentaries. Today the Bomb is at once the single greatest immediate threat humanity faces and the stuff of fandom, camp, and cartoons.

"LOOK!" the films of Lookout Mountain repeatedly exhort. As images of warfare circulate today from the cameras of drones, satellites, or bodies to the computer screens of analysts and demagogues and the phones of journalists, activists, and soldiers, we hope our history of Lookout Mountain Laboratory helps us to better look, and to look out. The history of Lookout Mountain Laboratory tells us that every act of looking implicates a history and a society, as well as power, ideology, and anxiety. For Lookout Mountain Laboratory, the pivotal anxieties were hermeneutic and heuristic, matters of understanding and order. Perhaps, just perhaps, our story might help make these anxieties acute again, such that visions of warfare—past or present, nuclear or otherwise—might finally fall within a governable human field.

EPILOGUE AND ACKNOWLEDGMENTS

On a cold Illinois winter day in 2014, we boarded an American Airlines flight for Dallas, where we caught a second plane for Guatemala City. The occasion was the Cold War Camera Conference, a remarkable, if small, gathering of photography scholars sponsored by the Toronto Photography Seminar and Durham Centre for Advanced Photography Studies. The late Andrea Noble [University of Durham] and the formidable Thy Phu [Western University] coorganized the conference in order to explore, in their words, "the global, interconnected networks of production, circulation and reception of photography" during the Cold War.[1] Perhaps the biggest takeaway from this conference for us was that *the Cold War isn't over*, especially in some sectors of the world. Andrea and Thy, together with the remarkable artist Daniel Hernández-Salazar, took us and a group of other scholars through the living history of the Cold War as it is still being played out in Guatemala.[2] Over the course of several days, in addition to listening to and presenting papers, we visited critical sites in Guatemala's violent Cold War past and present: the Museum of Martyrs from the Popular, Student, and Union Movement; the DNA Laboratory of the Guatemalan Forensic Foundation; the Bone Laboratory of the Guatemalan Forensic Foundation; the Catholic Church Human Rights Bureau; and the Guatemala National Police Historical Archive. Far from being memorials to a not-so-distant past, each one of the sites was and still is active in the prosecution of Guatemala's Cold War history, a prosecution that points not only to virtually every sector of Guatemalan society—given the thirty-plus-year civil war—but also to the United States, whose Cold War policies in Guatemala were directly responsible for the outbreak and endurance of genocidal violence.

Of the sites we visited, each dramatic and disturbing in its own right, the Guatemala National Police Historical Archive seemed to us the most representative of Guatemala's arduous search for justice in the blood-soaked trappings of the supposed Cold War. When the United Nations brokered a peace agreement in the 1990s, the National Police of Guatemala were told to turn over all their records to human rights investigators. The National Police were by then notorious for "disappearing" dissidents, journalists, professors, students, and anyone else who might undermine their reign of violence in Guatemala City. During the 1980s especially, the National Police—supported by the United States with materials and training—would regularly pull people off the streets and sidewalks in broad daylight and force them into the backs of vehicles to make them disappear forever. Bystanders would see these kidnappings, but would typically do nothing—for if they did, they were likely to be "disappeared" too. Indeed, for the police the act of disappearing was a public act, a means of terrorizing Guatemala's urban citizens and thus maintaining ruthless control over them. During the course of Guatemala's long Cold War/civil war some forty to fifty thousand persons were "disappeared."

When the United Nations called for their records, the National Police denied having any records at all. And so, for nearly a decade after the peace talks, the Guatemalan people, and the people who cared about them, lived as if no records existed. The archival history of the National Police, too, had been "disappeared." It was as if the violence against people in Guatemala—unlike that perpetrated by the Nazis against their victims, on which they kept notoriously meticulous records—had been so thoroughly perfected that not even a written trace could be found. The Guatemalan people lived with the horror of having their friends and loved ones "disappeared" so thoroughly that not even a record could be found.

This was the case until 2005, when the office of the Human Rights Ombudsman in Guatemala City received a phone call from citizens worried that explosives were being kept in an apparently abandoned old police building. There were, in fact, no explosives to be found in the building, but there was plenty that was politically explosive. The ombudsman found millions of police records, stacked floor to ceiling in decaying piles. The records, it turns out, dated back all the way to 1882, and included thousands upon thousands of ID cards, photographs, logs, notes, and case records, including endless records on the "disappeared." The ombudsman took immediate custody of the building and began what would become a massive archival project, the stakes of which are not just historical but political: the Archivo Histórico de la Policía Nacional, as it is called today, is not bringing the dead back to life, but it is resurrecting thousands of people politically as it is making them reappear as public figures.[3]

In what is undoubtedly one of the most beautiful and compelling books in political philosophy in the last century, *The Human Condition*, Hannah Arendt argues that politics is a world of "appearances." Far from a cynical commentary on the hypocrisy of politicians, Arendt's claim entails both a realistic acknowledgment that the only way we can do political business is by relying on appearances and a more value-laden argument for the virtue of publicity, in its classical republican sense of *making things public*. "For us," Arendt writes, "appearance—something that is being seen and heard by others as well as by ourselves—constitutes reality," by which she means a political reality.[4] To be a political being, to have a political existence, is to be a being that appears before others in public.

Therefore, perhaps the greatest form of *political* violence [as distinguished from broader forms of violence] is to be forcibly removed from the world of appearances, or to be "disappeared." To be "disappeared"—a perverse if starkly accurate use of the passive voice—is not just to be kidnapped or killed. We know of political hostages and martyrs who are absent in body but are still very present as public figures in memory and imagination. To be "disappeared" is something qualitatively different: it is to be removed from the political world in such a way that no public memory or imagination is allowed. The political violence of being "disappeared" is not just against a particular person, but against the whole of the political society in which that person had his or her public being.

A regime that engages in disappearances is a regime that so terrorizes its citizens that no memorial, no recognition, and no acknowledgment of an absence are allowed.

But what of an archive that has disappeared? Our time at the Archivo Histórico de la Policía Nacional raised for us this oddly resonant question, resonant because a disappearing archive is what we had been dealing with all along in our decade-long research on Lookout Mountain Laboratory. The basis for the history we have told in this book had to be discovered, pieced together, reconstructed, and otherwise reconceived, for though Lookout Mountain Laboratory was arguably the most important film studio of the US Cold War, it had no archives, at least not in the sense of a coherent collection of film and documents. As we described in the introduction, when the studio on Wonderland Avenue was closed in the late 1960s, its films and papers were shipped off to warehouses, thrown in dumpsters, and otherwise scattered across the official and unofficial networks of the national security state. As a result, to write this book we had to not only construct an archive but also build a network of contacts and sources, work that appears much more journalistic than scholarly, yet is precisely the sort of work scholars must learn to do if they are to begin to make visible the many histories of national security states that have been disappeared or that just happen to be invisible.

We first learned of Lookout Mountain Laboratory in 2007 when one of us [Ned O'Gorman] was working on another project at the Eisenhower Presidential Library and came across a memo that described President Eisenhower's strong reaction to news about Ivy "Mike," the first thermonuclear device ever to be detonated [discussed at length in chapter 4]. Curious about the incident and the film, we were able to locate a digitized version of *Operation Ivy* on the Internet in the Prelinger Archives' online collection at the Internet Archive. We watched and rewatched the film, noting that a unit called "Lookout Mountain Laboratory" had produced it. Searching the Internet, we turned up a two-page Department of Energy "fact sheet" about Lookout Mountain [a fact sheet that, as we would later determine, was not entirely factual], a few other digitized films shot by the unit, and references to Peter Kuran, who had made a documentary about Lookout Mountain. For the next two years, periodic digging around turned up bits of further information about Lookout Mountain here and there—in government memos, in some oral histories, in a conversation with an archivist, and so on—but the history continued to be elusive.

Indeed, as we discussed in chapter 9, if we had tried to learn about Lookout Mountain Laboratory in the 1980s rather than the 2000s, the task would have been far more difficult, for much of what we were learning and seeing was available only because of the Department of Energy's "Openness Initiative" in the 1990s. That initiative, an effort of the Clinton administration, sought to declassify documents, photographs, and films having to do with nuclear and other Cold War secrets. It was a slow process, requiring expert personnel to thoroughly review all materials, redacting what was deemed to be sensitive information, before releasing texts, images, and films to the public. And as things transpired, the events of September 11, 2001, quickly halted whatever momentum there was, putting a firm end to the declassification efforts of the Openness Initiative.

But our efforts, as events also turned out, were not in vain. In the summer of 2010, about three years into our work on Lookout Mountain Laboratory, we began to find what we were looking for. Our discovery began with the nondescript building in the Hollywood Hills that had been Lookout Mountain's headquarters. We wrote a letter to the owner at the time, John Ladner, asking if he might show us the site. [John would later sell the Wonderland Avenue property to actor and musician Jared Leto.] We were told in a phone call to be at the gate of the facility at a precise time, and that the gate would open only momentarily—such Hollywood drama! Arriving at the appointed time, we made it through the gate just as it was closing. We waited for more than a few minutes in the parking lot, wondering where all this would go. In time, John showed up at the door to his most unorthodox home [even by Hollywood standards], greeting us at the precise place where Lookout Mountain employees used to get cleared for entrance by security. With John we were able to walk at length through the building: we saw the old film vaults, viewing rooms, processing rooms, animation studios, and the soundstage. On-site, we were finally able to get a concrete sense of just how extensive the unit's work had been, as well as come to grips with the innovative and experimental nature of much of that work. And just as important, to our great surprise, before we left John handed us a small set of microfilm reels: on them, it turns out, were semiannual reports documenting Lookout Mountain's activities across many years of its history. "I don't know why I trust you guys," John said, "but I do." We hope we've proved ourselves worthy of his trust.

The microfilm not only gave us much of the historical material we needed, but helped us see what else we needed to look for. Over the next several years, we flew coast to coast and searched extensively online to gather fragments of the disappeared archives that came out of Lookout Mountain Laboratory and construct our own archive. Some of these archives remain inaccessible to us; these have not so much been disappeared as, in the words of Ariella Azoulay [whom we got to know while in Guatemala], been rendered "unshowable," so as to prohibit "others from acting and interacting with them, and with each other."[5] Or rather, *certain others*. For some reason, Peter Kuran, the Hollywood special effects professional, has been given access to images and documents that are classified. The walls of classification, it seems, are selective; and with respect to the nuclear state now, as always it seems, they remain more open to Hollywood, the Smithsonian, and the like than to academic scholars. The reasons for this are obvious and go back to the beginnings of Lookout Mountain Laboratory: the nuclear state needs story and spectacle to sustain itself far more than the truth. Indeed, the truth can be awkward.

For all that we do have, we want to thank not only John Ladner, but also the host of other people who have provided us with crucial photographs, moving images, documents, or memories: Martha DeMarre at the Nuclear Testing Archive; Miranda Gilmore and Tammy Horton at the Air Force Historical Research Archive; the people who built and run the Air Force Historical Research Archive Index [an unofficial and strictly volunteer effort]; the incredible archivists and lawyers at the George Washington University's National Security Archive; the staff at the National Archives and Records Administration [NARA], especially those who work with film and photography; Jimi Jones and Karin Hodgin Jones, who put us up when we were working at NARA; Mary Elizabeth Ruwell at the Air Force Academy's McDermott Library; the people behind the Department of Energy's OpenNet, especially Hazel O'Leary, who oversaw the initiative in the 1990s; Matthew Coolidge at the Center for Land Use Interpretation; Rick and Megan Prelinger at the Prelinger Archive, who have become friends; the many people who have contributed relevant films and documents to the Internet Archive; and Peter Kuran, who as much as anyone has helped preserve the legacy of Lookout Mountain Laboratory in Hollywood and elsewhere.

We especially want to thank those who provided us with access to their own personal archives and stories chronicling Lookout Mountain's many operations: not just John Ladner, but also former 1369th members Christopher Zenor, Al Homen, Terry Fail, Andy Trimm, and Dale Anderson; and former Lookout Mountain Laboratory employees Ken Hackman and Dennis Johnson. Without these people, this book simply could not have been written. They were not only part of Lookout Mountain's history, but are now part of its reappearance in the world. We also want to thank Byron Risvet and Virginia Sedillo at the Defense Threat Reduction Agency, who provided access to what unclassified documents they could, but more important, helped us better understand the history of Lookout Mountain's disappearing archives. Last but not least, we want to thank Peter Zavatarro of EG&G for remarkable insights into the work of that company.

To be sure, these people now find themselves part of our project in ways that may not be consistent with what they had imagined. What does it mean to make a disappeared history reappear? We have already suggested that this is a political act, necessarily so. Yet it is part of political phenomenology, "politics as such," rather than any particular political agenda. To be sure, we are also deeply concerned about the absurd politics of nuclear weapons, absurd because they are designed in such a way that there is no way to "win" with them, but only lose. Nuclear destruction is total, and everyone knows that any nuclear war is likely to become a total nuclear war, wiping all human life from the Earth. Nuclear testing has poisoned countless people and poisoned the Earth in irremediable ways. And yet the supposed "superpowers" of the world, the United States chief among them, cling to these weapons as amulets, teaching the world to believe that evil is good, or if not good then necessary. The unfolding dimensions of this absurd history may be unravelling before our very eyes. Who knows if these words we write will see the light of day? As we composed this epilogue near the end of 2017, Rex Tillerson, the embattled and underprepared US secretary of state, was trying to keep North Korea from facing off in a nuclear confrontation with a man Tillerson himself has reportedly dismissed as a "f—ing moron," Donald Trump, a faint shadow of a man who has chosen Twitter and television rather than film as his special means of propping up and projecting his thin self into the world—at what cost?[6]

Given the fraught status of memory and storage in a society of contested, congested, and contingent media platforms, it is little surprise that archives have recently become intensified sites of anxiety, energy, creativity, and labor. The library sciences are overwhelmed at present with questions about the future. What can be properly stored from the shifting torrents of data produced on today's platforms? What of yesterday's physical archives should be digitized before they degrade or disappear? And what is lost through the metadata we fail to capture in these efforts? The digital humanities have spurred manifold archival projects, each trying to reimagine the archive in a digital world. As we have learned through the generous support of the National Endowment for the Humanities, which has granted us two awards over the past decade to pursue our collaborative research on Lookout Mountain Laboratory, the humanistic disciplines are confronting questions of archives with a new intensity and profundity. Because archives are typically intentional sites of memory in a society otherwise typified by unintentional, automated forms of memory, it is little wonder archives have become such meaningful social, political, and cultural sites.

But what are the archives? The answer to that question depends on time, place, circumstances, and all those other things that go into the making of what we call "culture." We have something here too to learn from the Archivo Histórico de la Policía Nacional in Guatemala City, as well as another archive that has helped guide us, George Washington University's impressive National Security Archive. Both have large holdings from the Cold War. Both are run independently of the government. And both directly address the ends of democracy in their mission. And yet the meaning of these two archives is significantly different, especially with respect to what they assume about the nature of democracy.

George Washington University's National Security Archive was founded some thirty years ago "by journalists and scholars to check rising government secrecy," and the archive has a team of Freedom of Information Act [FOIA] lawyers among its staff. Indeed, one of its several claims of "extraordinary, quantifiable success over the past 25 years" is "40,000 FOIA and declassification requests to more than 200 offices and agencies of the U.S. government that have opened more than 10 million pages of previously secret U.S. government documents." As such, the National Security Archive, like the Archivo Histórico de la Policía Nacional, functions as a legal entity as much as a historical one.

Indeed, to walk into the Archivo Histórico de la Policía Nacional is to walk into a justice factory. It is to see groups of gowned and gloved workers organizing, processing, and digitizing documents and photos. Their goal is to take the archives dumped by the National Police as piles of trash in an abandoned building and to reconstruct, as nearly as possible, the structure and contents of the police records. Building archival structures that replicate the original institutional structures of the archived agency is standard archival practice. But here the mission is different from any North American archive we know of. For at the end of one hallway at the Archivo sits the bare office of the human-rights prosecutor. No computer sits on a desk. Rather, the Archivo is itself the prosecutor's "data" storage machine, his file system, his memory bank, his evidence repository. The reconstruction of the police archives, a massive and multiyear project, is being meticulously carried out so that the perpetrators of disappearances might be not only identified but also brought to justice. The democratic ethos of the Archivo is oriented toward political justice, a change in the state of affairs in Guatemala. In crucial respects, the Archivo "ends" in the prosecutor's office.

We have never been in the National Security Archive, so we cannot attest to what its facilities look like. [We imagine office cubicles, computer screens, watercoolers, and so on.] While it is staffed by lawyers and has collaborated in lawsuits and even prosecutions [including the prosecution of retired army general and former president Efraín Ríos Montt in Guatemala, ultimately stymied by the Constitutional Court of Guatemala], it is apparent that the National Security Archive is an information factory first, a judgment factory second, and a justice factory only remotely. Its democratic ethos is strongly informed by the idea of "freedom of information." In the 1950s the lawyer Harold Cross and the American Society of Newspaper Editors launched the "freedom of information" movement as a way to counter the growing secrecy of the federal government in the context of the Cold War. This movement would eventually help bring about the Freedom of Information Act, signed in 1966 by President Johnson and used widely by the National Security Archive. Cross wrote in his 1953 *The People's Right to Know: Legal Access to Public Records and Proceedings*: "Citizens of a self-governing society must have the legal right to examine and investigate the conduct of its affairs subject only to those limitations imposed by the most urgent public necessity. To that end, they must have the right to simple, speedy enforcement procedures geared to cope with the dynamic expansion of government activity."[7]

In most respects, Cross approached his work in a forensic spirit: "information" was needed for journalistic investigations and, more broadly, to make the government accountable to the people. Yet underlying Cross's efforts and those of the editors of the newspapers that he represented was a faith in the stand-alone democratic virtue of "openness." Exposure, closely related to exposé, was itself a kind of democratic good. The National Security Archives today continues this faith: most of its work ends in well-timed publicity statements.

Exposure, to be sure, is a democratic good. But is it therefore a democratic end? Are archives that expose government secrets inherently democratic? Is the opening of archives itself a democratic accomplishment? We confess that we ask the same of the book now in your hands. Is making the disappeared history of Lookout Mountain Laboratory reappear a democratic good? Of course, democratic societies need information, but liberal democratic culture in the United States is too prone not just to hold the rather crass assumption that more information is always better, but also to hold the more sophisticated Whitmanian and Deweyan assumption, more recently championed by Richard Rorty, that democracy is ultimately a matter of "experience." "Information," especially freedom of information, fits nicely with such a notion of democracy. "Information" is synonymous with exposure, and exposure is itself experienced as a kind of democratic good. Archives in this Deweyan cultural context become potential sites of exposé, disclosure, revelation, and so on—all aiming ideally toward a broadly distributed culture of critical judgment. Justice, in this Deweyan world, would seem to be a spontaneous outgrowth of the proliferation of democratic experience, rather than a particular end to be achieved through concerted and focused effort.

To be sure, judgment is both the beginning and end of justice. We move toward justice through acts of judgment, and justice is enacted in an authoritative act of judgment. But in Deweyan culture, judgment reigns so supreme that it can take the place of justice. If "experience" is at the heart of democracy, democratic experiences can proliferate quite apart from substantive changes in the state of affairs. Indeed, a curious connection can be drawn between Deweyan democratic culture, the activities of the National Security Archives, and surveillance agencies. Each approach "archives" as information for critical judgment and "data" as information for analysis in ways that can and often do operate quite apart from immediate concerns with justice.

The Archivo Histórico de la Policía Nacional challenges these Deweyan assumptions, as it insists that exposure is not enough. The democratic culture of the Archivo is one in which history, condensed in the archives, is proactively oriented toward justice through acts of exposure, yes, but more so through the construction of structures of accountability, of justice, even in a political context in which those structures are regularly frustrated by corruption, cronyism, and fear. Still, the people of the Archivo persist in their factory-like work, working toward a country not yet achieved. The goal of democratic politics, they attest, is not ultimately a broad realization of critical judgment and widespread forms of democratic "experience," but justice, an objective order, a state of affairs, indeed a state. Richard Rorty—and we might add much of the digital humanities—offers few categories for understanding the methodical labors of the Archivo.

Our point here is not to point fingers at anyone but ourselves. As we wrote this book and did the research to write it, we wrestled over and over again with what it means not only to make a disappeared history reappear, a political act, but to direct it toward justice. We have wished, at times, for a human-rights prosecutor's desk at the end of our academic hallway, especially as we considered the violence to peoples and land that nuclear testing did and that Lookout Mountain dramatized. Instead, we have this book and a prayer that someday, perhaps, it will help some people somewhere learn something that will be directed toward acts of justice. We are, to be clear, grateful for the opportunity to publish our work. Here we have to thank Mark Williams at Dartmouth College, and Richard Pult, Mike Burton, and Amanda Dupuis at the University Press of New England. For over three years we looked for a publisher who would be willing to embark with us on a history of Lookout Mountain Laboratory that would go beyond prose into images, visualizations, charts, and other design elements. The University Press of New England not only accepted the proposal, they embraced it with gusto. We can only say thank you, thank you, thank you. It is sad, very sad, that ours is among the last books this august press will publish.

Elizabeth Forsaith did an outstanding job copyediting this book for UPNE. This book owes much of its look and feel to the expertise of Michelle Bowers, who advised us on typography. Susan Becker, Linda Robbennolt, and Mary Pat McGuire also gave us invaluable advice on the the book's structure, look, and visual strategy. Alex Jerez lent expertise and labor to some of our visualizations. Ned's editor at the University of Chicago Press, Doug Mitchell, ended up declining our cumbersome "designed-book" project, but made it clear that he would be its cheerleader. We had, as well, good conversations with editorial pros at places such as the University of North Carolina Press and the University of Texas Press, which helped shape the book before you. But there is one person who stands out from the small chorus urging us on: Joe Masco of the Department of Anthropology at the University of Chicago. It was Joe who, at a point when we had all but given up on our "designed-book" aspirations, said *No! You can't give up!* And it was Joe who ended up providing crucial reader reports to help us refine and publish our project. Thank you, Joe!

Before we close, we also want to thank the host of others who helped us along the way, beginning with the remarkable graduate and undergraduate students at the University of Illinois who played significant roles in helping us see this project through: Ian Hill, Jessica Landau, Paul McKean, Laura Shea, Rohini Singh, and Jillian Klean Zwilling. We want to make special note of the amazing work Grace Hebert and Katie Bruner did for us: Grace read countless pages of Air Force documents and built us a database to match no other on Lookout Mountain's activities, and Katie spent a semester on the manuscript, crossing our "t's" and cross-checking our citations. Any errors that remain are ours, not hers. A host of current and former faculty colleagues here at Illinois have encouraged us too: the late Nancy Abelmann, Antoinette Burton, Jodi Byrd, John Caughlin, Anita Say Chan, Jon Ebel, Cara Finnegan, Colin Flint, Rayvon Fouché, Harriett Green, Ryan Griffis, Ben Grosser, Diane Harris, James Hay, Laurie Hogin, Sharon Irish, Masumi Iriye, Sally Jackson, Lilya Kaganovsky, Brett Kaplan, Karrie Karahalios, Ed Kolodziej, Prita Meier, Lisa Nakamura, Safiya Umoja Noble, Chris Prom, Christian Sandvig, Anna Westerstahl Stenport, David Tewksbury, Julie Turnock, Deke Weaver, and Terri Weissman. So, too, a number of different units at the University of Illinois, Urbana-Champaign, have supported our work: the Program for Arms Control, Disarmament, and International Security; the Illinois Program for Research in the Humanities; the Center for Advanced Study; and the Campus Research Board. We also owe great thanks to Marit McCluske and Janki Thakkar, who helped us realize a website on which to begin sharing our many digital resources with the world.

Colleagues at a number of other universities provided critical opportunities for developing, presenting, and refining the work represented in this book, beginning with Tara McPherson, Steve Anderson, Craig Dietrich, and Erik Loyer at the University of Southern California, who through the National Endowment for the Humanities and Mellon Foundation–supported Alliance for Networking Visual Culture invited us, along with several other scholars, to Los Angeles in the summer of 2010 to pursue our research. Other fellows there that summer—Wendy Hui Kyong Chun, Brian Goldfarb, Kara Keeling, Debra Levine, Nicholas Mirzoeff, Veronica Paredes, Joan Saab, Jentery Sayers, Karen Tongson, Marcela Fuentes Visintini, and Mark Williams—proved inestimable conversation partners about media theory, digital publishing, and the question of the archives. Also at University of Southern California, filmmaker and artist Jeanne Jo spent a day with Kevin creating lasting images of former 1369th photographers at Vandenberg Air Force Base; her eyes and ears helped greatly in our understanding that part of this book's material. Pippa Oldfield at the Centre for Visual Arts and Cultures in Durham, England, and her collaborator Tom Allbeson at Swansea University provided us with a fantastic occasion to present our work on EG&G. Robert Hariman, Kate Baldwin, and Dilip Gaonkar at Northwestern University gave us two occasions to present our work and offered in response incredibly valuable feedback and encouragement. Anne Demo and Bradford Vivian invited us to present at Syracuse University at a gathering of scholars of visual rhetoric in 2009, a trip that proved fruitful for our collaboration in many different ways. And several faculty in the Media Studies department at the University of Virginia provided Ned with some needed encouragement at a point when this project was losing steam: Bruce Williams, Aynne Kokas, Jennifer Peterson, and Siva Vaidhyanathan. Ned would also like to thank Chad Wellmon at UVA for his friendship and encouragement, and the Institute for Advanced Studies in Culture for helping support Ned's yearlong stay at UVA in 2015–16, when some of this book was written.

Our friend Tim Garrett lent us his office many moons ago so that we could begin to plan our ambitious project; Nathan Keay also hosted us on an early trip. As a neighbor to Ned, Ben Rund helped this work along with his enthusiasm and his knowledge of engineering and machines. Dave Tell at the University of Kansas gave us a wonderful opportunity to present our work in front of a lively and engaged group of faculty and graduate students connected to the Hall Center for the Humanities. Susan Courtney and Jennifer Fey invited us to present on a panel with them at the Society for Cinema and Media Studies, which ended up paying scholarly dividends well beyond the conference itself. Similarly, Doug Cunningham invited us to join him on a conference panel that led to a chapter on Lookout Mountain in the *Blackwell Companion to War Film* he coedited with John Nelson. Shiloh Krupar [Georgetown] and Sarah Kanouse [Northeastern] asked us to join them on a panel at the American Studies Association, which continues to lead to further interaction and collaboration. A group of scholars including Christina Tekie, Dana Powell, Brian Smithson, and Stephanie Friede helped shape aspects of this project's methodology through including Kevin in their Infrastructural Worlds conference at Duke University. Kyle Jensen and Jacqueline Foertsch at the University of North Texas invited Ned to give a keynote at their annual Postwar Faculty Colloquium, which proved to be not only a great time but the beginning of partnerships. Kevin presented on our work at the "Arctic Cinemas and the Documentary Ethos" conference at the University of Illinois, run by Anna Stenport, Scott MacKenzie, and Lilya Kaganovsky. Peter Asaro at the New School gave Kevin an occasion to present on our research, and Orit Halpern at Concordia University joined Kevin in a lively collaborative presentation on Cold War archives at the Media Art Histories Conference in Montreal. Bryan Taylor at the University of Colorado, Nate Atkinson at Georgia State University, Timothy Barney at the University of Richmond, Marty Medhurst at Baylor University, Danielle Endres at the University of Utah, and Ian Hill at the University of British Columbia all proved crucial conversation partners during the course of this work. We also want to thank folks at the Association for the Rhetoric of Science and Technology for giving us an opportunity to present our work. And finally, we thank Linda O'Gorman and Susan Becker for their encouragement and support along the long road this book has been.

As with any major project like this, we published bits and pieces along the way. We want to thank the editors at the journals *Rhetoric and Public Affairs*, *Visual Studies*, *Communication and Critical/Cultural Studies*, and *Journal of War and Culture Studies* for opportunities to publish work, as well as the editors of the volumes *Arctic Cinemas and the Documentary Ethos*, *Sighting Memory: The Intersection of Visual Practices and Practices of Memory*, and *The Blackwell Companion to War Film*. We had a couple of more informal occasions to publish our work via *Communication Current* and the National Science Foundation's *SBE 2020*, for which we are grateful. And we are, we should say, grateful for each other, for the remarkable opportunity to colabor, for friendship along the way, and for a common faith and hope that vain things cannot last.

NOTES

Preface

1. See Masco, *The Theater of Operations*; Scarry, *Thermonuclear Monarchy*; and Wills, *Bomb Power*.
2. The most noteworthy exception is Masco in "Nuclear Technoaesthetics"; "Survival is Your Business"; and *The Theater of Operations*.
3. Masco, "Target Audience," 23.
4. Shapiro, *Atomic Bomb Cinema*, 5, 7.

Introduction

1. Eisenhower, "Farewell Radio and Television Address"; Horkheimer and Adorno, *Dialectic of Enlightenment*.
2. Der Derian, *Virtuous War*, xxviii. See also Stahl, *Militainment, Inc*.
3. Phil Karn, comment on *Operation Ivy*, August 31, 2006, *Internet Archive*, https://archive.org/details/operation_ivy.
4. Rancière, *The Politics of Aesthetics*, 12. Rancière writes, "I call the distribution of the sensible the system of self-evident facts of sense perception that simultaneously discloses the existence of something in common and the delimitations that define the respective parts and positions within it. A distribution of the sensible therefore establishes at one and the same time something common that is shared and exclusive parts. This apportionment of parts and positions is based on a distribution of spaces, times, and forms of activity that determines the very manner in which something in common lends itself to participation and in what way various individuals have a part in this distribution."
5. Raymond Williams, *Marxism and Literature*, 128.
6. Geertz, *Local Knowledge*, 73–93. "Political aesthetics" has been resurrected from Walter Benjamin's deathly association of the "aestheticization of politics" with fascism in "The Work of Art in the Age of Mechanical Reproduction" [Benjamin, 242]. Critics from an array of fields—art history, visual studies, memory studies, political theory, media studies, and rhetorical studies—are recognizing anew that political orders implicate aesthetic orders, or that, in the words of Robert Hariman, "our political experience is styled" [Hariman, *Political Style*, 2]. But in its resurrection, political aesthetics has reappeared in new bodies. No longer tightly bound to the art object, political aesthetics has been moving into the sensorium, raising critical questions about what Fred Turner has recently called the "surround," the multimedia environments in which we live, move, and have our political being [Turner, *The Democratic Surround*].
7. See Scott, *Seeing Like a State*, 2–3.
8. On the use of maps for making sense of the Cold War, see Barney, *Mapping the Cold War*.
9. Habermas, *Legitimation Crisis*. See O'Gorman, *The Iconoclastic Imagination*, for an extensive discussion of the political and cultural implications of the fact that states must render themselves "as an image" to publics.
10. Raymond Williams, *Marxism and Literature*, 128.
11. See Carey, "The Roots of Modern Media Analysis," 39–40. As Carey writes of McLuhan, "McLuhan erased the distinction between art and utility, between aesthetic action and practical form. Everyday objects—cars, clothes, and lightbulbs—were governed less by utility than by aesthetics: their meaning was to be sought in a principle of taste rather than a principle of interest and action."
12. Anderson, *Imagined Communities*.
13. Kittler, *Optical Media*; Virilio, *War and Cinema*; Stahl, *Through the Crosshairs*.
14. Foucault, *Discipline and Punish*.
15. Azoulay, *Civil Imagination*, 12.
16. Lippit, *Atomic Light*.
17. Azoulay, *Civil Imagination*, 14–18.
18. Hariman and Lucaites, *The Public Image*, 58.
19. See Mirzoeff, *How to See the World*.
20. See Acland and Wasson, *Useful Cinema*; Bellows and McDougall, *Science Is Fiction*; Boon and Rotha, *Films of Fact*; Hediger and Vonderau, *Films That Work*; Kessler, "Visible Evidence–But of What?"; Orgeron, Orgeron, and Streible, *Learning with the Lights Off*; Reagan, Tomes, and Treichler, *Medicine's Moving Pictures*; Slide, *Before Video*; Streible, Roepke, and Mebold, "Introduction."
21. Hediger and Vonderau, *Films That Work*, 40.
22. Doherty, *Projections of War*, 4–5.
23. In addition to Doherty's *Projections of War*, see Atkinson, "Newsreels as Domestic Propaganda"; Cunningham, "Desiring the Disney Technique"; Koppes and Black, *Hollywood Goes to War*; Leskosky, "Cartoons Will Win the War"; Maslowski, *Armed with Cameras*; Moyes, *Battle Eye*; Thomas, "Cartoon Combat."
24. Mills, *White Collar*, 329.
25. Friedberg, *Window Shopping*, 125–36.
26. Tennessee Williams, *The Glass Menagerie*; Percy, *The Moviegoer*; Kirkham, *Charles and Ray Eames*.
27. Friedberg, *Window Shopping*, 144–45.
28. MacIntyre, *After Virtue*; MacIntyre, *Whose Justice?*
29. MacIntyre, *After Virtue*, 174–75.
30. Mills, *White Collar*, 80.
31. Wiener, *Cybernetics*, 8. The principles of cybernetics predated Wiener, as discussed in Giedion, *Mechanization Takes Command*; Mindell, *Between Human and Machine*.
32. See Edwards, *Closed World*.
33. Halpern, *Beautiful Data*, 83.
34. Ibid., 81.
35. Edwards, *Closed World*, 7.
36. Here we draw inspiration from Peters, "Information: Notes Toward a Critical History."
37. "Public Information Policy on Biological Warfare, Radiological Warfare, and Chemical Warfare"; "Excerpts from Report of the Secretary of Defense's Ad Hoc Committee on Chemical, Biological, and Radiological Warfare, 30 June 1950."

38. Stevens, *Worldwide Military Command and Control System*, 4.
39. Again, we would urge readers to see Edwards, *Closed World*.
40. Stevens, 2.
41. We know all of this because Dr. Risvet graciously invited us out to Kirtland as we were researching this book.

Chapter One: Hollywood's Nuclear Weapons Laboratory

1. "Secret U.S. Project Here Protested," 1. Several follow-up articles were published in the *Los Angeles Times*. See "Laboratory Complaints Answered by Air Force"; Hartmann, "Protests on Laboratory Bring Action"; and "Peace Seen in Operation of Air Force Lab."
2. "Secret U.S. Project Here Protested," 2.
3. Ibid., 2.
4. Ibid., 1.
5. Ibid.
6. Call, *Selling Air Power*, 15.
7. Ibid., 43; Air Power League, *Peace Through Air Power*, 2. The Air Power League was a proponent of air power as such, not just that of the Air Force. Indeed, they pushed quite hard for an air-oriented Navy unified under a single command with the Air Force. See ibid., 28–29.
8. Cumings, *Dominion from Sea to Sea*, 321–25.
9. Ibid., 341.
10. See for example, Smoodin, *Regarding Frank Capra*; Culbert, "'Why We Fight'"; German, "Frank Capra's *Why We Fight* Series."
11. See Saettler, *Evolution of American Educational Technology*, 184–90.
12. See Cunningham, "Imaging/Imagining Air Force Identity."
13. Ibid., 96.
14. "More Films Produced by AAF Than by Big Studios," 44.
15. Cunningham, "Imaging/Imagining Air Force Identity," 96.
16. See Lewis, *American Culture of War*, 45–56.
17. *The Last Bomb* [film].
18. Air Photographic and Charting Service, *Historical Summary*, 68; "Lookout Mountain Background." Indeed, in the planning reports for its first major assignment, Operation Sandstone, Lookout Mountain was referred to as the First Motion Picture Unit. See Winant et al., "Sandstone Report," Annex 2, 4; Hull, *Atomic Weapons Tests*, 10.
19. "Outline of History, Lookout Mountain Laboratory," 1.
20. *History of 1352, Jan. through June 1954*, 4.
21. See "The 34th Academy Awards, 1962," Academy of Motion Picture Arts and Sciences, https://www.oscars.org/oscars/ceremonies/1962/, and *History of 1352, July through Dec. 1956*, 19–20; Air Photographic and Charting Service, "Awards for Photographic Achievements," in *Chronology*, 35. There is some confusion in official Air Force lore about whether *Toward the Unknown*, a 1956 Lookout Mountain film, received an Academy Award nomination. "Awards" [cited in this note] suggests that it was, but the Lookout Mountain report cited here says only that Air Force headquarters sent the film to the Academy urging that it be nominated; and the academy's database itself cites only *Breaking the Language Barrier* as a nominee [see Academy of Motion Picture Arts, "Academy Award Database"]. Nevertheless, Lookout Mountain earned a wide array of awards and recognitions, among them from the Jury for the International Exhibition of Documentary and Short Films, held in Venice, Italy, in 1957; the International Exposition of Cinematographic Arts in Venice in 1960; an award at the First Annual Technical Film Festival in 1960; and CINDY [Cinema and Industry] awards in 1960 and 1961. See Air Photographic and Charting Service, *Historical Summary*, 34–35.
22. United States Congress, *Federal Audio-Visual Programs*, 52.
23. The *Perry Mason* relationship was reported by Al Homen in an interview with Kevin Hamilton, Oct. 31, 2014, Highland, California. Actor Dean Fredericks, who played Steve Canyon in the series, appears in photographs from the unit's January 1959 report; the series used extensive footage of Air Force activities almost certainly originating with Lookout Mountain's footage services.
24. See Humphries, *Hollywood's Blacklists*.
25. May, *The Big Tomorrow*, 4; Doherty, *Projections of War*, 4.
26. Doherty, *Projections of War*, 5.
27. May, *The Big Tomorrow*, 4.
28. Hoberman, *An Army of Phantoms*, 22, 224, 277.
29. Ronald Reagan's work with Lookout Mountain is not mentioned in any of its official reports; however, a photo in the possession of former employee Kenneth Hackman as well as a photo book self-produced by Lookout Mountain employees show Reagan on set at Desilu Studios doing spot work for Lookout Mountain.
30. In *Cinematic Cold War*, Tony Shaw and Denise Youngblood divide Hollywood's Cold War history into five periods: "1947–1953 [dominated by hard-line negative propaganda]; 1953–1962 [soft-core, positive propaganda mixed with the beginnings of negotiated dissent]; 1962–1980 [pro-détente propaganda]; 1980–1986 [New Right propaganda]; 1986–1990 [call for peace]" (19). Lookout Mountain's career spanned three of these five periods; and as we will see, their most intensive Hollywood activities took part during the second period, the period of "soft-core, positive propaganda mixed with the beginnings of negotiated dissent." In the 1960s, as Hollywood in many respects turned against the Cold War, Lookout Mountain turned more and more toward austere "documentary" work used primarily by engineers, war planners, airmen, and soldiers.
31. FBI to Nichols, "Re: Lookout Mountain Laboratory."
32. The Hollywood scriptwriter and humorist Leo Rosten once quipped that what the stars said was "reported to the world in greater detail than any other single group in the world, with the possible exception of Washingtonists. . . . People would know Clark Gable or Greta Garbo in parts of the world where they didn't know the name of their own prime minister or the mayor of their

own little town." Quoted in Ross, "The Politicization of Hollywood before World War II," 10.

33. Szczepanik, "Hollywood in Disguise," 172–73.
34. Shaw and Youngblood, *Cinematic Cold War*, 37.
35. Norberg to Johnson, "Subject: Motion Pictures and Propaganda."
36. For a thorough account of the "Atoms for Peace" campaign, see Osgood, *Total Cold War*.
37. The term "big science" was introduced to the literature in 1961 by Alvin Weinberg in his influential article "Impact of Large-Scale Science on the United States." In the article, Weinberg approached the term in an ironic more than an analytic manner [see Weinberg, "Impact of Large-Scale Science on the United States"]. Later scholars have used the term in a more analytical fashion, examining a diversified set of institutions and practices under the rubric, each sharing the quality of large scale. See, for example, Galison and Hevly, *Big Science*.
38. Arendt, *Life of the Mind*, 57.
39. See Herken, *Brotherhood of the Bomb*; Rhodes, *Making of the Atomic Bomb*; Rhodes, *Dark Sun*; Rhodes, *Arsenals of Folly*; and Younger, *The Bomb*.
40. On STS and "following the instruments," see Bijsterveld and Pinch, *Special Issue on Sound Studies*, 639; Hankins and Silverman, *Instruments and the Imagination*, 5. Similarly, sociologist Karin Knorr-Cetina has argued that following the history and uses of the material instruments of the laboratory "reveals the fragmentation of contemporary science" in a way that a focus on the role of scientific theory cannot [Knorr-Cetina, *Epistemic Cultures*, 3]. Most influentially, Bruno Latour has taught a generation of scholars in the history of science and technology to focus on the intersections and interactions among scientists, their theories, and their instruments [Latour, *Science in Action*]. For similar arguments see Appadurai, *The Social Life of Things*; Galison, *Image and Logic*; Haraway, *Simians, Cyborgs, and Women*; Latour, "Give Me a Laboratory and I Will Raise the World"; Pels, Hetherington, and Vandenberghe, "The Status of the Object"; Pels, *Unhastening Science*.
41. Edwards, *Closed World*; Mackenzie, *Inventing Accuracy*; MacKenzie, *Knowing Machines*.
42. "Outline of History of Lookout Mountain Laboratory," 1.
43. *History of 1352, Jan. through June 1955,* 1.
44. See Atkinson, "Newsreels as Domestic Propaganda," 72–75. Richard L. Miller, *Under the Cloud*, 75–76. Weisgall, *Operation Crossroads*, 83–94.
45. Weisgall, *Operation Crossroads*, 8, 13–17.
46. Ibid., 153.
47. Ibid., 280–82.
48. Ibid., 189.
49. Ibid., 280.
50. Quoted in Ibid., 284.
51. Thomas, "History," 7.
52. "Eniwetok" is now spelled "Enewetak" in closer keeping with Marshallese pronunciation. However, at the time of the Pacific nuclear tests it was spelled "Eniwetok" in official US documents. For the sake of historical accuracy, and even of marking the miscues between Americans and Marshallese, we use "Eniwetok."
53. Air Photographic and Charting Service, *Historical Summary*, 66.
54. "Outline of History of Lookout Mountain Laboratory," 2.
55. See Air Photographic and Charting Service, *Historical Summary*, 67.
56. *Lookout Mountain Air Force Station* [film].

Chapter Two: Colonels, Cameras, and Security Clearances

1. Goddard and Copp, *Overview*, 363.
2. Ballard, Bond, and Paxton, *Lowry Air Force Base*, 22–24.
3. Department of the Air Force, "Basic Photography," iii.
4. Kittler, *Gramophone, Film, Typewriter*; Kittler, *Optical Media*; Virilio, *War and Cinema*.
5. Masco, *Theater of Operations*, 3.
6. Ibid., 35.
7. Hull, *Atomic Weapons Tests*, iv.
8. Ibid., 10.
9. Ibid., Annex 1, sect. 18, 1.
10. Berkhouse et al., *Operation Sandstone: 1948*, 44.
11. Ibid., 4, 10.
12. Air Photographic and Charting Service, *Historical Summary*, 68–69.
13. Ibid., 69.
14. Department of the Air Force, *United States Air Force Academy Catalogue*, 1955–56, 41.
15. SAC remained one of Lookout Mountain's primary clients throughout the unit's existence. Training films for SAC pilots, missile operators, and technicians were regularly made; more cinematically, SAC commissioned a number of special report films about the emerging missile mission for Air Force and other government officials during the height of debates over whether planes or missiles would carry the day for American strategy. Lemay also struggled with how to respond and relate to depictions of the Air Force on popular screens, at times frustrated with the portrayals, but at other times intervening directly to see that films such as *Bombers B-52*, *Strategic Air Command*, or *A Gathering of Eagles* were made with the full, and at times expensive, cooperation of the Air Force, as outlined in Suid, *Guts and Glory*, 190.
16. Air Photographic and Charting Service, *Historical Summary*, 1.
17. Air Photographic and Charting Service, *Chronology*, 2.
18. Air Photographic and Charting Service, *History of Air Photographic and Charting Service, 1 January 1953–30 June 1953*, in *Historical Summary*, 16–18.
19. Ibid., 15, 17.
20. Air Photographic and Charting Service, *Historical Summary*, 3, 6.
21. "Guide to Lookout Mountain Air Force Station."
22. Air Photographic and Charting Service, *Historical Summary*, 67.
23. Ibid., 73–74.
24. Air Photographic and Charting Service, *History of Air Photographic and Charting Service, 1 January 1953–30 June 1953*, in *Historical Summary*, 5–6.

25. *History of 1352, April through June 1952*, 2; *History of 1352, Jan. through June 1955*, 1.
26. *History of 1352, Jan. through June 1957*, 3–4.
27. *History of 1352, July through Dec. 1957*, 37.
28. *History of 1352, Jan. through June 1954*, 7.
29. Ibid., 6.
30. Ibid., 6–7.
31. Ibid., 32.
32. Ibid., 32–34.
33. *History of 1352, July through Dec. 1957*, 3.
34. *History of 1352, July through Dec. 1963*, 7.
35. Second Lt. Dennis Johnson [ret.], phone interview with Kevin Hamilton, August 9, 2014.
36. *History of 1352, Jan. through June 1954*, 11.
37. Ibid., 2.
38. Ibid., 2–3.
39. *History of 1352, Jan. through June 1964*, 2.
40. Ibid., 7–9; *History of 1352, July through Dec. 1964*, 13–25.

Chapter Three: Strategies of Containment

1. *Lookout Mountain Air Force Station* [film].
2. Hau'ofa, Waddell, and Naidu, *A New Oceania*.
3. Ibid. Hau'ofa describes the islands as moving through a persistent, slow exchange of material transported by tides, volcanoes, and bird guano. Vincente Diaz builds on this conception of moving and connected islands in his scholarship on Austronesian navigation techniques. See Diaz, "Voyaging for Anti-Colonial Recovery," 25–26. Etak, Diaz explains, which often translates to "moving islands," is an Austronesian navigational technique for "calculating distance traveled, or position at sea by triangulating the speed of islands of departure and destination with that of a third reference island." "For the navigator, the canoe remains stationary and the islands zip by." To be sure, ways of charting make possible conceptions of the world and one's place within it.
4. Cosgrove, *Geography and Vision*. In his essay "Seeing the Pacific" in the volume, Cosgrove points out how nineteenth-century American cartography rendered this area a "distant group of scattered islands" and consistently pushed the Pacific to the left and right edges of a flat map, splitting the Pacific in a way that coincided with racial delineations. "Environmental determinists" even racialized latitude and longitude through the ascription of certain human proclivities and characteristics to particular locations on the grid, securing certain places not only in space but within evolutionary development. In Cosgrove's view, imperial perspectives on the Pacific did not reach for and achieve a unified pictorial frame for that part of the world until challenges to American hegemony emerged through conflict with Japan during World War II. See Cosgrove, *Geography and Vision*, 185–202.
5. Weeks and Meconis, *The Armed Forces of the USA in the Asia-Pacific Region*, 15–16; Cosgrove, *Geography and Vision*, 188–90; Wilson, *Reimagining the American Pacific*, 133–34.
6. Nixon, *Slow Violence*, 7.
7. The United Nations designated the region a "trust territory" of the United States, one that was officially ruled "non-self-governing." It was ruled at first by the US Navy—a spoil of war—and then by the US Department of the Interior. See United Nations, "Trust and Non-Self-Governing Territories." For Marshall Island history, see Deines et. al, "Marshall Islands Chronology"; and Maclellan, *Banning Nuclear Weapons*.
8. Johnston, "Database of Nuclear Tests."
9. Ibid. Though the United Nations made the United States chief steward of that trust, this arrangement provided at least some legal grounds for future appeals for cessation of nuclear testing. By the time the United States moved to conduct the later series of tests under Operation Dominic, opposition to bombing the trustees had so grown that Joint Task Force Eight, the organization responsible for the tests, had to move the operation to a new location outside the territory of the trust.
10. Mackland, "Operation Camera"; Office of the Historian, *Operation Crossroads*, 9. The National Archives and Records Administration [NARA] holds hundreds of separate 35 mm and 16 mm reels of unedited test footage. Around a hundred contact prints exist in NARA's Still Picture Branch of images of cameras and photographers at work in Crossroads. At Michigan State's archives, one can review the notebooks of one of the lead photographers; the July 15, 1946, issue of *Life* magazine covering the test included a photograph of the photographers.
11. Weisgall, *Operation Crossroads*, 116, 120, 121.
12. Office of the Historian, *Operation Crossroads*, 9.
13. Air Photographic and Charting Service, *Historical Summary*, 65.
14. Berkhouse et al., *Operation Crossroads: 1946*, 167–68. Another thirty-six Navy and civilian men [the latter largely from Los Alamos] served in the Technical Photography Group of the Instrumentation Division—see ibid., 74, 81.
15. Thomas, "History," 8.
16. Ibid., 7.
17. Hales, "The Atomic Sublime," 17.
18. Quoted in Boyer, *By the Bomb's Early Light*, 82.
19. Ibid., 91.
20. Markwith, "Farewell to Bikini," 97–116. The sanction of the forced removal of these people depended on not only the fantasy of their docility, but a view of them as island-oriented, rather than ocean-oriented.
21. Of course, such incongruity was quite consistent with the long-standing American habit of seeing every landscape as a new frontier for colonization. Before long, the moon itself would be subject to such an imperial imagination.
22. See Atkinson, "Newsreels as Domestic Propaganda," 72–75.
23. The search for an atomic bomb test site began in early 1946. Naval test planners looked all over the sea, seeking an anchorage protected from wind and waves, but with enough currents to disperse radioactivity broadly. It had to be within one thousand miles of a B-29 base, but no less than three hundred miles from any city; and they

wanted the test site to be uninhabited, or nearly so. A number of sites in the Atlantic, the Caribbean, and the Pacific were considered, but Bikini Atoll won out. The ring-shaped island could hold and protect plenty of ships, and the currents and tides in and around Bikini's lagoon would help disperse radioactivity. Kwajalein Atoll, some two hundred miles from Bikini, could serve as a B-29 launching site. And the Navy determined that Bikini Atoll's "mere" 167 inhabitants could be relocated to Rongerik Atoll, 125 miles away. See Shurcliff, *Bombs at Bikini*, 16–17, and Teaiwa, "Bikinis and Other S/Pacific N/Oceans," 89. The inhabitants of Bikini were rightly skeptical of Rongerik as haunted—the fish there almost certainly carried the ciguatera disease from eating certain food along the coral. It may in fact be the case that what made Bikini such a worthy refuge for nuclear test fleets and a dispersal system for irradiated water also made it a good place to live and fish, whereas nearby Rongerik, less desirable for the tests, also harbored conditions ripe for death-dealing fish populations [see Kiste, *The Bikinians*].

24. In fact, in the run-up to Crossroads, *two* Parisian designers, in a kind of fashion war, paid homage to America's Pacific atomic test with names for two-piece bathing suits. First Jacques Heim called his new two-piece bathing suit the "Atome," and then in a countermove, his competitor Louis Réard called his model the "Bikini." See Weisgall, *Operation Crossroads*, 263.
25. Bruce Williams, "American Military Exceptionalism."
26. In September 1945, *Life* magazine pictured Christians laid-out poolside in a two-piece, soaking up radiation, describing her as "Half-Mexican, Half-Dutch," the very admixture of familiar and exotic that the Crossroads bombs would come to represent in American culture. "Anatomic Bomb," *Life*, 53.
27. Weisgall, *Operation Crossroads*, 180. Orson Welles, Rita Hayworth's husband, decried in a commentary on ABC radio on June 30, 1946, "I want my daughter to be able to tell her daughter that grandmother's picture was on the last atom bomb ever to explode." See Welles, "Orson Welles Announces His Wife's Image on an Atomic Bombshell."
28. Weisgall, *Operation Crossroads*, 264–65.
29. For another image of the bar, see Naval History and Heritage Command, "Cross Spikes Club." https://www.history.navy.mil/our-collections/art/exhibits/conflicts-and-operations/operation-crossroads-bikini-atoll/cross-spikes-club.html
30. Hariman and Lucaites, "The Iconic Image of the Mushroom Cloud and the Cold War Nuclear Optic," 137.
31. Hales, "Atomic Sublime," 5–8.
32. The US government referred to the atoll as "Eniwetok" until 1974, when the spelling of the name was changed to "Enewetak" to more closely reflect Marshallese pronunciation. Because ours is a history of the US government in the 1940s, 1950s, and 1960s, we use the spelling that official documents used. On the spelling change, see Hacker, *Elements of Controversy*, 14.
33. Lilienthal to President Truman, "Subject: Test of Atomic Weapons," 67–68.
34. "A.E.C. Releases Eniwetok Atom Blast Pictures," 1.
35. In the summer of 1950, the Atomic Energy Commission reviewed Lookout Mountain's *Operation Sandstone* for possible public release. They wrote to President Truman, "This film recently has been given full security review and found to be publicly releasable without prejudice to the common defense and security." Yet, the Commission continued, "a change in the world situation [Truman had just sent troops to Korea] makes it appear inadvisable to make public release of this film at this time. The Department of State and the Department of Defense concur in this view. It is our feeling that the public release of this film would be objectionable both on the grounds of its possible usefulness in the current Communist propaganda campaign, and of its possible effect on the plans and operations of Joint Task Force Three [the group responsible for running another series of nuclear tests under the name Operation Greenhouse]." Dean to President Truman, "Subject: Operation Sandstone." Truman concurred, and the film was kept from public view until 1952 [see "Morristown Seeks $ Aid for Atom Ex from Biz Groups" for evidence of the 1952 release].
36. Ball, "Nation Gains New Power in Atomic Weapons."
37. Snapp, "Operation Sandstone—Classification Guide," 5–6.
38. Winant et. al, *Sandstone Report–43*, Annex 2, 1, 4.
39. Technical photography ranged from motion-picture footage of the assembly and handling of the bomb devices to fireball photography. See Udley, "Appendix A: Photographic Report."
40. Winant et. al, *Sandstone Report*, Annex 2, 1.
41. Hull, "Photographic Report," Annex 1, sect. 18, 4.
42. Davis, "Sandstone Documentary Film."
43. Winant et. al, *Sandstone Report*, Annex 2, 4; Hull, *Atomic Weapons Tests*, 47.
44. Hull, "Photographic Report," 4.
45. Disney used a similar, if animated, book prop in its 1943 *Victory through Air Power* [film].
46. *Lookout Mountain Air Force Station* [film].
47. In *Operation Sandstone*, unlike most subsequent Lookout Mountain nuclear test films, all the sound is nondiegetic.
48. Marx, *Machine in the Garden*.
49. Joe Masco writes, "While previous generations of scientists imagined the experimental laboratory as a model of the world, in the early Cold War period the world itself became the laboratory. Experiments across a wide range of disciplines demonstrated that each biological being on the planet was increasingly marked by the trace elements of the US nuclear testing program, as the earth, sea, and sky were transformed into experimental zones for nuclear science" [Masco, *Theater of Operations*, 87].
50. Hales, "Atomic Sublime," 10.
51. Byrd, *Transit of Empire*, 64.
52. Quoted in Rhodes, *Dark Sun*, 382.
53. Air Photographic and Charting Service, *Historical Summary*, 69.
54. Lookout Mountain Laboratory, *Joint Task Force Three Presents Operation Greenhouse* [film].
55. *Quarterly Report 1952, Lookout Mountain Laboratory, Jan. through March*, 1.

56. Defense Nuclear Agency, "Fact Sheet: Greenhouse"; Johnston, "Database of Nuclear Tests."

57. The public release version of the film was completed in the summer of 1952. Fifty prints of the film were sent to the Atomic Energy Commission; however, the prints were not publicly circulated until sometime later. See *Quarterly Historical Report, 1352d Motion Picture*, 2.

58. Lookout Mountain Laboratory, *Operation Greenhouse* [film]. As noted above, we refer to this title as *Operation Greenhouse*, although the film's full title in our bibliography and other indexes is *Joint Task Force Three Presents Operation Greenhouse*.

59. Hales, *Atomic Spaces*, 13, 37–38.

60. Ibid., xix.

61. *Quarterly Report 1952, Lookout Mountain Laboratory, Jan. through March*, 1.

62. DeLoughrey, "Myth of Isolates," 174.

63. "Interim Report by the Ad Hoc Committee of the NSC Planning Board on Armaments and American Policy."

64. For more on Operation Candor, see Chernus, *Eisenhower's Atoms for Peace*; Hewlett and Holl, *Atoms for Peace and War*. For more on Eisenhower and the paradox of nuclear deterrence, see O'Gorman, *Spirits of the Cold War*, chap. 4, and O'Gorman, *Iconoclastic Imagination*, chap. 6.

65. Trachtenberg, *History and Strategy*, 137.

66. Chernus, *Apocalypse Management*.

67. Weart, *Nuclear Fear*, 264.

68. *History of 1352, Jan. through June 1954*, 10, 11.

69. Ibid., 10, 14–16.

70. Ibid., 10.

71. *History of 1352, July through Dec. 1954*, 8.

72. Snapp, "Meeting 893," 5.

73. Fields to Clarkson, "New Outline."

74. Strauss to Wilson, "Subject: Documentary Film Entitled 'Commander's Report.'"

75. Clarkson, "History of Operation Castle," iv.

76. Salisbury, "Subject: Themes in Public Reporting."

77. *History of 1352, July through Dec. 1954*. 10.

78. *History of 1352, July through Dec. 1956*.

79. The structure of the photographic responsibilities at Dominic were confused. Lookout Mountain not only had to reorient their work to document a newly urgent series of tests, they also had to contend with changing mandates from changes in command of the task force, and confusing or even contradictory reporting arrangements within Joint Task Force Eight. For example, "technical control" of Air Force documentary units at Dominic was given to Task Unit 8.1.3 [Defense Atomic Support Agency, or DASA, the entity responsible for the weapons tests themselves], while operational and administrative control was given to Task Unit 8.4, the group responsible for coordinating Air Force contributions to the test. As a result, on at least one occasion, DASA requested "photo coverage of 69 [. . .] scientific project locations on 14 different islands," while the Air Force requested that the same photographers cover documentation of their air crews delivering the weapons the effects of which DASA projects were studying. See *History of 1352, July through Dec. 1962*, 14. The very command structure for these photographers spanned locations in Hawaii and Johnston and Christmas Islands. Similar confusion over responsibilities and reporting emerged over funding. On a number of occasions, Air Force documentary photographers also encountered other documentary film and photography units at work throughout Joint Task Force Eight [likely Navy units], which caused confusion among the multiple parties. And in still other challenges, Air Force photographers assigned to film the work of B-52 bombers in the tests were put on planes too slow to keep up with the B-52s.

80. It is important to note that unlike, for example, at Crossroads, the less-technical film and photographic work at Dominic was not intended for the public. None of the Dominic films were available to the public until the declassification effort of the late 1990s.

81. Kennedy had been loath to pursue atmospheric testing anyway, in light of the "Bravo" incident. In a later study of the period, William Ogle, the Los Alamos scientist in charge of Dominic's scientific mission, put it this way: "Atmospheric testing was a special horror in Kennedy's mind, even though he himself apparently did not believe that long-range fallout would seriously endanger anyone's health. His actions seem to imply a feeling that underground testing would not seriously affect the international balance of nuclear forces, but that atmospheric testing would lead to sudden and large changes in our posture vis-à-vis the Russians." Ogle, *Account of the Return to Nuclear Weapons Testing*, 303.

82. *History of 1352, July through Dec. 1962*, 10. Lookout Mountain photographers had earlier developed new techniques for remote photography at missile launchpads at Vandenberg. The same techniques, among the most technical the unit performed in its history, came into play at Johnston Island in support of the same Thor missiles. For Dominic, LML photographers sailed on ships to document the recovery of test instruments at sea, tracked missiles from specialized mounts, accompanied remote sensor outposts to small islands across the Pacific, and ascended Maui's Mt. Haleakala to document auroral effects of the tests. See *History of 1352, July through Dec. 1962*, 10–11.

83. As President Kennedy weighed a resumption of testing in late 1961, in response to the Soviet abrogation of a three-year moratorium, pressure against further Bikini testing built from the State Department and America's delegation to the United Nations. See "Trust Isles Raise Atom Test Issue," *New York Times*. Amid growing criticism of America's stewardship of the trust, the State Department feared it could not effectively manage the diplomatic effects of continued testing. James Carr, acting secretary of the interior, put the matter even more strongly in a November 3, 1961, letter to Glenn T. Seaborg, who as chairman of the Atomic Energy Commission was working closely with the Department of Defense to develop a proposed testing plan for the president's consideration. "Atomic testing at Eniwetok and Bikini in the past has led to great concern in the United Nations with respect to the discharge of our obligations to the Micronesians," he wrote, reminding Seaborg of the trusteeship agreement. "It is for these reasons—our obligations to the people of Micronesia, who would have

no voice, direct or indirect in a decision to test nuclear devices in the area, and our position before world opinion as trustee for these people—that we recommend against any further testing in the Trust Territory of the Pacific Islands." Carr to Seaborg, "Recommendation against Further Testing."

84. *Operation Dominic: Johnston Island* [film].
85. In the lead-up to the test, on May 4, 1962, *Life* magazine published an explanation of the tests that featured a spatial representation of Dominic's elaborate and decentralized plans ("Bomb Tests," Life, 44–45). The artist's rendering places readers in near orbit, with a view of the Pacific that locates Christmas and Johnston Islands as points within a network of trajectories, danger zones, and flight paths. The horizon curves behind to reveal glimpses of Hawaii and other lands, but the emphasis is on activity taking place not on earth or even sea, but in a nonplace above sky and before space.
86. *Operation Dominic: Nuclear Tests 1962* [film].

Chapter Four: Sense and Sensibilities

1. O'Keefe, *Nuclear Hostages*, 150.
2. Halpern, *Beautiful Data*.
3. Akira Mizuta Lippit argues that nuclear weapons must be seen within the broader historical development of "phenomenologies of the inside," noting that "psychoanalysis, X-rays, and cinema" each erupt into the scene in the late-nineteenth century and become, each in their own profound way, part of the history of atomic science and nuclear power (Lippit, *Atomic Light*, 5).
4. On idealism and nuclear deterrence, see O'Donovan, *Peace and Certainty*.
5. See Chernus, *Apocalypse Management*; Oakes, *Imaginary War*.
6. See O'Gorman, *Spirits of the Cold War*; Hogan, *Cross of Iron*.
7. American *allies*, not just enemies, feared an American-wrought nuclear World War III. The issue took on special importance during the war in Korea, in which the British, for example, were concerned about the eruption of a "general atomic war" if the United States decided to use nuclear force in Korea (Betts, *Nuclear Blackmail*, 34). Amid the advent of Eisenhower's "New Look," which placed a premium on nuclear deterrence, Eisenhower's National Security Council worried regularly about alarming allies, leaving them feeling that the United States was as much a threat to world order as a protector of it (see Gaddis, *Strategies of Containment*, 125–61).
8. Rancière, *Politics of Aesthetics*, 12.
9. Adm. William D. Leahy, who in his 1950 memoir would describe the United States' actions in Hiroshima and Nagasaki as commensurate with the "ethical standard common to the barbarians of the Dark Ages" (Leahy, *I Was There*, 441), expressed his reservations about ever dropping an atomic bomb again before the congressional Joint Committee on Atomic Energy and the Joints Chiefs of Staff on July 19, 1947. See Joint Committee on Atomic Energy, "Scale and Scope of Atomic Production."
10. Baldwin, "Atomic Weapon," 10.
11. Indeed, Oppenheimer's opposition to the "Super" was not strictly moral. His General Advisory Committee recommended the pursuit of smaller rather than larger nuclear weapons, shifting strategy away from what would become deterrence to a more traditional tactical approach. As for the technical difficulties of a fusion weapon, though the fusion process was well understood (Hans Bethe explained the fusion process as early as 1938—before the fission process was adequately understood), how to create it in a controlled manner was not. Edward Teller aggressively pursued fusion's experimental realization both during and after the war. He believed that the best way to create a fusion reaction was to create the exceptionally high temperatures it required through a fission reaction. This technical solution, however, would divert plutonium production away from fission bombs to an as yet unrealized fusion bomb—creating yet another set of problems for Teller and others pushing for the thermonuclear bomb. Then there were further problems having to do with the liquefaction of deuterium and tritium and, once liquefied, containing the liquid long enough to create a self-sustaining reaction. These problems were eventually resolved as a new means of assembly was devised (the "Teller-Ulam" design) and a solid, lighter-weight deuterium-tritium source was discovered in lithium deuteride (O'Keefe, *Nuclear Hostages*, 142–44, 151, 159, 162).
12. Alsop, "Matter of Fact."
13. Barrett to Webb, "Subject: Project for PSB."
14. Alperovitz, *Decision to Use the Atomic Bomb*, 164–66.
15. "Public Information Policy on Biological Warfare, Radiological Warfare, and Chemical Warfare" and "Excerpts from Report of the Secretary of Defense's Ad Hoc Committee on Chemical, Biological, and Radiological Warfare, 30 June 1950"; Fritchley, "Report of the Office of Public Information."
16. NSC 126; "Memorandum on Public Statements with Respect to Certain American Weapons." For background material on NSC 126, including Truman's December 5, 1950, directive "Public Discussion of Foreign and Military Policy" quoted previously, see White House Office, National Security Council Staff: Papers, 1948–61, Disaster File, box 6, Eisenhower Presidential Library, Abilene, Kansas. For more discussion of these memos, see O'Gorman, *Spirits of the Cold War*, 187–89.
17. For the best account of this streamlining process, see Parry-Giles, *Rhetorical Presidency*.
18. Panel of Consultants on Disarmament, "Draft Summary of the Line of Argument," 1038.
19. Ibid., 1039.
20. Ibid., 1038.
21. Ibid., 1040.
22. Ibid., 1041.
23. Chernus, *Eisenhower's Atoms for Peace*, 25.
24. Peterson, "Panic: The Ultimate Weapon," 100.
25. Ibid., 107.
26. Ibid., 106.
27. Oakes, *Imaginary War*.
28. Medhurst, "Eisenhower's 'Atoms for Peace' Speech"; Chernus, *Eisenhower's Atoms for Peace*.
29. Parry-Giles, *Rhetorical Presidency*, 131.

30. Ibid., 134.
31. Lay, "Official Statements Regarding Nuclear Weapons."
32. Stassen, "Comment on Thermonuclear and Atomic Weapons."
33. Osgood, *Total Cold War*, 156.
34. Burke, *Rhetoric of Motives*, 49–58.
35. Possony, *An Outline of American Atomic Strategy in the Non-Military Fields*.
36. Snapp, *Staff Study, Public Information Plan, Operation Ivy*.
37. Wills, *Bomb Power*.
38. Hogan, *Cross of Iron*, 70.
39. Scott, *Seeing Like a State*.
40. Snapp et al., "Letter to J. Edgar Hoover—Operation Ivy"; Snapp et al., *Security and Public Reporting Aspects of 1952 Pacific Tests*.
41. Snapp and Clarkson, "Information Plan for Operation Ivy," 3, 4.
42. Burriss, "Administrative Plan No. 1, Operation Ivy," A-3.
43. Burriss, *Operation Ivy, Report of Commander*, 37.
44. "First-hand" is how General Clarkson explained the impact of pictures of the nuclear tests in his letter to Gordon Dean in November 1952. See Clarkson to Dean, "Subject: Completion of Operation Ivy."
45. Azoulay, *Civil Imagination*, 23–24.
46. Henry, "Technological Priesthood."
47. Gaylord, *Operation Ivy, Report to the Scientific Director, Documentary Photography*, 65.
48. *History of 1352, July through Dec. 1952*, 3.
49. The reference to "deadpan" was made by Edward Barrett in a memo to James Webb at the Department of State concerning the Psychological Strategy Board's efforts in the wake of the Ad Hoc Committee report. Indeed, civil defense films during the early 1950s would lean heavily on a matter-of-fact "documentary" style (see Barrett to Webb, "Subject: Project for PSB"). An October 9, 1951, memo from the Department of Defense's Office of Public Information identified the civil defense "documentary" *Survival under Atomic Attack* as exemplary of its efforts. The film, made by United World Films' Castle Films, begins with its narrator, Edward R. Murrow, declaring, "Let us face without panic the reality of our times, the fact that atom bombs may someday be dropped on our cities, and let us prepare for survival by understanding the weapons that threaten us." *Survival under Atomic Attack* insists, "production must go on" in the factories of major cities even in the case of atomic attack and adds, "Our offices and homes will also be posts of duty not to be abandoned." See *Survival under Atomic Attack* (film).
50. *History of 1352, July through Dec. 1952*, 3.
51. For more on *Racket Squad*, see the episode entitled "The Salted Mine" at the Internet Archive, https://archive.org/details/RacketSquadTheSaltedMine1951. Television, of course, was exploding in the 1950s. In 1945 there were sixty-five hundred television sets; by 1950 there were more than eleven million (see Cumings, *Dominion*, 338).
52. Terrace, *Television Introductions*, 114 (emphasis added).
53. For more on the rhetoric of adventurism in the early US Cold War, see O'Gorman, *Spirits of the Cold War*, chap. 3.
54. On the rhetorical significance of nuclear technicians, see O'Gorman and Hamilton, "At the Interface."
55. *History of 1352, Jan. through June 1953*, 31–32; *History of 1352, Jan. through June 1954*, 8.
56. *History of 1352, Jan. through June 1953*, 32.
57. Clarkson, "Subject: Completion of Operation Ivy."
58. Howard to Jackson, "Subject: National Information Policy."
59. Dean to Eisenhower, June 17, 1953; "History of 1352, Jan. through June 1954," 8.
60. Herken, *Brotherhood of the Bomb*, 265–80; Monk, *Robert Oppenheimer*, 558–62.
61. Bird and Sherwin, *American Prometheus*, 417, 429–30, 435–36, 470–72. Lewis Strauss, in some respects, made his reputation in atomic energy by defending secrecy. See Strauss, "Some A-Bomb Fallacies Are Exposed," *Life*, June 24, 1950, 80–90. Strauss's commitment to secrecy was the subject of fierce public debate and a significant part of his eventual downfall. See John J. Steele, "Passions and Stratagems in the Fall," *Life*, June 29, 1959, 28–29.
62. Black, "Secrecy and Disclosure as Rhetorical Forms."
63. Dean to Eisenhower, "Atomic Energy Commission and Operation Ivy Film Review."
64. Strauss to Peterson, September 29, 1953. A "Q" clearance granted access to Top Secret Restricted Data. The viewing of a document rated as Secret Restricted Data should require the lesser "L" clearance.
65. Howard to Jackson, "Subject: National Information Policy."
66. Ibid.
67. *History of 1352, Jan. through June 1954*, 9.
68. Minutes from the 185th Meeting of the NSC, February 17, 1954.
69. Snapp, Peterson, and Strauss, "Subject: Film on Operation Ivy."
70. Ibid.
71. For evidence that Eisenhower himself pushed the lower classification versions of *Operation Ivy*, see Dean to Eisenhower, "Atomic Energy Commission and *Operation Ivy* Film Review."
72. *Report on the White House Conference of Mayors*, 1.
73. Ibid., 2.
74. Ibid., 53.
75. "Mayors Row over Federal Defense Role," *Baltimore Sun*, December 15, 1953, 2.
76. "H-Bomb Movie Shown to Them, 2 Mayors Claim," *Daily Boston Globe*, December 19, 1953, 3.
77. "Minutes," Operations Coordinating Board, January 27, 1954.
78. "Minutes," Operations Coordinating Board, March 20, 1954.
79. *History of 1352, Jan. through June 1954*, 8–9.
80. Richard L. Miller, *Under the Cloud*, 188–94.
81. "Excerpts from President Eisenhower's Press Conference," March 31, 1954, in Cantelon, Hewlett, and Williams, *American Atom*, 128.
82. Gould, "Government Film of H-Bomb Test Suffers from Theatrical Tricks," 35.
83. Black, "Secrecy and Disclosure as Rhetorical Forms," 147.

Chapter Five: Routine Reports

1. *Military Participation on Buster-Jangle* [film].
2. Masco, *Theater of Operations*, 46.
3. Fehner and Gosling, *Origins of the Nevada Test Site*, 4.
4. Solnit, *Savage Dreams*, 162.
5. *History of 1352, Jan. through June 1960*, 3; Air Photographic and Charting Service, *Historical Summary*, 5.
6. Solnit, *Savage Dreams*, 162.
7. Vanderbilt, *Survival City*, 27.
8. Paglen, *Blank Spots on the Map*, 51.
9. Solnit, *Savage Dreams*, 5–6.
10. We are relying in this chapter primarily on Bordwell, "Classical Hollywood Cinema: Narrational Principles and Procedures." However, Bordwell's best-known work on classical Hollywood cinema is cowritten with Janet Staiger and Kristin Thompson: *The Classical Hollywood Cinema*. Our concern here is less with showing that Lookout Mountain films "fit" the structure and style of classical Hollywood cinema than with showing how they drew on Hollywood conventions of the time to narrate America's nuclear test operations.
11. Susan Courtney's work has placed the treatment of the "screen West" by Lookout Mountain and Civil Defense films in the context of both the rhetorics of Hollywood cinema and the specific racialized aesthetics of the West as a space of white privilege. See Courtney, *Split Screen Nation*.
12. Fehner and Gosling, *Origins of the Nevada Test Site*, 36–46.
13. Ibid., 47.
14. Maag et al., *Operation Ranger*, 38, 41.
15. Quoted in Fehner and Gosling, "Origins of the Nevada Test Site," 36–46, 50.
16. Ponton et al., *Shots ABLE to EASY*, 59.
17. Ibid., 85.
18. *History of 1352, April through June 1952*; Ponton et al., *Operation Tumbler-Snapper*, 50, 103, 174.
19. Air Photographic and Charting Service, *Historical Summary*, 67. Lookout Mountain's workload at the Nevada Test Site would grow to such proportions that they eventually built a film-processing laboratory at Camp Mercury itself (*History of 1352, Jan. through June 1955*, 9–10).
20. Air Photographic and Charting Service, *Historical Summary*, 73.
21. Sherman, "Atomic Security Policy Seems Centered Around Little Faith in the Press," *Los Angeles Times*, November 12, 1951, A5.
22. Atomic Energy Commission, "Admission of Limited, Selected Group of Uncleared Observers to One Shot Spring 1952 Test Series in Nevada."
23. Ibid. See also Bryan-Wilson, "Posing by the Cloud."
24. Lookout Mountain's role in this test is discussed in Ponton et al., "Shots SUGAR and UNCLE," 92; Gilbert and Wilson, "Operation Buster," 16; Armed Forces Special Weapons Project, "Draft of Final Report for Operation Jangle," 112. The Los Alamos role in documentary photography is discussed in Ponton et al., "Operation Buster-Jangle," 37.
25. On "bureaucratic style," see Hariman, *Political Style*.
26. *History of 1352, Jan. through June 1954*, 22–23.
27. *History of 1352, Jan. through June 1953*, 44.
28. *History of 1352, July through Dec. 1953*, 27; *History of 1352, Jan. through June 1954*, 23.
29. History of 1352, Jan. through June 1954, 23.
30. Ibid.
31. Courtney, *Split Screen Nation*, 217.
32. Ibid., 219.
33. History of 1352, July through Dec. 1955, 40.
34. See, for example, *Operation Plumbbob: Weapons Development Report* [film].

Chapter Six: The Vectors of America

1. *History of 1352, July through Dec. 1953*, 18.
2. Sheehan, *A Fiery Peace in a Cold War*, 199.
3. In 1953, when Lookout Mountain shot its first missile film, the Air Force was just starting to get its act together with regard to a missile program. Under the leadership of Bernard Schriever, the Air Force commissioned Culver City's Ramo-Wooldridge Corporation to begin an intercontinental ballistic missile development program. See ibid., 209. The story of pilots competing with unmanned aerial vehicles is still, of course, a live one in the age of drones. An important intermediate chapter of this story took place in and around the Apollo program. For more on this, see Mindell, *Digital Apollo*.
4. *History of 1352, Jan. through June 1956*, 16.
5. *History of 1352, July through Dec. 1956*, 19.
6. Ibid. The film did, however, earn recognition at festivals and exhibitions in Venice, Edinburgh, and Berlin. (See *Chronology of the Air Photographic and Charting Service*, 33.
7. Sheehan, *A Fiery Peace*, 341.
8. Ibid., 342.
9. Lookout Mountain's sometimes spotty reports are not clear on this point, but it was common for them to make short promotional films for defense contractors in addition to their Air Force commissioned films. We know that Lookout Mountain did the film work for Thor 101 and have every reason to conclude that in producing film reports on the event they did one for Douglas Aircraft.
10. *History of 1352, Jan. through June 1957*, 30–33.
11. O'Gorman and Hamilton, "EG&G and the Deep Media of Timing, Firing, and Exposing."
12. *History of 1352, July through Dec. 1955*, 49.
13. Ibid., 2.
14. Sheehan, *A Fiery Peace in a Cold War*, 386.
15. Page, *Vandenberg Air Force Base*, 10.
16. For more on McGovern, see Mitchell, *Atomic Cover-up*.
17. *History of 1352, July through Dec. 1958*, 35.
18. Ibid., "Foreward [sic]."
19. The claim for unprecedented scale and ninety thousand persons is found in Lookout Mountain's film *Ballistic Missile Development: 1 January 1959*.
20. *History of 1352, July through Dec. 1958*, 41.
21. Ibid.

22. This information came from Kevin Hamilton's interview with two former 1369th "trackers," Terry Fail and Andy Trimm.
23. *History of 1352, Jan. through June 1959*, 22.
24. Ibid., 28–29.
25. Ibid., 26.
26. Ibid.
27. *History of 1352, July through Dec. 1959*, 3.
28. *History of 1352, Jan. through June 1960*, 23.
29. *History of 1352, July through Dec. 1960*, 27.
30. *History of 1352, Jan. through June 1961*, 44.
31. *History of 1352, July through Dec. 1962,* 55. The mission of the 1369th did not fundamentally change from the days of Operating Location 1 in 1958; it just expanded to entail motion-picture and still photographic work for "documentary, engineering sequential, surveillance, and tracking photography of operational training and R&D launches, flight readiness firings, fueling operations, missile weapon system checkout tests; documentary photography of missile site construction, ground and aerial, and systems equipment installation in Western United States for data analysis, human engineering studies, public information programs, training films, briefing films and briefing slide presentations and technical manual photography" (ibid., 51).
32. *History of 1352, Jan. through June 1962*, 26; *History of 1352, July through Dec. 1962*, 52.
33. *History of 1352, Jan. through June 1962*, 24–25; *History of 1352, July through Dec. 1962*, 51–52.
34. In 1962, also, several key 1369th personnel were sent to help cover the Operation Dominic nuclear tests in the Pacific. Given that they were pros at sky shots from the ground, they proved crucial to Lookout Mountain's work at Dominic. See *History of 1352, July through Dec. 1962*, 53.
35. *History of 1352, Jan. through June 1967*, 76–80; *History of 1352, July through Dec. 1968*, 15.
36. For the activities of Lookout Mountain's detachments, see *History of 1352, Jan. through June 1964*, 48–88; *History of 1352, July through Dec. 1964*, 72–137.
37. Air Photographic and Charting Service, *Historical Summary*, 21.
38. Ibid, 22.
39. *History of 1352, Jan. through June 1963*, 54–58, *History of 1352, July through Dec. 1965*, 94–103.
40. See Lookout Mountain Laboratory, *Ballistic Missile Development* (film).
41. *History of 1352, Jan. through June 1962*, 35–36.
42. *History of 1352, July through Dec. 1964*, 37–38.
43. *History of 1352, July through Dec. 1966*, 70.

Chapter Seven: Engineering Geographies

1. Barney, *Mapping the Cold War*, 27.
2. Ristow, "Air Age Geography," 333.
3. Ibid.
4. Cunningham, *Imagining Air Force Identity Masculinity*; Virilio, *Speed and Politics*.
5. Eisenhower and Treuenfels, *Eisenhower Speaks*, 278.
6. Quoted in Snead, *Gaither Committee, Eisenhower, and the Cold War*, 33.
7. Quoted in Hogan, *Cross of Iron*, 396.
8. Farish, "Frontier Engineering," 178.
9. Loomis, *Problems of Air Defense: Final Report of Project Charles*, xxiii–xxiv.
10. Drew, *NSC-68: Forging the Strategy of Containment*, 51.
11. Lackenbauer, *Canadian Arctic Sovereignty and Security*, 2; Jockel, *No Boundaries Upstairs*, 60–64.
12. Hediger and Vonderau, *Films That Work*, 40.
13. Barnes and Farish, "Between Regions," 808.
14. Grant, *Polar Imperative*, 14–17.
15. Mindell, *Between Human and Machine*, 231–59.
16. Schaffel, *Emerging Shield*, 207.
17. Twitchell, "Incomplete Shield."
18. Freedman, *Deterrence*.
19. Scarry, *Thermonuclear Monarchy*; Wills, *Bomb Power*.
20. Farish, "Frontier Engineering," 187.
21. Ibid., 188.
22. Kikkert, "Pragmatism and Cooperation."
23. Here it bears recalling that, as related in chapter 2, Lookout Mountain and indeed all Air Force photographic units were based within the Air Photographic and Charting Service (or APCS), an organization otherwise devoted at the time to racing the Soviet Union to produce the most accurate map of the globe for navigation in the new air age. Photography and vision played a key role in this work. Postwar aerial mapping techniques drew on radar and aerial photography to mathematically model the planet, culminating in 1960 in a standard coordinate system known as the World Geodetic System. (See Martin-Nielsen, *Eismitte in the Scientific Imagination*, 100–105). With the advent of the DEW Line, APCS, already familiar with the region and the work necessary to surviving the cold climates, assumed the role of chronicler of construction; APCS film units also created training and orientation films for DEW Line workers. In both cases, the DEW Line and BMEWS films of the APCS foregrounded the engineering feats of the projects while minimizing problems of sovereignty.
24. Barney, *Mapping the Cold War*; Farish, "Frontier Engineering," 187.
25. Like several of other films discussed in this book, attributing the photography in *Aleutian Skywatch* to Lookout Mountain is a matter of inference. Based on internal Air Force reports, we know that Detachment 1 at Elmendorf Air Force Base, which was established in 1961, was involved in DEW Line documentation; and that even before this Lookout Mountain crews were sent north to document DEW Line work. We know, moreover, that *Aleutian Skywatch* uses ample footage from the sites Lookout Mountain documented (see "History of 1352, Jan. through June 1960"). We do not, however, have direct documentation showing that the footage in *Aleutian Skywatch* is Lookout Mountain footage. As with the majority of Lookout Mountain's work, no precise records were preserved about every assignment they covered, at least not on the public side of security clearances. Therefore, we have inferred that the footage in *Aleutian Skywatch* is Lookout Mountain footage.

26. Edwards, *The Closed World*.
27. The visual architectural impact of DEW Line stations comes from a good pedigree; the domes bear the design of Buckminster Fuller; and Robert Leon Ratté, the project architect for the reconfigurable boxes that served as a base, would later work extensively with modernist Paul Rudolph, an architect known for modularity, industrial technologies, and functionalism. See "Robert Leon Ratté: Obituary."
28. Twitchell, "Incomplete Shield."
29. Farish, "Frontier Engineering," 188.
30. Edwards, *Closed World*; O'Gorman and Hamilton, "At the Interface."
31. The 1365th reports do not indicate that the film was approved for public release upon production; the narrative of the film itself strongly suggests a Congressional audience needing to be reassured of both the necessity and the functionality of the DEW Line and BMEWS systems. By the time of the 1978 "A Reference List of Audiovisual Materials Produced by the United States Government" [a NARA publication], *Eyes of the North* had been approved for public release. See National Audiovisual Center, "A Reference List of Audiovisual Materials."
32. Der Derian, "The (S)pace of International Relations." See also Virilio and Lotringer, *Pure War*.
33. Lackenbauer and Shackleton, "Inuit-Air Force Relations," 73–88.
34. The classic work on the Puritan "errand" is Perry Miller, *Errand into the Wilderness*.
35. *History of 1352, July through Dec. 1963*, 10.
36. Howe, a Yanktonai Dakota, was an internationally exhibited artist with a long career founded on both traditional and modern techniques and styles. See South Dakota State University, "Oscar Howe Biography."
37. See Lincoln Laboratory, "Early-Warning Radars."
38. O'Gorman, *Iconoclastic Imagination*, 3, 60–61, 108–10.

Chapter Eight: The Vietnamization of the Cold War Camera

1. Gaddis, *Strategies of Containment*, 201, 239.
2. Quoted in ibid., 20.
3. Masco, *Theater of Operations*, 22; Habermas, *Legitimation Crisis*, 70.
4. Jameson, *Postmodernism*, 355; Zelizer, *Covering the Body*.
5. Sheehan, *Bright Shining Lie*.
6. Quoted in Gaddis, *Strategies of Containment*, 213.
7. Foster, "Preface," in *Visuality and Vision*, ix.
8. Mirzoeff, *Right to Look*, 3.
9. Foster, "Preface," in *Visuality and Vision*, ix.
10. Metz, *Imaginary Signifier*, 49–50.
11. Peters, "Information," 14.
12. Ibid.
13. Foucault, *Discipline and Punish*.
14. Masco, *Theater of Operations*; Oakes, *Imaginary War*; Vanderbilt, *Survival City*.
15. Masco, *Theater of Operations*, 47.
16. "Outline of History, Lookout Mountain Laboratory," 1.
17. Freedman, *Strategy*, 618–29.
18. Gaddis, *Strategies of Containment*, 125–61.
19. Tadelis, *Game Theory*, 163–64.
20. Gaddis, *Strategies of Containment*, 224–26; Freedman, *Kennedy's Wars*, 13–26.
21. Gaddis, *Strategies of Containment*, 235.
22. Ibid., 236.
23. Ibid., 200–201.
24. Office of the Secretary of Defense, "IV.C.3. Evolution of the War," i.
25. Office of the Secretary of Defense, "IV.C.7[a], Volume I. Evolution of the War," 15.
26. Van Staaveren, *Gradual Failure*, 43.
27. *History of the Aerospace Audio-Visual Service*, January 1, 1967–June 30, 1968, 98–99.
28. Ibid.
29. *History of 1352, July through Dec. 1962*, 63.
30. Appel, "Bombing Accuracy in a Combat Environment."
31. *History of 1352, Jan. through June 1964*, 84.
32. Ibid.
33. *History of 1352, July through Dec. 1964*, 117; *History of 1352, Jan. through June 1965*, 8–9.
34. *History of 1352, Jan. through June 1965*, 11.
35. Ibid.
36. *History of 1352, July through Dec. 1965*, 3.
37. *History of 1352, Jan. through June 1965*, 153.
38. *History of 1352, July through Dec. 1965*, 249.
39. Ibid., 10.
40. *History of 1352, Jan. through June 1965*, 18.
41. Ibid., Appendix 4.
42. *History of 1352, July through Dec. 1965*, Col. Frank R. Amend to MATS and CINCPACAF, attached letter, September 16, 1965.
43. *History of the 600th, July through Dec. 1966*, 1–2.
44. Ibid., 7.
45. Ibid., 5.
46. Ibid., ii.
47. Ibid., 4, 6.
48. Warndorf, "Oral History Interview," 18.
49. *History of the 600th, July to Dec. 1966*, 21.
50. Warndorf, "Oral History Interview," 13.
51. *History of the 600th, July through Dec. 1966*, 21.
52. Warndorf, "Oral History Interview," 14.
53. Anderson, USAF Oral History Interview, 19–20, 23; Johnson, phone interview with Kevin Hamilton, August 9, 2014.
54. *History of the 600th, July through Dec. 1966*, 17.
55. Warndorf, "Oral History Interview," 11.
56. Ibid., 34.
57. Appel, "Bombing Accuracy in a Combat Environment."
58. See Graff, *Tuesday Cabinet*.

Chapter Nine: Mushroom Cloud Cameras

1. Rosenthal, "Nuclear Mushroom Cloud as Cultural Image," 71.
2. Azoulay, *Civil Imagination*, 23–24.

3. Hariman and Lucaites, "Iconic Image of the Mushroom Cloud and the Cold War Nuclear Optic," 142.
4. Jameson, *Political Unconscious*, 9.
5. Other proposed names, early on, were "geyser," "dome-shaped column," "great funnel," "cauliflower," and "parasol" (Weart, *Nuclear Fear*, 402). Both Weart (402–4) and Rosenthal ("The Nuclear Mushroom Cloud as Cultural Image," 86–88) have speculated as to why "mushroom cloud" stuck over the others.
6. See Boyer, *By the Bomb's Early Light*, 82, 87.
7. Rosenthal, "Nuclear Mushroom Cloud as Cultural Image," 86.
8. For the "calming" effect of the Crossroads imagery, see Boyer, *By the Bomb's Early Light*, 84.
9. Ibid., 84.
10. Ibid., 90.
11. *Operation Teapot: Military Effects Studies* (film).
12. See ibid. for discussion of the problem and its resolution.
13. Ibid.
14. Anonymous, "Terror—And the Terror Weapon."
15. In the middle of the 1950s, Eisenhower commissioned a panel to study, with all the acuity of laboratory science, the "human effects" of nuclear weapons. The study committee recommended a set of actions focused on the "involvement" and "knowledge" of the American people. Still, they claimed inadequate knowledge, writing as if the solution were bigger, better research programs: "We are acutely aware, however, that there are vast uncharted areas in these regions, and recognize that there is a substantial deficit in available information and in the needed basic social and psychological research. It is our hope that in the years ahead there may be found fruitful ways for private institutions and government to cooperate in the support of an accelerated program of both basic and applied social science research, which have not yet been sufficiently focused on these problems" ("Report to the President and the National Security Council by the Panel on the Human Effects of Nuclear Weapons Development," November 21, 1956).
16. Quoted in Saunders, *Cultural Cold War*, 1.
17. Quoted in O'Gorman, *Spirits of the Cold War*, 155.
18. Masco, "Nuclear Technoaesthetics," 354. See also Davis, *Stages of Emergency*.
19. The concern with microseconds in the nuclear testing regime was rooted in the phenomenon of the nuclear detonation itself. As Masco writes, "Nuclear explosions happen in billionths of a second, requiring weapons scientists to develop their own languages for dividing microseconds into understandable units. Since World War II, Los Alamos weapons scientists have examined nuclear explosions in units called 'shakes,' shorthand for 'faster than the shake of a lamb's tail': one shake equals 1/100,000,000th of a second, which is the time it takes one uranium atom to fission. A hydrogen bomb explosion, the most devastating military force on the planet, occurs in about one hundred shakes, or a millionth of a second. The internal complexity of a nuclear explosion can consequently be approached as a potentially endless universe of processes, interactions, pressures, and flows all happening in a split second. Put differently, if one were to add up the 2,053 nuclear detonations conducted in human history—a force thousands of times the total destructive power unleashed during World War II—collectively, these explosions would still not constitute a single second of time" (ibid., 356).
20. For the connection between nuclear photography and Hollywood special effects, see Kuran, *Atomic Filmmakers* (film). Kuran himself is a prominent Hollywood special effects artist, and he has devoted part of his career to arguing for the central place of Lookout Mountain Laboratory and EG&G in the advent of modern cinematic special effects.
21. As discussed briefly in chapter 6, the "E" in EG&G stood for Harold Edgerton, the MIT engineer responsible for a range of high-speed camera and "stroboscopic" techniques, and the "Gs" for Kenneth Germeshausen and Herbert Grier, Edgerton's graduate students and eventual business partners. In the 1930s Edgerton developed strobe-light techniques of high-speed photography, originally to enhance technical photography of rotating motors. In 1938 his work on the first electronic flash gained mass attention when a collaboration with MIT alum Gjon Mili, photographing tennis player Bobby Riggs in midserve, reached the pages of *Life* magazine. Edgerton would go on to publish, with James Killian, a popular book of his "stop-motion" images; he was later recognized for an Oscar-winning film in 1940. See O'Gorman and Hamilton, "EG&G and the Deep Media of Timing, Firing, and Exposing."
22. Rosenthal, "Nuclear Mushroom Cloud as Cultural Image," 79.
23. See Bryan-Wilson, "Posing by the Cloud"; *Atomic Filmmakers* (film) ; *Icarus* (film) ; and Stenovec, "George Yoshitake."
24. The July–Dec. 1964 Lookout Mountain report mentions outfitting some Type IV camera pods for Cinerama cameras, but it is unclear what film footage this produced. *History of 1352, July through Dec. 1964*, 38.
25. *History of 1352, July through Dec. 1959*, 6–7; "History of 1352, Jan. through June 1960," 7–8.
26. Belton, "Glorious Technicolor," 360.
27. Ibid., 360.
28. *History of 1352, Jan. through June 1953*, 27–28. As if to coordinate their use of CinemaScope with Twentieth Century Fox, Lookout Mountain, again working with Fox, installed a CinemaScope screen in their Wonderland Avenue facility in October 1953. Then on December 4—the same day Fox released the first commercial film using CinemaScope, the biblical epic *The Robe*—Lookout Mountain tested their new screen, no doubt featuring the "Grable" shot. See *History of 1352, July through Dec. 1953*, 33.
29. It is questionable whether this film was ever completed. No record of it exists in Lookout Mountain reports, but Peter Kuran discovered and reconstructed the film's aural and visual components, including titles, from the archives at the Defense Threat Reduction Agency's holdings. See *Atomic Filmmakers* (film).
30. *History of 1352, Jan. through June 1954*, 4.

31. See Hariman and Lucaites, "Iconic Image of the Mushroom Cloud and the Cold War Nuclear Optic"; Rosenthal, "Nuclear Mushroom Cloud as Cultural Image."
32. Edwards, *Closed World*, 19, 28.
33. Ponton et al., "Shot Apple 2," 52. Most journalists and television crews were stationed on "News Nob," some fourteen kilometers from ground zero, while a small cadre of reporters, including a television crew, was allowed to station themselves in a trench some three kilometers from ground zero [see Defense Threat Reduction Agency, "Fact Sheet: Operation Teapot," 5]. On white, middle-class suburbanites as the focus group, so to speak, of Operation Cue, see Masco, *Theater of Operations*.
34. *History of 1352, Jan. through June 1955*, 4.
35. Ponton et al., "Shot Apple 2," 10, 14.
36. Ibid., 52.
37. Edgerton, Germeshausen, and Grier, "Operation Teapot, Project 9.1," 14–15.
38. Masco, *Theater of Operations*, 58.
39. Edgerton, Germeshausen, and Grier, "Operation Teapot—Project 39.4C," 7.
40. Defense Nuclear Agency, *Operation Teapot—Report of the Test Manager*, 91.
41. Elliott, "Subject: Continental Test Information Plans"; Nichols to Atomic Energy Commission, "Subject: Release of Nevada Test Site Documentary Motion Picture"; Harbour, "Final Report: United States Air Force Information Program during Operation Teapot."
42. *History of 1352, Jan. through June 1955*, 4.
43. Ibid.
44. Hariman and Lucaites, "Iconic Image of the Mushroom Cloud and the Cold War Nuclear Optic," 142.

Chapter Ten: Closure

1. *History of 1352, Jan. through June 1967*, 31.
2. *History of 1352, Jan. through June 1968*, 26.
3. See US Congress, *Federal Audiovisual Materials Policy and Programs*; Pearson, "Combat Camera Heritage Series: James Elmer, Col, USAF Retired."
4. *History of 1352, Jan. through June 1968*, 36–37.
5. Warndorf, "Oral History Interview."
6. *History of 1352, Jan. through June 1969*, ix.
7. See Aerospace Audio-Visual Service, *History of the Aerospace Audio-Visual Service, Jan. 1967 to June 1968*, 97.
8. Ibid., 99.
9. Air Photographic and Charting Service, *Historical Summary*, 299.
10. *History of the Aerospace Audio-Visual Service, Jan. 1967 to June 1968*, 100–101.
11. *History of 1352, Jan. through June 1965*, 96.
12. *History of the Aerospace Audio-Visual Service, Jan. 1967 to June 1968*, 100–101.
13. Ibid., 105–6.
14. Ibid., 1.
15. *History of the Aerospace Audio-Visual Service, Jan. 1967 to June 1968*, i.
16. Ibid., ii.
17. See *History of the 600*th Photographic Squadron, Jan. through June 1966, 22–23.
18. *History of the Aerospace Audio-Visual Service, Jan. 1967 to June 1968*.
19. For more on the prominence of the photographers' own bodies in earlier depictions of nuclear tests, see Bryan-Wilson "Posing by the Cloud."
20. Warndorf, "Oral History Interview," 28–33.
21. Anderson, "United States Air Force Oral History Interview," 25.
22. Virilio, *Logics of Perception*.
23. *History of Aerospace Audiovisual Service, Jan. through Dec. 1980*, vol. 1, 1; Department of the Air Force, "Organization and Mission," 4.
24. Morrisroe, "Largest Filmmaking Machine in the World."
25. McGovern, "United States Air Force Oral History Program Interview," 161–62.
26. Brown, *"Managing" the Defense Department—Why It Can't Be Done*.
27. "Department of Defense Key Officials, 1947–2014," 16.
28. This information is based on Carol Brown's "History of Visual Information Records" and also the Administrative History Note in the Organization Authority Record, Defense Visual Information Center, National Archives, https://catalog.archives.gov/id/10488372.
29. Department of Defense, "Instruction: 5040.02," 38.
30. Ibid., 2.
31. "Information Operations," as defined in Department of Defense, "Directive: 3600.01," 12.
32. Department of Defense, "Instruction: 5040.02," 18.
33. Ibid.
34. Department of Defense, "Instruction: 5040.02," encl. 6, 23–25.

Epilogue and Acknowledgments

1. Toronto Photography Seminar, Cold War Camera Conference, February 20–23, 2014, Guatemala City, Guatemala, http://www.torontophotographyseminar.org/news/cold-war-camera-conference-guatemala.
2. We were joined in Guatemala by a truly outstanding group of scholars and critics, who each helped further our work through feedback and conversation: Marcos Armstrong, Ariella Azoulay, Sarah Bassnett, Elspeth Brown, John Curley, Mitchell Denburg, Heather Diack, Erina Duganne, Molly Geidel, Johanna Lozoya, Nicholas Mirzoeff, Darren Newbury, Pippa Oldfield, Eva Pluhařová-Grigienė, Jason Pribilsky, Eric Sandeen, Ileana Selejan, Joseph Slaughter, Dot Tuer, Laura Wexler, and Andrés Mario Zervigón.
3. For a scholarly study of the Archivo Histórico de la Policía Nacional, see Weld, *Paper Cadavers*.
4. Arendt, *The Human Condition*, 50.
5. Azoulay, "Actions, Non-actions, Interaction," 28.
6. Kaplan, "Trump's Nuclear Meltdown."
7. Cross, *People's Right to Know*, xiii. Thank you to Paul McKean for teaching us about Cross.

LOCATION
CONTROL

SOURCES

Films and Television Programs

The Air Force Missile Mission. 1352nd Motion Picture Squadron, Air Photographic and Charting Service, United States Air Force. College Park, MD: National Archives at College Park, 1959. Record group 342, no. 342-SFP-608. Film.

Air Force Photographic Highlights. 1352nd Motion Picture Squadron, Air Photographic and Charting Service, United States Air Force. College Park, MD: National Archives at College Park, 1959. Record group 342, no. 342-SFP-651. Film.

The Airman's World [25-part series]. Air Photographic and Charting Service, United States Air Force. College Park, MD: National Archives at College Park, 1962. Record group 342, nos. 342-SFP-1121A through -1121Z. Film.

Aleutian Skywatch. New York: Audio Productions, 1961. Film.

Atlas the ICBM. 1352nd Motion Picture Squadron, Air Photographic and Charting Service, United States Air Force. College Park, MD: National Archives at College Park, 1957. Record group 342, no. 342-SFP-583. Film.

Atomic Filmmakers: Hollywood's Secret Film Studio. Directed by Peter Kuran. Santa Clarita, CA: VCE, 2001. Film.

Atomic Proving Ground: The Story of Operation Sandstone. 4201 Motion Picture Squadron, United States Air Force. Las Vegas, NV: Nuclear Testing Archive, Department of Energy, 1948. No. 0800074. Film.

Atomic Tests in Nevada: The Story of AEC's Continental Proving Ground. 1352nd Motion Picture Squadron, Air Photographic and Charting Service, United States Air Force. College Park, MD: National Archives at College Park, 1955. Record group 434, no. 434.53. Film.

Ballistic Missile Development: Program Highlights 1958. 1352nd Motion Picture Squadron, Air Photographic and Charting Service, United States Air Force. College Park, MD: National Archives at College Park, 1958. Record group 330, no. 330-DVIC-434. Film.

Ballistic Missile Development: 1 January 1959. 1352nd Motion Picture Squadron, Air Photographic and Charting Service, United States Air Force. College Park, MD: National Archives at College Park, 1959. Record group 330, no. 330-DVIC-427. Film.

The Beginning or the End. Directed by Norman Taurog. Beverly Hills, CA: Metro-Goldwyn-Mayer, 1947. Film.

The Bird Watchers: Photo Instrumentation at Vandenberg. 1352nd Photographic Group, Air Photographic and Charting Service, United States Air Force. College Park, MD: National Archives at College Park, ca. 1965. Record group 342, no. 342-SFP-1398. Film.

Blast Measurement in Operation Sandstone. 4201 Motion Picture Squadron, United States Air Force. Las Vegas, NV: Nuclear Testing Archive, Department of Energy, 1948. No. 0800007. Film.

Bombers B-52. Directed by Gordon Douglas. Burbank, CA: Warner Bros., 1957. Film.

Borax: Construction and Operation of a Boiling Water Power Reactor. 1352nd Motion Picture Squadron, Air Photographic and Charting Service, United States Air Force. College Park, MD: National Archives at College Park, 1955. Record group 434, no. 434.80. Film.

Bwana Devil. Directed by Arch Oboler. Los Angeles, CA: Arch Oboler Productions, 1952. Film.

Cinemascope Featurette: Shot Number 12. Edited by Peter Kuran. From *Atomic Filmmakers DVD*. Santa Clarita, CA: VCE, 2003. Film.

Colossus: The Forbin Project. Directed by Joseph Sargent. Universal City, CA: Universal Pictures, 1970. Film.

Crossroads. Created by Bruce Conner. 1976. Film.

Dr. Strangelove or: How I Learned to Stop Worrying and Love the Bomb. Directed by Stanley Kubrick. Culver City, CA: Columbia Pictures Corporation, 1964. Film.

Dumbo. Directed by Samuel Armstrong, Norman Ferguson, Wilfred Jackson, Jack Kinney, Bill Roberts, Ben Sharpsteen, and John Elliottee. Burbank, CA: Walt Disney Pictures, 1941. Film.

EG&G in Operation Sandstone. 4201 Motion Picture Squadron, United States Air Force. Las Vegas, NV: Nuclear Testing Archive, Department of Energy, 1948. No. 0800004. Film.

Eyes and Ears of the Arctic: The DEW System. United States Air Force, 1960. Internet Archive, https://archive.org/details/342FR1344.

Eyes of the North. United States Air Force, 1966. Film. Internet Archive, https://archive.org/details/342.26433D

Fail-Safe. Directed by Sidney Lumet. Culver City, CA: Columbia Pictures, 1964. Film.

Fantasia. Directed by James Algar, Samuel Armstrong, Ford Beebe Jr., Norman Ferguson, Jim Handley, T. Hee, Wilfred Jackson, Hamilton Luske, Bill Roberts, Paul Satterfield, and Ben Sharpsteen. Burbank, CA: Walt Disney Pictures, 1940. Film.

A Gathering of Eagles. Directed by Delbert Mann. Universal City, CA: Universal Pictures, 1963. Film.

Hell and High Water. Directed by Samuel Fuller. Los Angeles, CA: Twentieth Century Fox Film, 1954. Film.

Hell's Angels. Directed by Howard Hughes. Hollywood, CA: Caddo Company, 1930. Film.

High Noon. Directed by Fred Zinnemann. Hollywood, CA: United Artists, 1952. Film.

Hiroshima Mon Amour. Directed by Alain Resnais. Paris: Argos Films, 1959. Film.

Icarus. Written and directed by César Pesquera. Barcelona: Story, 2014. Film.

Joint Task Force Three Presents Operation Greenhouse. 1352nd Motion Picture Squadron, Air Photographic and Charting Service, United States Air Force. Nuclear Testing Archive, Department of Energy, Las Vegas, NV, 1951. No. 0800088. Film.

The Last Bomb. First Motion Picture Unit, Army Air Force. College Park, MD: National Archives at College Park, 1945. Record group 330, no. 330-DVIC-320034. Film.

Lookout Mountain Air Force Station. 1352nd Photographic Group, Air Photographic and Charting Service, United States Air Force. Albuquerque, NM: Defense Threat Re-

duction Information Analysis Center, Kirtland Air Force Base, 1963. Film.
Let's Face It!. 1352nd Motion Picture Squadron, Air Photographic and Charting Service, United States Air Force. College Park, MD: National Archives at College Park, 1954. Record group 304, no. 304.8. Film.
Measuring and Mapping the World. Air Photographic and Charting Service, United States Air Force. College Park, MD: National Archives at College Park, 1961. Record group 342, no. 342.20227DF. Film.
Military Effects Studies on Operation Castle. 1352nd Motion Picture Squadron, Air Photographic and Charting Service, United States Air Force. Las Vegas, NV: Nuclear Testing Archive, Department of Energy, 1954. Film.
Military Participation at Tumbler/Snapper. 1352nd Motion Picture Squadron, Air Photographic and Charting Service, United States Air Force. Las Vegas, NV: Nuclear Testing Archive, Department of Energy, 1952. No. 0800011. Film.
Military Participation on Buster-Jangle. 1352nd Motion Picture Squadron, Air Photographic and Charting Service, United States Air Force. Las Vegas, NV: Nuclear Testing Archive, Department of Energy, 1952. No. 0800010. Film.
Navy's Part in Operation Sandstone. 4201 Motion Picture Squadron, United States Air Force. Las Vegas, NV: Nuclear Testing Archive, Department of Energy, 1948. No. 0800008. Film.
Night Flight. Directed by Clarence Brown. Beverly Hills, CA: Metro-Goldwyn-Mayer, 1933. Film.
Operation Castle: Commander's Report. 1352nd Motion Picture Squadron, Air Photographic and Charting Service, United States Air Force. Las Vegas, NV: Nuclear Testing Archive, Department of Energy, 1954. No. 0800013. Film.
Operation Dominic: Christmas Island. 1352nd Photographic Group, Air Photographic and Charting Service, United States Air Force. Las Vegas, NV: Nuclear Testing Archive, Department of Energy, 1962. No. 0800064. Film.
Operation Dominic: Johnston Island. 1352nd Photographic Group, Air Photographic and Charting Service, United States Air Force. Las Vegas, NV: Nuclear Testing Archive, Department of Energy, 1962. No. 0800065. Film.
Operation Dominic: Nuclear Tests 1962. 1352nd Photographic Group, Air Photographic and Charting Service, United States Air Force. Las Vegas, NV: Nuclear Testing Archive, Department of Energy, 1962. No. 0800061. Film.
Operation Greenhouse. 1352nd Motion Picture Squadron, Air Photographic and Charting Service, United States Air Force. College Park, MD: National Archives at College Park, 1952. Record group 434, no. 434.246. Film.
Operation Ivy [classified secret version, sanitized]. 1352nd Motion Picture Squadron, Air Photographic and Charting Service, United States Air Force. Las Vegas, NV: Nuclear Testing Archive, Department of Energy, 1952. No. 0800061. Film.
Operation Ivy [unclassified version]. 1352nd Motion Picture Squadron, Air Photographic and Charting Service, United States Air Force. College Park, MD: National Archives at College Park, 1952. Record group 304, no. 304.1. Film.
Operation Plumbbob: Military Effects Studies. 1352nd Motion Picture Squadron, Air Photographic and Charting Service, United States Air Force. Las Vegas, NV: Nuclear Testing Archive, Department of Energy, 1957. No. 0800022. Film.
Operation Plumbbob: Weapons Development Report. 1352nd Motion Picture Squadron, Air Photographic and Charting Service, United States Air Force. Las Vegas, NV: Nuclear Testing Archive, Department of Energy, 1957. No. 0800021. Film.
Operation Sandstone. 4201 Motion Picture Squadron, United States Air Force. Las Vegas, NV: Nuclear Testing Archive, Department of Energy, 1948. No. 0800003. Film.
Operation Teapot: Military Effects Studies. 1352nd Motion Picture Squadron, Air Photographic and Charting Service, United States Air Force. Las Vegas, NV: Nuclear Testing Archive, Department of Energy, 1955. No. 0800017. Film.
Perry Mason. New York: Columbia Broadcasting System, 1957–1966. Television Series.
Polar Strike. United States Air Force, 1352nd Photographic Group, Air Photographic and Charting Service. College Park, MD: National Archives at College Park, 1965. Record group 342, no. 342-NR-35-65. Film.
Racket Squad. Culver City, CA: Hal Roach Studios and Showcase Productions, 1950–1953. Television series.
The Reins of Command. 1352nd Motion Picture Squadron, Air Photographic and Charting Service, United States Air Force. College Park, MD: National Archives at College Park, 1961. Record group 342, no. 342-SFP-1285. Film.
The Return of Jesse James. Directed by Arthur Hilton. Santa Susana, CA: Lippert Pictures, 1950. Film.
Riders of the Ridge. Directed by Lesley Selander. Los Angeles, CA: RKO Radio Pictures, 1950. Film.
The Right Stuff. Directed by Philip Kaufman. Hollywood, CA: Ladd, 1983. Film.
The Robe. Directed by Henry Koster. Los Angeles, CA: Twentieth Century Fox Film, 1953. Film.
The Searchers. Directed by John Ford. Burbank, CA: Warner Bros., 1956. Film.
She Wore a Yellow Ribbon. Directed by John Ford. Los Angeles, CA: RKO Radio Pictures, 1949. Film.
Shield of Freedom. 1352nd Photographic Group, Air Photographic and Charting Service, United States Air Force. College Park, MD: National Archives at College Park, 1963. Record group 342, no. 330-DVIC-26377. Film.
Steve Canyon. Universal City, CA: Universal Studios, 1958–1960. Television series.
Strategic Air Command. Directed by Anthony Mann. Hollywood, CA: Paramount Pictures, 1955. Film.
Survival under Atomic Attack. Produced by US Office of Civil Defense. New York: United World Films, Castle Films Division, 1951. Film. Internet Archive, https://archive.org/details/0838_Survival_Under_Atomic_Attack_E01425_11_23_59_18.
Target Nevada. 1352nd Motion Picture Squadron, Air Photographic and Charting Service, United States Air Force. College Park, MD: National Archives at College Park, 1952. Record group 434, no. 434.362. Film.
Toward the Unknown. Directed by Mervyn LeRoy. Burbank, CA: Warner Bros., 1956. Film.

USAF Participation in Southeast Asia. 1352nd Photographic Group, Air Photographic and Charting Service, United States Air Force. College Park, MD: National Archives at College Park, 1964. Record group 342, no. 342.20661DF. Film.

U.S. Air Force Participation in Operation Sandstone. 4201 Motion Picture Squadron, United States Air Force. Las Vegas, NV: Nuclear Testing Archive, Department of Energy, 1948. No. 0800005. Film.

U.S. Army Engineers on Operation Sandstone. 4201 Motion Picture Squadron, United States Air Force. Las Vegas, NV: Nuclear Testing Archive, Department of Energy, 1948. No. 0800006. Film.

Victory through Air Power. Directed by James Algar and Clyde Geronimi. Burbank, CA: Walt Disney Pictures, 1943. Film.

Wings. Directed by William A. Wellman. Hollywood, CA: Paramount Famous Lasky, 1927. Film.

Yankee Doodle Dandy. Directed by Michael Curtiz. Burbank, CA: Warner Bros., 1942. Film.

Newspaper, Magazine, and Other Popular Sources

Academy of Motion Picture Arts and Sciences. "Academy Awards Database." http://awardsdatabase.oscars.org/.

"A.E.C. Releases Eniwetok Atom Blast Pictures." *New York Herald Tribune*, August 21, 1949, 1.

Alsop, Joseph. "Matter of Fact: Concerning Wonder Weapons." *Washington Post*, September 21, 1951, 25.

"Anatomic Bomb," *Life*, September 3, 1945, 53–54.

Baldwin, Hanson W. "The Atomic Weapon: End of War against Japan Hastened but Destruction Sows Seed of Hate." *New York Times*, August 7, 1945, 10.

Ball, John W. "Nation Gains New Power in Atomic Weapons." *Washington Post*, July 25, 1948, M1, 6.

Betancourt, Mark. "World War II: The Movie." *Air and Space Magazine*, March 2012. https://www.airspacemag.com/history-of-flight/world-war-ii-the-movie-21103597.

"Bomb Tests: This Job That Must Be Done." *Life*, May 4, 1962, 44–45.

Chavez, Patricia. "DTRIAC Celebrates 50th Anniversary." *CRBNIAC Newsletter* 12, no. 3 (2011): 4–6.

"Federal Audio-Visual Programs." *Business Screen Magazine* 22, no. 1 (1961), 52.

Gould, Jack. "Government Film of H-Bomb Test Suffers from Theatrical Tricks." *New York Times*, April 2, 1954, 35.

Hartmann, Robert T. "Protests on Laboratory Bring Action." *Los Angeles Times*, June 23, 1954, 2.

"H-Bomb Movie Shown to Them, Two Mayors Claim." *Daily Boston Globe*, December 19, 1953, 3.

Kaplan, Fred. "Trump's Nuclear Meltdown." *Slate*, October 11, 2017. http://www.slate.com/articles/news_and_politics/war_stories/2017/10/now_we_know_why_rex_tillerson_called_donald_trump_a_moron.html.

"Laboratory Complaints Answered by Air Force." *Los Angeles Times*, June 22, 1954, 19.

Leahy, William D. *I Was There*. New York: McGraw-Hill, 1950.

Mackland, Ray. "Operation Camera." *New York Times*, June 23, 1946, SM27.

Markwith, Carl R. "Farewell to Bikini." *National Geographic*, July 1946, 97–116.

"Mayors Row over Federal Defense Role." *Baltimore Sun*, December 15, 1953.

Michener, James A. *Return to Paradise*. New York: Random House, 1951.

———. *Tales of the South Pacific*. New York: Random House, 1946.

"More Films Produced by AAF Than by Big Studios." *Billboard*, September 2, 1944, 44.

Morrisroe, Patricia. "The Largest Filmmaking Machine in the World." *Boston Globe*, May 10, 1980, D16.

"Morristown Seeks $ Aid for Atom Ex from Biz Groups." *Billboard* (Cincinnati, OH), March 8, 1952, 57.

O'Brien, Nolan. "Physicist Declassifies Rescued Nuclear Films." *Lawrence Livermore National Laboratory News*, March 14, 2017. https://www.llnl.gov/news/physicist-declassifies-rescued-nuclear-test-films.

"Peace Seen in Operation of Air Force Lab." *Los Angeles Times*, June 29, 1954, 11.

Percy, Walker. *The Moviegoer*. New York: Vintage, 1998.

Peterson, Val. "Panic: The Ultimate Weapon." *Collier's Weekly*, August 21, 1953, 99–110.

"Robert Leon Ratte: Obituary." *New York Times*. October 10, 2014. http://www.legacy.com/obituaries/nytimes/obituary.aspx?pid=172764405.

"Secret U.S. Project Here Protested." *Los Angeles Times*, June 19, 1954, 1–2.

Sherman, Gene. "Atomic Security Policy Seems Centered around Little Faith in the Press." *Los Angeles Times*, November 12, 1951, A5.

Steele, John L. "Passions and Stratagems in the Fall of Strauss: Personal Feud, Partisan Wrath and Secretary's Own Faults Stop His Public Career." *Life*, June 29, 1959, 28–29.

Stenovec, Timothy. "George Yoshitake, Nuclear Test Photographer, Recalls Filming Nuclear Blast 55 Years Ago." *Huffington Post*, July 20, 2012. https://www.huffingtonpost.com/2012/07/20/george-yoshitake-nuclear-test-five-5-men-nevada_n_1687233.html.

Stover, Dawn. "Peter Kuran: Bringing Hollywood to History." *Bulletin of the Atomic Scientists*, October 23, 2014. https://thebulletin.org/peter-kuran-bringing-hollywood-history7752.

Strauss, Lewis L. "Some A-Bomb Fallacies Are Exposed." *Life*, July 24, 1950, 81–90.

"Trust Isles Raise Atom Test Issue: Mashalls' [*sic*] Use Complicated by Status under U.N." *New York Times*, December 3, 1961, 20.

Williams, Tennessee. *The Glass Menagerie*. New York: Signet, 1995.

Zhang, Sara. "Movies of Cold War Bomb Tests Hold Nuclear Secrets." *Wired*, December 3, 2015. https://www.wired.com/2015/12/nuclear-films/.

Personal Collections, Oral Histories, and Civilian Reports

Anderson, Darwin C. "United States Air Force Oral History Interview: 1/Lt. Darwin C. Anderson." November 21, 1968. Air Force Historical Research Agency, Maxwell Air Force Base, Montgomery, Alabama.

Appel, Bernard. "Bombing Accuracy in a Combat Environment." *Air University Review* (July-August 1975): n.p.

Brown, Carol. "History of Visual Information Records." 1995. "Army Pictorial Center," Signal Corps Photographic Center, http://www.armypictorialcenter.com/History%20of%20Records.htm.

Fail, Tommy, and Andy Trimm. Interviewed by Kevin Hamilton. November 2, 2014. Vandenberg Air Force Base, California.

Franck, James, Donald J. Hughes, J. J. Nickson, Eugene Rabinowitch, Glenn T. Seaborg, J. C. Stearns, and Leo Szilard. "Memorandum on Political and Social Problems of the Bomb by Scientists at the Metallurgical Laboratory of the University of Chicago." June 11, 1945. In Stoff, *Manhattan Project*, 140–47. *Franck Report*, http://www.nuclearfiles.org/menu/key-issues/ethics/issues/scientific/franck-report.htm.

"Guide to Lookout Mountain Air Force Station, Los Angeles, California." n.d. Internal document. Personal collection of Dennis Johnson.

"History of the 58th Wing Air Photo Unit, Crossroads." n.d. Personnel internal document. 58th Wing Air Photo Unit. Personal collection.

Homen, Al. Interviewed by Kevin Hamilton. October 31, 2014. San Bernardino, CA.

Johnson, Dennis [Retired 2nd Lt.]. Phone interview by Kevin Hamilton. August 9, 2014.

Lincoln Laboratory, Massachusetts Institute of Technology. "Early-Warning Radars." n.d. https://www.ll.mit.edu/about/History/earlywarningradars.html.

Loomis, F. W., director. *Problems of Air Defense: Final Report of Project Charles*. Cambridge, MA: MIT, 1951.

Maclellan, Nic. *Banning Nuclear Weapons: A Pacific Islands Perspective*. January 2014. International Campaign to Abolish Nuclear Weapons, http://www.icanw.org/wp-content/uploads/2014/01/ICAN-PacificReport-FINAL-email.pdf.

McGovern, Daniel A. Interviewed by James C. Hasdorff. "United States Air Force Oral History Program Interview of Lieutenant Colonel Daniel A. McGovern, USAF [Ret]." April 1988. Air Force Historical Research Agency, Maxwell Air Force Base, Montgomery, Alabama.

National Air Council. *Peace through Air Power: A Report by the Air Power League*. New York: 1946.

Naval History and Heritage Command. "Cross Spikes Club." 1946 painting by Arthur Beaumont. https://www.history.navy.mil/our-collections/art/exhibits/conflicts-and-operations/operation-crossroads-bikini-atoll/cross-spikes-club.html.

"Outline of History, Lookout Mountain Laboratory." Ca. 1963. Internal document. Lookout Mountain Air Force Station, Hollywood, CA. Personal collection of Dennis Johnson.

Pearson, Jim. "Combat Camera Heritage Series: James Elmer, Col, USAF Retired." Video interview. https://vimeo.com/57754473.

South Dakota State University. "Oscar Howe Biography." n.d. https://www.sdstate.edu/southdakotaartmuseum/collections/Oscar-Howe/oscar-howe-bio.cfm.

Thomas, Perry M. "History." 1946. Perry M. Thomas collection. Michigan State University Archives and Historical Collections, East Lansing, MI.

Warndorf, James P. Interviewed by Griffith S. Harrison. "United States Air Force Oral History Interview: Colonel James P. Warndorf." November 13, 1968. Air Force Historical Research Agency, Maxwell Air Force Base, Montgomery, Alabama.

Welles, Orson. "Orson Welles Announces His Wife's Image on an Atomic Bombshell." YouTube video. Posted by "CONELRAD6401240," 1:41, July 14, 2010. https://www.youtube.com/watch?v=9WT2Zte5ai4.

Government Sources

Note: Much of the knowledge we have of the activities of Lookout Mountain Laboratory comes from official and once classified semiannual reports that the unit's official historians produced for the Air Force. These reports were archived at the Air Force Historical Research Agency, Maxwell Air Force Base, Montgomery, Alabama. We were able to acquire thirty-four of what were probably forty-seven total reports that Lookout Mountain produced over the course of its twenty-one-year history. They are listed in the following section. In addition, we have relied on a number of official reports produced by Lookout Mountain's command, the Air Photographic and Charting Service [later named the Aerospace Audiovisual Service] as well as some unofficial documents produced for or by Lookout Mountain employees. All such sources are listed in the section that follows, or the "Personal Collections" section above. A significant set of documents came from the Depart ment of Energy's "OpenNet" initiative [https://www.osti.gov/opennet/], begun during the Clinton administration. However, we have noted that documents have slowly been removed from the site since we began our research in 2006.

Miscellaneous Government Sources

Armed Forces Special Weapons Project. "Draft of Final Report for Operation Jangle." August 1, 1952. Department of Energy OpenNet, accession no. NV0069100.

Atomic Energy Commission. "Admission of Limited, Selected Group of Uncleared Observers to One Shot Spring 1952 Test Series in Nevada." March 11, 1952. PSF: Subject File, 1940–1953, box 175, National Security Council-Atomic File, Papers of Harry S. Truman, Harry S. Truman Library, Independence, Missouri.

Barrett, Edward W., to James Webb. "Subject: Project for PSB." Memorandum. September 26, 1951. SMOF: Psychological Strategy Board Files, box 37, Papers of Harry S. Truman, Harry S. Truman Library, Independence, Missouri.

Berkhouse, L. H., J. H. Hallowell, F. W. McMullan, S. E. Davis, C. B. Jones, M. J. Osborne, F. R. Gladeck, and E. J. Martin. *Operation Crossroads: 1946*. Defense Nuclear Agency, report no. 6032F. May 1, 1984. Department of Energy OpenNet, accession no. NV0116892.

———, and W. E. Rogers. *Operation Sandstone: 1948*. Defense Nuclear Agency, report no. 6033F. December 19, 1983.

Burriss, Stanley W. "Administrative Plan No. 1, Operation Ivy." August 15, 1952. Department of Energy OpenNet, accession no. NV0404450.

———. *Operation Ivy, Report of Commander, Task Group 132.1*. November 1952. Department of Energy OpenNet, accession no. NV0051374.

Carr, James K., to Glenn T. Seaborg. "Recommendation against Further Testing in Eniwetok and Bikini Atolls." Las Vegas, NV: NNSA Nuclear Testing Archive, 1961.

Clarkson, P. W. "History of Operation Castle, Pacific Proving Ground." 1954. Department of Energy OpenNet, accession no. NV0039825.

———, to Gordon Dean. "Subject: Completion of Operation Ivy." December 5, 1952. Department of Energy OpenNet, accession no. NV0074003.

Davis, R. R. "Sandstone Documentary Film." January 17, 1948. Department of Energy OpenNet, accession no. NV0120896.

Dean, Gordon, to Harry S. Truman. "Subject: Operation Sandstone." Atomic Energy Commission to President Truman, July 27, 1950. Department of Energy OpenNet, accession no. NV0409506.

———, to Dwight D. Eisenhower. "Atomic Energy Commission and *Operation Ivy* Film Review." June 17, 1953. Department of Energy OpenNet, accession no. NV0407212.

Defense Imagery Management Operation Center. "How to Create a VIRIN." http://www.dimoc.mil/Submit-DoD-VI/Digital-VI-Toolkit-read-first/Create-a-VIRIN/.

Defense Nuclear Agency. "Fact Sheet: Greenhouse." January 1, 1980. Department of Energy OpenNet, accession no. NV0760115.

———. *Operation Teapot—Report of the Test Manager, Joint Test Organization—Nevada Test Site, Spring 1955*. November 1, 1981. Extract from Secret/Classified 1955 Report. US Department of Defense, Defense Technical Information Center, http://www.dtic.mil/docs/citations/ADA995154.

Defense Threat Reduction Agency. "Fact Sheet: Operation Teapot." May 2015. http://www.dtra.mil/Portals/61/Documents/NTPR/1-Fact_Sheets/16_TEAPOT.pdf.

Deines, Ann C., David I. Goldman, Ruth R. Harris, and Laura J. Kells. *Marshall Islands Chronology: 1944 to 1990. January 11, 1991*. Department of Energy. Department of Energy OpenNet, accession no. NV0400386.

Department of Defense. "Instruction: 5040.02." 2016 updated version. Defense Technical Information Center, http://www.esd.whs.mil/Portals/54/Documents/DD/issuances/dodi/504002p.pdf.

Department of Defense. "Directive: 3600.01." May 2, 2013. Defense Technical Information Center, http://www.esd.whs.mil/Portals/54/Documents/DD/issuances/dodd/360001p.pdf

Department of the Air Force. *United States Air Force Academy Catalogue*, 1955–69. 1956. https://catalog.hathitrust.org/Record/005882734.

———. "Basic Photography." Air Force Manual no. 95–1, September 15, 1959. Washington, DC: Department of the Air Force. http://hdl.handle.net/2027/uiug.30112107817006.

———. "Organization and Mission—Field: Aerospace Audiovisual Service." October 16, 1972. Air Force Historical Research Agency, Maxwell AFB, Montgomery, Alabama.

Dulles, John Foster. "Evolution of Foreign Policy." Speech before the Council on Foreign Relations, New York, January 12, 1954. Dulles Papers, box 322, Mudd Library, Princeton University, Princeton, New Jersey. https://babel.hathitrust.org/cgi/pt?id=umn.31951d024881358.

Edgerton, Germeshausen & Grier. "Operation Teapot—Project 9.1. Report to the Test Director, Technical Photography." August 12, 1957. Department of Energy OpenNet, accession no. NV0069119.

———. "Operation Teapot—Project 39.4C, Technical Photography of Physical Phenomena, February–May 1955." May 31, 1955. Department of Energy OpenNet, accession no. NV0051113.

Eisenhower, Dwight D. "Farewell Radio and Television Address to the American People." January 17, 1961. American Presidency Project, http://www.presidency.ucsb.edu/ws/?pid=12086.

Elliott, Richard G. "Subject: Continental Test Information Plans." Atomic Energy Commission Memorandum. October 13, 1954. Department of Energy OpenNet, accession no. NV0410505.

"Excerpts from Report of the Secretary of Defense's Ad Hoc Committee on Chemical, Biological, and Radiological Warfare, 30 June 1950." n.d. SMOF: Psychological Strategy Board Files, box 37, Papers of Harry S. Truman, Harry S. Truman Library, Independence, Missouri.

FBI to Mr. Nichols. "Re: Lookout Mountain Laboratory." Memorandum. July 22, 1954. FBI Freedom of Information Act, Reading Room, http://www.esd.whs.mil/Portals/54/Documents/FOID/Reading%20Room/Other/13-F-0865_Lookout_Mountain_Laboratory.pdf.

Fehner, Terrence R., and F. G. Gosling. *Origins of the Nevada Test Site*. December 2000. United States Department of Energy Report. Department of Energy OpenNet, accession no. NV0333360.

Fields, Kenneth E., to P. W. Clarkson. "New Outline on the Commission's File Requirements for Castle." August 13, 1953. Department of Energy OpenNet, accession no. NV0409345.

Fritchey, Clayton, to Secretary of Defense. "Report of the Office of Public Information on Carrying Out Recommendation VIII of the Report of the Secretary of Defense's Ad Hoc Committee on Chemical, Biological, and Radiological Warfare." October 9, 1951. SMOF: Psychological Strategy Board Files, box 37, Papers of Harry S. Truman, Harry S. Truman Library, Independence, Missouri.

Gaylord, James L. *Operation Ivy, Report to the Scientific Director, Documentary Photography*. February 1, 1953. Department of Energy OpenNet, accession no. NV0051050.

Gilbert, H. K., and R. Q. Wilson. "Operation Buster: Final Report." April 1, 1985. Defense Nuclear Agency. Extract version of 1952 report prepared by Armed Forces Special Weapons Project.

Harbour, David F. "Final Report: United States Air Force Information Program during Operation Teapot." May 10, 1955. Department of Energy OpenNet, accession no. NV0076564.

Historical Office, Office of the Secretary of Defense. "Department of Defense Key Officials, 1947–2014." June 2014. Historical Office of the Secretary of Defense, http://history.defense.gov/Portals/70/Documents/key_officials/Key%20Officials_June%202014.pdf.

Howard, Katherine G., to C. D. Jackson. "Subject: National Information Policy." Memorandum. September 16, 1953. Declassified Document Reference System, Gale Digital Collections.

———. *Atomic Weapons Tests, Eniwetok Atoll, Operation Sandstone, 1948*. Report to Joint Chiefs of Staff. December 31, 1948. Department of Energy OpenNet, document no. 16131191.

Hull, John Edwin. *Atomic Weapons Tests, Eniwetok Atoll, Operation Sandstone, 1948: Report to the Joint Chiefs of Staff*. December 31, 1948. Department of Energy OpenNet, accession nos. NV0411128, NV0411131 [includes Annex 1, "Photographic Report"].

"Interim Report by the Ad Hoc Committee of the NSC Planning Board on Armaments and American Policy." Enclosed within NCS-151, "Note by the Executive Secretary to the National Security Council on Armaments and American Policy." May 8, 1953. In *Foreign Relations of the United States, 1952–1954*, vol. 2, part 2, 1151–52.

Joint Committee on Atomic Energy. "The Scale and Scope of Atomic Production: A Chronology of Leading Events." January 30, 1952. National Security Council, Atomic File, Atomic Weapons: Stockpile, box 176, Harry S. Truman Library, Independence, Missouri.

Lay, James S. "Official Statements Regarding Nuclear Weapons." Memorandum for the National Security Council. October 8, 1953. In White House Office, National Security Council Staff Papers, 1948–1961, Disaster Series, box 26, Dwight D. Eisenhower Library, Abilene, Kansas.

Lilienthal, David, to President Harry S. Truman. "Subject: Test of Atomic Weapons." Memorandum. November 20, 1947. Department of Energy OpenNet, document no. 16050868.

"Lookout Mountain Background." 1962–1963. IRISNUM 01141313. Air Force Historical Research Agency, Maxwell Air Force Base, Montgomery, Alabama.

Maag, Carl, Stephen Rohrer, and Robert Shepanek. *Operation Ranger: 25 January–6 February 1951*. February 26, 1982. Defense Nuclear Agency, report no. 6022F.

"Memorandum of Discussion at the 152d Meeting of the National Security Council, Thursday, July 2, 1953." In *Foreign Relations of the United States, 1952–1954*, vol. 15, pt. 2: Korea, 1300–12.

"Memorandum on Public Statements with Respect to Certain American Weapons." Enclosed within NSC-126, "Public Statements with Respect to Certain American Weapons." February 28, 1952. In *Foreign Relations of the United States, 1952–1954*, vol. 2: *National Security Affairs*, 871–72.

"Minutes from the 185th Meeting of the National Security Council." February 17, 1954. NSC Series, box 5, Ann Whitman File, Dwight D. Eisenhower Presidential Library, Abilene, Kansas.

"Minutes from Meeting of the Operations Coordinating Board." January 17, 1954. White House Office, National Security Council Staff: Papers, 1948–1961, OCB Secretariat Series, box 11, Dwight D. Eisenhower Library, Abilene, Kansas.

"Minutes from Meeting of the Operations Coordinating Board." March 20, 1954. White House Office, National Security Council Staff: Papers, 1948–1961, OCB Secretariat Series, box 11, Dwight D. Eisenhower Library, Abilene, Kansas.

National Audiovisual Center. "A Reference List of Audiovisual Materials Produced by the United States Government, 1978." Washington, DC: National Audiovisual Center, National Archives and Records Service, 1978. Hathi Trust Digital Library, https://catalog.hathitrust.org/Record/000264432.

Nichols, Kenneth David, to Atomic Energy Commission. "Subject: Release of Nevada Test Site Documentary Motion Picture." Memorandum. March 25, 1955. Department of Energy OpenNet, accession no. NC0137111.

Norberg, Charles R., to Charles Johnson. "Subject: Motion Pictures and Propaganda." Memorandum. October 10, 1952. SMOF: Psychological Strategy Board Files, box 37, Papers of Harry S. Truman, Harry S. Truman Library, Independence, Missouri.

NSC-126, "Public Statements with Respect to Certain American Weapons." February 28, 1952. In *Foreign Relations of the United States, 1952–1954*, vol. 2, 869–70.

Office of the Historian, Joint Task Force One. *Operation Crossroads: The Official Pictorial Record*. New York: William H. Wise, 1946.

Office of the Secretary of Defense. "Part IV.C.3. Evolution of the War: The Rolling Thunder Program Begins." *United States Vietnam Relations, 1945–1969*. January 15, 1969. Report to the Secretary of Defense. National Archives Online, *Pentagon Papers*, http://www.archives.gov/research/pentagon-papers/.

———. "Part IV.C.7[a]. Volume I. Evolution of the War: The Air War in North Vietnam." *United States Vietnam Relations, 1945–1969*. January 15, 1969. Report to the Secretary of Defense. National Archives Online, *Pentagon Papers*, http://www.archives.gov/research/pentagon-papers/.

Ogle, William E. *An Account of the Return to Nuclear Weapons Testing by the United States after the Test Moratorium, 1958–1961*. Las Vegas, NV: United States Department of Energy, Nevada Operations Office, 1985.

Panel of Consultants on Disarmament. "A Draft Summary of the Line of Argument Agreed on November 15th [1952] at a Partial Meeting of the Panel in New York City." Memorandum. In *Foreign Relations of the United States, 1952–54*, vol. 2, National Security Affairs, 1038–41.

Ponton, Jean, Stephen Rohrer, Carl Maag, and Jean Massie. *Shots ABLE to EASY: The First Five Tests of the Buster-Jangle Series, 22 October–5 November 1951*. June 22, 1982. Defense Nuclear Agency, report no. 6024F.

———. *Shots SUGAR and UNCLE: The Final Tests of the Buster-Jangle Series, 19 November–29 November 1951*. June 23, 1982. Defense Nuclear Agency, report no. 6025F.

Ponton, Jean, Carl Maag, Mary Francis Barrett, and Robert Shepanek. *Operation Tumbler-Snapper: 1952*. June 14, 1982. Defense Nuclear Agency, report no. 6019F.

Ponton, Jean, Stephen Rohrer, Carl Maag, Robert Shepanek, and Jean Massie. *Operation Buster-Jangle, 1951*. June 21, 1982. Defense Nuclear Agency, report no. 6023F.

Ponton, Jean, Martha Wilkinson, Stephen Rohrer. *Shot Apple 2: A Test of the Teapot Series, 5 May 1955*. November 25, 1981. Defense Nuclear Agency, report no. 6012F. Department of Energy OpenNet, accession no. NV0017806.

Possony, Stefan T. *An Outline of American Atomic Strategy in the Non-Military Fields*. October 6, 1952. SMOF: Psychological Strategy Board Files, box 37, Harry S. Truman Library, Independence, Missouri.

Psychological Aspects of United States Strategy. November 29, 1955. C. D. Jackson Papers, box 73, Dwight D. Eisenhower Library, Abilene, Kansas.

"Public Information Policy on Biological Warfare, Radiological Warfare, and Chemical Warfare." n.d. SMOF: Psychological Strategy Board Files, box 37, Harry S. Truman Library, Independence, Missouri.

A Report on the White House Conference of Mayors on National Security: December 14–15, 1953. Washington, DC: United States Government Printing Office, 1954.

"Report to the President and the National Security Council by the Panel on the Human Effects of Nuclear Weapons Development." November 1956. Ann Whitman Files, Administrative Series, box 4, Dwight D. Eisenhower Library, Abilene, Kansas.

Salisbury, Morse, to Richard Hirsch. "Subject: Themes in Public Reporting on Operation Castle." Memorandum. April 22, 1954. Department of Energy OpenNet, accession no. NV0406802.

Shurcliff, William A. *Bombs at Bikini: The Official Report of Operation Crossroads*. New York: W. H. Wise, 1947.

Snapp, Roy B. "Operation Sandstone—Classification Guide." Atomic Energy Commission. Memorandum. March 9, 1948. Department of Energy OpenNet, accession no. NV0409248.

———. "Meeting 893." Atomic Energy Commission Meeting Minutes, July 23, 1953. Department of Energy OpenNet, accession no. NV0072317.

———. "Staff Study, Public Information Plan, Operation Ivy." September 26, 1952. Enclosed in *Atomic Energy Commission, Information Plan for Operation Ivy*. October 24, 1952. Department of Energy OpenNet, accession no. NV0409029.

Snapp, Roy B., and P. W. Clarkson. "Information Plan for Operation Ivy." Secretary of the Atomic Energy Commission. October 24, 1952. Department of Energy OpenNet, accession no. NV0409029.

Snapp, Roy B., Gordon Dean, Shelby Thompson, and Morse Salisbury. "Letter to J. Edgar Hoover—Operation Ivy." Atomic Energy Commission. November 18, 1952. Department of Energy OpenNet, accession no. NV0409009.

Snapp, Roy B., Thomas Keith Glennan, P. W. Clarkson, H. M. Page, and Robert T. Bryant Jr. *Security and Public Reporting Aspects of 1952 Pacific Tests*. Atomic Energy Commission. Department of Energy OpenNet, accession no. NV0408984.

Snapp, Roy B., Val Peterson, and Lewis Strauss. "Subject: Film on Operation Ivy." Secretary of the Atomic Energy Commission. December 8, 1953. Department of Energy OpenNet, accession no. NV0408960.

Stassen, Harold E. "Comment on Thermonuclear and Atomic Weapons." Director to General Staff, Foreign Operations Administration. Memorandum. White House Office, National Security Council Staff Papers, 1948–1961, Disaster Series, box 26, Dwight D. Eisenhower Library, Abilene, Kansas.

Stevens, Dean J. *The Worldwide Military Command and Control System: A Historical Perspective, 1960–1977*. Washington, DC: Historical Division Joint Secretariat, Joint Chiefs of Staff, September 1980.

Strauss, Lewis, to C. E. Wilson. "Subject: Documentary Film Entitled 'Commander's Report.'" n.d. Department of Energy OpenNet, accession no. NV0409750.

———, to Val Peterson. September 29, 1953. Department of Energy OpenNet, accession no. NV0408966.

"Terror—And the Terror Weapon." PSF: Subject File, 1940–1953, box 176, National Security Council-Atomic File, Papers of Harry S. Truman, Harry S. Truman Library, Independence, Missouri.

Truman, Harry. "Public Discussion of Foreign and Military Policy." Public directive. December 5, 1950. White House Office, National Security Council Staff: Papers, 1948–61, Disaster File, box 6, Dwight D. Eisenhower Presidential Library, Abilene, Kansas.

Udey, Edwin C. "Appendix A: Photographic Report on Atomic Weapon Assembly and Handling for X_Ray, Yoke, and Zerra Tests at Eniwtok [*sic*] Proving Grounds." January 1, 1948. In *Operation Sandstone, Nuclear Explosions, 1948*, 26–39. Department of Energy OpenNet, document no. 16340201.

United Nations. "Trust and Non-Self-Governing Territories [1945–1999]." n.d. United Nations and Decolonization, http://www.un.org/en/decolonization/nonselfgov.shtml.

"United States Air Force Basic Doctrine." *Air Force Manual 1-2*. April 1, 1955. Department of the Air Force. Hathi Trust, http://hdl.handle.net/2027/uiug.30112107816222.

United States Congress, House Committee on Government Operations, Government Activities and Transportation Subcommittee. *Federal Audiovisual Materials Policy and Programs: Hearings before a Subcommittee of the Committee on Government Operations, House of Representatives, Ninety-Fifth Congress, Second Session, September 21 and October 26, 1978*. Washington, DC: US Government Printing Office, 1979.

Winant, Frank I., John Edwin Hull, J. Barket, M. M. Anderson, A. H. Dahl, and J. P. Cooney. *Sandstone Report–43, Task Group 7.6, Operation Report Phases A, B, C, D, E*. March 20, 1948. Department of Energy OpenNet, document no. 16028740.

1352nd Motion Picture Squadron

Quarterly Report 1952, Lookout Mountain Laboratory, 1 January to 31 March. 1952. Air Force Historical Research Agency, Maxwell Air Force Base, Montgomery, Alabama.

Quarterly Historical Report, 1352d Motion Picture Squadron [Lookout Mountain Laboratory], 1 April 1952 through 30 June 1952. 1952. Air Force Historical Research Agency, Maxwell Air Force Base, Montgomery, Alabama.

Semi-Annual Historical Report, 1352 Motion Picture Squadron, Lookout Mountain Laboratory, 1 July 1952 through 31 December 1952. 1953. Air Force Historical Research Agency, Maxwell Air Force Base, Montgomery, Alabama.

History of the 1352 Motion Picture Squadron, Lookout Mountain Laboratory, 1 January 1953 through 30 June 1953. August 12, 1953. Air Force Historical Research Agency, Maxwell Air Force Base, Montgomery, Alabama.

History of the 1352 Motion Picture Squadron, Lookout Mountain Laboratory, 1 July 1953 through 31 December 1953. February 12, 1954. Air Force Historical Research Agency, Maxwell Air Force Base, Montgomery, Alabama.

History of the 1352 Motion Picture Squadron [Lookout Mountain Laboratory], 1 January 1954–30 June 1954. July 15, 1954. Air Force Historical Research Agency, Maxwell Air Force Base, Montgomery, Alabama.

History of the 1352 Motion Picture Squadron [Lookout Mountain Laboratory], 1 July 1954–31 December 1954. March 7, 1955. Air Force Historical Research Agency, Maxwell Air Force Base, Montgomery, Alabama.

History of the 1352 Motion Picture Squadron [Lookout Mountain Laboratory], 1 January 1955–30 June 1955. August 25, 1955. Air Force Historical Research Agency, Maxwell Air Force Base, Montgomery, Alabama.

History of the 1352 Motion Picture Squadron [Lookout Mountain Laboratory], 1 July 1955–31 December 1955. February 15, 1956. Air Force Historical Research Agency, Maxwell Air Force Base, Montgomery, Alabama.

History of the 1352 Motion Picture Squadron [Lookout Mountain Laboratory], 1 January 1956–1 July 1956. August 20, 1956. Air Force Historical Research Agency, Maxwell Air Force Base, Montgomery, Alabama.

History of 1352 Motion Picture Squadron [Lookout Mountain Laboratory], 1 July 1956–31 December 1956. February 1, 1957. Air Force Historical Research Agency, Maxwell Air Force Base, Montgomery, Alabama.

History of 1352 Motion Picture Squadron [Lookout Mountain Laboratory], 1 January 1957–30 June 1957. August 1, 1957. Air Force Historical Research Agency, Maxwell Air Force Base, Montgomery, Alabama.

History of 1352 Motion Picture Squadron [Lookout Mountain Laboratory], 1 July 1957–31 December 1958 [sic]. February 10, 1958. Air Force Historical Research Agency, Maxwell Air Force Base, Montgomery, Alabama.

History of 1352 Motion Picture Squadron [Lookout Mountain Air Force Station], 1 January 1958–30 June 1958. August 15, 1958. Air Force Historical Research Agency, Maxwell Air Force Base, Montgomery, Alabama.

History of 1352 Motion Picture Squadron, Lookout Mountain Air Force Station, 1 July 1958–31 December 1958. February 1, 1959. Air Force Historical Research Agency, Maxwell Air Force Base, Montgomery, Alabama.

History of 1352 Motion Picture Squadron, Lookout Mountain Air Force Station, 1 January 1959–30 June 1959. August 1, 1959. Air Force Historical Research Agency, Maxwell Air Force Base, Montgomery, Alabama.

History of 1352 Motion Picture Squadron, Lookout Mountain Air Force Station, 1 July 1959–31 December 1959. February 1, 1960. Air Force Historical Research Agency, Maxwell Air Force Base, Montgomery, Alabama.

History of 1352 Motion Picture Squadron, Lookout Mountain Air Force Station, 1 January 1960 through 30 June 1960. July 1, 1960. Air Force Historical Research Agency, Maxwell Air Force Base, Montgomery, Alabama.

History of 1352 Photographic Squadron, Lookout Mountain Air Force Station, 1 July 1960 through 31 December 1960. 1961. Air Force Historical Research Agency, Maxwell Air Force Base, Montgomery, Alabama.

History of 1352 Photographic Squadron, 1 January 1961–30 June 1961. 1961. Air Force Historical Research Agency, Maxwell Air Force Base, Montgomery, Alabama.

History of 1352 Photographic Squadron, 1 July 1961–31 December 1961. 1962. Air Force Historical Research Agency, Maxwell Air Force Base, Montgomery, Alabama.

History of 1352 Photographic Group, 1 January 1962–30 June 1962. 1962. Air Force Historical Research Agency, Maxwell Air Force Base, Montgomery, Alabama.

History of 1352 Photographic Group, 1 July 1962–31 December 1962. 1963. Air Force Historical Research Agency, Maxwell Air Force Base, Montgomery, Alabama.

History of 1352 Photographic Group, 1 January 1963–30 June 1963. 1963. Air Force Historical Research Agency, Maxwell Air Force Base, Montgomery, Alabama.

History of 1352 Photographic Group, 1 July 1963–31 December 1963. 1964. Air Force Historical Research Agency, Maxwell Air Force Base, Montgomery, Alabama.

History of 1352 Photographic Group, 1 January 1964–30 June 1964. 1964. Air Force Historical Research Agency, Maxwell Air Force Base, Montgomery, Alabama.

History of 1352 Photographic Group, 1 July 1964–31 December 1964. 1965. Air Force Historical Research Agency, Maxwell Air Force Base, Montgomery, Alabama.

History of 1352 Photographic Group, 1 January 1965–30 June 1965. 1965. Air Force Historical Research Agency, Maxwell Air Force Base, Montgomery, Alabama.

History of 1352 Photographic Group, 1 July 1965–31 December 1965. February 10, 1966. Air Force Historical Research Agency, Maxwell Air Force Base, Montgomery, Alabama.

History of 1352 Photographic Group, 1 January 1966 through 30 June 1966. August 15, 1966. Air Force Historical Research Agency, Maxwell Air Force Base, Montgomery, Alabama.

History of 1352 Photographic Group, 1 July 1966 through 31 December 1966. February 25, 1967. Air Force Historical Research Agency, Maxwell Air Force Base, Montgomery, Alabama.

History of 1352 Photographic Group, 1 January 1967 through 30 June 1967. August 28, 1967. Air Force Historical Research Agency, Maxwell Air Force Base, Montgomery, Alabama.

History of 1352 Photographic Group, 1 January 1968 through 30 June 1968. August 20, 1967. Air Force Historical Research Agency, Maxwell Air Force Base, Montgomery, Alabama.

History of 1352 Photographic Group, 1 July 1968 through 31 December 1968. February 14, 1969. Air Force Historical Research Agency, Maxwell Air Force Base, Montgomery, Alabama.

History of 1352 Photographic Group, 1 January 1969 through 30 June 1969. June 30, 1969. Air Force Historical Research Agency, Maxwell Air Force Base, Montgomery, Alabama.

600th Photographic Squadron

History of the 600th Photographic Squadron, 1 January 1966–30 June 1966. 1966. Air Force Historical Research Agency, Maxwell Air Force Base, Montgomery, Alabama.

History of the 600th Photographic Squadron, 1 July 1966–31 December 1966. 1967. Air Force Historical Research Agency, Maxwell Air Force Base, Montgomery, Alabama.

History of the 600th Photographic Squadron, 1 January 1967–31 July 1967 [sic]. 1967. Air Force Historical Research Agency, Maxwell Air Force Base, Montgomery, Alabama.

History of the 600th Photographic Squadron, 1 July 1967–31 December 1967. 1968. Air Force Historical Research Agency, Maxwell Air Force Base, Montgomery, Alabama.

Aerospace Audiovisual Service

History of the Aerospace Audio-Visual Service, 1 January 1967–30 June 1968. Air Force Historical Research Agency, Maxwell Air Force Base, Montgomery, Alabama.

History of the Aerospace Audiovisual Service, 1 January 1980–31 December 1980, Volume 1: Narrative. September 1980 [*sic*]. Air Force Historical Research Agency, Maxwell Air Force Base, Montgomery, Alabama.

Air Photographic and Charting Service

Chronology of the Air Photographic and Charting Service. October 1962. Air Force Historical Research Agency, Maxwell Air Force Base, Montgomery, Alabama.

Historical Summary of the Air Photographic and Charting Service, April 1951–December 1962. Air Force Historical Research Agency, Maxwell Air Force Base, Montgomery, Alabama.

General Sources

Acland, Charles R., and Haidee Wasson. *Useful Cinema*. Durham, NC: Duke University Press, 2011.

Air Power League. *Peace through Air Power: A Report by the Air Power League*. Washington, DC: Air Power League, 1946. http://hdl.handle.net/2027/mdp.39015035835530.

Alperovitz, Gar. *The Decision to Use the Atomic Bomb, and the Architecture of an American Myth*. New York: Knopf, 1995.

Anderson, Benedict R. *Imagined Communities: Reflections on the Origin and Spread of Nationalism*. London: Verso, 1991.

Appadurai, Arjun, ed. *The Social Life of Things: Commodities in Cultural Perspective*. Cambridge, UK: Cambridge University Press, 1986.

Arendt, Hannah. *The Human Condition*, 2nd ed. Chicago: University of Chicago Press, 1998.

———. *The Life of the Mind*. New York: Harcourt Brace Jovanovich, 1978.

Atkinson, Nathan S. "Newsreels as Domestic Propaganda: Visual Rhetoric at the Dawn of the Cold War." *Rhetoric and Public Affairs* 14, no. 1 (2011): 69–100.

Azoulay, Ariella. "Actions, Non-actions, Interaction, and So On and So Forth." *Journal of Visual Culture* 15, no. 1 (2016): 25–28.

———. *Civil Imagination: A Political Ontology of Photography*. Translated by Louise Bethlehem. New York: Verso, 2012.

Ballard, Jack S., John Bond, and George Paxton. *Lowry Air Force Base*. Charleston, SC: Arcadia, 2013.

Barnes, Trevor J., and Matthew Farish. "Between Regions: Science, Militarism, and American Geography from World War to Cold War." *Annals of the Association of American Geographers* 96, no. 4 (2006): 807–26.

Barney, Timothy. *Mapping the Cold War: Cartography and the Framing of America's International Power*. Chapel Hill: University of North Carolina Press, 2015.

Bellows, Andy Masaki, and Marina McDougall, eds. *Science Is Fiction: The Films of Jean Painlevé*. Cambridge, MA: MIT Press, 2001.

Belton, John. "Glorious Technicolor, Breathtaking Cinemascope, and Stereophonic Sound." In *The Classical Hollywood Reader*, 355–69. Edited by Stephen Neale. New York: Routledge, 2012.

Benjamin, Walter. "The Work of Art in the Age of Mechanical Reproduction," In *Illuminations*, 217–52. Edited by Walter Benjamin, Hannah Arendt, and Harry Zohn. New York: Harcourt, Brace and World, 1968.

Betancourt, Mark. "World War II: The Movie." *Air and Space*, March 2012. http://www.airspacemag.com/history-of-flight/world-war-ii-the-movie-21103597.

Betts, Richard K. *Nuclear Blackmail and Nuclear Balance*. Washington, DC: Brookings Institution Press, 1987.

Bijsterveld, Karin, and Trevor Pinch. *Special Issue on Sound Studies: New Technologies and Music*. London: SAGE, 2004.

Bird, Kai, and Martin J. Sherwin. *American Prometheus: The Triumph and Tragedy of J. Robert Oppenheimer*. New York: Knopf, 2005.

Black, Edwin. "Secrecy and Disclosure as Rhetorical Forms." *Quarterly Journal of Speech* 74, no. 2 (1988): 133–50.

Bogost, Ian. *Unit Operations: An Approach to Videogame Criticism*. Cambridge, MA: MIT Press, 2008.

Boon, Tim, and Paul Rotha. *Films of Fact: A History of Science in Documentary Films and Television*. New York: Wallflower Press, 2008.

Bordwell, David. "Classical Hollywood Cinema: Narrational Principles and Procedures." In *Narrative, Apparatus, Ideology: A Film Theory Reader*, 17–34. Edited by Philip Rosen. New York: Columbia University Press, 1986.

———, Janet Staiger, and Kristin Thompson. *The Classical Hollywood Cinema: Film Style and Mode of Production to 1960*. New York: Columbia University Press, 1985.

Boyer, Paul. *By the Bomb's Early Light: American Thought and Culture at the Dawn of the Atomic Age*. Chapel Hill: University of North Carolina Press, 1994.

Brown, Harold. *"Managing" the Defense Department—Why It Can't Be Done*. Ann Arbor: Graduate School of Business Administration, University of Michigan, 1981.

Bryan-Wilson, Julia. "Posing by the Cloud: US Nuclear Test Site Photography in Process." In *Camera Atomica*, 107–23. Edited by John O'Brian. London: Black Dog, 2015.

Burke, Kenneth. *A Rhetoric of Motives*. Berkeley: University of California Press, 1969.

Byrd, Jodi A. *The Transit of Empire: Indigenous Critiques of Colonialism*. Minneapolis: U. of Minnesota Press, 2011.

Call, Steve. *Selling Air Power: Military Aviation and American Popular Culture after World War II*. College Station: Texas A&M University Press, 2009.

Cantelon, Philip L., Richard G. Hewlett, and Robert C. Williams, eds. *The American Atom: A Documentary History of Nuclear Policies from the Discovery of Fission to the Present*, 2nd ed. Philadelphia: University of Pennsylvania Press, 1991.

Carey, James. "The Roots of Modern Media Analysis: Lewis Mumford and Marshall McLuhan." In *James Carey: A Critical Reader*, 34–59. Edited by Eve Stryker Munson and Catherine A. Warren. Minneapolis: University of Minnesota Press, 1997.

Chernus, Ira. *Eisenhower's Atoms for Peace*. College Station: Texas A&M University Press, 2002.

——. *Apocalypse Management: Eisenhower and the Discourse of National Insecurity*. Stanford, CA: Stanford University Press, 2008.

Cohen, Ira. "Rationalization." In *The Cambridge Dictionary of Sociology*. Edited by Bryan S. Turner. New York: Cambridge University Press, 2006.

Cosgrove, Denis E. *Geography and Vision: Seeing, Imagining and Representing the World*. New York: Palgrave Macmillan, 2008.

Courtney, Susan. *Split Screen Nation: Moving Images of the American West and South*. New York: Oxford University Press, 2017.

Cross, Harold. *The People's Right to Know: Legal Access to Public Records and Proceedings*. New York: Columbia University Press, 1953.

Culbert, David. "'Why We Fight': Social Engineering for a Democratic Society at War." In *Readings in Propaganda and Persuasion: New and Classic Essays*, 169–88. Edited by Garth S. Jowett and Victoria O'Donnell. Thousand Oaks, CA: SAGE, 2006.

Cumings, Bruce. *Dominion from Sea to Sea: Pacific Ascendancy and American Power*. New Haven: Yale University Press, 2009.

Cunningham, Douglas. "Imaging/Imagining Air Force Identity: 'Hap' Arnold, Warner Bros., and the Formation of the USAAF First Motion Picture Unit." *Moving Image* 5, no. 1 (2005): 95–124.

——. *Imagining Air Force Identity: Masculinity, Aeriality, and the Films of the U.S. Army Air Force's First Motion Picture Unit*. PhD diss., U. of California, Berkeley, 2009.

——. "'Desiring the Disney Technique': Chronicle of a Contracted Military Training Film." In *Learning from Mickey, Donald and Walt: Essays on Disney's Edutainment Films*, 27–39. Edited by A. Bowdoin Van Riper. Jefferson, NC: McFarland, 2011.

Davis, Tracy C. *Stages of Emergency: Cold War Nuclear Civil Defense*. Durham, NC: Duke University Press, 2007.

Deaile, Melvin G. "The SAC Mentality: The Origins of Strategic Air Command's Organizational Culture, 1948–51." *Air and Space Power Journal* (March–April 2015): 48–73.

DeLoughrey, Elizabeth M. "The Myth of Isolates: Ecosystem Ecologies in the Nuclear Pacific." *Cultural Geographies* 20, no. 2 (2012): 167–84.

Der Derian, James. "The (S)pace of International Relations: Simulation, Surveillance, and Speed." *International Studies Quarterly* 34, no. 3 (1990): 295–310.

——. *Antidiplomacy: Spies, Terror, Speed, and War*. Cambridge, MA: Blackwell, 1992.

——. *Virtuous War: Mapping the Military-Industrial-Media-Entertainment Network*, 2nd ed. New York: Routledge, 2009.

Diaz, Vicente M. "Voyaging for Anti-Colonial Recovery: Austronesian Seafaring, Archipelagic Rethinking, and the Re-mapping of Indigeneity." *Pacific Asia Inquiry* 2, no. 1 (2011): 21–32.

Doherty, Thomas Patrick. *Projections of War: Hollywood, American Culture, and World War II*. New York: Columbia University Press, 1993.

Drew, S. Nelson, ed. *NSC-68: Forging the Strategy of Containment*. Washington, DC: National Defense University, 1994.

Edwards, Paul N. *The Closed World: Computers and the Politics of Discourse in Cold War America*. Cambridge, MA: MIT Press, 1997.

Eisenhower, Dwight D., and Rudolph L. Treuenfels. *Eisenhower Speaks: Dwight D. Eisenhower in His Messages and Speeches*. New York: Farrar, Straus, 1948.

Eliot, Marc. *Jimmy Stewart: A Biography*. New York: Three Rivers Press, 2007.

Faith, William Robert. *Bob Hope, A Life in Comedy*. Cambridge, MA: Da Capo Press, 2003.

Farish, Matthew. "Frontier Engineering: From the Globe to the Body in the Cold War Arctic." *Canadian Geographer [Le Géographe canadien]* 50, no. 2 (2006): 177–96.

Fermi, Rachel, Richard Rhodes, and Esther Samra. *Picturing the Bomb: Photographs from the Secret World of the Manhattan Project*. New York: Harry N. Abrams, 1995.

Foster, Hal. Preface to *Vision and Visuality*, ix–xiv. Edited by Hal Foster. Seattle: Bay Press, 1988.

Foucault, Michel. *Discipline and Punish: The Birth of the Prison*. New York: Vintage Books, 1977.

Freedman, Lawrence. *Kennedy's Wars: Berlin, Cuba, Laos, and Vietnam*. New York: Oxford University Press, 2000.

——. *Deterrence*. Malden, MA: Polity Press, 2004.

——. *Strategy: A History*. New York: Oxford University Press, 2013.

Friedberg, Anne. *Window Shopping: Cinema and the Postmodern*. Berkeley: University of California Press, 1993.

Gaddis, John Lewis. *Strategies of Containment: A Critical Appraisal of American National Security Policy during the Cold War*, revised and expanded edition. New York: Oxford University Press, 2005.

Galison, Peter. *Image and Logic: A Material Culture of Microphysics*. Chicago: University of Chicago Press, 1997.

——, and Bruce William Hevly. *Big Science: The Growth of Large-Scale Research*. Stanford, CA, Stanford University Press, 1992.

Geertz, Clifford. *Local Knowledge: Further Essays in Interpretive Anthropology*. New York: Basic Books, 1983.

German, Kathleen M. "Frank Capra's *Why We Fight* Series and the American Audience." *Western Journal of Speech Communication* 54, no. 2 (1990): 237–48.

Giedion, Sigfried. *Mechanization Takes Command: A Contribution to Anonymous History*. New York: Oxford University Press, 1948.

Goddard, George W., and DeWitt S. Copp. *Overview: A Lifelong Adventure in Aerial Photography*. Garden City, NY: Doubleday, 1969.

Graff, Henry F. *The Tuesday Cabinet: Deliberation and Decision on Peace and War under Lyndon B. Johnson*. Englewood Cliffs, NJ: Prentice Hall, 1970.

Grant, Shelagh D. *Polar Imperative: A History of Arctic Sovereignty in North America*. Vancouver: Douglas and McIntyre, 2010.

Habermas, Jürgen. *Legitimation Crisis*. Boston: Beacon Press, 1975.

Hacker, Barton C. *Elements of Controversy: The Atomic Energy Commission and Radiation Safety in Nuclear Weapons Testing, 1947–1974*. Berkeley: University of California Press, 1994.

Hales, Peter B. *Atomic Spaces: Living on the Manhattan Project*. Urbana: University of Illinois Press, 1997.

———. "The Atomic Sublime." *American Studies* 32, no. 1 (1991): 5–31.

Halpern, Orit. *Beautiful Data: A History of Vision and Reason since 1945*. Durham, NC: Duke University Press, 2014.

Hankins, Thomas L., and Robert J. Silverman. *Instruments and the Imagination*. Princeton, NJ: Princeton University Press, 1995.

Haraway, Donna Jeanne. *Simians, Cyborgs, and Women: The Reinvention of Nature*. New York: Routledge, 1991.

Hariman, Robert. *Political Style: The Artistry of Power*. Chicago: University of Chicago Press, 1995.

———, and John Louis Lucaites. "The Iconic Image of the Mushroom Cloud and the Cold War Nuclear Optic." In *Picturing Atrocity: Photography in Crisis*, 135–46. Edited by Geoffrey Batchen, Mick Gidley, Nancy K. Miller, and Jay Prosser. London: Reaktion Books, 2012.

———, and John Louis Lucaites. *The Public Image: Photography and Civic Spectatorship*. Chicago: University of Chicago Press, 2016.

Hau'ofa, Epeli, Eric Waddell, and Vijay Naidu. *A New Oceania: Rediscovering Our Sea of Islands*. Suva, Fiji: School of Social and Economic Development, University of the South Pacific, 1993.

Hediger, Vinzenz, and Patrick Vonderau. *Films That Work: Industrial Film and the Productivity of Media*. Amsterdam: Amsterdam University Press, 2009.

Henry, David. "The Technological Priesthood: A Case Study of Scientists, Engineers, and Physicians for Johnson-Humphrey." In *Communication and the Culture of Technology*, 157–79. Edited by Martin J. Medhurst, Alberto Gonzalez, and Tarla Rai Peterson. Pullman: Washington State University Press, 1990.

Herken, Gregg. *Brotherhood of the Bomb: The Tangled Lives and Loyalties of Robert Oppenheimer, Ernest Lawrence, and Edward Teller*. New York: Henry Holt, 2002.

Hewlett, Richard G., and Jack M. Holl. *Atoms for Peace and War, 1953–1961: Eisenhower and the Atomic Energy Commission*. Berkeley: University of California Press, 1989.

Hoberman, James. *An Army of Phantoms: American Movies and the Making of the Cold War*. New York: New Press, 2011.

Hogan, Michael J. *A Cross of Iron: Harry S. Truman and the Origins of the National Security State*, 1945–1954. New York: Cambridge University Press, 1998.

Horkheimer, Max, and Theodor W. Adorno. *Dialectic of Enlightenment*. Edited by Gunzelin Schmid Noerr. Translated by Edmund Jephcott. Stanford, CA: Stanford University Press, 2002.

Humphries, Reynold. *Hollywood's Blacklists: A Political and Cultural History*. Edinburgh: Edinburgh University Press, 2008.

Illingworth, Valerie. *A Dictionary of Computing*, 4th ed. New York: Oxford University Press, 1997.

Jameson, Fredric. *The Political Unconscious: Narrative as a Socially Symbolic Act*. Ithaca, NY: Cornell University Press, 1981.

———. *Postmodernism, or, the Cultural Logic of Late Capitalism*. Durham, NC: Duke University Press, 1991.

Jockel, Joseph T. *No Boundaries Upstairs: Canada, the United States, and the Origins of North American Air Defense, 1945–1958*. Vancouver: University of British Columbia Press, 1987.

Johnston, Robert William. "Database of Nuclear Tests, United States: Part 1, 1945–1963." November 8, 2006. http://www.johnstonsarchive.net/nuclear/tests/USA-ntests1.html.

Kessler, Frank. "Visible Evidence–But of What? Reassessing Early Non-fiction Cinema." *Historical Journal of Film, Radio and Television* 22, no. 3 (2002): 221–23.

Kikkert, Peter. "Pragmatism and Cooperation: Canadian-American Defence Activities in the Arctic, 1945–1951." Master's thesis, University of Waterloo, Waterloo, Ontario, 2009.

Kirkham, Pat. *Charles and Ray Eames: Designers of the Twentieth Century*. Cambridge, MA: MIT Press, 1998.

Kittinger, Joe, and Craig Ryan. *Come Up and Get Me: An Autobiography of Colonel Joe Kittinger*. Albuquerque: University of New Mexico Press, 2010.

Kittler, Friedrich. *Gramophone, Film, Typewriter*. Translated by Geoffrey Winthrop-Young and Michael Wutz. Stanford, CA: Stanford University Press, 1999.

———. *Optical Media*. Translated by Anthony Enns. Malden, MA: Polity Press, 2010.

Kiste, Robert C. *The Bikinians: A Study in Forced Migration*. Menlo Park, CA: Cummings, 1974.

Knorr-Cetina, Karin. *Epistemic Cultures: How the Sciences Make Knowledge*. Cambridge, MA: Harvard University Press, 1999.

Koppes, Clayton R., and Gregory D. Black. *Hollywood Goes to War: How Politics, Profits, and Propaganda Shaped World War II Movies*. New York: Free Press, 1987.

Kozak, Warren. *Lemay: The Life and Wars of General Curtis Lemay*. Washington, DC: Regnery, 2009.

Kuran, Peter. *How to Photograph an Atomic Bomb*. Santa Clara, CA: VCE, 2006.

Lackenbauer, P. Whitney. *Introduction to Canadian Arctic Sovereignty and Security: Historical Perspectives*, 1–22. Edited by P. Whitney Lackenbauer. Calgary, Alberta, Ontario: Centre for Military and Strategic Studies, 2011.

———, and Ryan Shackleton. "Inuit-Air Force Relations in the Qikiqtani Region during the Early Cold War." In *De-icing Required! The Historical Dimension of the Canadian Air Force's Experience in the Arctic*, 73–94. Edited by P. Whitney Lackenbauer and W. A. Marsh. Ottawa, Ontario: Canadian Department of National Defense, 2012.

Latour, Bruno. "Give Me a Laboratory and I Will Raise the World." In *Science Observed: Perspectives on the Social Study of Science*, 141–70. Edited by Karin Knorr-Cetina and Michael Mulkay. London: SAGE, 1983.

———. *Science in Action: How to Follow Scientists and Engineers through Society*. Cambridge, MA: Harvard University Press, 1998.

Leahy, William D. *I Was There: The Personal Story of the Chief of Staff to Presidents Roosevelt and Truman*. New York, NY: Whittlesey House, 1950.

Lebow, Richard Ned, and Janice Gross Stein. *We All Lost the Cold War*. Princeton, NJ: Princeton University Press, 1994.

Leskosky, Richard J. "Cartoons Will Win the War: World War II Propaganda Shorts." In *Learning from Mickey, Donald and Walt: Essays on Disney's Edutainment Films*, 40–62. Edited by A. Bowdoin Van Riper. Jefferson, NC: McFarland, 2011.

Lewis, Adrian R. *The American Culture of War: The History of U.S. Military Force from World War II to Operation Iraqi Freedom*. New York: Routledge, 2007.

MacIntyre, Alasdair C. *Whose Justice? Which Rationality?* Notre Dame, IN: University of Notre Dame Press, 1988.

———. *After Virtue*, 3rd ed. Notre Dame, IN: University of Notre Dame Press, 2007.

Mackenzie, Donald A. *Inventing Accuracy: A Historical Sociology of Nuclear Missile Guidance*. Cambridge, MA: MIT Press, 1990.

———. *Knowing Machines: Essays on Technical Change*. Cambridge, MA: MIT Press, 1998.

Martin-Nielsen, Janet. *Eismitte in the Scientific Imagination: Knowledge and Politics at the Center of Greenland*. New York: Palgrave Macmillan, 2013.

Marx, Leo. *The Machine in the Garden: Technology and the Pastoral Ideal in America*. New York: Oxford University Press, 1964.

Masco, Joseph. "Nuclear Technoaesthetics: Sensory Politics from Trinity to the Virtual Bomb in Los Alamos." *American Ethnologist* 31, no. 3 (2004): 349–73.

———. "Survival Is Your Business: Engineering Ruins and Affect in Nuclear America." *Cultural Anthropology* 23, no. 2 (2008): 361–98.

———. *The Theater of Operations: National Security Affect from the Cold War to the War on Terror*. Durham, NC: Duke University Press, 2014.

Maslowski, Peter. *Armed with Cameras: The American Military Photographers of World War II*. New York: Free Press, 1993.

May, Larry. *The Big Tomorrow: Hollywood and the Politics of the American Way*. Chicago: University of Chicago Press, 2002.

McBride, Joseph. *Searching for John Ford*. Jackson: University Press of Mississippi, 2001.

McLuhan, Marshall. *Understanding Media: Extensions of Man*. Cambridge, MA: MIT Press, 1964.

Medhurst, Martin J. "Eisenhower's 'Atoms for Peace' Speech: A Case Study in the Strategic Use of Language." *Communication Monographs* 54, no. 2 (1987): 204–20.

Metz, Christian. *The Imaginary Signifier: Psychoanalysis and the Cinema*. Bloomington: Indiana University Press, 1981.

Miller, Perry. *Errand into the Wilderness*. Cambridge, MA: Harvard University Press, 1956.

Miller, Richard L. *Under the Cloud: The Decades of Nuclear Testing*. New York: Free Press, 1986.

Mills, C. Wright. *White Collar: The American Middle Classes*. New York: Oxford University Press, 1951.

Mindell, David A. *Between Human and Machine: Feedback, Control, and Computing before Cybernetics*. Baltimore, MD: Johns Hopkins University Press, 2004.

———. *Digital Apollo: Human and Machine in Spaceflight*. Cambridge, MA: MIT Press, 2011.

Mirzoeff, Nicholas. *How to See the World: An Introduction to Images, from Self-Portraits to Selfies, Maps to Movies, and More*. New York: Basic Books, 2016.

———. *The Right to Look: A Counterhistory of Visuality*. Durham, NC: Duke University Press, 2011.

Mitchell, Greg. *Atomic Cover-up: Two U.S. Soldiers, Hiroshima and Nagasaki, and the Greatest Movie Never Made*. New York: Sinclair Books, 2012.

Monk, Ray. *Robert Oppenheimer: A Life Inside the Center*. New York: Doubleday, 2013.

Moyes, Norman B. *Battle Eye: A History of American Combat Photography*. New York: MetroBooks, 1996.

Nadel, Alan. *Containment Culture: American Narratives, Postmodernism, and the Atomic Age*. Durham, NC: Duke University Press, 1995.

Nixon, Rob. *Slow Violence and the Environmentalism of the Poor*. Cambridge, MA: Harvard University Press, 2011.

Oakes, Guy. *The Imaginary War: Civil Defense and American Cold War Culture*. New York: Oxford University Press, 1994.

O'Donovan, Oliver. *Peace and Certainty: A Theological Essay on Deterrence*. Oxford: Clarendon, 1989.

O'Gorman, Ned. *Spirits of the Cold War: Contesting Worldviews in the Classical Age of American Security Strategy*. East Lansing: Michigan State University Press, 2011.

———. *The Iconoclastic Imagination: Image, Catastrophe, and Economy in America since the Kennedy Assassination*. Chicago: University of Chicago Press, 2015.

O'Gorman, Ned, and Kevin Hamilton. "At the Interface: The Loaded Rhetorical Gestures of Nuclear Legitimacy and Illegitimacy." *Communication and Critical/Cultural Studies* 8, no. 1 (2011): 41–66.

———. "EG&G and the Deep Media of Timing, Firing, and Exposing." *Journal of War and Culture Studies* 9, no. 2 (2016): 182–201.

———. "The Sensibility of the State: Lookout Mountain Laboratory's Operation Ivy and the Image of the Cold War 'Super.'" *Rhetoric and Public Affairs* 19, no. 1 (2016): 1–44.

O'Keefe, Bernard J. *Nuclear Hostages*. Boston: Houghton Mifflin, 1983.

Orgeron, Devin, Marsha Orgeron, and Dan Streible, eds. *Learning with the Lights Off: Educational Film in the United States*. New York: Oxford University Press, 2012.

Osgood, Kenneth Alan. *Total Cold War: Eisenhower's Secret Propaganda Battle at Home and Abroad*. Lawrence: University of Kansas, 2006.

Page, Joseph T. *Vandenberg Air Force Base*. Charleston, SC: Arcadia, 2014.

Paglen, Trevor. *Blank Spots on the Map: The Dark Geography of the Pentagon's Secret World*. New York: Dutton, 2009.

Parry-Giles, Shawn J. *The Rhetorical Presidency, Propaganda, and the Cold War, 1945–1955*. Westport, CT: Praeger, 2002.

Pels, Dick. *Unhastening Science: Autonomy and Reflexivity in the Social Theory of Knowledge*. Liverpool: Liverpool University Press, 2003.

——, Kevin Hetherington, and Frédéric Vandenberghe. "The Status of the Object: Performances, Mediations, and Techniques." *Theory, Culture, and Society* 19, no. 5–6 (2002): 1–21.

Peters, John Durham. "Information: Notes Toward a Critical History." *Journal of Communication Inquiry* 12, no. 2 (1988): 9–23.

Powell, Robert. *Nuclear Deterrence Theory: The Search for Credibility*. New York: Cambridge University Press, 1990.

Rancière, Jacques. *The Politics of Aesthetics: The Distribution of the Sensible*. London: Continuum, 2004.

Reagan, Leslie J., Nancy Tomes, and Paula A. Treichler, eds. *Medicine's Moving Pictures: Medicine, Health, and Bodies in American Film and Television*. Rochester, NY: University of Rochester Press, 2007.

Rhodes, Richard. *The Making of the Atomic Bomb*. New York: Simon and Schuster, 1986.

——. *Dark Sun: The Making of the Hydrogen Bomb*. New York: Simon and Schuster, 1995.

——. *Arsenals of Folly: The Making of the Nuclear Arms Race*. New York: Knopf, 2007.

Ristow, Walter W. "Air Age Geography: A Critical Appraisal and Bibliography." *Journal of Geography* 43, no. 9 (1944): 331–43.

Rosenthal, Peggy. "The Nuclear Mushroom Cloud as Cultural Image." *American Literary History* 3, no. 1 (1991): 63–92.

Ross, Steven J. "The Politicization of Hollywood before World War II: Anti-Fascism, Anti-Communism, and Anti-Semitism." In *The Jewish Role in American Life: An Annual Review*, vol. 5, 1–30. Edited by Bruce Zuckerman and Jeremy Schoenberg. West Lafayette, IN: Purdue University Press, 2007.

Saettler, Paul. *The Evolution of American Educational Technology*. Charlotte, NC: Information Age, 2004.

Sandeen, Eric. *Picturing an Exhibition: The Family of Man and 1950s America*. Albuquerque: University of New Mexico Press, 1995.

Saunders, Frances Stonor. *The Cultural Cold War: The CIA and the World of Arts and Letters*. New York: New Press, 2000.

Scarry, Elaine. *Thermonuclear Monarchy: Choosing between Democracy and Doom*. New York: Norton, 2014.

Schaffel, Kenneth. *The Emerging Shield: The Air Force and the Evolution of Continental Air Defense, 1945–1960*. Washington, DC: Office of Air Force History, United States Air Force, 1991.

Scott, James C. *Seeing Like a State: How Certain Schemes to Improve the Human Condition Have Failed*. New Haven, CT: Yale University Press, 1998.

Shaw, Tony, and Denise J. Youngblood. *Cinematic Cold War: The American and Soviet Struggle for Hearts and Minds*. Lawrence: University Press of Kansas, 2010.

Sheehan, Neil. *A Bright Shining Lie: John Paul Vann and America in Vietnam*. New York: Vintage, 1988.

——. *A Fiery Peace in a Cold War: Bernard Schriever and the Ultimate Weapon*. New York: Random House, 2009.

Slide, Anthony. *Before Video: A History of the Non-Theatrical Film*. New York: Greenwood Press, 1992.

Smith, Starr. *Jimmy Stewart: Bomber Pilot*. Minneapolis: Zenith Press, 2010.

Smoodin, Eric. *Regarding Frank Capra: Audience, Celebrity, and American Film Studies, 1930–1960*. Durham, NC: Duke University Press, 2005.

Snead, David L. *The Gaither Committee, Eisenhower, and the Cold War*. Columbus: Ohio State University Press, 1999.

Solnit, Rebecca. *Savage Dreams: A Journey into the Hidden Wars of the American West*. San Francisco: Sierra Club Books, 1994.

Stahl, Roger. *Militainment, Inc.: War, Media, and Popular Culture*. New York: Routledge, 2010.

——. *Through the Crosshairs: War, Visual Culture, and the Weaponized Gaze*. New Brunswick, NJ: Rutgers University Press, 2018.

Stoff, Michael B., ed. *The Manhattan Project: A Documentary History*. Philadelphia: Temple University Press, 1991.

Streible, Dan, Martina Roepke, and Anke Mebold. "Introduction: Nontheatrical Film." *Film History* 19, no. 4 (2007): 339–43.

Suid, Lawrence H. *Guts and Glory: The Making of the American Military Image in Film*, revised and expanded edition. Lexington: University Press of Kentucky, 2002.

Szczepanik, Petr. "Hollywood in Disguise: Practices of Exhibition and Reception of Foreign Films in Czechoslovakia in the 1930s." In *Cinema, Audiences and Modernity: New Perspectives on European Cinema History*, 166–85. Edited by Daniel Biltereyst, Richard Maltby, and Philippe Meers. New York: Routledge, 2012.

Tadelis, Steve. *Game Theory: An Introduction*. Princeton, NJ: Princeton University Press, 2013.

Teaiwa, Teresia K. "Bikinis and Other S/Pacific N/Oceans." *Contemporary Pacific* 6, no. 1 (1994): 87–109.

Terrace, Vincent. *Television Introductions: Narrated TV Program Openings since 1949*. Lanham, MD: Scarecrow Press, 2014.

Thomas, John D. "Cartoon Combat: World War II, Alexander de Seversky, and Victory Through Air Power." In *Learning from Mickey, Donald and Walt: Essays on Disney's Edutainment Films*, 63–83. Edited by A. Bowdoin Van Riper. Jefferson, NC: McFarland, 2011.

Thompson, Wayne. *To Hanoi and Back: The United States Air Force and North Vietnam, 1966–1973*. Washington, DC: Air Force History and Museums Program, 2000.

Trachtenberg, Marc. *History and Strategy*. Princeton, NJ: Princeton University Press, 1991.

Turner, Fred. *The Democratic Surround: Multimedia and American Liberalism from World War II to the Psychedelic Sixties*. Chicago: University of Chicago Press, 2013.

Twitchell, Samuel Edward. "The Incomplete Shield: The Distant Early Warning Line and the Struggle for Effective Continental Air Defense, 1950–1960." Master's thesis, Iowa State University, Ames, Iowa, 2011.

Van Staaveren, Jacob. *Gradual Failure: The Air War over North Vietnam, 1965–1966*. Washington, DC: Air Force History and Museums Program, 2002.

Vanderbilt, Tom. *Survival City: Adventures among the Ruins of Atomic America*. Princeton, NJ: Princeton Architectural Press, 2002.

Virilio, Paul. *Speed and Politics: An Essay on Dromology*. New York: Columbia University, 1986.

——. *War and Cinema: The Logistics of Perception*. Translated by Patrick Camiller. New York: Verso, 1989.

——, and Sylvère Lotringer. *Pure War*. New York: Semiotext(e), 1983.

Weart, Spencer R. *Nuclear Fear: A History of Images*. Cambridge, MA: Harvard University Press, 1988.

Weeks, Stanley Byron, and Charles A. Meconis. *The Armed Forces of the USA in the Asia-Pacific Region*. New York: I. B. Tauris, 1999.

Weinberg, Alvin M. "Impact of Large-Scale Science on the United States." *Science* 134, no. 3473 (1961): 161–64.

Weisgall, Jonathan M. *Operation Crossroads: The Atomic Tests at Bikini Atoll*. Annapolis, MD: Naval Institute Press, 1994.

Weld, Kristen. *Paper Cadavers: The Archives of Dictatorship in Guatemala*. Durham, NC: Duke University Press, 2014.

Whitfield, Stephen J. *The Culture of the Cold War*, 2nd edition. Baltimore, MD: Johns Hopkins University Press, 1996.

Wiener, Norbert. *Cybernetics: Or Control and Communication in the Animal and Machine*, 2nd edition. Cambridge, MA: MIT Press, 1961.

Williams, Bruce. "American Military Exceptionalism: How Popular Media Shapes Public Misunderstandings of Why and How We Fight." Academic talk, October 6, 2017, Department of Communication, University of Illinois, Urbana-Champaign.

Williams, Raymond. *Marxism and Literature*. New York: Oxford University Press, 1977.

Wills, Garry. *Bomb Power: The Modern Presidency and the National Security State*. New York: Penguin Press, 2010.

Wilson, Rob. *Reimagining the American Pacific: From the South Pacific to Bamboo Ridge and Beyond*. Durham, NC: Duke University Press, 2000.

Younger, Stephen Michael. *The Bomb: A New History*. New York: Ecco Press, 2009.

Zavattaro, Peter. *EG&G: Historic Involvement in the Nuclear Weapons Program*. Las Vegas, NV: NTS Historical Foundation, 2004.

Zelizer, Barbie. *Covering the Body: The Kennedy Assassination, the Media, and the Shaping of Collective Memory*. Chicago: University of Chicago Press, 1992.

ILLUSTRATION CREDITS

Note: All National Archives materials are in the Photography or Motion Picture collections in College Park, Maryland.

xii [top] Charles T. Forsyth operating two high-speed cameras in the left fire-control blister of an F-13 photo aircraft for Operation Crossroads, 1946. National Archives, RG 342 [B44579].

xii [bottom] Operation Crossroads, Baker test, July 25, 1946. National Archives, RG 342 [B44649].

xiv [top] Launch of Discoverer 14 satellite, August 18, 1960, on a Thor booster, Vandenberg Air Force Base, California. National Air and Space Museum, Archives Division [NASM-9A11846].

xiv [bottom] Camera operators from the 1365th Photographic Group operate M-45 camera mounts developed at Lookout Mountain to track missiles at Cape Canaveral, 1959. National Archives, RG 342 [K-KE-11906].

xvi [top] US Air Force Airman First Class Hunter D. Tucker Jr. is shown downloading a DBM-4 camera from an F-4C aircraft at Cam Ranh Bay Air Base, South Vietnam, 1968. Photo by John E. Bets, USAF. National Archives, RG 342 [KE-37282].

xvi [bottom] North Vietnamese gunners run to hide and man their gun positions after being surprised by an Air Force reconnaissance plane, 1966. National Archives, RG 342 [95920-USAF].

xx Val Peterson, director of the Federal Civil Defense Administration, on set at Lookout Mountain Laboratory, 1953. Ken Hackman Archives.

2 [bottom] Still from *Radiological Safety in Operation Sandstone*. 4201 Motion Picture Squadron, United States Air Force, 1948. Nuclear Testing Archive, Department of Energy [0800075].

3 [top left] Still from *Operation Greenhouse*, produced by 1352nd Motion Picture Squadron, Air Photographic and Charting Service, United States Air Force, 1952. National Archives, RG 434 [434.246].

3 [top right] Still from *Another Day of War*, produced by 1352nd Motion Picture Squadron, Air Photographic and Charting Service, United States Air Force, 1967. National Archives, RG 342 [SFP-1639].

5 Illustration from *Basic Photography*, Air Force Manual 95-1. Washington, DC: US Government Printing Office, 1959, 3. https://babel.hathitrust.org/cgi/pt?id=uiug.30112107817006.

6 Civilian specialists of the 1350th Motion Picture Squadron examine and classify films, 1967. National Archives, RG 342 [KE-27974].

7 [top] An archivist at the 1350th Motion Picture Squadron at Wright-Patterson Air Force Base, Ohio, helps a producer find a scene, 1967. National Archives, RG 342 [KE-27972].

7 [bottom] Jeanie Ottaviano at work in the still photo depository at Lookout Mountain Laboratory [date unknown]. Ken Hackman Archives.

8 Illustration from *Basic Photography,* Air Force Manual 95-1. Washington, DC: US Government Printing Office, 1959, 60. https://babel.hathitrust.org/cgi/pt?id=uiug.30112107817006.

9 Illustration from *Basic Photography,* Air Force Manual 95-1. Washington, DC: US Government Printing Office, 1959, 80. https://babel.hathitrust.org/cgi/pt?id=uiug.30112107817006.

10 [top] Composer Bill Lavender at work on a film score at Lookout Mountain [date unknown]. Ken Hackman Archives.

10 [bottom] Lookout Mountain artists at work on storyboards, mid-1950s. Ken Hackman Archives.

11 [bottom] Lookout Mountain artists at work on storyboards, mid-1950s. Ken Hackman Archives.

12 Still from *Operation Greenhouse*, produced by 1352nd Motion Picture Squadron, Air Photographic and Charting Service, United States Air Force, 1952. National Archives, RG 434 [434.246].

13 Still from *Data for Deterrence*, produced by 1352nd Motion Picture Squadron, Air Photographic and Charting Service, United States Air Force, 1965. National Archives, RG 342 [342-FR-490].

14 [top] Briefing room in the US Air Force Command Post, the Pentagon, ca. 1963. National Archives, RG 342 [168733-USAF].

14 [bottom] Visual display system at the underground control center of Strategic Air Command, Offutt Air Force Base, Nebraska, ca. 1963. National Archives, RG 342 [171234-USAF].

15 Pilots, briefing and intelligence officers see combat pictures taken in flight by the wing-gun cameras installed in F-51 "Mustangs," 1951. National Archives, RG 342 [NASM-4A-35272].

18 [top] US Air Force master archival reference card for the film *The Atomic Bomb Assembly*, 1954. National Archives, RG 342.

18 [bottom] US Air Force master archival reference card for the film *Air Strikes, Southeast Asia 1966*, 1966. National Archives, RG 342.

22 [left] Sound recording during a production at the 1365th Photographic Squadron, Orlando, Florida, 1965. National Archives, RG 342 [KE-22740].

22–23 Dean Fredericks portrays his popular television character Steve Canyon at Lookout Mountain Laboratory for an Air Force Academy recruitment TV short, 1959. National Archives, RG 342 [177182-USAF].

23 [right] Sound recording for motion-picture film at Lookout Mountain Laboratory [date unknown]. Ken Hackman Archives.

24 Front entrance of Lookout Mountain Laboratory in its early years [date unknown]. Air Force Historical Research Agency, Maxwell Air Force Base, Montgomery, Alabama [IRISNUM 01141313].

26 View of original radar station acquired for use by Lookout Mountain Laboratory, ca. 1947. Air Force Historical Research Agency, Maxwell Air Force Base, Montgomery, Alabama [IRISNUM 01141313].

27 Still from *The Army Nurse*. US Army Pictorial Service, 1945. Prelinger Archives. https://archive.org/details/ArmyNurs1945.

28 On location with the First Motion Picture Unit, 1944. National Archives, RG 342 [NASM-4A-15984].

30–31 Stills from *Lookout Mountain Air Force Station*, produced by 1352nd Motion Picture Squadron, Air Photographic and Charting Service, United States Air Force, 1963. National Archives, RG 342 [342-USAF-48721A].

33 John Ford on location directing for Lookout Mountain's *People to People* series of orientation films about Southeast Asia, 1959. National Archives, RG 342 [172093-USAF].

34–35 Visualization by Alex Jerez for the Imaging Technology Group, Beckman Institute, University of Illinois, based on research by Kevin Hamilton [CC BY-SA 4.0].

38 Illustration by Kevin Hamilton [CC BY-SA 4.0]. Data from http://www.johnstonsarchive.net/nuclear/tests/ and https://www.osti.gov/opennet/manhattan-project-history/Resources/maps/MED_facilities_map.htm.

40 View of first stage of construction at Lookout Mountain Laboratory, ca. 1948. Air Force Historical Research Agency, Maxwell Air Force Base, Montgomery, Alabama [IRISNUM 01141313].

42 View of Lookout Mountain Laboratory, ca. 1953. Air Force Historical Research Agency, Maxwell Air Force Base, Montgomery, Alabama [IRISNUM 01141313].

44–45 [left] Cameras showing variety of lenses used to photograph atomic bomb tests at Bikini Atoll, July 1946. National Archives, RG 342 [B44563].

44–45 [top] Atomic bomb, ca. 1964. National Archives, RG 342 [49704-AC].

44–45 [bottom] Status board in the Production Control Division at Lookout Mountain Laboratory, 1957. Defense Threat Reduction Information Analysis Center [98016].

46 Col. Paul T. Cullen [*left*], Maj. John D. Craig [*center*], and Lt. Col. Richard J. Cunningham [*right*] beneath a photo plane at Operation Crossroads, 1946. National Archives, RG 342 [342-FH-83-B44459].

49 [left] Still from *Atomic Proving Ground, the Story of Operation Sandstone*, produced by 4201 Motion Picture Squadron, United States Air Force, 1948. Nuclear Testing Archive, Department of Energy [0800074].

49 [right] Still from *Radiological Safety in Operation Sandstone*, produced by 4201 Motion Picture Squadron, United States Air Force, 1948. Nuclear Testing Archive, Department of Energy [0800075].

50–51 Stills from *Operation Sandstone*, produced by 4201 Motion Picture Squadron, United States Air Force, 1948. Nuclear Testing Archive, Department of Energy [0800003].

53 Air Photographic and Charting Service Command Structure, 1953. From *History of the Air Photographic and Charting Service, April 1951–December 1962*. Air Force Historical Research Agency, Maxwell Air Force Base, Montgomery, Alabama, 4.

54 Hiran survey of the Southwest Pacific, 1962. From *History of the 1370th Photo-Mapping Wing, 1 July 1962–31 December 1962*. Air Force Historical Research Agency, Maxwell Air Force Base, Montgomery, Alabama, 81.

56 Lookout Mountain award recipients at an annual banquet [date unknown]. Ken Hackman Archives.

59 1352nd Motion Picture Squadron Command Structure, 1953. from *History of the Air Photographic and Charting Service, April 1951–December 1962*. Air Force Historical Research Agency, Maxwell Air Force Base, Montgomery, Alabama, 71.

60–61 Illustration by Kevin Hamilton [CC BY-SA 4.0]. Lookout Mountain data from unit reports; nuclear test data from http://www.johnstonsarchive.net; missile launch data from http://www.spacearchive.info/vafblog.htm.

64 Marilyn Monroe at a Lookout Mountain shoot on Harold Lloyd's Greenacres Estate, photograph by Harold Lloyd. Courtesy the Harold Lloyd Trust, all rights reserved.

66 [top] Mushroom cloud from a United States nuclear test in the Marshall Islands [date unknown]. Ken Hackman Archives.

66 [bottom] The people of Bikini Atoll and the surrounding islands are informed about their forced migration as camera crews look on, 1946. National Archives, RG 374 [374-ANT-18-CR-113].

66–67 Images of the "Able" test at Operation Crossroads are inspected, 1946. National Archives, RG 342 [342-FH-K-2518].

67 [right] Atomic test at Eniwetok Atoll during Operation Sandstone, 1948. National Archives, RG 342 [B44695].

68 The aftermath of the "Baker" shot, the second of two nuclear detonations at Bikini Atoll during Operation Crossroads, 1946. National Archives, RG 342 [B44654].

70 [left] Still from *Lookout Mountain Air Force Station* produced by 1352nd Motion Picture Squadron, Air Photographic and Charting Service, United States Air Force, 1963. National Archives, RG 342 [342-USAF-48721A].

70 [right] Still from *USAF Participation in Operation Dominic*, produced by 1352nd Motion Picture Squadron, Air Photographic and Charting Service, United States Air Force, 1962. National Archives, RG 342 [342-SFP-1173].

71 Marshallese transporting an American resurvey party in a *tipnol* canoe, Rongerik Atoll, 1947. University of Washington Libraries, Special Collections [UW39273].

72–73 Illustration by Kevin Hamilton [CC BY-SA 4.0]. Military Air Transport service routes from http://www.timetableimages.com/ttimages

/mats/mats5308/mats53-3.jpg, https://catalog.hathitrust.org/Record/008463078, https://commons.wikimedia.org/wiki/File:Wtaf-routes-1964.jpg, and http://www.amc.af.mil/Portals/12/documents/AFD-131018-047.pdf.

75 Cameras and equipment lined up by Boeing B-29 "Suella J." on the flight line at Kwajalein during Operation Crossroads, 1946. National Archives, RG 342 [B44539].

76 Emblem for Joint Task Force One, responsible for Operation Crossroads, 1946. From brochure prepared for test observers, found at http://crossroads.alexanderpiela.com/files/Operation_Croassroads_Pamphlet.pdf.

77 Eastman high-speed cameras custom mounted in a Douglas C-54 for Operation Crossroads, 1946. National Archives, RG 342 [B44546].

78 A makeshift bar on Enyu Island during Operation Crossroads, 1946. From *Operation Crossroads: The Official Pictorial Record*. Office of the Historian, Joint Task Force One, 96.

79 The aftermath of the Baker shot, the second of two nuclear detonations at Bikini Atoll during Operation Crossroads, 1946. National Archives, RG 342 [B44650].

82–83 Visualization by Kevin Hamilton (CC BY-SA 4.0). Film annotation Sharon Messmore, made possible by National Endowment for the Humanities grant HD-51246-11.

84 Test workers at Operation Castle prepared for radiological study. National Archives, RG 374 [374-ANT-22-D-269-01].

85 Test workers at Operation Castle washing down for radiation. National Archives, RG 374 [374-ANT-22-D-269-02].

88 [left] Still from *Operation Greenhouse*. 1352nd Motion Picture Squadron, Air Photographic and Charting Service, United States Air Force, 1952. National Archives, RG 434 [434.246].

88 [right] Still from *Operation Greenhouse*, produced by 1352nd Motion Picture Squadron, Air Photographic and Charting Service, United States Air Force, 1952. National Archives, RG 434 [434.246].

89 Illustration from *Report by the Commander, Joint Task Force Three on Completion of Operation Greenhouse*, 1951. Nuclear Testing Archive, Department of Energy [NV0059457], 81.

92–93 Stills from *Military Effects Studies on Operation Castle*, produced by 1352nd Motion Picture Squadron, Air Photographic and Charting Service, United States Air Force. 1954. Nuclear Testing Archive, Department of Energy.

95 Radiological survey of islands Eberiru, Aomon, and Biijiri for *Operation Greenhouse, 1951. from Operation Greenhouse, Scientific Director's Report, Annex 9.3*. Nuclear Testing Archive, Department of Energy [NV0767713], 64.

96 Illustration from *The Effects of Nuclear Weapons*, 1962. Samuel Glasstone, (Washington, DC: United States Atomic Energy Commission, 1962), 83.

97 A technician monitors effects of atmospheric nuclear tests during Operation Dominic, 1962. Ken Hackman Archives.

100 [left] Lookout Mountain's mobile camera boom in use for Operation Ivy, 1952. Defense Threat Reduction Information Analysis Center [21-PLK-45-2].

101 [top] Personnel from Joint Task Force 132 on a site visit to Eniwetok Atoll, 1952. Defense Threat Reduction Information Analysis Center [21-PAK-78-7].

101 [bottom] Operation Ivy, "Mike" shot, November 1, 1952. The Official CTBTO [Flickr photostream], https://www.flickr.com/photos/ctbto/6476282811.

101 [right] Actor Reed Hadley surveys the view from above a camera bank at Operation Ivy, 1952. Defense Threat Reduction Information Analysis Center [21-PLK-45-6].

102 Actor Reed Hadley aboard the USS *Estes* for the filming of *Operation Ivy*, 1952. Defense Threat Reduction Information Analysis Center [21-PAK-37-4].

105 Diagram for auto-remote camera designed and built by Lookout Mountain for Operation Ivy, 1952. *Operation Ivy, Report to the Scientific Director, Documentary Photography*, 1953. Nuclear Testing Archive, Department of Energy [NV0051050], 26.

107 A view of the two-mile-long structure housing helium for the "Ivy Mike" device at Operation Ivy, 1952. National Archives, RG 342 [B44709].

111 Diagram for mobile camera boom designed and built by Lookout Mountain for Operation Ivy, 1952. *Operation Ivy, Report to the Scientific Director, Documentary Photography*, 1953. Nuclear Testing Archive, Department of Energy [NV0051050], 27.

113 Reed Hadley at the remote-control console for the Operation Ivy test aboard the USS *Estes*, 1952. Defense Threat Reduction Information Analysis Center [21-PAK-46-5].

115 Reed Hadley and others don protective goggles for viewing the Operation Ivy test from aboard the USS *Estes*. Defense Threat Reduction Information Analysis Center [21-PAK-46-1].

116–17 Stills from *Operation Ivy*. 1352nd Motion Picture Squadron, Air Photographic and Charting Service, United States Air Force. 1952. Nuclear Testing Archive, Department of Energy [0800012].

118 Still from *Operation Ivy* demonstrating how 14 Pentagon buildings could fit in the crater left by "Ivy Mike," 1952. National Archives, RG 342 [4A-22013].

120 Lookout Mountain drawing demonstrating depth of "Ivy Mike" crater in terms of a seventeen-story building, 1952. *Operation Ivy—Pacific Proving Grounds—Report to the Scientific Director, Project 3.7—Photographic Crater Survey*, 1952. Testing Archive, Department of Energy [NV0411677], 14.

122 View of the "Ivy Mike" detonation, captured by a Lookout Mountain photographer. National Archives, RG 342 [K8329].

125 A Lookout Mountain photograph of Operation Ivy, on display at the *Family of Man* exhibition at the Museum of Modern Art, 1955. © Wayne Miller/Magnum Photos.

128 [left] A crew chief guides a sampler aircraft into a decontamination area after it has flown through an atomic cloud in Nevada, 1955. National Archives, RG 342 [154609AC].

128 [right top] One test worker evaluates another for radiation during a nuclear test operation. National Archives, RG 374 [374-ANT-19-21].

128 [right bottom] A mushroom cloud rises over the Desert Rock exercises during the Buster-Jangle nuclear tests in Nevada, 1951. National Archives, RG 374 [M289-10].

129 M/Sgt Carmie M. Zaccardi and T/Sgt Gerald T. Boylan photograph an X-15 flight at Rogers Dry Lake, Edwards AFB, California, 1960. National Archives, RG 342 [342-171205-USAF].

130 Lookout Mountain photographers at work during an Operation Teapot test in the Nevada desert, 1955. National Archives, RG 374 [374-ANT-30-35-PLK-219-1].

133 Crater left from a nuclear detonation in the Nevada desert, ca. 1955. National Archives, RG 374 [374-ANT-68].

135 A high-speed photograph of a Nevada nuclear detonation captured by Edgerton, Germeshausen, and Grier for the Atomic Energy Commission, 1952. © 2010 MIT. Courtesy of MIT Museum [HEE-NC-52011].

137 Illustration by Alex Jerez for the Imaging Technology Group, Beckman Institute, University of Illinois, based on research by Kevin Hamilton [CC BY-SA 4.0].

138 Lookout Mountain press photo of a mannequin in a test shelter during the Upshot-Knothole tests in Nevada. Courtesy of Kevin Hamilton.

140 Operation Ranger, Baker-1 shot, January 28, 1951. National Archives, RG 374 [374-40-11-PL-9-5].

141 Outline of cloud from Operation Buster's "Dog" at one-hour intervals, 1952. *Technical Air Operations, Operation Buster-Jangle*, 1952. Testing Archive, Department of Energy [NV0068075], 49.

142–43 Stills from *Target Nevada*, produced by 1352nd Motion Picture Squadron, Air Photographic and Charting Service, United States Air Force, 1953. Nuclear Testing Archive, Department of Energy [0800096].

146 Still from *Military Participation on Tumbler/Snapper*, produced by 1352nd Motion Picture Squadron, Air Photographic and Charting Service, United States Air Force, 1952. Nuclear Testing Archive, Department of Energy [0800011].

147 Workers at the Lookout Mountain vault catalog films for storage and distribution. Ken Hackman Archives.

149 [left and right] Stills from *Military Participation on Tumbler/Snapper*, produced by 1352nd Motion Picture Squadron, Air Photographic and Charting Service, United States Air Force, 1952. Nuclear Testing Archive, Department of Energy [0800011].

150 Lorraine Hamlin at work painting an animation cel at Lookout Mountain [date unknown]. Ken Hackman Archives.

153 [left] Still from *Atomic Tests in Nevada*, produced by 1352nd Motion Picture Squadron, Air Photographic and Charting Service, United States Air Force, 1955. National Archives, RG 434 [434.53].

153 [right] Still from *The Searchers*, directed by John Ford. Warner Brothers, 1956.

154 Lookout Mountain photographers at work on a Nevada nuclear test, ca. 1952. National Archives, RG 374 [374-ANT-30-65-PZK-26-2].

156–57 [left] Ejection seat test filmed by Lookout Mountain photographers at Edwards Air Force Base, California, 1961. National Archives, RG 342 [169799-USAF].

157 [right] Airman Second Class Billy G. Johnson boresights a 16mm Mitchell camera at a remote camera site at Vandenberg Air Force Base, California, for the launch of a Thor missile, 1966. National Archives, RG 342 [KE-22190].

158 Photographers of the 1369th Audiovisual Squadron record the launch of a Minuteman missile, August 28, 1969. National Archives, RG 342 [KE-50571].

161 Lookout Mountain photographers test their new custom-built M-45 tracking camera mount for a film of the Thunderbirds aerial demonstration team in Arizona, 1956. National Archives, RG 342 [K-KE-5334].

162 Lookout Mountain cameraman Airman First Class Ronald L. Nadeau operates an M-45 tracking mount camera at Vandenberg Air Force Base, California, 1961. National Archives, RG 342 [K-KE-25001].

164 Still from *Atlas Test Vandenberg AFB July 18, 1963*, produced by 1369th Photographic Squadron, Air Photographic and Charting Service, United States Air Force, 1963. Archives of the San Diego Air and Space Museum [HACL 01065]. https://www.youtube.com/watch?v=ldEWWa1krq4.

165 Still from *Atlas USAF Film Report 1959*, produced by 1369th Photographic Squadron, Air Photographic and Charting Service, United States Air Force, 1959. Archives of the San Diego Air and Space Museum [HACL 01005]. https://www.youtube.com/watch?v=ldEWWa1krq4.

166 Exterior view of building 9340, Vandenberg Air Force Base, home to the 1369th Photographic Squadron, 1970. National Archives, RG 342 [KE-40671].

167 Contemporary view of a Lookout Mountain camera control unit installed at Space Launch Complex 10, Vandenberg Air Force Base, 2015. Photograph by Kevin Hamilton [CC BY-SA 4.0].

168–69 Stills from *Ballistic Missile Development: Program Highlights 1958*, produced by 1352nd Motion Picture Squadron, Air Photographic and Charting Service, United States Air Force, 1958. National Archives, RG 330 [330-DVIC-434].

170 Photographers with the 1369th prepare pad cameras to document a launch from under an Atlas missile tower at Vandenberg Air Force Base [date unknown]. National Archives, RG 342 [K-KE-25004].

171 An Atlas missile is lifted from the transporter and placed in launch facility at Vandenberg Air Force Base, 1970. National Archives, RG 342 [KE-51707].

173 1369th photographers at their remote camera operation station in a missile launch blockhouse at Vandenberg Air Force Base [date unknown]. National Archives, RG 342 [KE-51707].

174 A composite photo by the 1369th Photographic Squadron demonstrates the progress of a missile out its silo during launch. National Archives, RG 342 [K-52343].

176 Brigadier General James "Jimmy" Stewart on set during a shoot at Lookout Mountain, ca. 1959. Ken Hackman archives.

178 [left] Lookout Mountain's Colorado detachment captured this construction photo of the tunnel into the new North American Air Defense headquarters in Cheyenne Mountain, ca. 1961. https://commons.wikimedia.org/wiki/File:Cheyenne_Mountain_Const_-_tunnel_with_pipes.jpg.

178 [right] Aerial view of the Dye III site of the Distant Early Warning Line [DEW Line] station in Greenland, 1977. National Archives, RG 342 [KKE-66354].

179 [left] An automatic camera in a balloon gondola captures Air Force Captain Joseph W. Kittinger Jr. during his record-setting jump from 102,800 feet, August 16, 1960. National Archives, RG 342 [342-B-04–071–164261AC].

179 [right] A photographer for the 1352nd shoots a practice run for a midair capture of a Discoverer space capsule over the Pacific, 1961. National Archives, RG 342 [172469-USAF].

180 Air Force photograph of a fiberglass radome sixty-eight feet in diameter, as used in the DEW Line radar stations in the Arctic, 1959. National Archives, RG 342 [160802-AC].

183 An Air Force diagram shows the approximate locations of a planned line of DEW Line radar stations, 1959. National Archives, RG 342 [157118-AC].

185 A view inside the NORAD headquarters in Cheyenne Mountain, Colorado, 1966. Image courtesy of the Charles Babbage Institute, University of Minnesota Libraries, Minneapolis, Minnesota.

186 A newly constructed DEW Line station, 1957. National Archives, RG 342 [158051-AC].

187 [top, bottom] Stills from *Aleutian Skywatch*, produced by Audio Productions, New York, 1961. https://archive.org/details/AleutianSkywatch.

189 A Lookout Mountain photographer records a C-130 during Operation Polar Siege at Six Mile Lake, Alaska, 1964. National Archives, RG 342 [K-23174].

190 Aerial view of the Ballistic Missile Early Warning System [BMEWS] location in Thule, Greenland, by Lookout Mountain photographer Ken Hackman, 1968. National Archives, RG 342 [K-8673].

191 Diagram of a DEW Line station's layout and organization [year unknown]. Capt. Pamela G. Rooney, *Distant Early Warning [DEW] System Operations Handbook* [http://antiquehistory.net/beach/Distant-Early-Warning-[DEW]-System-Operations-Handbook.pdf].

193 A DEW Line station and totem pole at Point Barrow, Alaska, 1970. National Archives, RG 342 [K-56028].

196–97 Stills from *Shield of Freedom*, produced by 1352nd Motion Picture Squadron, Air Photographic and Charting Service, United States Air Force, 1963. National Archives, RG 330 [330-DVIC-26377].

198 An automatic camera in a balloon gondola captures Air Force Captain Joseph W. Kittinger Jr. during his record-setting jump from 102,800 feet, August 16, 1960. National Archives, RG 342 [342-B-04–071–170303AF].

200 President John F. Kennedy views U.S. Air Force Academy falcon mascot, 1963. Cecil Stoughton. White House Photographs. John F. Kennedy Presidential Library and Museum, Boston, Massachusetts.

202 [top] Airman Second Class Robert Hatcher and Airman First Class Richard Hatcher, twin brothers, work in a darkroom at Tan Son Nhut Air Base, Vietnam, 1965. National Archives, RG 342 [95224-USAF].

203 [top] Master Sgt. Rodger E. Stockard, stationed in Korea, displays one of his photographs along with the *Newsweek* cover on which it appeared, 1951. National Archives, RG 342 [NASM-4A 35354].

202–3 [bottom] Onboard camera captures two missiles just fired from a US Air Force aircraft, ca. 1964. Courtesy of Al Homen.

204 Still from gun camera footage captured from an F-105 Thunderchief flown by Major Ralph Kuster during a raid over North Vietnam, 1967. National Archives, RG 342 [342-C-KE26311].

207 Illustration from *Night Vision Trainer*, Air Force Manual 50-10. Washington, DC: US Government Printing Office, 1959. 2. https://babel.hathitrust.org/cgi/pt?id=uiug.30112107098771.

208 Illustration from *Basic Photography*, Air Force Manual 95-1. Washington, DC: US Government Printing Office, 1959. 66. https://babel.hathitrust.org/cgi/pt?id=uiug.30112107817006.

209 Diagram of camera placement for exterior photography of model residences during Operation Teapot, 1955. *Technical Photography of Physical Phenomena*, 1955. Nuclear Testing Archive, Department of Energy [NV0521535], 36.

211 A reconnaissance laboratory technician examines negatives at Tan Son Nhut Air Base, Vietnam. Photographed by 600th Photographic Squadron, 1968. National Archives, RG 342 [KE-3039].

215 Airman First Class Larry G. Hannan of the 600th Photo Squadron inserts a Milliken camera into its pod under an F-100 aircraft at Bien Hoa Air Base, Vietnam, 1969. National Archives, RG 342 [104968-USAF].

216–17 Stills from *USAF Participation in Southeast Asia*, produced by 1352nd Motion Picture Squadron, Air Photographic and Charting Service, United States Air Force, 1963. National Archives, RG 342 [342.20661DF].

219 Camera placements on an F-105D Thunderchief. Illustration by Alex Jerez for the Imaging Technology Group, Beckman Institute, University of Illinois, based on research by Kevin Hamilton [CC BY-SA 4.0].

220 Illustration by Kevin Hamilton [CC BY-SA 4.0].

221 Bob Hope and his cast arrive at Pleiku Air Base, Vietnam, for one of their annual Christmas shows, 1966. National Archives, RG 342 [342-AF-99731USAF].

222 At Korat Air Base, Thailand, Sgt. Richard C. DeGraeve loads a KB-71 strike camera into an F-105 Thunderchief, 1968. National Archives, RG 342 [342-KE-35290].

223 Lookout Mountain flow chart for processing and distribution of motion-picture film from Southeast Asia, ca. 1966. Courtesy of Dennis Johnson.

224 A U.S. Air Force C-47 releases psychological warfare leaflets near Nha Trang, South Vietnam. National Archives, RG 342 [342-C-KE35295].

225 President Lyndon B. Johnson meets with foreign policy advisers at one of his weekly Tuesday Luncheons, 1967. Lyndon Baines Johnson Library photo by Yoichi Okamoto, no. C6151-12.

226–27 Re-creation of search results for *mushroom cloud* on a popular stock photography website, 2018. Illustration by Kevin Hamilton [CC BY-SA 4.0].

228 Operation Dominic, Frigate Bird shot, 1962. National Archives, RG 374 [374-G-62-17].

230 Diagram of camera locations for islands Japtan and Parry during Operation Ivy, 1953. *Operation Ivy, Report to the Scientific Director, Documentary Photography*, 1953. Nuclear Testing Archive, Department of Energy [NV0051050], 48.

231 One of the ubiquitous classification restrictions one encounters in reviewing government documents on nuclear weapons testing, ca. 1950.

232 Gallery installation view of CROSSROADS by Bruce Conner. The Conner Family Trust and Kohn Gallery, Los Angeles.

234 Lookout Mountain photographers at work during Operation Coulee Crest, 1963. National Archives, RG 342 [342-179177-USAF].

235 Photographer at Vandenberg Air Force Base, 1969. National Archives, RG 342 [342-K-KE-60262].

236 President John F. Kennedy observes an Atlas missile launch at Vandenberg Air Force Base with Secretary of Defense McNamara and General Thomas S. Power, 1962. Courtesy of Al Homen.

238 Cover of *Cinefantastique* v.15, no.2, featuring Peter Kuran, March 1985.

241 A view of the Command Post at Headquarters, Strategic Air Command, Offutt Air Force Base, 1961. National Archives, RG 342 [342-B-11-082 -164994-AC].

243 Historical [*left*] and current [*right*] emblems for the Defense Threat Reduction Information Analysis Center [DTRIAC], 2018. Defense Threat Reduction Agency Office of Public Affairs.

244–45 Stills from *CinemaScope Featurette: Shot Number 12*, restored and reconstructed footage by Peter Kuran from historical footage. From Atomic Filmmakers DVD [Santa Clarita, California: VCE], 2003. Used with permission.

246 Two-story house at Operation Cue, 5,500 feet from blast, after the blast, 1955. National Archives, RG 304 [6234461].

248 Archival nuclear test footage awaiting restoration at Lawrence Livermore Laboratories, 2014. Lawrence Livermore Laboratories [CC BY-SA 4.0].

250 [top] Abandoned headquarters, Aerospace Audio-Visual Service, Norton Air Force Base, San Bernardino, California, 2014. Photo by Kevin Hamilton [CC BY-SA 4.0].

250 [bottom] Aging camera mounts designed and built by Lookout Mountain technicians for SLC-10 Thor missile launch facility at Vandenberg Air Force Base, California, 2014. Photo by Kevin Hamilton [CC BY-SA 4.0].

251 [top] Remnants of prototype DEW Line station, Streator, Illinois, 2015. Photo by Kevin Hamilton [CC BY-SA 4.0].

251 [bottom] Former headquarters, 1369th Audiovisual Squadron, Vandenberg Air Force Base, California, 2014. Photo by Kevin Hamilton [CC BY-SA 4.0].

252 Lookout Mountain Laboratory facility in Laurel Canyon, Hollywood, California, 2014. Photo by Kevin Hamilton [CC BY-SA 4.0].

255 Parcel map for 8935 Wonderland Avenue, Hollywood, California, 2017. Los Angeles County Office of the Assessor.

256 Staff in front of the newly redesignated headquarters of the Aerospace Audio-Visual Service, Norton Air Force Base, ca. 1968. Courtesy of Al Homen.

260 Emblem from the Facebook page of the Defense Imagery Management Operations Center [DIMOC], 2018.

284 A film vault attendant of the 1350th Motion Picture Squadron at Wright-Patterson Air Force Base in Ohio assigns a location to newly accessioned film, 1967. National Archives, RG 342 [KE-27970].

INDEX

N

O

P

Q

R

S